Emanuel Swedenborg

A Treatise Concerning Heaven and Hell

Emanuel Swedenborg

A Treatise Concerning Heaven and Hell

ISBN/EAN: 9783337389352

Printed in Europe, USA, Canada, Australia, Japan

Cover: Foto ©Lupo / pixelio.de

More available books at **www.hansebooks.com**

A

TREATISE

Concerning

HEAVEN and HELL,

Containing

A RELATION of many WONDERFUL THINGS THEREIN, as heard and seen by the AUTHOR,

The HONOURABLE

EMANUEL SWEDENBORG,

Of the SENATORIAL ORDER of NOBLES in the Kingdom of SWEDEN.

Now First Translated from the ORIGINAL LATIN.

——This is a rebellious people——which say to the Seers, See not. Isai. xxx. 9, 10.

Where there is no Vision, the people perish. Prov. xxix. 18.

I have multiplied Visions, and used Similitudes, by the ministry of the Prophets. Hof. xii. 10.

For the invisible things of Him from the creation of the world are clearly seen, being understood by the things that are made. Rom. i. 20.

LONDON:

PRINTED AND SOLD BY JAMES PHILLIPS, GEORGE YARD, LOMBARD STREET.

AND SOLD ALSO BY

S. LEACROFT, CHARING CROSS; T. MILLS, BRISTOL; AND E. SCORE, EXETER.

M DCC LXXVIII.

THE
PREFACE
TO THE
FOLLOWING TRANSLATION.

BESIDES the more general provisions made by the Father of Lights for the instruction of his church and people in divine things, under the publick dispensations of the Law and the Gospel, He has also been graciously pleased, at sundry times and in divers manners, as occasions and the needs of the church might require it, to make extraordinary discoveries and revelations to particular persons, either for more private or publick use, and to answer various ends of his wisdom and goodness: and indeed, were it so that all things proceeded according to one invariable rule of government in his administrations, in grace, in providence, and also in the natural world, without his interposing any particular acts of his divine authority and power, God's government of the world would be less attended to and believed in, his cognizance of human affairs be questioned by many, and such a settled sameness in the course of things be construed into a blind fatality. Nor is it easily to be conceived by us, how one unchangeable mode of proceedings could be adapted to the present condition of mankind, as free agents, under their continual fluctuations and deviations from the rule of obedience, their backslidings, rebellions and apostacy; and accordingly we read how the Lord varied his particular dealings with the Israelites,

according

according to their states and circumstances respectively, for direction, for warning, for corrections, &c. by visions, by voices, by signs and wonders, and by the mission of angels, to reclaim and convert them: and this is so far from arguing any variableness in God, that it evidences his unchangeableness in mercy and goodness, by accommodating his dealings and dispensations to the needs and requirements of his poor frail creatures, agreeably to that his declaration; " I am the Lord, I change not, " therefore ye sons of Jacob are not consumed." Mal. iii. 6.

How things went with the Antediluvians in regard to divine manifestations, the sacred records give us but little intelligence; but thus much we may collect from them, that in the line of Seth, as contradistinguished from that of Cain, there was a church of devout worshippers then on earth, in which Enoch was highly favoured of God, and a man of renown, whose prophetick writings continued in the church down to the times of the apostles, as appears from the Epistle of Jude. In this line of Seth (from what is mentioned of Enoch and Noah) we may conclude, that the church of God, before the general apostacy brought on the flood, was instructed and conducted by particular revelation from heaven; and that an intercourse between angels and the holy men of those early days (called the Sons of God) was no unfrequent thing.

On the call of Abraham heaven was again opened to man in the way of divine communications externally, and he was taught of God the things that be of God, by the ministry of angels; so that what we now call extraordinary dispensations were then the ordinary way of conveying divine knowledge (1): and from these more immediate discoveries of himself to the patriarchs we apprehend it was, that God stiled himself the God of Abraham, the God of Isaac, and the God of Jacob.

Nor was the delivery of the law, as a stated directory to the Israelites for duty and worship, intended to supersede particular revelations from heaven, or communications with angels; nay, the promise of an angel to " go before them in the way" was

(1) See *Bromley on extraordinary Dispensations*, at the end of his *Way to the Sabbath of Rest*. A book which I much recommend to the reader.

imme-

immediately annexed to it (2); and the prophetick difpenfation under the law appears as a fupplement of fuperior excellency to the law itfelf, by expounding and illuftrating the typical parts of it, in reference to that miniftration of righteoufnefs by Jefus Chrift, which fhould far exceed it in glory. Thus the law and the prophets made together, as it were, but one difpenfation; and all ferious Jews looked upon divine manifeftations, by prophecy and vifion, as fuch ftanding tokens of God's favour towards them, that any occafional ceffation of them was confidered as a mark of the divine difpleafure: thus the Pfalmift; "We fee not our tokens, there is not one prophet more (3):" and hence it was that the feers or true vifionaries were held in fuch honour by the godly of that church. Thus, "The word of the Lord was precious in thofe days; there was no open vifion (4):" "her prophets find no vifion from the Lord (5)." And it is obfervable, that from the time of Malachi to a little before the advent of Chrift, during which period prophecy and vifion ceafed in the Jewifh church (at leaft in perfons of a publick character) was the moft horrid degeneracy of that people from all things facred and moral; inteftine divifions, bribery, and libertinifm diffufed their poifon through church and ftate; the very temple was often polluted with the blood of hoftile factions; and the high priefthood bought and fold, nay, the nomination to it fubmitted to heathen princes, who conferred the fame on the higheft bidder: thus fulfilling the truth of Solomon's words (6): "Where there is no vifion, the people perifh;" meaning thereby, that where there is a ceffation of all divine communications, the fenfe of religion decays, and all things tend to ruin.

When the time was fully come, as foretold by the prophets, for the Sun of Righteoufnefs to arife with healing in his wings; for God to manifeft himfelf in the flefh to deftroy the works of the Devil, and to fupply what was lacking in all preceding difpenfations; then the heavens were again opened, and cœleftial communications renewed with men; an angel foretold the birth

(2) Exod. iii. 20. (3) Pfal. lxxiv. 10. (4) 1 Sam. iii. 1.
(5) Ifai. iii. 2. (6) Prov. xxix. 18.

of him, who should be the harbinger to this Prince of Peace; the same heavenly messenger was sent to the highly favoured Virgin with a salutation on her miraculous conception of him; and a host of angels proclaimed the joyful news of his gracious advent; angels ministered unto him during his abode on earth, and announced his resurrection from the dead. But when all was finished relating to our adorable Redeemer's ministry, sufferings, and life in the flesh, and that the dispensation of the Holy Ghost took place according to this promise, were all extraordinary dispensations then to cease? By no means; for this very publick solemnity on the day of Pentecost was attended with a gracious promise of their continuance in the church to future generations, as declared to all present by Peter, who, on quoting the prophecy of Joel (7) concerning the same vouchsafements, applies them to the times of the Gospel dispensation; " For " the promise is to you and to your children, and to them that " are afar off (8)." And they certainly continued with the apostles, as more particularly appears from the visions of angels by Peter, Paul, Philip, and John the Divine, plainly evincing, that they were not superseded by the giving of the Holy Ghost.

Such as are no friends to the belief of extraordinary gifts and communications, have laboured all they could to confine them to the times of the apostles; but in so contradicting the current testimony of the church history, they shew much prejudice, and little modesty. The apostolical fathers, Barnabas, Clement, and Hermas (whose writings were reverenced as of canonical authority for four hundred years, and were read, together with the other Canonical Scriptures, in many of the churches) confirm the truth of prophecy, divine visions, and miraculous gifts continuing in the church after the apostolical age, both by their testimony and experience; and to pass over many other venerable names (among whom Tertullian and Origen are witnesses of eminence to the same truth afterwards) Eusebius, Cyprian and Lactantius, still lower down, declare, that extraordinary divine manifestations were not uncommon in their days: Cyprian is very express on this subject, praising God on that behalf, with

(7) Joel ii. 28, 29.   (8) Acts ii. 39.

respect

respect to himself, to divers of the clergy, and many of the people, using these words: " The discipline of God over us " never ceases by night and by day to correct and reprove; for " not only by visions of the night, but also by day, even the " innocent age of children among us is filled with the Holy " Spirit, and they see, and hear, and speak in ecstacy such " things as the Lord vouchsafes to admonish and instruct us " by (9):" and it was the settled belief of the early fathers of the church, that these divine communications, for direction, edification, and comfort, would never wholly cease therein.

That extraordinary gifts became more rare in the church about the middle of the third century is allowed by Cyprian himself, and such other both cotemporary and subsequent writers, as at the same time testified to the reality of them; and they account for it from the encouragement given to the pernicious doctrines of Epicurus, and other materialists at that time, which disposed many to turn every thing supernatural and spiritual into mockery and contempt. In the next century, when the profession of Christianity became established by Constantine as the religion of the empire, and millions adopted it from its being the religion of the court, the fashion of the times, or the road to temporal emoluments, then Christianity appeared indeed more gorgeous in her apparel, but became less glorious within; was more splendid in form, but less vigorous in power; and so what the church gained in superficies, she lost in depth. She suffered her faith to be corrupted by the impure mixtures of heathenish philosophy, whilst the honours, riches, and pleasures of the world insinuated themselves into her affections, stole away her graces, and so robbed her of her best treasure, insomuch that many have made it a doubt, whether in the times here spoken of, Paganism was more christianized, or Christianity more paganized.

In this condition of things, no wonder that we hear so little of divine visions and extraordinary spiritual gifts in those days: for however outward men are apt to glory in the pompous appearance of a visible church, yet the true spiritual church may

(9) Epist. 16.

be confidered at that time, and indeed ever fince, as in her wildernefs ſtate, withdrawn from the multitude to keep herſelf unſpotted from the world, and to preſerve a holy intercourſe with her Beloved, in a life and converſation becoming the Goſpel of Chriſt; nor were her heavenly vouchſafements leſs than before, but only leſs proper to be divulged, as leſs likely to be received, or to be received only with deriſion, as were the dreams of Joſeph by his brethren. We always mean to except under this diſtinction many excellent perſons mixed with carnal profeſſors in common life, yet walking in all good conſcience, fearing God, and working righteouſneſs. Nor is any thing here ſaid with a deſign to ſuggeſt, as though the eſtabliſhment of Chriſtianity in the Roman empire were without its great beneficial effects; for it was a means appointed by Providence for ſpreading the knowledge of the Truth over a great part of the known world, whereby great numbers under very defective and corrupt adminiſtrations of it were converted from the error of their ways, and by paſſing through the outward forms and ordinances to the inward power, became burning and ſhining lights in the church: beſides, Divine Truth is of a diffuſive nature, like the precious ointment upon the head of Aaron, that fell down to the ſkirts of his garments. Thus the Chriſtian religion, in the weakeſt adminiſtrations of it, was not without good influence on the nations that received it, by civilizing their manners, improving their ſyſtems of morality, repreſſing their enormous vices, and regulating their polity by more wholeſome laws and inſtitutes.

To trace the Chriſtian religion in the various revolutions of its progreſs, from its firſt civil eſtabliſhment down to the preſent times, would be the province of an hiſtorian; we ſhall therefore paſs over all the intervening periods of it, to conſider the ſubject before us in the way both of ſcriptural and rational enquiries in relation to ourſelves. And here it muſt be owned, that the belief of all extraordinary or ſupernatural diſpenſations is at a very low ebb with us, and that from ſeveral aſſignable cauſes, two or three of which ſhall here be noticed.

And firſt, from an undue exaltation of man's natural rational faculties and powers, as the ſufficient teſt of revealed Truths;

and

and this grofs error has prevailed more among men of human learning for this paſt century, than perhaps ever before; to which it is owing, that almoſt every thing in religion has been run into queſtion and controverſy, and that a general diſbelief of all things ſupernatural has in a great meaſure baniſhed faith, and introduced Sadduciſm amongſt us, to the denying of all ſpiritual viſions and apparition of angels as things incredible.

Secondly, This doubting and unbelief in things of a ſpiritual nature has ſpread to a greater extent among all claſſes, from an exceſſive attachment to worldly intereſt, and the love of money in the trading nations of Chriſtendom, through the vaſt increaſe of commerce and navigation in the laſt two centuries; whereby the affections and purſuits of ſuch great numbers have been ſo engaged on the ſide of filthy lucre, as to turn an employment, in itſelf innocent and uſeful, into the occaſion of ſin. Hence a ſordid avarice, and making haſte to be rich by frauds, extortion, and injuſtice, which lays an invincible obſtacle in the way of faith; ſince we are told, that every one that would name the name of Chriſt, as his Saviour, muſt firſt depart from iniquity.

Another great hinderance to the belief of all communications with the world of ſpirits, is a life of pleaſure, which the apoſtle calls a ſtate of death (10), as it chains down the mind to the object of the ſenſes, and things of outward obſervation, and totally indiſpoſes it for the conſideration of things inward and ſpiritual: and this is not only the caſe of the voluptuous and libertine part of mankind, but of thoſe alſo, who, from an indulged levity and diſſipation of mind, abandon themſelves to vain paſtimes and amuſements, are carried away with every wind of faſhion and folly, or, like the Athenians, ſpend their time in nothing elſe, but either to tell or to hear ſome new thing. Should an apoſtle reveal any thing concerning heaven or hell to perſons thus indiſpoſed to receive his report, is it not to be expected that they would reply in deriſion, like the philoſophers or Athenians before mentioned, at the preaching of St. Paul? " What will this babbler ſay?" Nor can it be expected that the

(10) 1 Tim. v. 6.

contents of the following volume should meet with a more favourable reception from such. All things relating to the other world, and the condition of departed souls, are of a most interesting nature, and call for great seriousness and awful attention; and they that bring not with them minds so prepared for the consideration of these subjects, however they may boast of their reason, they are not as yet qualified for judges in these matters. And this leads to an observation or two on the subject of reason.

There is nothing more talked of and pretended to than reason, and yet nothing in which people of every rank and age are less agreed in; that which generally passes for reason being of a vague, uncertain nature, varying according to the tempers, inclinations, and circumstances of men. Thus it happens, that the reason of one of thirty years of age is seldom the reason of the same person at fifty; the reason of the majority is not the reason of the minority; nay, in every profession, art, and science, men reason differently, and often oppositely, except where reason has least place, as in mathematicks, geometry, and arithmetick. And yet there is a right reason in all things, where men are qualified to find it out; but these are few, and we see by far the greater part perpetually wrangling, disputing, and contradicting one another in relation to right and wrong in most things; and the main cause of it is the want of simplicity, and a right disposition of the will and affections, which are absolutely necessary, in order to a right judgment: but whilst men dignify their passions, humours, and false interests with the venerable name of reason, it remains in them no other than the operations of their present state of mind on the errors, prejudices, and wrong principles they have before imbibed, and which they are resolved to maintain with the most words, and such arguments as they are masters of; and hence it is, that we have so many criticks, politicians, and divines, which are utter strangers to the truth of the matters they take in hand.

But reason has also its specifick differences and measures, according to the nature of the subject to be investigated; thus ethicks, physicks, and metaphysicks have each their respective principles, and consequently a distinct kind of reason, and he that

that is a good proficient in the knowledge of one, may be very deficient in another. Thus every part of knowledge has its standard, adequate and proper to itself; so natural things are known by natural reason, and spiritual things are discerned by a spiritual light; and this distinction is founded on the authority of Scripture, in which we are told, that " the natural man " receiveth not the things of the Spirit of God, for they are " foolishness unto him; neither can he know them, because they are spiritually discerned (11);" that is, the animal or foulish [ψυχικ⊕] man, with all his natural faculties and endowments, cannot of himself attain to the knowledge of spiritual things, they being too far above his reach, and therefore it must be given him from above, or he cannot have it: nay, so contrary are they to the propensities and apprehensions of his sensual fallen nature, that whilst he presumes on a fancied sufficiency in himself to comprehend these things, the deeper he plunges himself into the darkness of human ignorance concerning them, and the more accounts them foolishness; and thus God is said to make foolish the wisdom of this world, by leaving such to their wilful blindness, who chuse darkness rather than light.

Nothing is here said to depreciate the external rational knowledge, even in its lowest sphere, when joined with the fear of God in men of humble minds; for this also is the gift of God, and is not only helpful to us in all the purposes of this life, but in due place and subordination subservient to the divine life; it is the abuse of this knowledge only that falls under our censure, as when natural knowledge and human learning are employed to unsettle mens minds with respect to the things of the other world, and to rob them of the precious hopes of a glorious immortality through the redemption that is in Christ Jesus. All such kind of sophistry, mistaken for reason, is no better than vain deceit, and science falsely so called, and all that exercise themselves therein are disturbers of the peace of mankind, as well as enemies to the church of God. Nor can we here forbear to pass a reproof on all those, who, whilst they profess a

(11) 1 Cor. ii. 14.

reverence

reverence for the Gospel Revelation, patronize at the same time the infidelity of the Sadducees, as touching angels and spirits, and all extraordinary dispensations: for to deny all communication with the spiritual world, whether by vision, or any other means, naturally leads to atheism; and their pernicious reasonings in this way have had dreadful effects upon the present times, by weakening the sense of religion and conscience in the lower classes of the people. The belief of an intercourse with the other world, according to the truth of it, keeps alive and cherishes faith in the immortality of the soul in all ranks of people, and familiarizes the mind to its existence separate from the body; and it is not to be doubted, that such gracious vouchsafements were granted to the Jews under the Law, and have been continued since to the church under the Gospel, in aid and assistance to men's faith in the written traditions of both dispensations: such being the goodness of the Lord in compassion to the weakness of our nature, and the dulness of our minds, which stand so much in need of fresh, awakening incitements to call off our attention from earthly to heavenly things. And therefore we cannot but lament, that any men of name in the church, though little deserving of it on this account, have gone so far beyond this line, as to assert, that all extraordinary gifts and supernatural dispensations have totally ceased since the third century; but we have no authority for this but their own, and therefore do upon much better grounds assert, that extraordinary gifts and vouchsafements never did nor will cease in the church, till that which is perfect shall come, that is, till such extraordinary become ordinary dispensations, and angels shall converse with men as familiarly as they did with Adam before the fall: and in the mean time we confidently rely upon the divine promise, that the same Lord, who " gave some apostles, and some pro-
" phets, and some evangelists, and some pastors and teachers,
" for the perfecting of the saints for the work of the ministry,
" for the edifying of the body of Christ," will fulfil the same promise, " till we all come in the unity of the faith, and of the
" knowledge of the Son of God, unto a perfect man, unto the
" measure of the stature of the fulness of Christ (12)."

(12) Eph. iv. 11, 12, 13.

But

But it may be said here, that see-ers of visions are not mentioned along with prophets, &c. in the foregoing quotation from the apostle; and therefore, as the first are principally referred to in this preface, it will be here apposite to observe, that the name Prophet in Scripture is not confined to the gift of prediction or foretelling things to come, but signifies one to whom any divine manifestation was made for the use of others; and as this was generally by vision, so we read that prophets in ancient times were usually called Seers, that is, see-ers of visions; thus in 1 Sam. ix. 9. " Before time in Israel, when a man went " to enquire of God, thus he spake, Come, and let us go to " the Seer; for he that is now called a Prophet, was before " time called a Seer." And afterwards, in the same chapter, Samuel calls himself a Seer. And in 2 Sam. xxiv. 11. we read, " that the word of the Lord came unto the prophet Gad, Da- " vid's Seer." Of such honourable repute was the name Seer, or visionary, in those times. When therefore the apostle gives it in charge to the church, not to despise prophesyings, we have no warrant to exclude visions from the general charge, especially as we are well informed from ecclesiastical history, that the custom of communicating to the church the visions of holy persons, particularly such as were of authority in the ministry, continued down at least to the days of Cyprian, the good bishop of Carthage, who speaks of manifestations by vision throughout his Epistles, and also of his own; for he was a man of many visions, and among others had one concerning his own martyrdom, and the particular manner of it, which happened accordingly.

St. Paul (Heb. xii. 22.) speaking of the superior excellence and blessedness of the New Covenant, says, " But ye are come " unto mount Sion, and unto the city of the living God, " the heavenly Jerusalem, and to an innumerable company of " angels," &c. By which words, we cannot suppose him to mean less, than that by Christ, the mediator of this better covenant, a more free intercourse with heaven, and a more intimate fellowship with saints and angels, is now opened for us, if we debar not ourselves of this blessed privilege. What then hinders our conversing with angels now, as the patriarchs
and

and prophets did of old? what but our own fault and unfitnefs for fuch glorious company? Why do we not now fee them defcending and afcending between heaven and earth, as Jacob did on the typical ladder? Why, but for our own unbelief, our fottifhnefs, our earthly-mindednefs; from which deep fleep, as to the things of God, if we were truly awakened, we fhould fee caufe to own in the words of the fame patriarch, when he awaked from the vifion of the night; " Surely the Lord is in " this place, and I knew it not (13)." Heaven is as near to the heavenly, as the foul is to the body; for we are not feparated from it by diftance of place, but only by condition of ftate: thus when Elifha was furrounded in Dothan by the Syrians, his fervant faw not the chariots and horfemen [the angelical hoft] that furrounded his mafter for defence, as Elifha did, till the Lord opened his eyes. Juft fo it is with us; unbelief and fin keep us from feeing the things that are about us and near to us, and alfo from giving credit to the reports of thofe who are in the experience of them.

The fame apoftle, who cautions againft defpifing prophefyings, does alfo give us to underftand, that angels were not to difcontinue their vifits to men in future times of the church, as where exhorting us not to " be forgetful to entertain ftrangers ;" he adds, " for thereby fome have entertained angels unawares (14)." Now there would be no encouragement nor argument in the latter part of the verfe, unlefs the fame might happen to be the cafe with us alfo. But wherefore fhould we doubt, that thofe bleffed friendly beings fhould take delight in exercifing their good will to men by many kind offices both vifible and invifible, according to the good pleafure of our common Lord, as by preferving us in many dangers, protecting us againft the affaults of evil men and evil fpirits, and by counfelling, warning, and helping us by various ways and means we know not of? We ought not fo to doubt of this, as we are apt to do, nor wonder at it; " For are they not all miniftering fpirits, fent forth to " minifter for them, who fhall be heirs of falvation (15)?" We fhould rather wonder that good men, when they walk out

(13) Gen. xxviii. 16.   (14) Heb. xiii. 2.   (15) Heb. i. 14.

to meditate in the field, as Isaac did (16), should not often meet those cœlestial strangers to join them in sweet conversation on heavenly things, and be accompanied by them in their journies, as Tobias was. But whether manifested to us or not, sure it is, that we are more indebted to them for their kind assistance and ministrations than is generally believed, as evidently appears to have been the sense of our church, heretofore at least, as thus expressed in her collect for St. Michael and all Angels. " O
" everlasting God, who hast ordained and constituted the service
" of angels and men in a wonderful order, mercifully grant,
" that as thy holy angels alway do thee service in heaven, so
" by thy appointment they may succour and defend us on earth,
" through Jesus Christ our Lord."

As to the argument offered by those, who maintain the total cessation of these and other extraordinary dispensations on the establishment of the Christian religion, or its protection by the civil powers; viz. that the extraordinary gifts of the Spirit, together with its settled ecclesiastical œconomy, are sufficient for salvation, and the welfare of the church, and therefore what is more is needless, and not to be expected; for if men now will not believe Moses and the prophets, Christ and his apostles, so neither would they be persuaded, though one should rise from the dead. Be it answered, first, that the opposers of extraordinary dispensations do here take for granted the very point in question, viz. that they are ceased, which it is impossible for them to prove; nay, we appeal for the reality of them to the authority of universal ecclesiastical history, as also to the records of every particular church and nation in Christendom, not to insist on the testimony given thereto in numberless books, tracts, and narratives, some or other of which have fallen in the way of every person of any reading and conversation: what credit is to be given to or withheld from them respectively, is another matter of enquiry; but that all should be invention and forgery, requires a higher degree of credulity than is sufficient for believing the greater part of them; and as to the reproachful epithets of monkish and legendary, so liberally bestowed on well

(16) Gen. xxiv. 63.

d attested

attested narratives of this kind, by such as resolve to believe nothing but what they can see with their eyes, or touch with their hands, they are not to be regarded, where the grounds of credibility and evidence are the points in question. Many of the Roman Catholick writers stand confessedly chargeable with an over credulity; and it is to be wished, that many of the Protestant writers were less censurable than they are for incredulity; and the medium between both these extremes will be found the proper ground from whence to take the clearest view of these matters. Sure it is, that we are at this time very dangerously infected with doubting and unbelief, as to things supernatural; and that the general idea of reformation amongst us means rather a departure from certain Popish errors and superstitions, than any advances in true faith and godliness.

Secondly, As to what is alleged for the sufficiency of the ordinary means of grace under a legal establishment of religion for faith and salvation, may we not ask such bold pronouncers, by what commission they take upon them to determine concerning sufficiency in this matter, and who gave authority to teach, that the Lord is become more sparing of his benefits and gifts to his church than in former times, nay, than He has promised to be towards it; or do they suppose, that what is called an establishment of religion by the civil powers, is equivalent to the extraordinary gifts bestowed on the primitive Christians? Wherefore should they go about to limit the loving kindness of the Lord by their own scanty measure of sufficiency, since it is his usual way to give not only for mere necessity, but also for delectation; his gracious attribute, not only to be good, but abundant in goodness in all his works both of nature and grace, where men render not themselves unqualified for the same: and He that giveth one talent, is as ready to bestow ten talents on a due improvement of the former; for so He giveth grace for grace.

Thirdly, The inference they draw against the usefulness of miraculous gifts, and other extraordinary dispensations, from those words of Abraham, in the parable of Dives and Lazarus, " If they hear not Moses and the Prophets, neither will they " be persuaded, if one should rise from the dead," is not at all

conclusive

conclusive in this case; as that saying appears to respect such only as have hardened themselves in unbelief, by departing from faith in the written Word, under the ordinary means of salvation; and not such as are weak in the faith, but not obdurate, as was the case with the disciples, who, though under our Lord's own teachings, yet, through the dulness of their apprehension, seemed to need some mighty work to make an impression on their feeble minds: and accordingly, when Jesus was on the way with them to raise Lazarus from the dead, He speaks of the ensuing miracle as useful for them among others, and takes satisfaction on their account, that He was not present with Lazarus in his sickness to heal him: " I am glad for your sakes, that I was not there, " to the intent that ye may believe (17);" that is, by seeing him raised from the dead. So then we are to make a wide distinction between an evil heart of unbelief, as where men, through an incorrigible attachment to sinful courses, or by taking pains to confirm themselves in infidelity, are proof against evidence sufficient for their conviction; and where they are in unbelief through present inattention, distraction of mind from worldly hinderances, dulness of apprehension, and the like causes, but without any wilful opposition to the truth. In these last cases extraordinary means have often salutary effects, by calling off the mind from its wandering, by alarming and converting the sinner from the error of his ways. History supplies us with numberless instances of this kind; and, among others, I see no cause to doubt what is recorded of Bruno, founder of the Carthusian order, viz. that he was converted on the following occasion. As he attended the corps of a certain ecclesiastick (who had been a followed preacher) to his grave, the deceased raised himself up from the funeral bier, and pronounced himself condemned by the just sentence of God; upon which he was interred without the solemnity of Christian burial, and the effect upon Bruno in particular was, that he became impressed with so piercing a sense of his own danger, that he retired from the world, and devoted himself, during the remainder of his life, to a religious retirement and vigorous discipline.

(17) John xi. 15.

From what has been observed on the foregoing subject, we shall conclude, that the same Lord, who in times past sent his prophets, wise men, and seers, and gave extraordinary tokens and warnings to awaken a careless world to a sense of its danger, has not wholly ceased in these last ages to manifest his power and goodness for the same end, in various instances, to cooperate as assisting means with the more general and stated provisions of his revealed will, for our incitement and benefit: and though some, through their unbelief and obduracy in sin, refuse to profit by any methods of his goodness, whether ordinary or extraordinary; yet many others may not be so far departed from the faith and fear of God, as to continue unreclaimable by his more particular and alarming visitations. Thus we read, that many were converted on seeing the miracles which Jesus did, whilst the Scribes, Pharisees, and Rulers endeavoured to stifle their report, and remained wilful unbelievers to the end; and we well know what like opposition we have to expect from men of the same leaven to every thing that may here be advanced in favour of extraordinary manifestations: but were their names and number greater than they are, it would have no weight with us, being no strangers to their little length and breadth, and their want of depth, and ready to meet them in the field of argument, as well as prepared to answer every objection they have to offer; wishing them at the same time more modesty for their own sakes, than to dictate to the church what is sufficient, and what is needless to the purposes of salvation, without scriptural authority. In the general division I am speaking of, there is a class of modest well-meaning men, who are no further concerned in the matter before us, than to justify the ways of God to man, upon a supposition that all things are left to one settled scheme of things and means, as not seeing any thing beyond it, who are established in the faith under the use of ordinary means, and have no invincible prejudice against the extraordinary, but only think them not granted in these ages of the church: and with such I have no controversy; but address myself only to those, who declare open war against all supernatural manifestations, whether they are in the profession of Christianity or not.

And

And here I must ask all such, to what purpose is this your opposition to the belief of any fresh discoveries of the other world? Is it not a subject of the highest importance to us to know, what and where we shall be to all eternity after a short passage over this bridge of time? Are there not different degrees of evidence in these matters; and supposing that your conviction were at all times so full in relation thereto, as to exclude all shadow of doubting, yet are there not infinite particulars and circumstances relating to the world of spirits, which may serve as an inexhaustible fund of fresh discoveries, many of which may have been revealed to others, though not to us, and for us to receive from them? How comes it then, that you are so void of all reasonable curiosity, as to prefer ignorance to information in these things, nay, to study objections to the belief of them? Were any prejudice allowable in this case, it should rather be for, than against them, especially where they have a tendency to promote faith, virtue, and godliness. If any knowledge is to be coveted, surely it is that of the laws, ways, and accommodations of that good country, which we hope to go to and live in for ever. Besides, such extraordinary manifestations are greatly conducive to the good of this world, by laying before us fresh motives and encouragements in our way through it, to strive lawfully for the high prize that is set before us in a better, and by rousing every power and faculty of the mind by fresh news from heaven. If we believe the Scriptures, we must allow of such an intercourse between heaven and earth in former times; and if it be less frequent now, it is owing to the infidelity and apostacy of the times, for God's goodness endureth the same for ever, and good spirits are equally desirous of holding communication with men now, as formerly; but then there must be a suitableness for it on the part of the latter, something of that innocence and simplicity of life, which in ancient times served for the basis of such fellowship.

But neither are instances of extraordinary dispensations so very few now, as most are apt to imagine; for among the many estimable and excellent men and women in the Christian church now that hold fast sound doctrine, walking in the fear of God, and in all good conscience, there is a select company of the inner court

court worshippers, to whom the Lord revealeth his secrets, and maketh known the hidden things of his kingdom. Some of these are favoured with secret communications for their own sakes, or for the benefit only of some few others. They are generally persons of a retired life, little known of their brethren, and sometimes, like Joseph, persecuted by them; an instance of which kind has been well attested to me by a person of veracity, who knew the party, viz. a gentlewoman of fortune; who having declared at different times that she conversed with angels, her relations applied to a late chancellor for a statute of lunacy against her; and though she was allowed upon examination to be reasonable and of sound mind in all other things, yet, upon her confessing this article of her charge, she was ordered to a private madhouse, and her fortune committed to the management of her relations. May it not be asked here, if they, who can favour such prosecutions, are not to be suspected of thinking that the Seers of old were at times beside themselves? Can we be at a loss then how to account for our hearing so seldom of such extraordinary dispensations in these times of unbelief, when it is become so dangerous to own them, or at least when the recital is likely to meet with nothing better than mockery and derision?

But whatever cautionary reserves may be justifiable, nay, prudent, where the manifestation appears to respect only the party to whom it is made, or for private use to some few others, according as discretion may direct; yet, where it is evidently given for publick notoriety and use, as in the case of this author; more especially if by express command; here the person is to be considered as standing in the prophetick character, and therefore is not to consult with flesh and blood in this matter, nor to regulate his measures by human prudence; but to deliver his message boldly, and leave the event to God, lest he suffer for his disobedience, as Jonah did, and be obliged to deliver it at last. But it may be asked here, if it be not reasonable to expect that every such message from heaven should have the attestation of a miracle to evince the truth of it; to which it might suffice to answer, in the words of Job (18), that " the Lord giveth not

(18) Job xxxiii. 13.

" an

" an account of his matters." This however is certain, that wherever He sends a message, He also gives power sufficient with it to convince, or to condemn the rejection of it. Our Lord, in the days of his flesh, wrought miracles, sometimes to convince the understanding, sometimes to take away all excuse from the hardened and impenitent, and sometimes He refrained from doing them, to prevent the greater condemnation of unbelievers; thus He is said not to have done many mighty works in Galilee, because of their unbelief.

But the foregoing query may be further urged into an objection of such apparent strength, as may be thought deserving of a more particular answer. Thus it may be asked, If any particular revelation for publick use and benefit, either in the way of instruction, direction, or warning, rests only on the credit and authority of the revealer, are we not liable to much deception in the matter; and though the messenger may be a true one, yet might not our receiving him as such give encouragement to pretenders and impostors to assume the like character in order to deceive, and to come with, " Thus saith the Lord," in their mouths, when the Lord hath not spoken it? In this case, what rule have we to go by, and how shall we tread firm on such slippery ground? To this it is replied, that as in old times there were false as well as true Prophets and Seers, so nothing hinders but there may be like counterfeits now o'days; for in this mixed world of good and evil, where men stand in their liberty of speaking and acting, no infallible provision against hypocrisy and imposture can take effect, but the enemy will sow his tares in the same field where the good husbandman has sowed his wheat, and Satan will at all times transform himself into an angel of light. Every thing has its contrary here, where good and evil are set one against the other; but then help and means are provided for our direction and safety; if offences are many, so also are our defences; if errors are manifold, there are diversities of gifts to detect and refute them; and if the Father of lies and his emissaries are busy to deceive us, the good Spirit of God is ever ready to lead us into all Truth: so that we have not only light in the Scriptures, but through supplication and prayer may also have **Light** within us from above for

the

the difcerning of fpirits, and for our fecurity againft all the powers of darknefs. We are not therefore to reject truth and error indifcriminately in whatever forms they may appear, becaufe the latter may wear a like garb with the former; but try the fpirits, and hold faft to that which is good, herein imitating the fifhers mentioned in the Gofpel (reprefentative of the wife in Chrift's kingdom) who, " when they had filled their net " with fifh of every kind, gathered the good into veffels, and " caft the bad away (19):" nay, the moft illiterate Chriftian walking humbly in the fear of God, and working righteoufnefs according to his beft knowledge, never was nor will be fuffered to fall into any fatal delufion: fimplicity and uprightnefs of heart place him under the protection of the Almighty, and he is in the effence of truth, though without the formal ideas of it; for " all the paths of the Lord are mercy and truth to fuch " as keep his covenant and his teftimonies (20);" miftake he may, but cannot dangeroufly err, for his very errors are innocent, and love fanctifies all he thinks, fays, and does. Thus the pure in heart fee God in all things, and from all things reap benefit without hazard of lofs; whilft the perverfe and ungodly " change even the truth of God into a lie (21), by turning that which was defigned for their good into the occafion of their fin. But to refume the fubject: If it were allowed to be a juftifiable caufe for the rejecting every extraordinary difpenfation that comes fupported by credible evidence, becaufe fome may falfely pretend to the fame, the objection would be of equal force on the fide of numbers againft liftening to their eftablifhed paftors and teachers, becaufe fome among them are ignorant, fome unfound in doctrine, and fome handle the word of God deceitfully; and though this muft be allowed to be a pitiable cafe where it happens, yet the falvation of the confcientious worfhipper does by no means lie upon any fuch hazard, for ordinary and extraordinary means are all one with the Lord, and rather than any fincerely pious and feeking foul fhould perifh for lack of knowledge, He would fend, if need were, an angel from heaven to be its teacher; but all fuch have an unerring guide, even the

(19) Matt. xiii. 48.   (20) Pfal. xxv. 10.   (21) Rom. i. 25.

good

good Spirit of God, and "them that are meek shall He guide in judgment, and such as are gentle, them shall He learn his way (22)."

Lastly, It is to be observed under this article, that all who professedly oppose every kind of communication with the world of spirits, do not only deny the authority of the sacred records, but also set aside that evidence which is given to the truth of this matter, by the concurrent testimony of every age and nation; so that matter of fact is against them, and proves all their pretensions to reason and philosophy to be vain, whilst they go about to invalidate all authority, except that of their own senses, and I may add, even to render that doubtful likewise; nay, I have heard one of this sceptical class declare, that he would not believe the testimony of his own senses in such a case. It is well known, that the Heathens believed themselves to be under the care of their gods through the ministry of genii or tutelary spirits, and held the existence both of good demons, and of evil or caco-demons; for dark as their dispensation was, they had shadows of truth among them sufficient to keep alive their belief of the soul's immortality, and they have transmitted down to us in their histories many instances of supernatural visions and apparitions, and of warnings by dreams; so that many of our modern unbelievers have less of faith in things of the other world than the very Gentiles, several of whom have declared themselves indebted to good and visible agents for the wisdom of their laws, for many valuable discoveries in physick, for warnings, predictions, and extraordinary deliverances (23). To give only one saying of Cicero, among many, to the same purpose: "I know not," says he, "any one nation, polite, or barbarous, which does not hold, that some persons have the gift of foretelling future events (24)."

But I chiefly confine myself here to cœlestial visions, answerable to the following work, and which are by no means to be considered on the level with apparitions, whether of ghosts departed, or of spirits of any other order, these last being of a far inferior kind to the first; and yet it will not be going far

(22) Psal. xxv. 8. (23) Cicero de Divinatione. (24) Ibid. Lib. 1.

out of my way to speak a few words of the latter. There is a climax in God's works of nature, or a scale ascending from the lowest to the highest of them, till they terminate in the great adorable Original, who is the Alpha and Omega of the universe. From these gradations, discovered or discoverable in the natural world, we may from analogy (which is our best rule here to go by) conclude, that the like progression takes place in the spiritual worlds, and that there is not that wide chasm between one and the other that is generally supposed, but that the most refined part of the material meets the grossest part of the immaterial system of beings, visible thus ending where invisible begins; and consequently, that there are spirits very near us, though not discernible by us, except when according to certain unknown laws of their existence, or the particular will of the Lord, they become manifested to us, either visibly or audibly; and highly credible it is, that all nature is peopled with them in its several regions of the air and earth, and its subterraneous dwellings, according to their different classes, subordinations, and allotments. Milton finely expresses himself on this subject as follows:

" ———Think not, though men were none,
" That heaven would want spectators, God want praise:
" Millions of spiritual creatures walk the earth
" Unseen, both when we wake, and when we sleep," &c.

Now to argue against their existence from their being inconspicuous, is an absurd conclusion for men who pretend to philosophy, especially when all know what a new world of animalcula, invisible before, has been discovered to us by the improved microscope: and who will say, that the natural eye of man is incapable of such further assistance, as may enable us to discern the subtle vehicles of certain spirits, whether consisting of air or ether; certain it is, that either by condensation, or some other way, they can make themselves visible, and converse with us, as man with man; and so innumerable are the instances hereof, as also of their discoveries, warnings, predictions, &c. that I may venture to affirm, with an appeal to the publick for
the

the truth of it, that there are few ancient families in any county of Great Britain, that are not possessed of records or traditions of the same in their own houses, however the prevailing Sadducism of these times may have sunk the credit of them, as well as in a great measure cut off communications of this kind.

These spirits are of both sorts, like men on earth, good and bad; as to the latter, they are the agents of Satan, to promote the interests of his kingdom, and, like their chief, " go to and " fro in the earth, walking up and down in it (25)," seeking whom they may deceive and destroy. These are enemies to good men, and the willing associates of men of evil dispositions, over whom they have great power through the consent of their will, but none otherwise, practising upon their minds and understanding " with all deceivableness of unrighteousness in them that " perish, because they received not the love of the truth, that " they might be saved (26)." This power of enticing, prompting, and instigating such as become their willing captives to all kinds of evil; and the heinous sin of the latter, in freely surrendering themselves into their hands to be practised upon, stands confessed even in the form of proceeding in our courts of judicature in the case of atrocious delinquents, it being part in the charge of indictment, that they did such and such things at the instigation of the Devil, inferring it as the aggravation of their crime, that they could chuse the service of so bad a master.

To continue insensible of our danger from evil spirits, whether from ignorance, inattention, or the disbelief of them, is one of the sorest evils that can befall us, and is in the church at this day a misery to be lamented with tears of blood, as it leads to a fatal carelessness, exposes us to their subtle devices, and gives them an advantage over us every way. Nor are they an enemy lightly to be accounted of, being watchful, diligent, and full of stratagems for our ruin; and they have moreover a hold on the corrupt part of our nature, and well know how to use it, being furnished with traps of all sorts to catch the unwary, and with baits adapted to every vicious appetite and inclination; having a great part of the honours and riches of this

(25) Job i. 7.   (26) 2 Thess. ii. 10.

world

world at their difpofal, through the power and influence of thofe that are fubject to them: and therefore it behoves us to be well furnifhed for this part of our fpiritual warfare, and to put on the whole armour of God, feeing thofe we have to do with are not to be fubdued with carnal weapons; for here, as the apoftle tells us, " we wreftle againft principalities, againft " powers, againft the rulers of the darknefs of this world, " againft fpiritual wickednefs in high places (27)." But we come now to fpeak of better fpirits, and more to fatisfaction.

If there be legions of fpirits about and near us to deceive, tempt, and annoy us, can we doubt of there being as many appointed to ferve, help, and defend us, according to their feveral claffes and offices in this our world? The conclufion is natural from parity of reafon, and the law of oppofites, according to which the Great Governor of the world has contrafted evil with a counterbalance of good; confequently, fuch beneficent beings there doubtlefs always have been, and are, in readinefs to fuccour the fallen human race by their friendly miniftrations, and to fill up the diftance in the fcale of created beings between men and angels. The darknefs of the Heathen world moft certainly did not feparate them from the care of that good God, who is loving to every man, and whofe mercy is over all his works; and though their condition might not admit of communion with angels, but in rare inftances, yet the good offices of thefe kindly affectioned minifters in their refpective provinces, might, in a fort, be angelical to them anfwerably to their difpenfation, and ferve as the loweft ftep in Jacob's ladder for their communication with the heavenly world: and by what is handed down to us by authors of credit concerning communications of this kind to eminent perfons in the ancient Heathen world, as Socrates and others, whether by checks and warnings, impulfes, dreams, voices or vifions, we are not at liberty to doubt of an intercourfe between good fpirits, and the well difpofed Heathens of all ranks, as a difpenfation not fo unfrequent as many fuppofe; feeing that the inftances of this kind amongft ourfelves, that come to publick knowledge, bear no proportion

(27) Eph. vi. 12.

in number to those that are concealed from us. This, however, we are assured of upon the best authority, that "many shall come from the east and from the west" [in the Gentile world] "and sit down with Abraham, Isaac, and Jacob, in the kingdom of heaven; and that many of the children of the kingdom" [professors of the truth] "shall be cast out (28)."

Though we now stand in a far higher dispensation than the Heathens, and are called to an innumerable company of angels, and to the fellowship of the Holy Ghost, yet we are not therefore to suppose, that all intercourse with good spirits of an inferior order is now ceased amongst us; as many, who have not yet attained to the glorious privileges of the Gospel, and the immediate guardianship of angels, may nevertheless stand indebted, under God, to the ministry of such good spirits for many important services, both in their spiritual and temporal affairs; nay, they may be to all of us in the natural world what the good angels are in that which is purely spiritual, and by their great knowledge in the laws and powers of this mundane system, and by various impressions on our animal spirits and faculties, may contribute much to our relief, comfort, and preservation in many difficulties, distresses, and dangers; and perhaps few that take a serious review of the most remarkable occurrences of their past lives, will not be led to ascribe much of assistance to the instrumentality of such invisible friends; nay, who can say, that they are not constituted subordinate agents on various occasions in conducting the scheme both of general and particular providences? There is nothing in this supposition that offers violence to reason or religion; and sure it is, that we have abundant credible testimonies to wonderful discoveries made by them of a very interesting nature both to individuals, and also to society, as of concealed writings and treasure, of murders, conspiracies, and other matters leading to the administration of justice both distributive and punitive (29), as is well known of all conversant with men and books; so that to give the lie to all such relations as credited by the learned, the wise,

(28) Matt. viii. 11, 12.
J. Aubrey, Esq. F. R. S.

(29) See, in particular, Miscellanies, by

the good of all classes, must appear nothing less than impudence joined with infidelity.

It has been made a common objection to the credibility of many apparitions, that they have been either silent, or not delivered any thing worthy of such extraordinary visits; and, consequently, that such visions were no other than the effect of imagination and fancy, as not answering to any use or purpose. To which be it answered, that the use of such visits may be very important, though nothing should pass in the way of conversation between the parties during the interview; as first, by convincing the spectator of the reality of such beings as spirits, and so removing doubts concerning a future state, as by preparing him for the return of such visits to further purpose. Secondly, by affecting the conscience with a tender sense of duty, or with remorse for past offences, and impressing the mind with awful thoughts of its own existence in a separate state. Thirdly, by giving us to know, that we are the objects of regard to beings in the other world, and visible to them when we think not of it, which may serve as a means to restrain us from indecent and offensive liberties in our most retired hours, when the more weighty consideration of the Divine Omnipresence may not be attended to, and so lose its proper effect upon us.

But here we are called off from answering more objections on this subject, to observe, that this laboured opposition to the belief of all intercourse betwixt us and the other world, too often proceeds both from a practical and a speculative kind of atheism, and consequently the disbelief of a future state. Hence proceeds that countenance given to some late writers in favour of infidelity, as also that dreadful apostacy amongst so many in these last days, of exalting I know not what natural religion, in order to lessen the authority of Divine Revelation; whereas it may truly be affirmed, that all such resistance to or departure from the faith under the light of the Gospel, however it may be covered, or coloured with the name of natural religion, is nothing better than atheism. O wretched men, here spoken of, what are you doing? What but the greatest possible injury to your own souls? What but robbing yourselves of every comfort that reason and religion can supply to make this life a blessing?

And

And all for the miserable, mad hope, that when you die, you shall be of no more account than a dead dog in a ditch. If there be any folly, it is yours; if any insanity in the world, you are possessed of it: for if there be a God, you make Him your enemy through your unbelief; if a heaven, what lot have you to hope for in such inheritance? If a hell, how will you escape it? And here also let it be asked, what is your character and estimation in society, if true members of society you can be called, who have no pledge to give of your obedience and fidelity to government, as acknowledging no sanctity in an oath, which is inseparably connected with the belief of a future state? Thus void of faith, void of conscience, void of honour (for what is honour without conscience) what have you left for a support to the slenderest virtue, what have you to engage the smallest confidence from man? Can any firm bond of compact or friendship find place in that heart, which has no interest in *Hereafter* to care for, and wherein every motive and measure must take its rise and direction from the love of self, and the love of this world? In this case, it is more for our comfort to go by our hopes than our fears; and therefore one would be willing to believe, from tenderness to human nature, and also from charity, that the number of those who are in this horrible degree of infidelity is but small; but however that may be, it will be proper to observe here, that to the many general causes of infidelity, some of which have been briefly touched on before, as the undue exaltation of natural reason, a life of pleasure, and confirmed habits of vice, we may add the spirit of controversy and dispute long ago introduced into the church by the artificial logick of Aristotle, and encouraged and kept up in the schools as a necessary part of education in theology, to the engendering perplexity and doubting on every subject, and keeping back the mind from fixing in any settled principles of religion. The several churches of Christendom have confessedly been long infected with this poison of fierce contention and debate, to the banishing of sweet peace and brotherly love, whilst a pretended zeal for truth has served for a cloak to that " wrath of man, " which worketh not the righteousness of God." But such carnal weapons ill befit the Christian warfare; all such kind of

striving

striving for victory among ourselves gives advantage to the enemies of our holy faith, and causes the Philistines to rejoice. The best way of healing differences is by composedness and gentleness of mind, and the Truth of the Gospel of peace is most suitably offered, and most readily received by humble men, and such as are of a meek and quiet spirit. It is obvious to remark in this place, that Deism, Sadducism, and Atheism did never more abound amongst us than since the itch of controversy and wrangling, on all occasions, has filled the world so full of false reasoning and perverse disputings; nay, the contagion has descended to private life, and turned much of our conversation into contradiction and a strife of words, and introduced a bold behaviour and an assuming talkativeness, offensive to all modest persons; insomuch that we are now in general fallen under that reprehension of the apostle applied to the contentious, who " come together, not for the better, but for the worse (30)."

After what has been replied to objections against the credibility of extraordinary manifestations, and also offered as concerning some causes of unbelief in this case, we are here led to declare not only our belief, but full assurance, that extraordinary communications, however now less frequent than formerly, are still continued to several particular members of the different churches, though not publickly revealed by them; and that they are not to be considered only as a particular privilege, but as making part of the state of certain persons (not all) of eminent purity and piety; and to be inwardly convinced of this ourselves, is to make some approach to their state; for however we may come short of them as to like vouchsafements, yet both in the ordinary and extraordinary gifts and graces of the Spirit, we are led, not only to rejoice with them, but by mutual fellowship do participate with them in the blessing; for as in the natural body, so also in the mystical body of Christ, the inferior as well as the superior members jointly contribute to the nourishment and welfare of the whole, by a circulation of that which every one supplieth, so that the highest cannot say to the lowest, I have no need of thee. Thus the meekness, the pati-

---

(30) 1 Cor. xi. 17.

ence, and the humble condefcenfion in fome, may countervail the high illuminations and fplendid miniftrations of others, whilft a common fenfe of their mutual dependence and relation joins them all in the unity of the Spirit to the edifying of the church in love; and therefore where any, whether in the ftated office of the miniftry, or others, go about to vilify or obftruct the fuccefs of any extraordinary way that has a manifeft tendency to promote true godlinefs, they would do well to confider and ftand in awe, left they be found to oppofe themfelves to a work of God; for neither can they be fure that we are not now come to the near approach of that glorious ftate of the church fpoken of in fo many places by the prophets; when the Lord fhall do great things for her in the latter days by a revival of his work in righteoufnefs and peace, fhall pour out his Spirit upon all flefh, reftore the old paths of heavenly communications, and make his Sion a praife in the earth. However unpromifing the times are, yet, praifed be God! we can draw comfort from the promifes of better days, even under the " prefent falling away, " and the revelation of the man of fin foretold (31)," to precede the day of the Lord's coming in the power of his Spirit, to fanctify and cleanfe his church, and to purify unto himfelf a peculiar people zealous of good works; trufting in hope that this time is near at hand, i. e. that he that fhall come, will come, and will not tarry. And though there has been for a feafon a withholding, in a meafure, from Sion the ordinary confolations of the Spirit, in the way of a judgment work [under grace] for felf-condemnation, humiliation, and fubfequent glorification, yet we are affured that fuch judgment is fent forth unto victory over the remainder of indwelling fin : for there is a judgment unto righteoufnefs, as well as a judgment unto condemnation; and accordingly in the former fenfe it is faid, that " Zion fhall be " redeemed with judgment, and her converts with righteouf- " nefs (32);" fo that her tribulation is for purification, and exaltation; as it is faid in another place, " For a fmall moment " have I forfaken thee, but with great mercies will I gather " thee, faith the Lord, thy Redeemer (33):" and as to the

(31) 2 Theff. ii. 3. (32) Ifai. j. 27. (33) Ifai. liv. 7.

reftitution

restitution of her gifts, graces, and extraordinary dispensations, signified by precious stones, under her figurative denomination of the Lord's house or temple, the prophet proceeds thus: "O thou afflicted, tossed with tempest, and not comforted, behold, I will lay thy stones with fair colours, and thy foundations with sapphires, and all thy borders with pleasant stones; and all thy children shall be taught of the Lord, and great shall be the peace of thy children; in righteousness shalt thou be established (34)."

The above is but a small part of the glorious things that are spoken by the evangelical prophet, of the city of God, the spiritual church under the Gospel dispensation in the latter days, when she shall have filled up the measure of her persecutions and sufferings both from her open enemies, and also in the house of her friends. And we trust that the time draws very nigh for this glorious dispensation of the New Jerusalem to take place; and particularly, among other important considerations, from instances of extraordinary communications from above, by visions and otherways, to godly men and women of different churches within this last century, and who may be considered as the harbingers or forerunners of it. Nor did ever any extraordinary revolution come to pass in the church of God, without previous notices of it first given to some chosen vessels for a testimony to the times, to strengthen the weak in faith, to comfort the afflicted, to alarm the careless and impenitent, or to answer other good purposes of the Divine Providence and goodness.

Instances of the kind above mentioned of both sexes are ready at hand to offer, and which were received in their day, according to the dignity of their character, by such as were qualified to profit by their message and ministry; but, as is usual in these cases, they were rejected by the greater part, and their names are here passed over, as it is one design of this preface to guard, as far as possible, against giving occasion for critical cavilling and dispute; it being sufficient for the main intent of it, to recommend and enforce, to the best of our power, the

(34) Isai. liv. 11, 13.

credibility

credibility and authority of the following treatise by the honourable and learned author Emanuel Swedenborg, a native of Sweden, of eminence and diſtinction in his country, having had an honourable employment under the crown, and being of the firſt ſenatorial order of the kingdom; of reſpected eſtimation in the royal family during the late reigns; of extenſive learning, as his voluminous writings demonſtrate; and as to private life and character, irreproachable. Something more particular, as to his perſonal character, has been ſpoken in the Preface to the *Theoſophick Lucubration*, printed and ſold by M. Lewis in Pater-Noſter Row; and Mr. Swedenborg's *Letter to a Friend*, giving a particular account of himſelf and family, annexed to that Preface, is poſtfixed to this, the original of which is in my hands.

It muſt be owned, that the following treatiſe contains ſo many wonderful particulars relating to the worlds of ſpirits, warranted for truth by the ocular teſtimony of the writer, according to his ſolemn affirmation, as would appear impoſſible for man in this mortal body to come at the knowledge of, but for the like inſtances delivered down to us on the authority of the ſacred records, and the promiſe therein made to the church of the continuance of ſuch manifeſtations in it: and the viſions of our author muſt appear to us the more extraordinary, when we conſider that they were of the moſt exalted nature, as not being exhibited objectively to the bodily organs or external ſenſes; nor yet merely intellectual, by repreſentations in the mind, but purely ſpiritual, whereby ſpiritual beings and things were actually ſeen and perceived by his ſpiritual ſenſes, as one ſpirit beholds another, and anſwering to thoſe expreſſions in Scripture, of " being in the Spirit," and of being " caught up by the Spirit;" as likewiſe to that rapt, trance, or ecſtacy of the apoſtle, during which he ſays, " whether he was in the body, or out of the body, he could not tell (35)."

The ſame queſtion that will be aſked here has been briefly noticed already, viz. If a teſtimony to ſo extraordinary a diſpenſation does not require the extraordinary ſeal of miracles to

---

(35.) 2 Cor. xii. 2.

render

render it credible? To which be it further anfwered, that many of the prophets worked no miracles, and yet were believed upon their own private teftimony; and that we believe many things of the higheft confequence in religion upon human authority, where the perfons tranfmitting and delivering them appear properly qualified and circumftanced to give credibility to what they relate. But this argument has been confidered in the Preface to the *Theofophick Lucubration* before mentioned; and from the reafons adduced, and fuch as are ready to be further produced, if called for, we look upon our author's teftimony as worthy of our acceptation in this matter, and venture to rely on his known integrity and piety, and his difinterefted and indefatigable labours to inftruct the world in the moft important truths relating to falvation, at the expence of his fortune, and the facrifice of all worldly enjoyments, during more than the laft thirty years of his life. And if we further reflect, that the whole fcope and tendency of his writings is to promote the love of God and of our neighbour; to inculcate the higheft reverence to the Holy Scriptures; to urge the neceffity of practical holinefs, and to confirm our faith in the Divinity of our Lord and Saviour Jefus Chrift: thefe confiderations, I think, may be allowed of as fufficient credentials (as far as human teftimony can go) of his extraordinary miffion and character, and as convincing marks of his fincerity and truth; efpecially as we have to add, upon the credit of two worthy perfons (one of them a learned phyfician, who attended him in his laft ficknefs) that he confirmed the truth of all that he had publifhed relating to his communications with the world of fpirits, by his folemn teftimony a very fhort time before he departed this life in London, Anno Dom. MDCCLXXII.

Reader, might it not feem a wonder, if a perfon of fo extraordinary and apoftolical a character fhould better efcape the imputation of madnefs than the prophets of old? And accordingly fome have given out, that he was befide himfelf, and in particular, that it was occafioned by a fever which he had about twenty years before his death. Now it is well known by all his acquaintance, that our author recovered of that fever after the manner of other men; that his extraordinary communications
commenced

commenced many years before that time, and that his writings, both prior and subsequent to it, entirely harmonize and proceed upon the same principles with an exact correspondence; and that in the whole of his conversation, transactions, and conduct of life, he continued to the end of it the same uniform, excellent man. Now if to write many large volumes on the most important of all subjects with unvaried consistency, to reason accurately, and to give proofs of an astonishing memory all the way, and if hereto be joined propriety and dignity of character in all the relative duties of the Christian life; if all this can be reconciled with the true definition of madness, then there is an end of all distinction between sane and insane, between wisdom and folly. O fie upon those uncharitable prejudices, which have led so many in all ages to credit and propagate slanderous reports of the best of men, even whilst they have been employed in the heavenly work of turning many from darkness to light, and from the power of Satan unto God.

Were an angel from heaven to come and dwell incarnate amongst us, may we not suppose that his conversation, discoveries, and conduct of life, would in many things be so contrary to the errors and prejudices, the ways and fashions of this world, that many would say with one consent, that he is beside himself; and where any one of our brethren, through the divine favour, attains to any high degree of angelical illumination, and communications, may he not expect the like treatment? I forget the name of the philosopher, whose precepts and lectures were so repugnant to the dissolute manners of the Athenians, that they sent to Hippocrates to come and cure him of his madness; to which message that great physician returned this answer: that it was not the philosopher, but the Athenians that were mad. In like manner, the wise in every city and country are the smaller part, and therefore must be content to suffer the reproachful name that in truth belongs to the majority. This has been the case of all extraordinary messengers for good to mankind, and the world is not altered in this respect. But it may be said, that though it be thus with the ignorant and profane, yet men of education and learning will form a more righteous judgment of the matter, and be determined impar-

tially

tially according to the nature of the evidence; and it would be well if this were so; but in general it is far otherwise. Human learning, considered merely in itself, neither makes a man a believer, nor an unbeliever, but confirms him in truth or error, according to his prejudices, inclinations, or interest; at least it is commonly so: and therefore we find, that in all ages such among the learned as devoted themselves to support the credit and interest of their particular professions, were always the most violent persecutors of the truth; for though truth has its conveyance through the intellectual part in man, yet it never gains its effect, or operates as a principle, till it be received into the affection and will; and so man is said in Scripture to be of an understanding heart. So that knowledge is productive of the greatest good, or the greatest evil, according to the ground or disposition in which it resides; when joined with piety and humility, it adds both lustre and force to truth; when joined with the corrupt passions of our nature, it is the most violent persecutor of it: and this was the case with the Scribes and Pharisees, and Doctors of the Law; no greater enemies to Christ than they; the pride of reputation for learning, and the authority of publick teachers, unfitted them for becoming learners at the feet of the lowly Jesus; and therefore to them were directed those words of our Lord: " How can ye believe, who " receive honour one of another, and seek not the honour that " cometh of God only (36)?" Giving us hereby to understand, that the dominion of any wrong passion over the mind, will prove a certain hinderance in our way to divine truth.

Great as our loss is by the fall, yet something of that correspondent relation, which originally subsisted between the human soul and divine truth, is still remaining with us (through grace) otherwise we should no more be capable of receiving it when offered, than the brute beasts, which have no understanding; but then, that all may not be lost by wilful sin, and we rendered thereby incapable of conversion, we must be careful not to set up idols in our hearts, nor suffer any false interest to mislead us, as thereby the mind is tinctured with prejudice against

(36) John v. 44.

the truth, and the underſtanding receives a wrong bias, and ſo we become like the falſe wiſe ones ſpoken of in Job (37), who " meet with darkneſs in the day-time, and grope in the noon day " as in the night." This difference in the ſtate of the heart and the affections, occaſions the difference we ſee both in the unlearned and learned of equal natural and acquired abilities, that whilſt ſome readily receive the truth in the light and love of it, others are always diſputing, and always ſeeking, without ever coming to the knowledge of it.

As there is correſpondency, or a mutual relation between rightly diſpoſed minds and truth in the general, ſo likewiſe there is a particular correſpondency or congruity between certain minds and certain truths in particular, producing an aptitude in the former to receive the latter as ſoon as offered, and that by a kind of intuition without reaſoning; and hence it comes to paſs, that ſuch as have a remarkable fitneſs for this or that particular claſs of truths (which we uſually term genius) are leſs qualified for any conſiderable proficiency in certain others. Thus the mathematician ſeldom excels in metaphyſical knowledge; and he that may be very expert in ſyſtematical divinity, is oftentimes a ſtranger to myſtical theology; one member thus ſupplying what another lacketh, whilſt all may learn thereby to eſteem and love one another, and praiſe the Lord for his diverſity of gifts for the common benefit of his church. Let not then ſuch as walk in the ſimplicity of a naked faith, without needing any other evidence; let not ſuch, I ſay, cenſure in the following book what they do not underſtand, or cannot receive, as it may be of uſe to others, who are led more in the way of knowledge than themſelves. We judge not them, nay, love them; wherefore then ſhould they come ſhort of us in charity? Are we not brethren, and travelling to the ſame good land, why then ſhould we fall out by the way? Even the Scribes could ſay, as touching Paul: " If a ſpirit or an angel hath ſpoken to " him, let us not fight againſt God (38):" and who can ſay, that what this our author delivers to us, as from viſion and revelation in the other world, is not the very truth?

(37) Job v. 14.   (38) Acts xxiii. 9.

Let it be observed here, in regard to the ensuing work, that though the narrative part of it should appear to the reader of doubtful authority, yet the doctrinal part, where confirmed by plain Scriptures, certainly merits his serious attention, nay, many things therein, touching which the Scriptures are silent, carry weight and internal evidence along with them in the judgment of impartial minds; and though they claim not a place among the *Credenda* of religion, yet will often be found useful to illustrate them, as also to enrich the mind, to familiarize heavenly things to the thoughts, and to wean the affections from the toys and vanities of a miserable world lying in wickedness. It is allowed that our author does not, in all places throughout his writings, follow the commonly received interpretations of the Scriptures; but so neither do all churches, nor all expositors in the same church. Though as to life and godliness, and consequently what pertains to salvation, the Scriptures are sufficiently plain, yet with respect to many difficult and mysterious parts of them, they continue wrapped up in a venerable obscurity, to be opened according to the needs and states of the church to the end of the world; and we doubt not to affirm, that the highly illuminated Swedenborg has been instrumental in bringing hidden things to light, and in revealing the spiritual sense of the sacred Records above any other person, since the church became possessed of that divine treasure. In the present dark night of general apostasy has this new star appeared in our northern hemisphere, to guide and comfort the bewildered traveller on his way to Bethlehem.

It is further to be remarked on our author's writings (of which the following treatise is little more than a twentieth part) that the representation he therein gives us of the heavenly kingdoms, sets before us that world of desires so objectively to the human intellect and reason, nay, even to our sensible apprehension, as to accommodate the description of it to the clear ideas of our minds, whether they be called innate, acquired, or (as he pronounces them) influxive from the spiritual world. He gives us to know from autopsy, or his own view of it, that heaven is not so dull a place, as some foolishly suppose it, who having no ideas of it, so neither desire to have any, and this

through

through a superstitious fear in some of profaning the subject by any association of natural ideas; whereas nature, in the state of man's innocence, was constituted a fair representation of the first or lowest heaven, and will again bear the same resemblance in the millennial kingdom (39); and though it be now sadly corrupted and deformed through the entrance and dominion of sin, yet as far as we can separate the evil from the good, so far it adumbrates to us cœlestial things; nay, even the art and ingenuity of man, as displayed in works of nature, is a ray of the divine skill manifested in the human mind. Thus Bezaleel and Aholiab are said to have wrought curious work, for the service of the sanctuary, by wisdom and understanding given them from the Lord (40). If then we receive innocent satisfaction here from viewing beautiful houses and gardens, why should we be so averse from thinking that there are cœlestial mansions and paradises in the kingdom of our Father? Does musick delight us? why may we not hope to be entertained with more ravishing harmony from the vocal and instrumental melody of the angels in heaven? How cheering both to the mind and senses, and also helpful to pious meditations in good men, are the sweetly variegated scenes of nature in the prime of the year; and can we be unwilling to believe that corresponding heavenly scenes are provided for the delectation of departed happy souls in the land of bliss? Especially when we understand (as understand we may) that all that is truly pleasing, beautiful, and harmonious in nature, is by influx from the spiritual into the natural world; in which latter, archetypal glories are faintly represented to us by earthly images. It was a profane saying of a late well known jester and epicure, who was also a noted performer on the dramatick stage; that " as to heaven, he had no great longing for " the place, as he could not see what great pleasure there could " be in sitting ——— (41) on a cloud, and singing of psalms." But had that impious man reflected, that heaven or hell must be the everlasting portion of every one in the other world; and

(39) See *Paradise Restored*: Sold by *Robinson* in *Pater-Noster Row*.
(40) Exod. xxxvi. 1.
(41) The expression here left out is so gross, and unbecoming the subject, that we forbear giving it to the reader.

had

had he been acquainted with our author's writings, he would not have treated the glories of the place with such ludicrous profaneness; but have thought, and spoken, and lived better than he did: nay, he might have wished his lot to be there, even from a principle of epicurism in a certain sense; for all spiritual beings must have spiritual senses, and if in heaven, those senses must be gratified with delights adapted thereto: but where any one is so grossly sensual, as to place the supreme felicity of a spirit in such gratifications as suit only with the corporeal part of our present degraded nature, may it not be said of such a one, that he has degraded it still lower, even to the level of an ass in his understanding, and to that of a swine by his affections? The work before us will help such a one to very different conceptions of the heavenly kingdom, even as to those particular beatitudes which are most nearly accommodated to the ideas of sense; and he may also therein learn, that all the relative duties, all the social virtues, and all the tender affections that give consistence and harmony to society, and do honour to humanity, find place and exercise in the utmost purity in those delectable abodes, where every thing that can delight the eye, or rejoice the heart, entertain the imagination, or exalt the understanding, conspire with innocence, love, joy, and peace, to bless the spirits of just men made perfect, and to make glad the city of our God.

Such, dear reader, and so excellent are the things here offered for thy entertainment and instruction by this wonderful traveller. But if, after all, thou canst not read him as the enlightened Seer, and the extraordinary messenger of important news from the other world, read him as the Christian divine and sage interpreter of the Scriptures; read him as the judicious moralist, and acute metaphysician; or read him as the profound philosopher; or if he cannot please in any of these characters, read him at least as the ingenious author of a divine romance: but if neither as such he can give content, I have only to add; Go thy way, and leave the book to those that know how to make a better use of it; and such, I trust, are not a few among the serious, being willing to hope, for the honour of our country, that if such a ludicrous representation of hell, as passes under the

the title of, *The Visions of Don Quevedo*, could make its way amongst us through no less than ten editions, there will not be wanting in the land a sufficient number of persons of sober reflexion and contemplative minds, to give all due encouragement to a work so well calculated, as this is, to promote true wisdom and godliness, by credible testimony to the realities of the world of spirits, and to the respective states and conditions of departed souls.

As to the persons concerned in translating and conducting the publication of the following extraordinary work, I may venture to say, that they deserve well of the publick, as far as the most disinterested pains and benevolent intentions can justify the expression; and though we are far from obtruding the contents of this book on any, as demanding an implicit faith therein, yet we cannot but zealously recommend them to the most serious attention of those who are qualified to receive them, as subjects of the greatest importance, high as heaven, and deep as hell, and comprehending all that is within us and without us; as a key that unlocks all worlds, and opens to us wonderful mysteries both in nature and grace; as displaying many hidden secrets of time and eternity, and acquainting us with the laws of the spiritual worlds; as leading us from heaven to heaven, and bringing us, as it were, into the company of angels, nay, into the presence chamber of the King of Saints, and Lord of Glory. In a word, whatever is most desirable to know, whatever most deserving of our affections, and whatever is most interesting in things pertaining to salvation; all this is the subject of the following volume.

We are not unprepared for the opposition that may be expected to any fresh discoveries of truth, especially, as has been observed before, where the credit or interest of any considerable profession or body of men is concerned. Established doctrines and opinions are considered as sacred, and the sanction of custom gives them the firmness of a rock with most; as is known to have been the case in physick, astronomy, and natural philosophy, in which, truth, though supported by the evidence of demonstration, has scarcely been able to make its way in a century. Besides, the pride of learning is strong on the side of established

established institutes, and for men to part with what they have been building up with much study and pains for a great part of their lives, is a mortifying consideration; they are startled at the thoughts of becoming thus poor, and some would be as willing to part with their skins, as with their acquisitions of this kind; and hence it is, that we read of so many martyrs to error and folly in all ages. These things considered, we are not to wonder that our author's publications have met with no better encouragement hitherto in his own country (as is usually the case with prophets) we being informed some time ago by a worthy merchant residing at Gottenburg, that but few of the clergy (as far as had come to his knowledge) had then received them; and that the Reverend Dr. Beyer, a learned man, and professor in divinity in that university, had suffered much persecution for adopting and propagating the truths contained in his writings, and was not suffered to print his explication and defence of them in Sweden. But to the honour of our constitution, we can as yet call the liberty of the press (and a liberty within the bounds of decency may it always be) as the privilege of Englishmen, and therefore may reasonably hope for better success to our author's writings in this land of freedom; not that we expect any encouragement on their behalf from our pharisees and bigots of any denomination, for they are the same every where; but our hopes are from men of unprejudiced minds, dead to self and the world, of a simplified understanding, and such as are friends to wisdom wherever they find her; in a word, whose spirit harmonizes with truth, and whose hearts are unison to heavenly things.

I cannot think of concluding this preface without speaking somewhat particularly to a point of doctrine, the knowledge of which is the more necessary to the reader for the right understanding of the author's writings, as in the vast variety of subjects and new discoveries that he presents to us, it has a principal connexion with most of them; nay, is the true key in his hand that opens the secrets of the visible and invisible worlds, explains man to himself, and also reveals the spiritual sense of the Sacred Writings. The doctrine I am here speaking of, is that of cor-

respondency

respondency or correspondence, which are terms nearly of the same signification.

Correspondence or correspondency, in a philosophical sense, is a kind of analogy that one thing bears to another, or the manner in which one thing represents, images, or answers to another; and this doctrine, as it refers to things in heaven and in earth according to their mutual relations, is given us in the following adage of the renowned Hermes Trismegistus—*Omnia quæ in cælis, sunt in terris terrestri modo; omnia quæ in terris, sunt in cælis cælesti modo.*

This natural or material world, in which we live as to the body, proceeds derivatively (in a sense consistent with the Mosaick account of the creation) from the spiritual world, and subsists by continual influx from it; it is as a spiritual thing formed into a palpable and material thing, as an essence cloathing itself with a form; or as a soul making to itself a body. Therefore this world, and all things in it, as far forth as they stand in the divine order, do correspond to heaven and heavenly things; but now (through the fall of man) standing in evil as well as good, the dark, evil, or hellish world has gained a form in outward nature. Hence it is, that so many evil men, evil beasts, and poisonous things, together with all the disorders in the natural world, bear its impressions and properties, and make this world a kind of torment-house to us. Man, considered in himself, is a little image of heaven or hell, and also of this outward world, which no other being is; and therefore he is the most wonderful of all God's creatures. At death he puts off his part in this material kingdom, and passes into one of the other two, being its servant to which he obeys or unites himself here by his will and affections; and therefore he is commanded to set his " affections on things above (42)," as they constitute the band of union betwixt heaven or hell, and the soul of man. These three worlds are called Principles, as first, the light or heavenly world; secondly, the dark or hellish world; and thirdly, this natural or material world; and man's reasoning faculty stands in the center of the three, and receives

(42) Col. iii. 2.

impreſſions from each, as it turns to one or other of them; then ſpeculates on the materials it derives thence, and contends for or againſt right and truth, even as the affections are ſet, for theſe bias, lead, or bribe it; and therefore, if reaſon be not enlightened from above, under the conduct of good affections, it is a meer mercenary, ready to enliſt on any ſide.

The human nature was ſo almoſt univerſally corrupted at the time of our Saviour's advent in the fleſh, that unleſs Jeſus Chriſt had come into the world when He did, to reſtore the heavenly principle of light and grace, or truth and goodneſs, through the medium of his humanity (all immediate communication between God and the ſoul being well nigh ceaſed) the human race muſt have periſhed, by falling irrecoverably into the evil principle, to the utter extinction of truth, and the loſs of all free will to good; but by the entrance of this Divine Friend into the human nature, He opened the ſhut gate of communication betwixt heaven and earth, God and the ſoul, and ſo became our great Mediator and gracious Redeemer. But ſtill we are at liberty to receive or reject Him as our Sanctification and complete Redemption, for man can only be ſaved conſiſtently with choice and free will.

Men had loſt the true original language of nature (which expreſſed things according to their qualities and properties) before the flood, even ſo much of it as had remained among the poſterity of Seth and Enoch for a conſiderable time; and this ignorance they fell into on their loſing the knowledge of nature in its correſpondence to divine and heavenly things; for nature in its proper order, as obſerved before, is the book of God, and exhibits ſpiritual things in material forms. In the room therefore of this was ſubſtituted a language by letters and reading in books, to help him this way for attaining to divine knowledge, as rudiments leading thereto in our preſent ſtate of ignorance, in which literature is miſtaken by moſt for wiſdom itſelf; however, to ſome the door was and ſtill is open for immediate heavenly communications, but what through unbelief, earthly mindedneſs, and other ſad impediments, few at this time are qualified for ſo high a privilege.

The

The early ancients after the flood had some knowledge of correspondency derived down to them by tradition, though without any perception of it in themselves; and it remained longest among the Egyptians, of which their hieroglyphicks or sacred sculptures were a principal part; but by degrees they became so far corrupted and blind, as to lose sight of the things represented, and to worship their representatives or images. Hence the original of their foolish idolatry of beasts, birds, fishes, and vegetables. Our enlightened author, had he lived longer, designed, as he told me, to give us the key to the ancient hieroglyphical learning, saying, at the same time, that none but himself could do it; but of this the world was not worthy.

The knowledge of correspondences is now almost entirely lost, especially in Europe, where even the name is little understood; and this is one main cause of the obscurity of the Scriptures of the Old Testament, which were chiefly written by the rules of this science; nay, man also, as an image of the spiritual and natural worlds, contains in himself the correspondences of both, of the former in his interior, and of the latter in his exterior or bodily part, and so is called the Microcosm, or Little World. Thus for example; all the organs of his senses, his features, bowels, and vessels, even to the minutest vein and nerve, correspond to something in the soul or spiritual part. On the other hand, the affections and passions of the mind represent themselves naturally in the face and features, so that the countenance would be the natural index to the mind, were men in a state of simplicity, without guile and dissimulation; and yet, as matters stand at present, so much still appears of the mind in the correspondent features of the face, as to serve for a type, signature, or impression thereof. Thus love, hatred, hope, fear, joy, sorrow, assent, contempt, surprize, &c. do naturally, and often involuntarily, manifest themselves in the visage; in like manner the will, by the actions and motions of the body; the understanding expresses itself in the speech, and the affections in the sound or voice; and all these by influx from within, and correspondence from without: and as the features correspond to the affections, so does the eye to the intellect, the nose to the faculty of discerning, and the ears to attention

attention and obedience; accordingly we use the word *quick-sighted*, to signify a ready apprehension; and penetration or discernment is sometimes expressed by *smelling a thing out*; and *to hearken* in Scripture means *to obey*. Be it likewise observed, that the heart corresponds to sincerity of love; the loins, &c. to conjugal affection; the bowels to commiseration; the hands and fingers to operation, &c. and so much of the language of nature still remains, as to express by these outward representatives the corresponding powers, passions, and affections of the soul, which influences and actuates these several members and parts, as every one experiences. And as the body in its several parts and offices corresponds to the soul and its operations, so does the soul in its several faculties and powers to the heavenly world in all things good, and to the hellish world in all things evil. Thus wisdom, love, purity, innocence, &c. have reference to the cœlestial kingdom, as being communications by influx from thence, and therefore it is that heaven bears a near analogy to man (as standing in his right order) and is called by our author, *The Grand Man:* for the human form is the most perfect of all, and accordingly, God assumed it in condescension to man, represents Himself to us by it, and manifests Himself in it, at times, to the holy angels; so likewise the angelical societies, according to their distinguishing qualities and excellence, bear a particular relation to this or that part of the human form. Thus, as our author informs us, one society corresponds to, or is in, the province of the head, and they are such as excel in wisdom; another to the heart, being such as excel in love; and some to the arms, as being of superior strength, and so on. Thus, as the body corresponds to the soul, so the soul in its true state and order corresponds to heaven, and heaven to God, who is the only original fountain of goodness and truth, of all blessedness and perfection, from whom they descend, in their different kinds and degrees, through the heavenly and spiritual worlds down to this last and lowest form of creation, the earth in which we now dwell.

The earth likewise, in its different kingdoms, animal, vegetable, and mineral, corresponds to things in the spiritual world. Thus, not only the beasts of the field, and the birds

of

of the air, according to their different properties, have a representative meaning in Scripture, but also trees and plants of
various kinds; so in particular, those of the aromatick kind,
as also the olive, the vine, and the cedar, do figure divine gifts
and graces, and other rare endowments in the human heart
and mind; and in like manner, gold, silver, precious stones,
and other particulars of rich furniture in the tabernacle and
temple, are mentioned in Scripture with a corresponding reference to goodness, truth, purity of affection, holiness, &c. and
so the wisest interpreters expound them, and this not by arbitrary significations, but as outward proper signs of things inward
and spiritual. Thus all nature is a theatre of divine wonders,
representative of the invisible world to such as are of a right
understanding and discernment, as our author has exemplified
in a thousand instances. It is hoped, that what has been here
offered on the subject of correspondency, will be found useful
to such as are in a disposition to give the following book an
attentive perusal.

From the great variety of important subjects and discoveries
to be met with in our author's writings, I cannot refrain from
observing on one more, as deserving our particular regard, as
also to prepare the reader for what he is to meet with in this
volume, viz. the doctrine of the intermediate state of departed
souls, called here, *The World of Spirits*, as being that in which
they all meet after death (except a very few, who pass directly
to heaven or hell) in order to their last preparation for final
bliss or misery. This doctrine has long been received in the
church, and revealed to many by their departed friends; but
having been much disfigured and misrepresented, like some other
truths, by erroneous additions and lucrative figments in the
church of Rome, it was not admitted by our first reformers,
who, instead of reforming the doctrine, totally rejected it under
the opprobrious name of a Popish purgatory; however, it has
been retained by most of the spiritual, otherwise called myftick,
writers in all churches, and I have seen a judicious defence of
it by the Hon. Archibald Campbell in our own; but the book,
I believe, is scarce. Sure it is, that as far as our author's credit
and authority extend, the truth of the doctrine will not be

m   questioned,

questioned, as he relates, that he had frequent rapts or tranflations of spirit to that intermediate world, and had there seen and converfed with moft, if not all, his departed friends and acquaintance, befides a great number of others, to the amount of very many thoufands. In this intermediate world, which he calls a ftate of vaftation, the good fpirits are gradually purified from all the ftains and defilements of fin which they had contracted in this naughty world, whilft the good principle predominating in them takes full poffeffion of all their faculties and powers, confirms them in good habits, and renders them meet to be partakers of heavenly joys; on which they are tranflated to heaven. On the other hand, the bad fpirits are gradually divefted of thofe fuperficial and apparent virtues, and all that adventitious, external good, which before had ferved as covers to the evil principle within, which now predominates without referve or controul, confirming them in their evil habits, and their repugnancy to all good; which being effected, they precipitate themfelves into the infernal pit, to join company with fuch as are like themfelves. Thus what is a ftate of purification to the good, is to bad fpirits a ftate of feparation of all extraneous good from that radical evil which conftitutes the effence of their nature.

Now this doctrine appears confonant; firft to reafon, as it accords with the tenor of the divine adminiftration in the government of this world, in which all things proceed to their limit or completion in a regular and gradual procefs. Secondly, It is confonant to religion, as it vindicates the divine attributes from all imputation of undue feverity, by laying man's deftruction at the proper door, and as the inevitable confequence of his own free choice. Thirdly, This doctrine yields confolation to the humble pious Chriftian, as the time of his departure draws nigh. Few fuch, upon a ftrict examination of themfelves, are fo well fatisfied with their ftate, as to find nothing lacking, but that they are already fitly qualified for the fociety of the holy angels; whereas the belief, that an intermediate ftate is appointed, wherein every thing that now hindereth fhall be removed out of the way, and their fouls purified from every pollution and fpot contracted by their union with this fleshly

nature,

nature, through the prevailing power and energy of the divine principle within them, and so bringing them into the state of just men made perfect, they can take comfort from this consideration, and meet their change with a holy confidence.

If this be so, and that the same intermediate state, which purifies the good spirits, leaves the bad under the total dominion of evil by their own free choice, that so both may be possessed by their own proper principle respectively, and go to their own proper place; how say some, that the devils will be essentially transformed into angels of light, at a certain time appointed by the Father? We desire here to oppose with the greatest tenderness, a doctrine which we heretofore judged favourably of, and modestly to offer the reasons of our present dissent, wishing rather that we could agree with some excellent men on the other side of the question; but human wishes are no rule of the divine proceedings, and even charity must be directed by the principle of truth, and the established laws and nature of things. We find ourselves in a sort called upon to offer a few observations on this subject, at a time when there is much reason to believe, that many have revived this doctrine more to quiet their fears, and so lull themselves into a false peace, than from any conviction of their understanding; whereas they may be supplied with a much surer remedy against those fears in the comfortable promises to the truly penitent delivered in the Gospel of our most compassionate Saviour, whose last declaration to his disciples before his ascension was, " that re-
" pentance and remission of sins should be preached in his name
" among all nations (43)."

It is evident, that the plainest Scriptures (and such we are to go by) are against the doctrine before mentioned; and that the same force of words that is therein used to express the eternal happiness of those that are saved, is also made use of to express the eternity of their state who are lost. But the advocates for that side of the question rest their plea and stress of their argument on the foot of divine mercy; and God forbid that we should go about to straiten that mercy towards others (though

---

(43) Luke xxiv. 47.

even devils) to which the very best of us stand indebted both for all they have, and all they have to hope for; and did the matter of the question turn merely upon mercy, in like manner as a gaol delivery depends on the arbitrary clemency of an earthly prince, I doubt not, that either one single soul would not go to hell, or if any, that a host of angels would be sent thither with a message of mercy; nay, if necessary to their salvation, that even Jesus Christ himself would condescend so far, as to visit those unhappy prisoners with a free offer of peace and reconciliation for their redemption. But here it must be observed, that mercy misunderstood and misapplied, is no other than man's own false idea of mercy. God's mercy in regard to man respects him as a creature that He has endowed with freedom of will, and whose happiness or misery depends on the right or wrong direction of his choice and affections, by which he becomes capable or incapable of the divine mercy. Now to compel such a creature, is to undo him, to unmake him what he is; and therefore mercy, with regard to him, is to provide for him such means and motives as may influence his understanding, will, and affections to what is good as his free choice. Now through the mercy of God every thing is done in this life (which is man's only state of probation) in order to this end, though man knoweth it not; how then are we to expect, that any means of this kind should be more effectual in the other world, wherein all things are represented to us as unchangeable, where the tree lieth as it falls for heaven or hell, and where all things increase in good or evil to eternity in their respective kingdoms? Praised be the name of the Lord, for his mercy endureth for ever! And as it is infinite, so it extends to all possible cases; but to make us good, that we may be qualified for happiness *against our will*, is no possible case, seeing that to be good, is to *will* good with desire and affection, which the self-hardened and impenitent are averse to, and therefore render themselves unreceptive of mercy. Now the very idea of diabolism carries in it repugnancy and hatred to God and goodness, and consequently the greatest contrariety to the possibility of conversion. Were it otherwise, and that the most malignant spirit in hell could sincerely say, " Lord, I am weary and ashamed of this evil

" nature,

"nature, and forry for the fins that have brought me into it; O
"help and deliver me through thy mercy from it, that I may be
"converted, and become thy fervant!" In this cafe, he would
inftantly ceafe to be a devil, and become an object of the divine
mercy; but repentance, prayer, and the defire of good, is all
from the grace of God, and dwelleth not in thofe who are the
willing fervants of fin, and therefore only free from, not to,
righteoufnefs (44).

It is fuppofed by fome, that length of fuffering will at laft
fubdue the reluctance of the will, melt the heart into tendernefs,
and turn the worft of evil fpirits to repentance and fupplication
for pardoning mercy, and qualify them for it; but this, as juft
now obferved, is the fole effect of that grace which they are not
admiffive of, and not the effect of fuffering, which has no fuch
power belonging to it; but has its different effects relative to
the different ftates of thofe who are the fubjects of its operations. Thus we fee, that as the fame fire which melts the wax,
hardens the clay, fo the fharpeft fufferings have contrary effects
on different perfons. They who have any remnant of grace in
their inmoft foul (however unrighteous they have been outwardly) any fpark of the divine life ftill remaining in their interiour, are foftened and meliorated by them, and become obedient to the heavenly voice, crying within them, Why will ye
die? Turn unto the Lord, that iniquity may not be your ruin:
whilft the obdurate and impenitent fay in their hearts with
Pharaoh, Who is the Lord, that we fhould obey him? And
turn that punifhment, which fhould be for their amendment,
into the occafion of their blafphemy and defpair. Could length
of fuffering produce the effect before mentioned, we might naturally fuppofe that fome change for the better would, in the
courfe of thoufands of years, have taken place in him who is
called in Scripture (45), "That old Serpent, which is the
"Devil and Satan;" and yet, as he had the prefumption to
tempt our Saviour in the wildernefs, and ftill continues to practife his wicked devices, in order to work our ruin; fo of him
it is foretold, that after being bound a thoufand years, during

(44) Rom. vi. 2c.   (45) Apoc. xx. 2.

Christ's millennial reign on earth, and being loosed from his prison, he will again go out to deceive the nations (46); so little of likelihood, if any possibility, there is, that they, who have confirmed themselves in enmity and hatred to all goodness, should become capable of repentance to salvation. I desire not to strain any argument beyond its proper strength against an hypothesis, which I find myself more ready to receive, upon any satisfactory grounds, than to reject; but let truth be ever held sacred and inviolable, whether it be according or contrary to our natural inclinations and wishes; nor let that be called a want of charity, where charity is not concerned, or would suffer perversion and abuse: for charity, which in its proper signification is love, cannot extend to that which is essentially evil; otherwise we must condemn that solemn appeal of the man after God's own heart: " Do not I hate them, O Lord, " that hate thee (47)?" And it was charged upon Jehoshaphat for sin (though otherwise a good king) that he had joined himself in confederacy with the wicked Ahaziah, as in those words of Jehu: " Shouldest thou help the ungodly, and love them " that hate the Lord? therefore is wrath upon thee from before " the Lord (48)." Whence we are to learn a caution how we bring dishonour upon this divine grace of charity, by misapplying it to false and unworthy objects, to the lessening of our zeal and affections for the honour of God, and the things that be of God.

We are encouraged to hope, that many things which have been offered in the course of this Preface will be found properly introductory to the following volume, and shall now conclude it with two or three short remarks to the serious reader, as no other is capable of reaping any benefit from our author's writings; nor to others have we any thing to say, unless it be to caution them against treating with derision or scurrility such matters as they may be more nearly concerned in than they at present suppose. Even the very dreams of good men, in relation to things of the other world, have at times something divine in them, and are not lightly to be regarded; but where such

(46) Apoc. xx. 7, 8.   (47) Psal. cxxxix. 21.   (48) 2 Chron. xix. 2.

communicate

communicate to us important instructions and discoveries as by commission, and from their own experience, and that with deliberation, consistency, and clearness, they demand our attention and reverence. And here it is to be observed, that what this author has published to the world concerning the states of departed souls respectively, the laws of the invisible worlds, and a thousand particular circumstances belonging thereto, appear to be such as could never enter into the heart of man to conceive, unless they had been given to him from above; and yet carry something of an internal evidence along with them, as soon as they are received by a serious mind; for, after all, it is more the right temper and disposition of the mind, than its sagacity, that gives us to see these things in their proper light. It is every wise man's care to guard against a stubborn incredulity on the one hand, as well as against any delusion that an over hasty belief might expose him to on the other; and in this age of doubting and disputing all things of a spiritual nature, our greater danger is confessedly from the former side, and therefore it behoves us to give the more heed, that we lean not to the error of the times. Besides, the weight and importance of the subjects here treated of adds to the credibility of the message, as coinciding with our confidence in the promises of the Lord, that He will reveal his secrets to his servants, and not forsake his church in the time of her extremity; but send his extraordinary messengers and ministers endued with light and power from on high to alarm the careless, to call back the wanderers, to confirm the wavering, and to comfort the spirit of the humble and contrite ones with glad tidings from the heavenly Canaan, the lot of their inheritance; and this in order to make ready a people prepared for the Lord against his second advent in spirit to build up the walls of the New Jerusalem: and when should such messengers be more expected, or when more entitled to a better welcome than in this our time of desolations, when faith and charity have so far failed amongst us, and when darkness is on the face of the deep, darkness in the church, and darkness in the state, darkness in the minds of good men, and darkness on all the dispensations of providence, so as to give emphatical application of those words of the Psalmist to our present condition:

dition: " It is time, O Lord, that thou have mercy upon Sion, " yea, the time is come (49)." But who are they that moſt reject the teſtimony of thoſe ſpecial meſſengers, and thoſe faithful witneſſes to the Truth, which the Father of Lights has ſent from time to time for the edification of his church, and the confirmation of the faith of many in it? Who but ſuch as are ever calling out for more evidence for believing, and pleading the want of it in juſtification of their unbelief, whilſt at the ſame time they labour all they can to invalidate the evidence of all human teſtimony, which is the ordinary medium through which divine truth is conveyed to us.

And now, dear reader, I bid you farewell, ſincerely wiſhing that you may be of the number of thoſe who take the Holy Scriptures for their guide, as their authentick outward rule of faith and life, and in an honeſt and good heart receive the Word of God, and keep it: and may the Spirit of Wiſdom give us a right judgment in all things pertaining to ſalvation, that ſo we may be preſerved from error through an over haſty credulity on the one hand, and an obſtinate incredulity on the other; neither rejecting the teſtimony of men fearing God, and of good report, as to what great things the Lord hath done for them, and to be communicated by them for the benefit of their brethren; nor ſuffering ourſelves to be impoſed on by the cunning craftineſs of ſuch as lie in wait to deceive: and as it is more profitable for us to have the heart eſtabliſhed in grace, and to glorify God in our lives, than to be gifted with viſions and particular revelations (through danger of being exalted above meaſure thereby) ſo let us not be high-minded, but fear; nor, becauſe others have been ſo favoured, expect or deſire the ſame ourſelves, but walk humbly and contentedly in the way of God's ordinary diſpenſations, leſt preſumption or a vain curioſity ſhould expoſe us to the danger of deluſion from our ſpiritual enemy: and as to thoſe that cannot receive many of the things delivered in the following book, and alſo as to thoſe that do receive them, let them not judge one another, but follow the rule of moderation laid down by the apoſtle, Rom. xiv. every one abiding

(49) Pſal. cii. 13.

by that of which he is perfuaded in his own mind, in a candid forbearance towards others. In men of a Chriftian fpirit, charity eafily beareth all fuch things, believeth all things for good, and hopeth all things for the beft: and as we are all brethren on a journey to the fame heavenly country, fo let us hold on our way together in peace, and that love, which is more than knowledge; and may the God of peace and love be with us!

AN ANSWER

TO A

LETTER FROM A FRIEND.

BY THE AUTHOR.

I TAKE pleasure in the friendship you express for me in your letter, and return you thanks for the same; but as to the praises therein, I consider them as belonging to the truths contained in my writings, and so refer them to the Lord our Saviour as his due, who is in himself the Fountain of all Truth. It is the concluding part of your letter that chiefly engages my attention, where you say as follows: " As after your departure
" from England disputes may arise on the subject of your wri-
" tings, and so give occasion to defend their author against such
" false reports and aspersions, as they who are no friends to
" truth may invent to the prejudice of his character, may it
" not be of use, in order to refute any calumnies of that kind,
" that you leave behind you some short account of yourself, as
" concerning, for example, your degrees in the university, the
" offices you have borne, your family and connexions, the ho-
" nours which I am told have been conferred upon you, and
" such other particulars as may serve to the vindication of your
" character,

"character, if attacked; that so any ill-grounded prejudices may be obviated or removed? For where the honour and interest of truth are concerned, it certainly behoves us to employ all lawful means in its defence and support." After reflecting on the foregoing passage, I was induced to comply with your friendly advice, by briefly communicating the following circumstances of my life.

I was born at Stockholm, in the year of our Lord 1689, Jan. 29. My father's name was Jesper Swedberg, who was Bishop of Westrogothia, and of celebrated character in his time. He was also a member of the Society for the Propagation of the Gospel, formed on the model of that in England, and appointed President of the Swedish churches in Pensylvania and London by King Charles XII. In the year 1710 I began my travels, first into England, and afterwards into Holland, France, and Germany, and returned home in 1714. In the year 1716, and afterwards, I frequently conversed with Charles XII. King of Sweden, who was pleased to bestow on me a large share of his favour, and in that year appointed me to the office of Assessor in the Metallick College, in which office I continued from that time till the year 1747, when I quitted the office, but still retain the salary annexed to it as an appointment for life. The reason of my withdrawing from the business of that employment was, that I might be more at liberty to apply myself to that new function to which the Lord had called me. About this time a place of higher dignity in the state was offered me, which I declined to accept, left it should prove a snare to me. In 1719 I was ennobled by Queen Ulrica Eleonora, and named *Swedenborg*; from which time I have taken my seat with the nobles of the equestrian order in the triennial assemblies of the states. I am a fellow, by invitation, of the Royal Academy of Sciences at Stockholm, but have never desired to be of any other community, as I belong to the Society of Angels, in which things spiritual and heavenly are the only subjects of discourse and entertainment; whereas in our literary societies the attention is wholly taken up with things relating to the body and this world. In the year 1734 I published the *Regnum Minerale* at Leipsick,

Leipsick, in three volumes, folio; and in 1738 I took a journey into Italy, and staid a year at Venice and Rome.

With respect to my family connexions: I had four sisters; one of them was married to Erick Benzelius, afterwards promoted to the Archbishoprick of Upsal; and thus I became related to the two succeeding Archbishops of that See, both named Benzelius, and younger brothers of the former. Another of my sisters was married to Lars Benzelstierna, who was promoted to a provincial government, but these are both dead; however, two Bishops, who are related to me, are still living; one of them is named Filenius, Bishop of Ostrogothia, who now officiates as President of the Ecclesiastical Order in the General Assembly at Stockholm, in the room of the Archbishop, who is infirm; he married the daughter of my sister; the other, who is named Benzelstierna, Bishop of Westermannia and Dalecarlia, is the son of my second sister; not to mention others of my family who are dignified. I converse freely, and am in friendship with all the Bishops of my country, which are ten in number, and also with the sixteen Senators, and the rest of the Grandees, who love and honour me, as knowing that I am in fellowship with angels. The King and Queen themselves, as also the three Princes their sons, shew me all kind countenance; and I was once invited to eat with the King and Queen at their table (an honour granted only to the peers of the realm) and likewise since with the hereditary Prince. All in my own country wish for my return home; so far am I from the least danger of persecution there, as you seem to apprehend, and are also so kindly solicitous to provide against; and should any thing of that kind befall me elsewhere, it will give me no concern.

Whatever of worldly honour and advantage may appear to be in the things before mentioned, I hold them as matters of low estimation, when compared to the honour of that sacred office to which the Lord himself hath called me, who was graciously pleased to manifest himself to me his unworthy servant, in a personal appearance in the year 1743; to open in me a sight of the spiritual world, and to enable me to converse with spirits and angels; and this privilege has been continued to me to this day. From that time I began to print and publish various unknown

known *Arcana*, that have been either seen by me, or revealed to me, concerning heaven and hell; the state of men after death; the true worship of God; the spiritual sense of the Scriptures; and many other important truths tending to salvation and true wisdom: and that mankind might receive benefit from these communications, was the only motive which has induced me at different times to leave my home to visit other countries. As to this world's wealth I have sufficient, and more I neither seek nor wish for.

Your letter has drawn the mention of these things from me, in case, as you say, they may be a means to prevent or remove any false judgment or wrong prejudices with regard to my personal circumstances. Farewell; and I heartily wish you prosperity both in things spiritual and temporal, of which I make no doubt, if so be you go on to pray to our Lord, and to set him always before you.

EMAN. SWEDENBORG.

London, 1769.

CATALOGUE

CATALOGUE

OF THE

THEOLOGICAL BOOKS

Publiſhed by the Author EMANUEL SWEDENBORG.

ARCANA CŒLESTIA, quæ continent Explicationem ſuper Geneſin et Exodum, 8 vol. Londini An. 1747 ad 1758, ed.

DE COELO ET INFERNO. De Nova Hieroſolyma et ejus Doctrina Cœleſti. De Ultimo Judicio. De Equo Albo. De Telluribus in Univerſo, Londini An. 1758, ed.

DOCTRINA NOVÆ HIEROSOLYMÆ. De Domino. De Scriptura Sacra. Doctrina vitæ pro Nova Hieroſolyma. Continuatio de Ultimo Judicio, et de Mundo Spirituali, Amſtelodami An. 1763, ed.

SAPIENTIA ANGELICA de Divina Providentia, et de Divino Amore et Divina Sapientia, Amſtelodami An. 1763, ed.

DELITIÆ SAPIENTIÆ DE AMORE CONJUGIALI. Poſt quas ſequuntur voluptates inſaniæ de Amore Scortatorio, Amſtelodami An. 1768, ed.

APOCALYPSIS REVELATA, Amſtelodami An. 1764, ed.

VERA CHRISTIANA RELIGIO, continens Univerſam Theologiam Novæ Eccleſiæ, à Domino apud Danielem, Cap. vii. 13, 14. et in Apocalypſi, Cap. xxi. 1, 2. prædictæ, Amſtelodami An. 1771.

CONCERNING

HEAVEN AND HELL.

IN our Lord's discourse with his disciples on the *Consummation of the age* (1), or last time of the church, at the end of his prophecies concerning its successive states in regard to love and faith (2), he says thus: "Immediately after the "tribulation of those days shall the sun be darkened, and the "moon shall not give her light, and the stars shall fall from "heaven, and the powers of the heavens shall be shaken; and

---

☞ References for explanation, illustration, and proof, to a Latin work of the author, in eight volumes in quarto, entitled, *Arcana Cœlestia*, or, *Heavenly Secrets*, printed in numbers, or short sections, to which the references direct. n. with the figures following that letter, denotes the number of the sections referred to, from the beginning to the end of that work.

N. B. As the references under many articles are too numerous to be inserted, the translator often passes over the preceding numbers, and only gives two or three of the last; as the author, in the body of that work, by a most stupendous strength of memory, generally refers the reader to the foregoing numbers, in which the subject matter before him is treated of.

(1) The words here translated, *The consummation of the age*, is the true rendering from the Greek, and not, *The end of the world*, as in our common translation, the word 'Αἰων never signifying the *world*, but an age or period of time, or a dispensation of things; and here particularly, of the church, as explained by the author: and that it here signifies the end of the church under its present dispensation. See n. 4535. 10672.

(2) Our Lord's predictions concerning the consummation of the age, his second advent, the successive desolation of the church, and the last judgment, as in Matt. xxiv. xxv. are explained in the work entitled, *Arcana Cœlestia*, in the prefixes to Genesis, from the fifth to the twenty-fourth chapter, n. 3353 to 3356, &c. and 5063 to 5071.

A "then

" then shall appear the sign of the Son of Man in heaven: and
" then shall all the tribes of the earth mourn, and they shall
" see the Son of Man coming in the clouds of heaven with
" power and great glory: and he shall send his angels with a
" great sound of a trumpet, and they shall gather together his
" elect from the four winds, from one end of heaven to the
" other." Matt. xxiv. 29, &c. They who understand these words according to the sense of the letter, suppose that all these things are to come to pass, as they are literally described, at that time which is called the last judgment; and accordingly not only that the sun and moon shall be darkened, the stars fall from heaven, the sign of the Lord appear in heaven, and that they shall see him in the clouds, and with him his angels with trumpets; but also, according to predictions of like sound in other parts of the sacred writings, that the whole visible world shall perish, and be succeeded by a new heaven and a new earth; and this is the general belief of Christians at this time: but all such are strangers to the interior of the scriptures, which have a hidden sense throughout, holding forth to us things spiritual and heavenly, by such as are natural and mundane in the expression of the letter, and this not only in sentences taken collectively, but also in every particular word (3): for the scriptures are written entirely according to correspondences (4), in order to represent to us inward and spiritual things, by such as are outward and natural, as will evidently appear by what is delivered and shewed in many places concerning this inward sense, in a work intitled, *Arcana Cælestia*, and also by a collection of instances of this kind taken thence, in a small treatise, *De Equo Albo*; or, *Of the White Horse*, mentioned in the Revelations: and according to this sense we are to understand the things of which our Lord speaks, in the place before cited, concerning his coming in the clouds of heaven; viz. by the sun there being

---

(3) That there is an inward or spiritual sense throughout the whole of the scriptures. See n. 1143, 1984, 2135, &c. 9063, 9086.

(4) That the *Word* is written by the strict rules of correspondences, and that spiritual things are therein signified throughout, n. 1404, 1408—2900, 9086. See chapters on correspondences in this work.

darkened,

darkened, is signified the Lord in regard to love (5); by the moon, the Lord with respect to faith (6); by stars, the knowledges of goodness and truth, or love and faith (7); by the sign of the Son of Man in heaven, the manifestation of divine truth; by the tribes of the earth mourning, all particulars and circumstances relating to goodness and truth, or love and faith (8); by the coming of the Lord in the clouds of heaven with power and glory, his presence in the word, and right interpretation of it (9), clouds signifying the literal (10), and glory the inward and spiritual sense of the word (11); and by angels with a trumpet giving a loud sound, is signified heaven and divine truth proceeding thence (12). Hence we are given to understand by these words of our Lord, that at the consummation of the age, or end of the church period, when there shall no longer be faith and charity on earth, that the Lord will open the scriptures in their spiritual sense, and reveal the heavenly secrets therein contained. The secrets revealed in the following work are concerning heaven and hell, and the life of man after death, subjects which the church now o'days hardly knows any thing of, though described in the written word; nay, many who were born and live within the pale of it deny them, saying in their hearts, Who ever came from thence to shew us of these things: lest therefore the like incredulity, which chiefly reigns among the learned and worldly wise, should infect the simple in heart, and the simple in faith; to me it has been granted to

---

(5) That *sun* in the Word signifies the Lord, in reference to love, and thence love to the Lord, n. 1529, 1837—7083, 10809.

(6) That *moon* in the Word signifies the Lord, in reference to faith, and thence faith in the Lord, n. 1529, 1530—4996, 7083.

(7) That *stars* in the Word signify knowledges *(cognitiones)* of things good and true, n. 2495, 2849, 4697.

(8) That *tribes* signify all truths, and things good in their complex, and so the whole of faith and love, n. 3858, 4060, 6335.

(9) That the *coming of the Lord* signifies his presence in the word, and revelation of it, n. 3900, 4060.

(10) That *clouds* in the Word signify the written word in its literal sense, n. 4060—10551, 10574.

(11) That *glory* in the Word signifies divine truth, as it is in heaven, and as it is in the internal or spiritual sense of the word, n. 4809—9429, 10574.

(12) That *trumpet* signifies divine truth in heaven, and as revealed from heaven, n. 8815, 8823. In like manner, *voice*, n. 6971, 9926.

associate

associate with angels, and to converse with them, as man does with man; and also to see the things that are in the Heavens and in the Hells, and this now for thirteen years together; and also now to describe the things so seen and heard, in order that hereby the minds of the ignorant may be enlightened, and an end put to incredulity. By the vouchsafement of this immediate revelation we are given to know, that the coming of the Lord is at hand.

That the Lord is the God of Heaven.

2. The first and principal thing to know is, who is the God of heaven, as all other things depend thereon; how throughout the universal heaven no other is acknowledged for the God of heaven, but the Lord alone: it is there confessed by all, as he himself taught on earth; that he is " One with the Father;" that " the Father is in him, and he in the Father;" and that " he who seeth him, seeth the Father;" and that " all holiness " proceeds from him," John x. 30, 38. ch. xiv. 10, 11. ch. xvi. 13, 14, 15. I have frequently discoursed with the angels on this subject; and they constantly affirmed, that they knew not how to divide the Godhead into three, inasmuch as they know and perceive that it is one, and that in the Lord: moreover, they said, that such of the church as passed from this world into the other with the idea of three Deities in their minds, cannot be admitted into heaven, their thoughts being distracted, as it were, between one God and another; whereas it is contrary to the laws of the kingdom to believe in three, and confess but one (13): for in heaven every one declares his real sentiments, language there being the expression of the mind, or as thinking audibly; and therefore there is no admittance for such as have formed their ideas of the Godhead according to such a threefold division and separation, without concen-

(13) That on certain Christians being tried in the other life, as to the idea they had of God, it was found, that they had the idea of three gods, n. 2329, 5256, 10736, 10738, 10821. That a Divine Trinity in the Person of the Lord, is acknowledged in heaven, n. 14, 15, 1729, 2005, 5256, 9303.

trating

trating them into one in our Lord; besides, as among the angels there is a communication of their thoughts, should any one, whose belief and confession were so contradictory, come among them, he would immediately be discovered, and eliminated from their society: let it be noted, however, that all those, who in their life-time here did not separate between truth and goodness, or faith and love, do in the other world, under the instruction of the angels, [*whatever mistakes they may have innocently imbibed here*] readily receive the true and heavenly doctrine of our Lord being the God of the universe: but it is otherwise with those, who, in this state of mortality, separated between faith and good life, or, in other words, whose practice was not according to true faith.

3. They who in this life (though outwardly professing members of the church) did not believe in our Lord, but in the Father only, and confirmed themselves by arguments in such their unbelief, find no place in heaven; and forasmuch as they are without all influx from heaven, where the Lord only is worshipped, they are gradually divested of the faculty of thinking rightly on any subject, and at length either become like mutes, or else talk foolishly, moping about with their arms hanging dangling down before them, like paralyticks or ideots. They who have openly denied the divinity of our Lord, believing only in his human nature, as do the Socinians; they likewise are excluded from heaven, and being carried forward a little towards the right (*), are let down into a deep pit, and so separated from the rest that come from the Christian world: but as to such as profess to believe in an unmanifested divinity, which they call the Great Being, or Spirit of the Universe, from which all things proceeded, and renounce all faith in the Lord; these, on examination, are found to believe in no God, forasmuch as their unmanifested deity, or unknown God, is, according to their creed, no other than a mysterious something like

---

(*) The place of spirits in the other world, as also their ascent into heaven, or descent into hell, is all along described by the author in reference to the body of the spectator; and the meaning in this passage is, that the spirits here mentioned appear to sink down in front, a little towards the right, into the particular place appointed for them. Transl.

nature in its first forms, which, as they have no conception of it (14), cannot be any object of faith or love to them: these have their lot amongst those who are called Naturalists. The case is different with those that are born without the church, and are called Heathens, of whom we shall speak hereafter.

4. All infants, which constitute a third part of the society in heaven, are initiated in the doctrine and faith of the Lord being their Father, and afterwards of his being Lord of all, and consequently the God of heaven and earth. That they increase in stature and knowledge, even to angelical understanding and wisdom, will be shewed in what follows.

5. That the Lord is the God of heaven will admit of no doubt with those that are true members of the church, as he himself hath told us: " All things that the Father hath are " mine"—" All power is given unto me in heaven and in earth." Matt. xi. 27. John xvi. 15. xvii. 2. Matt. xxviii. 18. It is said " in heaven and in earth," for he who governs heaven, governs the earth also, as the latter is subject to the former (15). Now in quality of Governor of heaven and earth, we receive from him all the good of love, and all the true of faith, consequently all understanding, wisdom and happiness, and, to sum up all, eternal life, according to that declaration of our Lord, " He that " believeth on the Son, hath eternal life; but he that believeth " not the Son, shall not see life." John iii. 36. And elsewhere: " I am the resurrection and the life; he that believeth " in me, though he were dead, yet shall he live; and he that " believeth in me shall never die." John xi. 24, 25. And in another place: " I am the way, the truth, and the life." John xiv. 6.

6. There were certain spirits, who, whilst they lived in the body, professed only faith in the Father, without having any

(14) That a deity, not conceivable by any idea, is no object of faith, n. 4733, 5110, 5633, 6982, 6996, 7004, 7211, 9267, 9359, 9972, 10067.

(15) That the universal heaven is the Lord's, n. 2751, 7086. That he hath all power in heaven and earth, n. 1607, 10089, 10827. That as the Lord governs heaven, and all things depending thereon, so consequently all things in this world, n. 2026, 2027, 4523, 4524. That the Lord alone has the power of defending us against the evil spirits of darkness, of guarding us against all evils, and of confirming us in all good, and so consequently, of saving us, n. 10019.

other

other idea of our Lord than as of another man, and consequently did not believe in him as the God of heaven; wherefore they had leave to go about and enquire as they would, whether there were any other heaven than that of our Lord; but after continuing their enquiry for some days, they could procure no information of any other. They were of that class, who suppose the happiness of heaven to consist in pomp and dominion; and because they could not obtain their wishes, but were told, that the joys of heaven did not consist in such things, they were highly displeased, as not desiring any other heaven than wherein they might domineer over others in a pre-eminence after the fashion of this world.

That the Divinity of the Lord constitutes Heaven.

7. The angels considered collectively are called Heaven, as being the constituents of it, though in truth the divine virtue proceeding from the Lord by influx, and received by the angels, does really constitute it essentially, both in general, and also in its particular distinctions: now this divine influence proceeding from the Lord, is the good of love, and the true of faith, and according to the measure of their recipiency of these from him, in such degree is the excellence of their angelical nature, and so far do they constitute the forms of their respective heavens.

8. Every angel throughout the heavens knows, and intimately perceives, that he cannot will and do any good, nor think and believe any truth from mere self, but only from the divine influx, and consequently from the Lord; and that whatever of good and true they do and think from themselves, are only apparently, not really so, forasmuch as they have in them no principle of divine life that they can call their own. The angels of the inmost or highest heaven have a clear perception, and also a sensation of this influx, and in proportion thereto is their degree of bliss, which consists in love and light [wisdom], and as these are derived from the Lord's divinity, it is evident that this constitutes heaven, and not any thing proceeding from the

the nature of angels, as of themselves (16). Hence it is that heaven is called in scripture his dwelling and throne, and that the blessed inhabitants of it are therein said to be in the Lord (17). How heaven is replenished with divine virtue proceeding from him, will be explained in what follows.

9. The angels go still farther in this matter, affirming from the wisdom that is in them, that not only all goodness and truth, but likewise the whole of life proceed from the Lord by way of continual emanation, confirming their position by this argument, viz. That nothing can exist from itself, but from some prior cause, and all things from the first cause, which they call the original essence of the life of all things; and that they subsist in like manner, as subsistence is no other than a continuation of existence, and whatever loses its connexion with the first cause, through the intermediate links, must lose its existence: as then there is but one fountain of life, and man subsists only as a stream issuing therefrom, consequently, should the communication cease, so also must his life: moreover, they affirm, that as from this one only fountain (the Lord) of life proceed divine goodness and truth, so do they operate in every one according to the reception of them: they who receive them into their faith and life, in such they constitute heaven; but they who reject or pervert them, convert good into evil, and truth into error (*), and so they become hell to them. They farther establish this truth by the following argument, viz. That all things in the universe have some relation to goodness and truth, the

---

(16) That the angels of heaven acknowledge all good to be from the Lord, and nothing of it from self, and that the Lord dwells with them, though in his own divine principles, and not in any thing that is proper to them, or which they can call their own, n. 9338, 10125, 10151, 10157. And that therefore in the word, by angels, is understood some attribute of the Lord, n. 1925, 2821—8192, 10528: and they are also sometimes called gods, from the indwelling of the divinity in them, n. 4295, 4402, 8301, 8192. That also all good and all truth, essentially such, consequently, all peace, love, charity and faith, are only from the Lord, n. 1614, 2016—2892, 2904: as likewise all wisdom and understanding, n. 121, 124.

(17) That they who are in heaven, are said to be in the Lord, n. 3637, 3638.

(*) Thus we read of those, " who changed the truth of God into a lie." Rom. i. 25. and of the Lord being a " lying spirit in the mouth of Ahab's prophets," 1 Kings xxii. 22. Tr.

life of man's will (which is that of his love) to the former, and man's intellectual life (which is that of his faith) to the latter: now as all goodness and truth comes from above, so does also every vital principle in man: this being the creed of angels, they of consequence reject all gratitude and thanks directed to them, even for their most beneficent ministrations, and are highly displeased, and withdraw themselves, when any one ascribes good to them as the authors of it; nay, they are astonished to think that any one should be so besotted, as to imagine that he can be wise, or do any good from himself; nor do they call that good, which has self for its end, but that alone which is done from a disinterested love of goodness; this they call good from the divine fountain, and the principle that constitutes heaven, as having the Lord for its essence and root (18).

10. There are certain spirits, who, in the body, had confirmed themselves in this faith, that the good which they did, and the truths which they believed, were from themselves, and as such to be appropriated to them: of this class are all they who place merit in their good works, and value themselves on their own fancied righteousness: such have no admittance into heaven, for the angels shun their company, and look upon them either as stupid, or as thieves; as stupid, because they set themselves, and not the Lord, always before them; as thieves, because they rob him of the honour that belongs to him: all such are professedly enemies to the assurance of faith that obtains among the saints above, viz. That divine virtue, proceeding from the Lord alone, and received by the angels, constitutes both the sanctity and happiness of heaven.

11. That they who are in heaven, and also they who are true members of the church on earth, are in the Lord, and the Lord in them, appears from his own words: " Abide in me,
" and I in you: as the branch cannot bear fruit of itself, except
" it abide in the vine, no more can ye, except ye abide in me:
" I am the vine, ye are the branches: he that abideth in me,
" and I in him, the same bringeth forth much fruit; for with-
" out me ye can do nothing." John xv. 4—7.

(18) That all good in the angels from the Lord, has in it the divine nature of the Lord, but not the good that is from themselves, n. 1802, 3951, 8478.

12. Hence it may appear, that the Lord is with the angels in his own divine essence, and is all in all in heaven, because the good that is there is from him, and what proceeds from his divine nature is properly himself, and constitutes heaven, and not any thing that belongs to the angels as their proper own.

That the Divine Influx of the Lord in Heaven produces Love to him, and Charity to one another.

13. The divine efflux emaning from the Lord is called in heaven divine truth on the following account: it issues from his divine love; and this divine love and divine truth are to each other as the heat and light of the sun in our world, love being expressed and signified by the former, and truth proceeding from it (19) by the latter, and this by the law of correspondence: so then divine love is the essence, and divine truth is the form, and thus united, they enliven all things in heaven, as the heat and light of our sun, in conjunction, fructify the earth in the spring and summer seasons: but it is otherwise where they are not united, or the light not sufficiently impregnated with heat, for then all is benumned and lifeless. This divine good, which is represented by heat, is the good of love in the angels, and divine truth is that through and by which it operates and is manifested.

14. That the divine virtue which constitutes the nature of heaven is love, is because love is a principle of spiritual union, and joins the angels to the Lord, and to one another, insomuch that they are but as one in his sight: besides, love is the very essence to every life, and consequently both to men and angels: and this answers to experience, for how is every one animated and warmed by the fire of love! how languid and cold under

---

(19) That *fire* in the word signifies love in both senses, n. 934, 4906, 5215. That the holy and cœlestial fire signifies divine love, and every particular affection of it, n. 934, 6314, 6832. That the light therefrom signifies the truth proceeding from the good of love: and light in heaven, divine truth, n. 3395, 3485, 3636—9548, 9684.

the

the abfence of it! and how lifelefs under the total privation of it (20)! But it muft be remembered by the way, that the life of every one correfponds to the particular kind of love that actuates him.

15. There are two diftinct kinds of love that more particularly actuate the angels in heaven, love to the Lord, and love to their neighbour: in the inmoft or higheft heaven the former has the afcendant; in the fecond or middle heaven, the latter, yet both proceeding from the Lord, and conftituting their heavens refpectively: how both thefe kinds of love operate diftinctly, and how jointly, is clearly difcerned in the light of heaven, but obfcurely in this world. By love towards the Lord, in heaven, they do not mean the love of him in a perfonal confideration of the word, but to love the good that proceeds from him, and this is evidenced by the willing and doing good from the principle of love: and by the love of their neighbour, they do not mean merely a perfonal love of their fellows, but the love of truth proceeding from the Divine Word, manifefting itfelf in willing and acting according to truth in its feveral relations: hence it is evident, that thefe two loves are to be diftinguifhed as goodnefs and truth feparately confidered, and when conjoined, as goodnefs united with truth (21). But thefe things are of difficult comprehenfion by thofe who have not clear ideas of what is meant by love, by good, and by neighbour (22).

16. I have fometimes converfed with the angels on this fubject, who feemed to wonder that any in the Chriftian church fhould not know, that to love the Lord, and their neighbour, is to love goodnefs and truth, and to practife them from incli-

---

(20) That *love* is the fire of life, and the real efficient caufe of it, n. 4906, 5071, 6032, 6314.

(21) That to love the Lord and our neighbour, is to keep the divine commandments, n. 10143, 10153, 10310, 10578, 10648.

(22) By love to our neighbour, we are not to underftand the love of his perfon, but the good and the true which conftitutes his character, n. 5025, 10336. They who confine their love to the perfon, without regard to his principles, love equally the evil and the good that is in him, n. 3820. That charity is to will and to be well affected to the truth for its own fake, n. 3876, 3877. That charity towards our neighbour, is to do what is good, juft, and right in every relation we ftand in to him, n. 8120, 8121, 8122.

nation,

nation; when they may so easily know, that every one testifies the sincerity of his love for another, by a ready compliance with his will, and that this alone is the bond and cement of mutual love among men; as also that good proceeding from the Lord must be like him, as having his nature in it; and consequently that they are in his image and likeness, whose lives are formed on principles of goodness and truth, by will and practice: for to will a thing, is to love to do it, according to those words of our Lord: " He that hath my commandments, and keepeth " them, he it is that loveth me; and he that loveth me, shall " be loved of my Father, and I will love him, and will mani- " fest myself to him, and we will make our abode with him." John xiv. 21, 23. ch. xv. 10, 12. and elsewhere.

17. That the virtue proceeding from the Lord, which influences the angels, and constitutes heaven, is love, is confirmed by the experience of all in heaven; for all there are so many forms of love and charity, and appear in beauty beyond description, for their looks, their speech, their every action (23), are so many expressions of love: moreover, there are certain spiritual spheres which issue from and surround every angel and spirit, which make known by sensible evidence (and that sometimes to a considerable distance) the kinds and degrees of their particular affections; for these spheres are so many emanations from their vital affections, and the sentiments they produce, or, in other words, from the life of their love and faith: the spheres thus exhaling from the angels, are so replete with love, that they sensibly affect the spirits that are in company with them: I myself at times have been so affected by them (24). That love is the predominant principle in the life of angels, is manifest also from hence, that is, in the other world every one turns his face to the object of his love, so they who are principled with love towards the Lord, and towards their neigh-

(23) That the angels are so many forms of the love of charity, n. 3804, 4735, 9878, 10177.
(24) That a spiritual sphere, called the sphere of life, exhales from every man, spirit and angel, and is diffused around him, like to an atmosphere, n. 4464, 5179, 7454, 8630. That it streams from the vital affections, and their thoughts issuing therefrom, n. 2489, 4464, 6206.

bour,

bour, have their faces always turned towards the Lord; whereas they who are in the love of self, have their faces always turned from him, whatever be the movement of their bodies; for as in the other world, space corresponds to the inward state of spiritual beings respectively, so also the four quarters of the heavens (which have not their fixed determinations there as in this world) are determined with reference to the aspect of the spectators respectively (*). It is here to be noted, that it is not by any virtue or power in the angels of themselves, that they always turn their faces to the Lord, but by a holy instinctive power derived from him in those who love to obey his will (25): but more of this hereafter, where we shall speak of the four quarters of the heavens in the other world.

18. That the divine influencing virtue of the Lord in heaven is love, is because love is recipient of all things proper to heaven, as peace, understanding, wisdom, and happiness; for love attracts to itself whatever is congenial to it, as by a natural instinct, for they are its riches and perfection (26): and this we all can witness to, as knowing how love in ourselves ransacks whatever is laid up in the memory, and takes to itself whatever it there finds suitable to itself, which it disposes of in subserviency to its gratification and end, rejecting and banishing all that is contrary to it. That there is inherent in love a strong attractive power, with the desire of appropriating to itself such truths as accord with its nature, I had full experience of in certain spirits

(*) This will be farther explained in the sequel of this work, and may be understood thus: As the Lord has his personal manifestation in heaven always in the east, according to what our author relates, the angels and angelical spirits, which way soever they turn themselves, front always to the east, and so have the Lord always before them. Quere, If the belief of this among Christians in early days of the church, however they might come by it, did not first give occasion to the custom of turning to the east on repeating the creed. Tr.

(25) That spirits and angels constantly turn their faces towards the objects of their loves, and consequently all that are in the heavens towards the Lord, n. 10130, 10189, 10420, 10702. That the four quarters of the heavens in the other life are not fixed as in this, but are determined by the aspect of the spectator, and always the same, which way soever he turns, n. 10130, 10189, 10420, 10702.

(26) That in love are affections and things innumerable, and that love attracts to itself all things that are concordant with it, n. 2500, 2572, 3078, 3189, 6323, 7490, 7750.

that were tranflated to heaven, who, though of great fimplicity, and but of moderate capacity whilft in this world, prefently, upon their admiffion into the fociety of angels, attained to angelical wifdom, and the refined enjoyments of their kingdom; and that, becaufe they loved goodnefs and truth as fuch, and had, as it were, incorporated them into the very principles of life, whereby they became qualified for the immediate reception of the celeftial treafures: but as to thofe, who in this life had immerged themfelves in the love of felf and the world, they are fo far from being receptive of them, that they have an antipathy to them, and fo rejecting them upon the firft fenfations of them, they immediately affimilate in fellowfhip with fuch of the infernals, whofe affections accord with their own. There were certain fpirits, who doubted of the beatitudes of celeftial love, and therefore were defirous of being certified concerning the reality of this matter; wherefore they were permitted to be let into the ftate of it by the removal of that which difqualified for it, and accordingly they were conducted on to the angelical heaven, from whence they told me, that they felt an inward joy, which they could not exprefs, lamenting at the fame time, that they muft return to their former condition. Others alfo were as highly exalted to the participation of heavenly light, as their interior capacity would admit (*); and confeffed that they underftood and perceived things that before were utterly incomprehenfible by them. Let thus much fuffice to fhew, that love proceeding from the Lord is the only proper difpofition for, and recipient of, heaven, and all things proper to it.

19. That love towards the Lord, and love towards our neighbour, comprehend all divine truths, is manifeft from the following words of our Lord concerning thefe two loves: " Thou " fhalt love the Lord thy God with all thy heart, and with all " thy foul: this is the firft and great commandment. And the " fecond is like unto it: thou fhalt love thy neighbour as thy- " felf: on thefe two commandments hang all the law and the " prophets. Matt. xxii. 37, &c. Now the law and the pro-

(*) High in fenfible appearance, anfwers to inward in fpiritual things, and higheft to inmoft, and this by correfpondence between nature and fpirit.

phets comprehend the whole revealed world, and consequently all divine truth.

That Heaven is divided into Two Kingdoms.

20. Inasmuch as there are infinite varieties in heaven, and no one society, nor indeed any one angel, exactly like another (27), therefore heaven is to be considered under the threefold distinction of general, special, and particular: in general, into two kingdoms; specifically, into three heavens; and, in particular, into innumerable societies; to each of which shall be spoken in what follows: they are called kingdoms, because heaven is called the kingdom of God.

21. Some angels receive the divine influx more deeply or interiorly, others less; the former are called *celestial* angels, the latter, *spiritual* angels: hence it is that heaven is divided into two kingdoms, whereof the one is called the *celestial* kingdom, the other the *spiritual* kingdom (28).

22. The angels which constitute the celestial kingdom, inasmuch as they receive the divine efflux from the Lord more inwardly, are called interior, and also superior angels, from whom the heavens which they constitute derive the same distinctions (29); superior and inferior answering to interior and exterior (30).

(27) That there is an infinite variety in the works of God, and no one thing exactly like another, n. 7236, 9002. That there is also an infinite variety in the heavens, n. 684, 690, 3744, 5598, 7236. That the varieties in heaven are in the principle of good, n. 374, 4005—7836, 9002. That hereby all the societies in the heavens, and every angel in each society, have some distinguishing characteristick, n. 690, 3241, 3519—7833, 7836: and yet, that all are fellow members in the mystical body of Christ, and, as such, united to the Lord, n. 457, 3986.

(28) That heaven, in the full extent of the word, is distinguished into two kingdoms, the celestial and spiritual kingdoms, n. 3887, 4138. That the angels of the celestial kingdom receive the divine influx in their will-part, and consequently more interiorly than the spiritual angels, who receive it in their intellectual part, n. 5113, 6367, 8521, 9935, 9995, 10124.

(29) That the heavens, which constitute the celestial kingdom, are called the superior heavens, and those which constitute the spiritual kingdom, the inferior, n. 10068.

(30) That *interior* things are expressed by superior, and that *superior* signifies interior, n. 2148, 3084, 4599, 5146, 8325.

23. The

23. The love principle in the celestial angels is called celestial love; and that of the spiritual angels, spiritual love: celestial love has the Lord for its object, and spiritual love is the same with charity towards our neighbour: and as all good has relation to love, for whatever any one loves, that is good to him; therefore the good of the one kingdom is called celestial, and that of the other spiritual good: hence it appears in what respects these two kingdoms differ, viz. as the good of love towards the Lord, and the good of charity towards our neighbour (31); and as the former is more inward or deeper than the latter, therefore the celestial angels are more interior, and as such called superior.

24. The celestial kingdom is also called the sacerdotal kingdom of the Lord, and in scripture his *dwelling-place*; and the spiritual his *regal kingdom*, and in scripture his *throne:* from the divine-celestial principle the Lord is in this world called JESUS, and from the divine-spiritual, CHRIST.

25. The celestial angels far excel the spiritual in wisdom and glory, from their more intimate reception of the divine influx; and as their predominant principle is love to the Lord, they are consequently more closely joined to him (32). This higher excellence of the angels of this kingdom, is owing to their reception of divine truth immediately into the principle of life, and not as the spiritual angels, through the previous instrumentality of memory and reflection; insomuch that divine verities are written in their hearts, and they see them by intuition as within themselves, as in a kind of source, without having any occasion to reason concerning them, whether the matter be so or otherwise (33): like unto those described by Jeremiah; " I

---

(31) That the good of the celestial kingdom, is the good of love to the Lord; and the good of the spiritual kingdom, the good of charity towards our neighbour, n. 3691, 6435, 9468, 9680, 9683, 9780.

(32) That the celestial angels far excel the spiritual angels in wisdom, n. 2718, 9995. The difference between the celestial and the spiritual angels, n. 2088, 2669, 2708—8121, 9277, 10295.

(33) That the celestial angels reason not concerning the truths of faith, forasmuch as they perceive them intuitively in themselves, whereas the spiritual angels reason concerning them, whether the matter be so or not, n. 202, 337, 397—9277, 10786.

" will

" will put my law in their inward parts, and write it in their
" hearts; and they shall no more teach every man his neigh-
" bour, and every man his brother, saying, Know the Lord;
" for they shall all know me, from the least of them unto the
" greatest of them," xxxi. 33, 34. And they are called in
Isaiah, " *The taught of Jehovah,*" liv. 13. Now that the
taught of Jehovah are the taught of the Lord, he himself declares, John vi. 45, 46.

20. We have said, that they excel the other angels in wisdom and glory, as receiving divine truths immediately in their
life-principle (*), for as soon as they hear them, they immediately will and do them, without having any occasion to lay
them up in their memory to reflect and reason upon, in order to
know whether such things be true or not; for they who are of
this kingdom know immediately by influx (inspiration) from
the Lord, whether that which they hear be true or not, as this
influx passes immediately into the will, and mediately through
the will into the thinking faculty; or, in other words, immediately into the good [*bonum*] and mediately through the good
into the true [*verum*] (34); for that is called good which appertains to the will, and thence proceeds to work; and that true,
which appertains to the memory, and thence proceeds to thought
and reflection: so likewise all true [*omne verum*] (*) becomes
good, as being implanted in the love-principle, as soon as it
enters

(*) The will is here meant by the life or life-principle, being the same with love, which is the fire, and also the efficient cause of life: see note (u) before. It will be of great use to keep in memory this definition of our author, for the better understanding of his writings throughout. Tr.

(34) That the divine influx is into the property of good, and through the good into the true, and not contrarywise, consequently, into the will, and through that into the intellect, and not contrarywise, n. 5482. 5649, 6027—10153.

(*) The over delicate and critical reader will likely take offence at the words *good* and *true* being so often introduced in this translation for substantives, as not agreeing with ordinary usage in our language, though it is far from being un-grammatical in the Latin: but let it be observed here once for all, that neither the expression nor sense of the author could have been preserved without it, as *good-ness* and *truth* in the abstract and universal, would not have answered to his mean-ing, where it is needful to distinguish or particularize the kind or quality of what is good or true in any thing: thus, the good of peace, the good of love, the good of grace, &c. denotes the specifick goodness appertaining to those distinct subjects, and enters into the will; but so long as it rests only in the memory, and thence in the thoughts, it is not called good, as not having life, or the force of a principle, neither is it appropriated to man, seeing that man has his denomination from the will and intellect thence proceeding, and not from intellect separate from the will (35).

27. Such being the distinguishing difference between the angels of the celestial, and those of the spiritual kingdom, therefore they are separate, and form different societies, though there is a communication between them by means of certain intermediate angelical societies called celestial-spiritual, through which the celestial kingdom operates by influx on the spiritual kingdom (36): hence it is, that though heaven (in the complex sense of the word) be distinguished as two kingdoms, yet in effect they may be considered as one, forasmuch as the Lord has established an order of such intermediate angels, for the sake of forming a communication and conjunction between them.

28. As much is spoken in the following work concerning

---

and also the particular divisions that come under their several denominations: so also, the true of faith, the true of knowledge, the true of history, &c. specify the particular quality or quantity of truth that results from those kinds of evidence respectively: but the objection will vanish of itself on a little familiarity with the sense and application in which our author uses these expressions. Tr.

(35) That the will of man is the very essence of his life, and the receptacle of the good of love, and that the intellect is the existence or form of life from thence, and the receptacle of the true and good of faith, n. 3619, 5002, 9282. Consequently that the life of the will is the principal life of man, and that the life of the intellect proceeds from thence, n. 585, 590, 3619—10109, 10110. That those things are said to appertain to the life of man, and to be appropriated to him, which are received in his will, n. 3161, 9386, 9393. That man is denominated such from his will and his understanding thence proceeding, n. 8911, 9069, 9071—10110. That every one therefore is beloved and esteemed according to the goodness of his will, and not that of his understanding, nay, that he is despised who has an evil will, however great his share of understanding, n. 8911, 10076. That man continues after death according to the state of his will and intellect from thence, and that those things which are only ideally in his understanding without any share of the will in them, vanish at his death, as constituting no part of the man, n. 9069, 9071, 9282, 9386, 10153.

(36) That there is a communication and conjunction between the two kingdoms, by means of certain intermediate angelical societies, called celestial-spiritual, n. 4047, 6435, 8787, 8881. Of the divine influx through the celestial kingdom into the spiritual, n. 3969, 6366.

the

the angels of both thefe kingdoms, we forbear to be more particular on the fubject in this place.

That there are Three Heavens (*).

29. There are three heavens, and they entirely diftinct from each other; the higheft or inmoft, called the third heaven; the middle or fecond; and the loweft or firft heaven; and they rank in order, like the fupreme part in man, called the head, the middle called the body, and the loweft or feet; or as the uppermoft, middle, and loweft apartments in a houfe: in like order is the divine influx proceeding and defcending from the Lord; and from the fame law of order it follows, that heaven is tripartite, or divided into three.

30. The interior of man, as his underftanding and mind, fublift in like manner, and confifts of inmoft, middle, and loweft; for at the creation the whole of divine order was imaged in man, infomuch that he was divine order itfelf in a human form, and fo heaven in epitome (37): therefore it is, that man

is

(*) Although the author in the foregoing chapter tells us, that heaven (taken in the largeft or univerfal extent of that word) is divided into three diftinct heavens, and but two kingdoms, the kingdoms called the celeftial and fpiritual, and anfwering to the properties or principles of love and intellect, or goodnefs and truth (as being the predominant attributes in the angels of thofe kingdoms) yet we are not therefore to underftand, that the angels of the third heaven [paradife] are not highly tinctured with thefe divine qualities (for they receive both by influx through the fuperior heavens) but only that thefe are not their diftinguifhing characterifticks: they partake of both, otherwife they could not be angels; but their beatitudes confift chiefly in a kind of fpiritual gratifications more exterior, and approaching nearer to fenfe and external nature; as in emblematical reprefentations of divine and fpiritual things, under forms of exquifite beauty in endlefs varieties, and fucceffions of wonderful difplays of divine wifdom and power; and though their enjoyments be lefs inward and refined than thofe of more exalted fpirits, yet they are abundantly fuited to the capacities of their nature, and to fill them with joy and gratitude to the gracious author of their happinefs. It is to be noted, that (as *Omne majus continet minus*, fo) the fuperior angels enjoy the fum total of the felicity of the inferior angels, together with other fupereminent beatitudes appropriated to their ranks in glory refpectively. Tr.

(37) That the whole of divine order was imaged in man, infomuch that by creation he became divine order itfelf in a human form, n. 4219, 4220—10156, 10472.

is capable of communication with the heavens, as to his interior, and of affociating with angels after death, either with the angels of the higheft (inmoft) middle, or loweft heaven, according to his reception of the divine goodnefs and truth from the Lord, during his life in this world.

31. The divine influx from the Lord, as received in the third or inmoft heaven, is called celeftial, as are likewife the angels of that heaven; the fame divine influx, as received in the fecond or middle heaven, is called fpiritual, as alfo are the angels of the fame heaven: and as it is received in the loweft or firft heaven, it is called natural; but it muft be noted, that as what is called the natural of this heaven is very different from the natural of this our world, as the former partakes both of the fpiritual and celeftial properties, therefore this heaven is called the fpiritual and celeftial-natural, and its angels likewife (38): fuch of its angels as are called fpiritual-natural, are they who receive their influx from the middle or fecond, which is alfo the fpiritual heaven; as they are called the celeftial-natural, who receive their influx from the third or inmoft, which is alfo the celeftial heaven; though the angels called fpiritual-natural, and thofe called celeftial-natural, are of different denominations and orders, yet they both conftitute but one heaven, as being in the fame degree of blifs.

32. The diftinction of internal and external takes place in each heaven: they who are in the internal are called interior angels, as they who are in the external are called exterior angels. External and internal in the heavens anfwer to the will-part, and to the intellectual part in man, internal to the will, and external

---

10472. That the inner man in the human nature was formed in the image of heaven, and the external in the image of this world, and accordingly that man was named the microcofm by the ancients, n. 4523, 5368—10156, 10472. That man by creation was an epitome of heaven, as he is alfo now by his new creation or regeneration from the Lord, n. 911, 1900, 1982—6057, 9279, 9632.

(38) That there are three heavens, the higheft or inmoft, the middle, and the loweft; or the third, fecond, and firft, n. 684, 8594, 10270. That the goods (good things) there are in the fame order and degree, n. 4938—10017. That the good of the inmoft or third heaven, is called celeftial; the good of the middle or fecond, fpiritual; and that of the loweft or firft, fpiritual-natural, n. 4279, 4286—10017, 10068.

to the intellect: every will hath its proper intellect; the one is never without the other; the former may be compared to a flame, the latter to its light.

33. It is well to be remembered, that the interior state of the angels is that which determines their being of this or that heaven, for the more open their interiour is to the Lord, the more interiour is the heaven they belong to. There are three degrees of the interiour in every angel, spirit, and man; they in whom the third degree is opened, are in the inmost heaven; and they in whom only the second or first, are in the middle or lowest heaven accordingly. The interiour is opened according to the reception of divine goodness and truth in the inward parts: they who are so affected with divine truths, as to receive them into the life-principle or will, so that they become operative, are in the inmost or third heaven, and there in rank according to the degree of their affection for truth; but they who give them not so immediate an admission into the will, but only into their memory and understanding, and then afterwards frame their will according thereto, and then proceed to act; these are in the middle or second heaven: but they who add to their faith good life, though without any extraordinary earnestness and sedulity after divine knowledge; they are in the lowest or first heaven (39). Hence it is manifest, that it is the interiour or inward disposition that constitutes heaven, and consequently that heaven is something internal, and not external, according to those words of our Lord: " The kingdom of God " cometh not with observation; neither shall they say: Lo here, " or lo there; for behold, the kingdom of God is within you." Luke xvii. 20, 21.

34. Every human perfection [virtue and grace] increases towards the interiour of man, as being nearer to the Deity, and purer in itself, but decreases towards the exteriour, as this is

---

(39) That there are as many degrees of life in man, as there are heavens, which are opened to every one after death according to their past lives respectively, n. 3747, 9594. That heaven is in man, n. 3884: that therefore he who hath received heaven in himself in this life, is received into heaven after death, n. 10717.

more remote from the Deity, and more grofs in itfelf (40). Angelical perfection confifts in underftanding, wifdom, love, and in every good, and in happinefs from them; for without them happinefs is merely external, and not internal. Forafmuch as the interiour [the inward difpofitions and properties] of the angels of the inmoft heaven, are open in the third degree, therefore their perfection is of a far higher nature than that of the angels of the middle heaven, whofe interiour is open only in the fecond degree: in like proportion the perfection of the angels of the middle heaven exceeds that of the angels of the loweft heaven.

35. Such being the difference between the angels, it follows, that the angels of one heaven cannot find admiffion into the heaven of other angels, or any of them afcend from an inferior, or defcend from a fuperior heaven; for fhould any of them afcend to a higher heaven, he would immediately be feized with anguifh, neither would he be able to fee any of its inhabitants, much lefs to converfe with them; and he who fhould defcend from a fuperior to a lower heaven, would lofe his wifdom, ftammer in his fpeech, and be in the greateft diftrefs. Certain angels which belonged to the loweft heaven, and had not yet learned that heaven was a ftate adapted to the interiour, imagined that they fhould partake of the fuperior happinefs of the celeftial angels, could they be admitted into their heaven; accordingly this was permitted, but when they were there, they could not fee fo much as one angel, though they looked about for them, and, notwithftanding, a multitude of them was prefent; for the interiour of thefe ftrangers was not opened in the fame degree with the interiour of the celeftial angels, nor confequently their light: and prefently after they were feized with a heart-felt anguifh, fo that they fcarcely knew whether they were alive or not; wherefore they immediately betook themfelves to their

---

(40) That what is more interior is more perfect, as nearer to the Deity, n. 3405, 5146, 5147. That in the interiour are many thoufand particulars, which appear only in the general in the exteriour, n. 5707. That in proportion as any one advances from external to internal things, is his progrefs in light and underftanding, and is as it were exalted above the mifts into the higher and purer regions, n. 4598, 6183, 633.

own

own proper heaven, rejoicing that they were got again among their own companions, and promising that they would no more seek after things that were too high for them, and discordant to the condition of their nature (*). Some others I saw, who had descended from a superior to an inferior heaven, and became for a time so confused and lost to their wisdom, that they scarcely knew what heaven they belonged to. The case is quite otherwise when the Lord is pleased to exalt any from an inferior to a superior heaven, to shew them the glories of the latter, which often happens, for then they are first prepared, and surrounded with the intermediate angels, through whom they enjoy the communication with their superiors. From what has been already related, it appears that the three heavens are entirely distinct one from the other.

36. They who are in the same heaven can associate with all that are there; but the delights of their association are in proportion to the similarity of their affections, and affinity in good: but concerning these, in the following articles.

37. Though the heavens are so distinct, that the angels of one heaven cannot associate with the angels of another, yet the Lord connects them all by influx immediate and mediate; by immediate influx, from himself into all the three heavens; and by mediate influx, from one superior heaven to another (41), that so the three heavens may become one, by their connexion from first to last; nor indeed is there any thing absolutely unconnected; for were any thing to lose its connection by the intermediate links with its first cause, it would no longer subsist, but immediately lose its existence (42).

(*) However strange the above article may appear at first, yet probably the reader upon recollection will find, that he has at one time or other experienced something of like uneasy sensations, when in company with persons entirely unsuitable to his particular genius and disposition. Tr.

(41) That divine influx is both immediate from the Lord, and also mediate through one heaven to another, and also into the interior of man, n. 6063, 6307, 6472, 9682, 9683. Of divine influx as immediate from the Lord, n. 6058, 6474, to 6478, 8717, 8728. Of mediate influx through the spiritual into the natural world, n. 4067, 6982, 6985, 6996.

(42) That all things derive their existence from things prior to themselves, and so back from the first cause, and subsist in like dependence, as subsistence is continuation of existence; and that therefore there is nothing absolutely unconnected, n. 3626, 3628—6040, 6056.

38. He, who has no idea of divine order in respect to degrees, cannot form any conception how the heavens are distinct, nor yet what is meant by the inward and outward man; nor have the greater part any other notion of interior and exterior, or superior and inferior in this respect, than as something cohering by continuity from a higher to a lower degree of purity; whereas things interior and exterior, as here treated of, proceed not by the rule of CONTINUUM, so called, but the rule called DISCRETE (*). Degrees are of two kinds, *continuous*, and *discontinuous*, or *discrete*; the former are as the degrees of light decreasing on to obscurity, or as the different degrees of purity between the upper and lower regions of the atmosphere; and these degrees are determined by the distances respectively. Degrees that are not continuous, but discrete, are distinguished from the former, as prior from posterior, as cause from effect, and as what produces from the production. He that closely attends to this matter will find, that in all things throughout the universe, things are so ordered in their productions and compositions, that one thing proceeds from another, and that from a third, and so on; and he that has no perception of these degrees of order, can have no idea of the distinction of the heavens, nor of the distinct faculties of the interiour and exteriour of man, neither of the difference betwixt the spiritual and natural world, nor yet between the spirit and body of man, and consequently can know nothing of correspondences and emblematical representations, nor of the important doctrine of influx. Mere sensual men cannot receive these distinctions, making

(*) It will be somewhat difficult for a common reader, rightly to apprehend our author's meaning in this section; and yet a very important meaning belongs to it, and in particular, as it detects the gross error of those who assert the materiality of the soul, affirming it to be homogeneous, and continuous with the body; whereas it is heterogeneous, and *discrete*. A *continuum*, or *continued quantity*, is expressed by lines, and is the subject of geometry: a *discrete quantity* is expressed by numbers, and is the subject of arithmetick. In another light, *continuous* may be considered, answerably to the familiar sound of the word, as a unit, or any thing of the same kind continued without division, and giving but one idea; and *discrete*, as things of different kinds and natures, and disjoined, and so giving different ideas: so man, as consisting of soul and body, or spirit and matter, the parts or degrees of his composition are not only discontinuous or discrete, but also dissimilar. Tr.

nothing

nothing more of them than higher or lower in their scale of the degrees of continuity; and therefore have no other conception of what is spiritual, than as something natural in a more refined degree; thus they are quite beside the mark, and far from all true understanding of the matter (43).

39. Lastly, I find myself here at liberty to mention a certain secret concerning the angels of the three heavens, which is entirely unknown to every one, through ignorance as to the degrees here spoken of, viz. That there is in every angel, and also in every man, a certain inmost or supreme degree or part, which is the immediate subject of the divine influx, from whence the Lord regulates and governs their other interior faculties and powers successively, according to their degrees of order: this inmost or supreme part may be called the Lord's entrance into angel or man, and his dwelling-place in them: it is also by this inmost or supreme part in man, that he has his particular denomination, and is distinguished from the brute animals, for they have it not; and hence it is the peculiar privilege of man above other animals, that with respect to the interior faculties of his soul and spirit, he is capable of being raised by the Lord up to himself; that he can believe in him, be affected with love towards him, and so see him; as also that he is susceptible of understanding and wisdom, and can converse rationally; and hence likewise he has the privilege of eternal life: but how or what the Lord operates in this supreme part of the soul, which communicates with his divinity, is not clearly known even to the angels, as being above their thoughts and highest wisdom.

40. So much for these general truths concerning the three heavens: in what follows we shall speak of each heaven in particular.

(43) That the interiour and exteriour of man are not continuous, but distinct and discrete according to their respective degrees, and that every degree has its termination or limit, n. 3691, 4145, 5114, 8603, 10099. That one thing receives its form from another, and that the things so formed are not more pure or more gross according to any rule of *continuity*, n. 6326, 6465. That he who is a stranger to the distinction between things interior and exterior according to the degrees laid down, can neither form any just conceptions of the internal and external man, nor of the interior and exterior heavens, n. 5146, 6465, 10099, 10181.

That the Heavens consist of innumerable Societies.

41. The angels of each heaven are not all together, but are divided into societies greater or smaller, according to their degrees of difference with respect to the good of love and faith: they who are in the like good, and also degree of it, form one and the same society: the goods [species or kinds of good] in the heavens are of infinite variety; and every angel is to himself the condition or quality of his own good (44).

42. The angelical societies in the heavens have also their distances one from another, according to their different kinds of good, both in general and in particular; for distances in the spiritual world are determined by the difference of the interior states, and consequently in the heavens by the difference of the states with respect to love: they are at the greatest distance which differ most herein, and they at the least who differ least; whereas similitude of degree in this property connects them in the same society (45).

43. All likewise in the same society have their particular distinctions of place; they who are more perfect, or excel in good, in love, in understanding, and in wisdom, have their stations in or nearer to the center; and they who are less perfect,

---

(44) That there is an infinite variety in the works of God, and no one thing exactly like another in all respects, n. 7236, 9002. That there is the same infinite variety in the heavens, n. 684, 690, 3744, 5598, 7236. That the varieties in the heavens, which are infinite, are varieties in good, n. 3744, 5598—7836, 9002. That these varieties exist in the multifarious forms of truth, which specificate in every one the different kinds and degrees of good, n. 3470, 3804—7236. Whence it is, that not only every society in the heavens, but every angel in each society, have their particular distinction, n. 690, 3241—7236, 7833, 7836. But notwithstanding, that they all act consentaneously to the good of the whole by one principle of love from the Lord, n. 457, 3986.

(45) That all the societies of heaven have their constant situation according to their different inward states of life, and consequently according to their respective differences in good and faith, n. 1274, 3638, 3639. Wonderful things in the other life or spiritual world concerning distance, situation, place, space and time, n. 1273 to 1277.

round

round about them, according to their different degrees of perfection: in which respect they may be compared to light, decreasing in proportion to its distance from its center or luminous body; so they, who are in the middle, are in the greatest light; they, who are at the circumference, in the least; and others according to their respective distances.

44. The angels, who are of a similar disposition or interiour, come together as by sympathy; for with their fellows they are as at home with their friends, and with others as abroad and with strangers: also in company with the former they enjoy freedom of spirit, and consequently the true relish of life.

45. Hence it appears, that good is the bond of society in the heavens, and that the angels are of distinct societies, according to the kind or quality of their good [*secundum ejus quale*]; however, it is the Lord, from whom all good comes, that forms them into societies, and not the angels themselves: he it is that leads them, joins them, distinguishes them, and preserves them in liberty according to their degree of good, and so every one in the life of his love, faith, understanding, and wisdom, and thence in their proper happiness (46).

46. All who are in similar good, though they never met before, know one another as well as men know their friends and familiar acquaintance in this world, and that because in the other life all propinquities, affinities, and friendships are spiritual, and stand in relation to love and faith (47). This I have sometimes seen myself when absent from the body, and in company with angels: at such times some of them appeared as if we had been acquainted from our childhood, and others as perfect strangers: now the former were in a similar state of spirit with myself, but that of the latter was dissimilar.

(46) That all liberty is from love and affection, as what a man loves he does freely, n. 2870, 3158—9585, 9591. That as liberty is from love, therefore it is the life and life's delight in every one, n. 2873. That nothing appears to be our proper own work that proceeds not from liberty, n. 2880. That it is the very perfection of liberty to be led by the Lord, as this is to be led by the love of goodness and truth, n. 892, 905, 2872—9096, 9586 to 9591.

(47) That all proximities, relations, affinities, and, as it were, consanguinities in heaven, are from good, and according to its concordances and varieties, n. 605, 917, 1394, 2739, 3612, 3815, 4121.

47. All

47. All of the same angelical society agree in a common likeness of countenance, though with a difference in particular; now we may easily conceive of such a likeness in common, and of such variations in particular, by what is familiar to us in this world, it being well known, that in every different nation respectively there is a general similitude in the features and eyes of its inhabitants, that distinguishes them from those of another country; and this holds true more particularly in families: but this is much more remarkable in the heavens, where the affections of the mind are translucent through the face; for there the countenance is the external form of the affections within, and no counterfeit nor dissimulation is allowed of there. It was also shewed to me how the general likeness, which appears through the whole of a society, passes through its particular differences in the individual members of that society, and that under the following representation: there appeared to me as the face of an angel, which varied the forms of its countenance, so as to express the different affections of good and truth that distinguished a particular society; and each of these variations continued for some time, so as to give me leisure to observe, that the same common likeness served as the plane or ground of all the variations, and that these were as so many derivations therefrom: in such manner did this face represent to me the affections of the whole society under their particular differences in the individuals of it; for, as was said before, the faces of the angels are so many external forms of their affections within, and consequently of their love and faith.

48. Hence it follows, that any angel, who excels in wisdom, can presently read the state of another in his countenance, for no one there can conceal his interior state, much less lie or deceive by craft and hypocrisy. It sometimes happens, that hypocrites from beneath insinuate themselves into some angelical societies, who have learned to conceal their interior state to the form of good peculiar to such societies respectively, that they may pass for angels of light; but such can make no long tarrying there, for they presently begin to feel an inward anguish and pain, to change countenance, and to be struck in a manner lifeless, through the influx of the life-powers of the angels so
contrary

contrary to their own; on which they cast themselves headlong into hell among their fellows, without daring to ascend again (*): these are signified by the "man found among the guests bidden to the marriage feast, not having on a wedding-garment, and cast into outer darkness." Matt. xxii. 11, &c.

49. All the heavenly societies communicate with one another, but not in the way of open converse, for few go out of their own society to another, as such a departure would be like departing from themselves, or their proper life into another, unsuitable to their nature; but they hold communication by extending their spheres, which proceed from their vital affections of love and faith (†), and extend themselves far to the societies around them, and the farther in proportion to the degree of their interior excellence.(48). In proportion to this extension is the understanding and wisdom of angels: they who are in the inmost heaven, and the center thereof, extend their spheres throughout the universal heaven; and hence there is a communication of all heavenly things with every one, and of every one with all (49). But concerning this extension we shall treat

---

(*) That evil spirits may sometimes be permitted to appear among the angels, like Satan in paradise, is easy to believe; but this is no mitigation of their misery, as their hell is within them; nay, it greatly adds to their sufferings, as appears in the instance before us; so that it is not the place, but the state and condition of the parties that constitutes the happiness of heaven: thus the devils could not endure the pain that proceeded from the contrariety between their state, and the holy presence of our Lord; and yet to answer a divine purpose, this law of the nature of spirits was suspended during his temptation in the wilderness. Tr.

(†) By faith here we are not to understand mere believing, for there can be no unbelievers in heaven; but resignation, trust, reliance, together with a holy exercise of such of the intellectual powers as have respect to the divine attributes and to divine truths. It is here to be noted, that the author frequently uses the word faith, as expressive of intellect, and its object, truth; as on the other hand, he uses love and will as synonymous terms, where he speaks of the two great distinctions or principles in men and angels. Tr.

(48) That the spiritual sphere, or sphere of life, proceeds from every man, spirit, and angel, and surrounds them, as the atmosphere does the earth, n. 4464, 5179, 7454, 8630. That it issues from their vital affections and thoughts, n. 2489, 4464, 6206. That these spheres extend far to the angelical societies, in proportion to their quality and quantum of good, n. 6598 to 6613, 8063, 8794, 8797.

(49) That in the heavens there is a communication of all kinds of good, it being natural to celestial love to communicate of all it hath, n. 549, 550, 1391, 1399, 10130, 10723.

more fully in the sequel, where we speak of the celestial form, according to which the angelical societies are disposed; and where we treat of the wisdom and understanding of the angels, for all extension of the affections and thoughts proceeds according to that form.

50. It has been observed above, that in the heavens there are greater and lesser societies: the greater consist of myriads; the lesser, of some thousands; and the least, of some hundreds of angels: there are also some who dwell in a kind of solitude, as in single houses and families; but though these live in so dispersed a way, yet they are under subordination and government, as well as those who are in societies, the wiser of them being in the center as governors, and the more simple in the circumferences: these are under the Lord's more particular care and direction, and are the best of the angels.

That every angelical Society is a Heaven in a lesser Form, and every individual Angel a Heaven in the least Form.

51. That every society is a heaven in a lesser form, and every individual angel a heaven in the least form, is because the good of love and faith is that which constitutes heaven, and is in every society and angel in heaven: nor does it alter the matter, that the good here spoken of is different in quality or degree in every one, for still it is the good of heaven, and such difference or distinction only causes it to be a heaven of this or that denomination or quality: and therefore it is a common saying among them, when any one is exalted to this or that angelical society, that he is come to heaven; and, when speaking of those that are of it, that they are in heaven, and every one in his own heaven: this is well known to all in the other life; and therefore when any, who are out of or beneath heaven, behold any companies of the angels afar off, they readily say, There is heaven, or there: the case may be compared to the officers or ministers in a king's palace or court, who, though

they

they have different apartments, one above another, yet are all in the fame palace or court, according to their feveral ranks and offices; which anfwers to thofe words of our Lord: " In my " Father's houfe are many manfions," John xiv. 2. And alfo to what we read in the prophets, of the *habitations* of heaven, and the heaven of *heavens*.

52. That every angelical fociety is a heaven in a lefler form, may alfo be evinced from hence; that every particular fociety is formed after the likenefs of the whole heaven, wherein they, who moft excel, are fituated in the middle, and they, who are lefs in excellence, round about them, in diftances proportionate to their inferiority, as is mentioned in a preceding article, n. 43. This truth is farther confirmed from hence, that the Lord governs the univerfal heaven by the laws of an uniform oeconomy, as if they were all but one angel, and confequently thofe in every particular fociety; whence it fometimes follows, that a whole angelical fociety is reprefented under the appearance of a fingle angel, which the Lord has vouchfafed to grant me the fight of. When it pleafes the Lord to manifeft his perfonal appearance in the midft of the angels, he does not appear under the particular diftinction of being furrounded by many of them, but as one of them in an angelical form: hence it is, that he is fometimes in fcripture called an angel; as is alfo a whole fociety of them by a fingle name; thus Michael, Gabriel, and Raphael, fignify fo many angelical focieties, deriving thofe names from their different functions (50).

53. As an entire fociety is heaven in a lefler form, fo is every individual angel in its leaft form; for heaven is not without the angel, but within him, his interior affections and powers being fo difpofed, according to the form of heaven, as to be fitted for the reception of all external heavenly good things; his receptivity of which is according to the quality of divine

(50) That the Lord is called angel in the word, n. 6280, 6831, 8192, 9303. That a whole angelical fociety is alfo called angel in the fingular, and that Michael and Raphael are entire focieties, fo called from their particular offices, n. 8192. That the heavenly focieties, and alfo particular angels, are diftinguifhed only by the quality of their good, and its idea, n. 1705, 1754.

good

good in him from the Lord, and by which alone an angel is a form of heaven (*).

54. It is by no means to be said, that heaven is without any one, but within him, for it is according to the kind or quality of the heaven within, that every angel receives the heavenly influx from without him. Hence will appear the great error of those, who suppose that it is sufficient, in order to be in heaven, for any one to be exalted to the company of angels, whatever life he may be of, as to his interior state; and that therefore to be in heaven is nothing more than a grant by an immediate act of mercy (51); whereas, if heaven is not within, no heavenly influx is received from without. Many spirits under this erroneous persuasion, in order to convince them of their error, were permitted to ascend into the place of heaven; but they were no sooner there, but (as their interior state of life was contrary to that of the angels) their understanding became confused and darkened, all their inward powers disturbed, and they reduced to such a state of suffering, that they behaved like ideots, or insane persons: in a word, they who are ill-principled in their life's properties, and are translated to angelical society, feel a kind of suffocation, and suffer an anguish, like that of fishes when out of their element, or like that of animals in an air-pump, out of which the air is extracted: which shews that heaven consists in a state within, and not in a place without us (52).

55. As all receive the influences of the external heaven, according to the quality of the heaven that is within them, in

---

(*) The truth here laid down by our author in this and the following section, is of infinite importance, and adds light to that most concerning doctrine of our holy religion, the necessity of regeneration, or of being born again, in order to an entrance into the kingdom of heaven. Tr.

(51) That heaven is not a mere gratuitous grant by an immediate act of mercy, but according to the principle of life in every one, and that this vital principle of good and godliness, by which any one is qualified for heaven, is by gift and mercy from the Lord, and that mercy is to be understood in this sense alone, n. 5057, 10659. That if heaven were merely a gift by an immediate act of mercy, it would be given to every one, n. 2401. Concerning some evil spirits being cast down from heaven, who believed that heaven was nothing more than a mere gratuitous grant of immediate mercy to every one, n. 4726.

(52) That heaven is in man, 3884.

like

like manner alfo do they receive the Lord, as it is his divinity that conftitutes heaven: hence it is, that when he vouchfafes a perfonal manifeftation of himfelf to any fociety, his appearance is according to the quality of good in that particular fociety, and therefore he appears not to any two exactly alike (*); not that there is any variablenefs in him; but the diffimilitude is in them who behold him, from their own particular kind or degree of good, and according to it; and likewife according thereto are they affected with fuch beatifick vifion; they who love him moft are moft affected with delight, they with lefs that love him lefs; and as to the evil who are without heaven, they are tormented at his prefence. When the Lord manifefts himfelf to any fociety, he appears therein (as was faid before) as an angel, though diftinguifhable from the angels by fomething of a divine tranflucent glory.

56. There alfo is heaven, where the Lord is acknowledged, believed in, and loved: the various modes of worfhipping him in this or that fociety has no other effect than for the better, for it conftitutes a perfection in heaven. This will hardly be received without our taking in here fomething in the literary way for explanation and diftinction, to fhew how every thing that is perfect confifts of various other things: every thing, however fimple or *one* it may be fuppofed to be, exifts from various others, otherwife it would not be any thing, but be void of form, and confequently without particular quality or mark of diftinction; but where it exifts as a whole, from various parts and properties uniting with friendly compofition in a perfect form, it is then an entire thing, having its own peculiar quality and diftinction. Juft fo it is with heaven; it is a one or whole, confifting of variety, but of variety ordered and difpofed in the moft perfect form, for the heavenly form is of all the moft perfect. That all perfection is thus conftituted, appears from hence, that every thing moft beautiful, pleafing, and delightful to the mind and fenfes, do all proceed from confent of parts, and a harmonizing variety (whether they co-exift in

---

(*) This may in a fort be illuftrated in nature by the objects of vifion, which appear to the fpectator according to the quality of the eye, and the condition of its organs refpectively. Tr.

simultaneous order, or follow in succession) and not from any thing that is but merely one; whence comes the common adage, that in variety is delight; now we know that this must be according to the different qualities in things: and this may teach us that perfection, even in heaven, consists in variety; for this natural world is a kind of mirrour or glass, representing to us the things that are in the spiritual world (53).

57. The same may be predicated of the church in this matter, as the church is the Lord's heaven on earth; now the church is manifold, consisting of many churches, each of which is called and is a church, in proportion to the good of love and faith that is in it: and here also the Lord forms unity out of variety, and one church out of many (54). And the same may be affirmed of every member of the church in particular, that has been spoken of the church in common, viz. that the church is within, and not without the man; and also that every one, who is a true member of the church, is likewise a church himself, in whom the Lord is present in the good of his love and faith (55): and farther, it may be said of every one in whom the church is, as was said of every angel in whom heaven is, that he is the church in its least form, as an angel is heaven in its least form; and still farther; that man in whom the church is [as to its essential principle] is heaven in epitome, or its least form, in like manner as an angel is such, and that because man is created for heaven, that he may become an angel; consequently he, who lives in the principle of good from

---

(53) That every one entire thing is from harmony and consent of its several parts and properties, and that otherwise it would be without its particular quality and note of distinction, n° 457. That in this sense it is, that the universal heaven is one, n. 457: and that because all there have respect to one and the same end, which is the Lord, n. 9828.

(54) That if the principle of good were the only essential character of a church, without respect to separate truths, then there would only be one [external] church, n. 1285, 1316—3451, 3452. That all external churches, according to the principle of good in them, make one church before the Lord, n. 7395, 9276.

(55) That the church (as to its essential principle) is in man, and not without him, and that such men constitute the church considered collectively, n. 3884.

the

the Lord, is an angel-man (*) (56). I may here mention what man hath in common with angels, and what he hath more than the angels : now *man hath in common with angels*, that his interiour is formed like theirs, according to the model of heaven, and also that he is a real image of heaven, as far as he is in the good of love and faith: and *man has this more than the angels*, that in his exteriour he is formed after the image of this world; and that as far as he is in the principle of good, this world in him is subordinate, and subservient to heaven (57); and that so the Lord is present with him in both worlds, according to his divine order in each, for God is order (58).

58. Lastly, we are here to observe, that he who hath heaven in him, hath heaven, not only in his principal powers and properties, but also in the least things, as these in their proportion resemble the greatest; and this for the following reason, because every one is in reality the same with his own proper prevailing love, as this influences and regulates the whole man (59), and produces its likeness therein (*). In the heavens

---

(*) However inconclusive the foregoing method of reasoning used by our author may appear to the generality of our readers, it is not therefore to be lightly accounted of, as it is of weighty consideration in the spiritual subject before us. Tr.

(56) That the man, who is the church in epitome, is also heaven in its least form, after the likeness of heaven in its greatest form, and that, because all his interior faculties and powers are ordered and disposed according to the form and œconomy of heaven, and consequently fitted for the reception of all heavenly things, n. 911, 1900, 1982—6057, 9279, 9632.

(57) That to man belong both an interiour and exteriour, or an internal and external system; the former originally created an image of the heavenly world; and the latter an image of this mundane system; and that therefore man was called by the ancients the microcosm, or little world, n. 4523, 4524—9706, 10156, 10472. That consequently man was so formed, that the principle of this natural world in him should be subject to the heavenly world's principle, as is the case with all good men; but that it is quite the reverse with bad men, in whom the principle and things of this world are uppermost, n. 9283, 9278.

(58) That the Lord is order itself, inasmuch as divine goodness and truth proceeding from him constitute order, n. 1728, 1919—10336, 10619. That divine truths are the laws of order, n. 2247, 7995. That as far forth as any one lives in order, that is, in divine good according to the laws of divine truth, so far is he man, truly speaking, and so far has both the church and heaven a form in him, n. 4839, 6605, 8067.

(59) That the ruling love in every one enters into the whole of his life, and consequently into every thought and act of his will, n. 8067, 8853, 10110, 10284.

That

vens love to the Lord is the governing principle, because there the Lord is loved above all things, and consequently is all in all; he influences, guides, and forms the blessed angels into a similitude of himself, and constitutes heaven by his divine presence: hence it is, that every single angel is heaven in the least and lowest form; every angelical society in a greater form; and all the angelical societies collectively, in the greatest form. That the divinity of the Lord constitutes heaven, and is all in all things there, see above, n. 7 to 12.

That the universal Heaven in Complex resembles a Human Form.

59. That the universal heaven resembles the human form, is a secret hitherto unknown in this world, though well known there; nay, the knowledge of it in its several parts and particulars, constitutes the main of the intellectual entertainment of angels, as many truths depend thereon, which, without this common principle of science, they would never be able to form any clear conceptions of. Now, forasmuch as they know that the whole of heaven, together with its several societies collectively, are in the form of a man, therefore they call heaven the GRAND (MAXIMUM) and DIVINE MAN (60): divine, because it is the divinity of the Lord that constitutes heaven; *see above*, from n. 7 to 12.

60. That heavenly and spiritual things should be formed into such an image and likeness, will not be conceived by those

---

That where love and faith prevail as principles, they have a part in all that a man thinks and does, though he knows it not, n. 8854, 8864, 8865.

(*) The meaning of the author herein is as follows: The good principle in any one (which is and can be only from the Lord) enters into, sanctifies and blesses every thing that such a one thinks, says, and does from that principle: as, on the other hand, the evil principle that prevails in any one, infects with malignity even those things which outwardly appear most indifferent or innocent, according to that saying of the wise man; " The ploughing of the wicked is sin," Prov. xxi. 4. Tr.

(60) That the universal heaven is in a human form, and therefore called, *The Grand Man*, n. 2996, 2998—3741 to 3745, 4625.

who

who have no competent idea of them: such are apt to suppose, that what is earthly and material in the external part of the human composition, is so essential to man, that he would cease to be man without such materials; but let them know, that he receives not his denomination of man from thence, but from his capacities of knowing truth, and willing good: these spiritual and heavenly properties constitute his character as man: nay, all know that every one is called such or such a man, according to his understanding, and the disposition of his will; and also may know, that this terrestrial body is formed, in order to its subserviency to those faculties in this world, and through the instrumentality of its several organs contribute to their operations and usefulness in this lowest sphere of nature; for to the body belongs no principle of self-motion, but only to be passive and obsequiously obedient to the motions of the intellect and will, which are the only agents and principals in all that the man speaks or does, making use of the body only as their instrument; and consequently these are the principles that constitute the man, and also are in similar form, as appears by their instantaneous operations on all the bodily members, as an internal agent on an external instrument, whence man is denominated internal and spiritual: as such, a man in the greatest and most perfect form is heaven.

61. Such is the idea of the angels concerning man, and therefore they do not consider him in relation to the mere bodily acts, but with respect to the will that directs them, and with respect to his understanding, as far as this co-operates with the will (61).

62. The angels do not, it is true, behold the universal heaven in such a form, because it comes not within the reach of any angel's ken; but they sometimes behold very distant societies (consisting of many thousands of angels) as one in such a form; and from a society as a part, they conclude concerning the whole, that being the most perfect form in which

---

(61) That the will of man is the very essence of his life, and his understanding the existence or form of it, n. 3619, 5002, 9282. That the life of the will is the principal life of man, and that the life of his intellect proceeds from thence, n. 585, 590—10076, 10109, 10110.

the aggregates, and the parts of which they confift, refemble each other, without any other difference than betwixt greater and lefs (*) : wherefore they fay, that the Lord, as the center and great original of all creation, beholds the univerfal heaven in this form.

63. Such being the conftitution of heaven, it is accordingly actuated and governed by the Lord as one man, or one thing: now it is well known, that though man is a very complicated fyftem, confifting of a great variety of parts, as well in the principals, as in the particulars of his compofition; in the former, of members, organs, and bowels; in the latter, of fibres, nerves, and blood-veffels of different claffes and orders; and fo of members within members, and parts within parts; yet notwithftanding this his multifarious compofition, when he acts, he acts but as one fimple agent or man: fo in like manner may we confider the univerfal heaven, notwithftanding its infinite variety, to be uniformly governed by the will, and at the good pleafure of the Lord.

64. That fo many different parts in man act with fuch unity and conformity is, becaufe every thing in his compofition performs its office of ufe, as moft contributes to the good of the whole, the community miniftring ufe to the particular parts, and the latter theirs to the fervice of the community; for the community is made up of the parts, and the parts conftitute the community, wherefore they all confpire with mutual confent to promote the common good of the whole; whence arifes uniformity. Juft fo it is in refpect to ufe and co-operation with the confociations in the heavens, and they that fhould not contribute their refpective fervices to the common good, would be ejected as unprofitable members: by being profitable or unprofitable here is meant the being well affected to others for the fake of the common good, or only for the fake of our own private good in particular; of the latter fort are they who are actuated only by felf-love in all things; of the former clafs are

---

(*) This may be illuftrated by the configuration of falts of the fame fpecies: thus for example, whether they confift of parts of a triangular, hexagonal, cylindrical, or any other form; it is well known, that the minuteft particles of thofe parts are of the fame figure. Tr.

they

they who love the Lord above all things: hence it is, that all who are in heaven have only one principle of acting, and that, not from themselves, but from the Lord; for up to him they look, as the source of all good, and to his kingdom as that community, the good of which they are to promote in all things, according to those words of the Lord: " Seek first the " kingdom of God, and his righteousness, and all things shall " be added unto you," Matt. vi. 33. Righteousness (62) here means good from the Lord, as the source of all good. They who in this world love the good of their country above their own private good, and the good of their neighbour as their own, are they who in the other life love and seek the kingdom of the Lord, which is to them instead of their country: and they who love to do good to others from the love of good, and not for selfish ends, are they who love their neighbour; for among the angels *good* and *neighbour* mean the same (63): now all who are of this character are in what is called the Grand Man, or heaven.

65. As the universal heaven represents or resembles one man, and also is a divine spiritual man in the greatest form and image, therefore heaven is distinguished, like man, by human members and parts, and after the same names; accordingly the angels well know what particular member this or that society belongs to, and it is common for them to say, such a society is in a certain member or province of the head, another in such a part or province of the breast, and a third in such a member or province of the lungs, and so of the rest. In general, the supreme or third heaven forms the head to the neck: the middle or second heaven forms the breast down to the loins and knees: and the lowest or first heaven forms the inferior parts down to

---

(62) That *righteousness* in scripture is predicated of good, and *judgment* of truth; and that therefore to keep righteousness and judgment, is to adhere to goodness and truth, n. 2235, 9857.

(63) That the Lord is our neighbour in the highest sense of the word, and hence, that to love the Lord, is to love all that proceeds from him, as having his divine nature in it, consequently goodness and truth, n. 2425, 3419—6823, 8123. Consequently, that all good proceeding from the Lord [in the abstracted sense of the word] is our neighbour, and that to will and do it, is to love our neighbour, n. 5026, 10336.

the feet, and also the arms to the fingers; for the arms and hands are the extremities of the body, though at the sides: hence also proceeds the distinction of three heavens.

66. The spirits, who are beneath heaven, greatly wonder when they hear and see that heaven is beneath as well as above; for they are of the same opinion with the people of this world, that heaven is no where but above, not knowing that the situation of the heavens is as the situation of the members, organs, and bowels in man, some of which are above, and some beneath; some within, and some without; whence arise their confused ideas concerning heaven.

67. So much for what we had to say concerning heaven considered as the *Grand Man*; as without this previous knowledge, the things which follow relating to heaven could not be understood, nor any idea be conceived of the form of heaven, of the conjunction of the Lord with heaven, nor of the conjunction of heaven with man, nor yet of the influx of the spiritual into the natural world, much less of the laws of correspondence betwixt both; of which in their order in the sequel of this work; and for the better understanding of which subjects these things are premised.

That every Society in the Heavens resembles a Human Form.

68. That every society of heaven resembles the human form, and is in the likeness and image of man, has sometimes been given me to see. There was a society into which many had insinuated themselves, who knew how to counterfeit the appearance of angels of light, but they were hypocrites: upon the separation of these from the angels, the whole society appeared at first as an obscure body; afterwards, by degrees, in a human form, but indistinctly; and at last, clearly in the form of a man: they who formed this figure, as the several members or constituent parts of it, were such as were in the good (*)

(*) By the good of any thing, we are to understand the peculiar good quality or property that prevails in it, and distinguishes it from the kind of good in another thing:

of this fociety; but they who conftituted no part of this human form, were not of the fociety, nor in the good property that diftinguifhed it, but intruding hypocrites, and as fuch feparated from it. Such here are called hypocrites, who have good words, and outwardly good works, but at the fame time have a view to felf in every thing: they can talk like angels, of the Lord, of heaven, of love, and of fpiritual things, and are alfo in the outward practice of what is good, that they may be thought to be in deed what they are in word; whereas their thoughts are far different, and they have neither faith, nor good will to any but themfelves; and if at any time they do good to others, it is for fome felfifh end.

69. That a whole fociety of angels, when the Lord manifefts his prefence to them, appears as one in a human form, has been given me to fee; and once in particular, fuch a fociety appeared high towards the eaft, like a cloud of a pale red colour, furrounded with little ftars, and defcending; and as it defcended gradually, it appeared brighter, and at length in a perfect human form: the little ftars that furrounded the cloud were fo many angels under that appearance by light from the Lord.

70. It is to be noted, that though all of the fame fociety, when together, appear as one in a human form, yet no one fociety is exactly like another, but differs as different families

thing: fo here; the good of the fociety mentioned in this place, means the particular characteriftick of that fociety, whether as in the good of humility, of charity, of gratitude, and fo on. And as all the virtues, graces, relative duties, and perfections of every kind, give diftinction to the angelical focieties, fo do the different degrees of them, infomuch that they are innumerable: not that any one fociety is without any other virtue, but that it takes its particular denomination and diftinction from that in which it moft excels: and farther, it is to be noted, that every particular angel in every particular fociety has fomething of diftinction peculiar to himfelf, that differences him from every other angel in the fame fociety, but only as one member in the fame body differs from another, whilft each contributes, by one common harmonizing variety, to the perfection of the whole: the fame is obfervable in every fociety of good men on earth in proportion refpectively: and thus we call the latter by the name of a body; and what is there incredible in the fuppofition, that fuch focieties in heaven fhould be reprefented at times, even to the view of the beholder, under the appearance of a human form, as of all the moft excellent, and that which the Lord of all Lords has affumed for the manifeftation of his divinity. Tr.

from the same stock here on earth, and that from the like cause mentioned, n. 47. viz. that they differ according to the various kinds and degrees of good in which they are, and from which they derive their distinct appearances, though under one common form. In the most beautiful and perfect human form are the societies of the inmost or highest heaven, and more especially they who are in the center of it.

71. It is worthy of notice, that the greater the number in any of the angelical societies, and the greater their harmony, the more perfect is their human form; for the greater the variety or number, when acting by consent in a heavenly disposition, strengthens the unity of the whole, see n. 56. Thus every society in heaven, as it daily increases in number, advances in perfection, and not only every society in particular, but heaven in common, as the whole of heaven consists of its several particular societies. As heaven thus advances in degrees of perfection in proportion to the increase of its inhabitants, we may hence learn the error of those, who suppose that it may be so completely furnished with guests, as to leave no room for more; but imagine the greatest number you can, and yet there is room; nor do the angels desire any thing more than to have their number increased by the arrival of fresh angels from other worlds.

72. That every society, when together, appears as one human form, is because the universal heaven has the same form, as may be seen in the foregoing article; and in the most perfect form, as that of heaven, there is a resemblance between the parts and the whole, between the lesser and the greatest; now the lesser, or the parts of heaven, are the societies of which it consists, which are so many heavens in a lesser form; see above, n. 51 to 58. That there is such a perpetual similitude in the heavens, is because the various species of good [*bona*] in all there, proceed from one love or origin; now the one love from which all those goods originate, is love to the Lord in the angels proceeding from the Lord: hence it is that the universal heaven is a likeness of him in common; every society a similitude of him in a lesser community; and every angel a likeness or image of him in particular; see above on this subject, n. 58.

That

That every Angel is in a perfect Human Form.

73. It has been shewed before, that the universal heaven resembles the human form, as does likewise every society in heaven; and from the chain of causes and effects there produced, it follows, that every particular angel has the same figure; the universal heaven as a man in the greatest, each society in a lesser, and every particular angel in the least human form; for in the most perfect form, as is that of heaven, there is a mutual likeness between the whole and its parts; and that because heaven is a communion, and so communicates of its whole perfection to every one, whilst every individual is a receiver from that whole, and so is heaven in its least form, as has been shewed before. Man also in this world, as far as he is a recipient of the efflux from heaven, is so far a heaven, and an angel; see above, n. 57. This is described in the Apocalypse in the following words: " And he measured the wall thereof," [of the holy Jerusalem] " an hundred and forty and four cubits, according " to the measure of a man, that is, of the [*an*] angel;" xxi. 17. *Jerusalem* there means the church of the Lord, and in a higher sense, heaven (64); the *wall* signifies truth, as its defence against the attacks of error and evil of every kind (65) [*ab insultu falsorum et malorum*]; *an hundred and forty-four* means every species of what is good and true in the complex (66); the measure is its particular kind or quality [*quale ejus*] (67); *man* is he, or

(64) That Jerusalem signifies the church, n. 402, 3654, 9166.
(65) That wall signifies the defence of truth against the attacks of falsehoods and evils, n. 6419.
(66) That the number twelve signifies the whole complex of things good and true, n. 577, 2089—3858, 3913. The same is likewise signified by the numbers seventy-two, and one hundred and forty-four, because 144 is the product of twelve multiplied by itself, n. 7973. That in the Scripture, numbers stand for things, n. 482, 487, 647—4264, 4495, 5265. That multiplied numbers signify the same with the simple from which they proceed in multiplication, n. 5291, 5335, 5708, 7973.
(67) That *measure* in the scripture signifies the quality of a thing with respect to good and true, n. 3104, 9603.

that society, in which all those things are in general and in particular, consequently in which heaven is; and because an angel is also a divine man from these divine qualities, therefore it is said; *The meafure of a man, which is that of an angel.* This is the spiritual meaning of these words; and who, without this interpretation of them, would be able to find out the sense of the wall of the heavenly Jerusalem being the meafure of a man, that is, of an angel (68)?

74. But to come to experience: That angels are human forms or men, I have seen a thousand times, and have conversed with them, as one man with another, sometimes singly, sometimes with many together; nor did I ever see in them any thing that differed from the human form; at which I have sometimes wondered; and that this might not be suspected of being a deception, or vision of the imagination, it has been given me to see them when quite awake, and in all clearness of sensible perception. I have often told them, that in our Christian world, the generality were so grossly ignorant in respect to the nature of angels and spirits, as to take them for minds without form, mere invisible thinkers, and of which they had no other idea than as of vital æther; and that consequently, having nothing in them human but the power of thinking, they could neither see, hear, nor speak, as being without eyes, ears, and tongues. To which the angels replied, that they knew it to be so with many in this world, particularly among the learned, and (which they much wondered at) also with the clergy: and they assigned for the cause of it as follows, viz. that the learned, who first broached this error, being mere natural men, and borrowing all their ideas of substance from their external senses, and not from any interior light, or from those common notices of things which are implanted in the human mind, refined spiritual things and beings, as it were, into nothings; not seeing, from the grossness of their ideas, how any thing could exist spiritually in form and substance, that is not material and palpable to sense,

---

(68) Of the spiritual or internal sense of the word, see the explanation of the *White Horse* in the Apocalypse, and the Appendix to the *Heavenly Doctrine*.

as in this natural world (69). From such leaders in error this false notion concerning angels was derived down to others: now they who resign up their minds to others, and believe on their own authority alone, seldom recover their liberty, but for the most part acquiesce in confirming themselves in what they so imbibe. Moreover they said, that men of simplicity in faith and heart thought far otherwise of the angels, and conceived of them as heavenly men, and that because they did not extinguish the heavenly idea of them by human learning, nor admit of any thing into their minds, but under some form: hence it is that angels in churches, whether as carved or painted, have always been represented as men: by heavenly ideas, or ideas from heaven of celestial things, they said, was meant a divine influx or light in those who are in the good of faith and life.

75. From all my experience, which is now of many years, I can truly affirm, that the angels, in respect to their form, are perfect men, having like faces, eyes, ears, breasts, arms, hands, feet, &c. that they hear, see, and converse with one another; and, in a word, that nothing human is wanting to them, but these material bodies of flesh that we are invested with: I have beheld them in their own light, which far exceeds our greatest meridian lustre, and have therein discerned all the features and variations of their faces more distinctly than those of my fellow inhabitants of this earth. It was also granted me to see an angel of the inmost or highest heaven, who appeared with a more resplendent countenance than the angels of the lower heavens, and was of a human form in all perfection.

76. It is here to be observed, that the angels cannot be seen by any mortal man with the eyes of his body, but with those only of the spirit which is in man (70), and that because this

(69) That till a man be elevated above the carnal or sensual part, as to his apprehensions, he has but little wisdom, n. 5089. That a wise man's thoughts are of a more exalted nature, n. 5089, 5094. That when any one is elevated above sense, he comes into a clearer light, and at length advances to heavenly light, n. 6183, 6313—9730, 9922. That such elevation and abstraction from the things of sense was known to the ancients, n. 6313.

(70) That man, as to his interiour, is a spirit, n. 1594. And that such spirit is properly the man, and that the body derives its life from it, n. 447, 4622, 6054.

is in the spiritual world; but all things appertaining to the body, in the natural world: for like only sees like in the same common nature. Moreover, the organ of bodily vision, or the material eye, is so gross, that it cannot discern the more minute parts of nature without the assistance of optical glasses, as is well known; how much less those things which are above the sphere of nature, as are all things in the spiritual world: and yet these are manifested to his view, when he is withdrawn inwardly from the bodily sense, and the eye of his spirit is opened, which is done in an instant, when it pleases the Lord to give him a sight of things in the spiritual worlds; and then they appear as if he saw them with his bodily eyes: it was thus that the angels appeared to Abraham, Lot, Manoah, and the Prophets; and thus also was the Lord seen by his disciples after his resurrection: in like manner have I also been favoured with the sight of angels. From this kind of vision it was, that the Prophets were called *Seers*, and the " men whose eyes were open," 1 Sam. ix. 9. Num. xxiv. 3. And to cause them to see thus, was called, *Opening their eyes*, as in the instance of Elisha's servant, of whom it is said, " That Elisha prayed, and said, " Lord, I pray thee, open his eyes, that he may see: and the " Lord opened the eyes of the young man, and he saw: and " behold! the mountain was full of horses and chariots of fire " round about Elisha," 2 Kings vi. 17.

77. Some good spirits with whom I discoursed on this subject, expressed much grief at such ignorance in the church concerning the state of heaven, and that of angels and spirits, and with some sharpness charged me to declare, that they were not mere minds without form, nor like to a breath of æther, but men in human form, and that they saw, heard, and enjoyed senses, as well as the dwellers upon earth (71).

(71) That every angel, as a recipient of divine order from the Lord, is in a human form, perfect and beautiful, in proportion to his recipiency, n. 323, 1880, 1881—9879, 10177, 10594. That divine truth constitutes the form or existence of order, and divine good its essence, n. 2451, 3166—10122, 10555.

That

That Heaven, both in its Whole and Parts, resembles the Human Form; and that from the Divine Humanity of the Lord.

78. That heaven, both in its whole and parts, resembles the human form, and that from the divine humanity of the Lord, follows by consequence from the preceding articles; in which has been declared and shewed, i. *That the Lord is the God of Heaven.* ii. *That the Divinity of the Lord constitutes Heaven.* iii. *That Heaven consists of innumerable Societies, and that every Society is Heaven in a lesser Form; and every Angel in its least Form.* iv. *That the universal Heaven in Complex resembles one Man.* v. *That every Society in the Heavens also resembles one Man as to its Form.* vi. *That likewise every particular Angel is in a perfect Human Form.* From all these premises we may conclude, that the Deity, or Divine Nature, as constituting heaven, is also in a human form (*) : and that such human form is the Divine Humanity of the Lord, though otherwise

(*) The undiscerning reader is here to be cautioned against falsely imputing to our author the error of the ancient Anthropomorphites, whose heresy did not consist in ascribing a human form to the Deity, for every true believer acknowledges this in the WORD made flesh, but in ascribing a separate personal form to the Father or Divine Essence, in distinction from the Son : and it is to be wished that they who are most apt to fix such a charge upon our author may not be of that number, who outdo the ancient Anthropomorphites in their heresy, by a gross misunderstanding of the doctrine of the Holy Trinity, in assigning to the Godhead THREE distinct personal forms, and so plunge themselves into Polytheism, or the belief of a plurality of gods.

I shall conclude this note with another taken from a pamphlet intitled, " The " Cause of the Petitioners examined," &c. Printed for Robinson, Pater Noster Row, 1773. and to which I refer the reader for further satisfaction on this subject.

" I cannot but take occasion in this place, to condemn as highly offensive, " heathenish and profane, the manner of some to represent the Trinity as three " human persons sitting in council, and making decrees : see among others a book " intitled, *Lux in Tenebris*, with such a print. All they who figure the like " representations of the Godhead, whether in their minds, or on paper, whether " by sculpture, or painting, are Tritheists with a witness, however they may " (in order to cover the absurdity of their error) profess to believe in the Unity."
Tr.

thought

thought of by many in the church, will more fully appear from the many quotations extracted from the *Arcana Cælestia*, and collected together in this work; and also from the *Doctrine* of the *Holy Jerusalem*, towards the end of that work, where it treats of the Lord.

79. That this is the real truth, has been confirmed to me by much experience, of which I shall speak in what follows. All the angels in the heavens have no perception of the Divine Majesty under any other than a human form; and what is still more to be admired, they which belong to the superior heavens cannot think of him otherwise, being necessarily led thereto by a divine influx, and also by the form and laws of the heavenly world, according to which their thoughts extend themselves around them; for the thoughts of angels have such extension, and in proportion thereto is their understanding and wisdom: hence proceeds their unanimous consent to the truth of the Divine Humanity of our Lord, and in him only. These things were not only told me by the angels, but it was allowed me to have a perception of them during the elevation of my spirit into an interior sphere of heaven: hence it appears, that the more highly the angels are graduated in wisdom, the more evident is their perception of this truth, and the better qualified for the beatifick vision; for the Lord appears in an angelical, that is, a human form, to those who acknowledge and believe in his divinity as visible, but not to those who think it invisible; the former are capable of beholding his glorious Majesty, but the latter are not.

80. Forasmuch as the angels have no idea of the divine invisible essence, which they call the divinity without form, but only of the visible divinity in a human form; therefore it is a usual way of speaking with them to say, that the Lord alone is the true perfect Man, and that they are only so far men as they receive him, by which they mean their receiving good and truth from him, as therein he himself is, and which they call wisdom and understanding; for these (say they) all may know, constitute the man, and not his mere face and figure without them: and that this is so appears evidently from the angels of the more interior or higher heavens, who, being in the higher

degrees

degrees of good and truth from the Lord, are also of a more beautiful and perfect form than the lower angels: but the reverse of this is the case of the inhabitants of the infernal regions, who, when viewed in the light of heaven, scarcely exhibit any thing of the human form, but appear as monsters; forasmuch as they are in the properties of evil and false, which are opposite to wisdom and truth; for which reason their kind of life is not called life, but spiritual death.

81. As heaven, both in whole and in part, thus resembles a man, from the Divine Humanity of the Lord; therefore the angels commonly say, that they are in the Lord, and some of them, that they are in his body, meaning, in the good of his love; according to those words of the Lord. " Abide in me, " and I in you: as the branch cannot bear fruit of itself, ex- " cept it abide in the vine, no more can ye, except ye abide in " me: I am the vine, ye are the branches: without me, ye " can do nothing—Continue ye in my love: If ye keep my " commandments, ye shall abide in my love." John xv. 4—10.

82. Such being the perception of the divinity in the angels, it is, as it were, congenial to every one that is a recipient of the divine influx, to form an idea of God under some species of humanity: thus did the ancients, and so the moderns both within and without the church, whilst the more simple of both, figure him in their thoughts, as the ancient of days in a vesture of light; but many extinguish every idea of God in their minds, either by carnal reasonings, or an evil life (*); and so in the former case dispute against him as a revealed God; or in the latter, disown his existence; and thus having extinguished in themselves the light from heaven, will not allow that any others have it: whereas it is given from above to every man as a creature born into this world for heaven, and whither no one goes that is entirely without any idea of a Deity.

83. Hence it is, that he, who is devoid of every idea of heaven, and so of the Divine Creator of it, is incapable of

(*) Hence it is that so many amongst us run into Naturalism, ascribing all things to blind nature, avoiding even the mention of the name of God, nay, banishing every idea of him from their minds, and so become atheists; for that of which we have no manner of idea ceases to be an object of our faith.   Tr.

entrance into heaven, but finds a refiftance and repulfe on the firft approach; and that becaufe his interiour, which fhould be the receptive and qualifying condition, is not adapted to the ftate of heaven, but is as a fhut gate within him, and the clofer fhut, by how much nearer he approaches to the holy abode. Such is the fate of thofe in the outer church, who deny the Lord, or with the Socinians difown his divinity: as to the lot of thofe who were not born nor educated within the pale of the church, nor favoured with the light of the written Word; this fhall be fpoken to hereafter.

84. That the ancients had an idea of the Divine Humanity, is manifeft from the divine appearances to Abraham, Lot, Jofhua, Gideon, Manoah, his wife, and others, who, though they beheld God as man, yet they worfhipped him as the God of the univerfe, calling him the God of heaven and earth, and Jehovah; and that it was the Lord that appeared to Abraham, he tells us, John viii. 56. and alfo to others in old times, John i. 18. v. 37.

85. But that God is alfo Man, will hardly be believed by thofe who judge of heavenly things by their external fenfes, and the things of this world, and confequently of the divine and fpiritual, by the corporeal and natural man; for fuch a one will immediately conclude, that if God were alfo Man, he muft (from his ubiquity) be as large as the univerfe, or, in order to be Governor of heaven and earth, ftand in need of many lieutenant governors, like earthly monarchs; or if we fhould tell them, that there is no fuch extenfion of fpace in heaven, as with us in this world, they could not receive it; for they who think only from outward nature on this fubject, and apply thofe thoughts as a meafure to heavenly things, fall into grofs delufion and abfurdity: extenfion in heaven is of a far different nature from what is here; in this world it is fomething determinate, and, as fuch, meafureable; but there indeterminate and unmeafurable (*): but concerning extenfion in heaven we fhall speak

---

(*) We are fenfible that this diftinction of our author, though of highly important ufe in this fubject, will be of difficult comprehenfion with many, not only among the unlearned, but the learned alfo, as it is above the fphere of metaphyfical

speak hereafter, where we treat of space and time in the spiritual world. Every one knows the great extent of vision by the bodily organ of sight, even as far as to the sun and stars, though at so immense a distance; and every man of thought can testify to the incomparably greater extent of sight by the eye of the mind, and that in proportion to the interior capacity of him that speculates. What then shall we say of him, who gave sight both to body and mind, and is the inmost and supreme over all! Such being the extent of our thoughts, how easy is it to believe, that the knowledge of all heavenly and divine things is communicated from angel to angel from the first divine fountain of knowledge, according to their capacities of receiving respectively, as has been declared in the preceding articles.

86. The angels wonder that men should account themselves wiser than their brethren for rejecting the belief of the Deity, as manifesting himself under a human form; whereas, if the truth be searched into, they will be found to have substituted nature in the room of the Creator, and as totally ignorant of what relates to God, angels, spirits, and even their own immortal souls; concerning all which, the simple and unlearned, whom they so despise, have ideas more conform to truth than themselves, whilst they conceive of the Deity as having assumed a human form; of angels, as heavenly men; and that they themselves shall be like unto them, if they lead holy lives according to God's commandments: these persons the angels call intelligent, and not the others (*).

That

taphysical knowledge in general; and yet it may readily be understood by those who can abstract their thoughts entirely from natural to spiritual things, and also may be illustrated by what passes within us in the spiritual part of our composition : *Ex. gr.* That the ideas and powers of the human mind have their extent and limits is agreed by all; for what is more common than to say of such or such a one, that he is a man of extensive knowledge, or of a very limited capacity; and yet to think of applying any determinate rule from outward nature, as an adequate measure of these, how grossly absurd would be the thought! As well might we go about to measure imagination by the gallon, or intellect by the carpenter's rule. The attentive mind, by improving this hint, will discern the difference between degrees and extension in the natural and spiritual worlds. Tr.

(*) We have omitted here to translate a large collection of references on the subject of the Lord's Divine Humanity, as many of them have been already given; and as they refer to books in the hands of exceeding few: and also as it may be

judged

That there is a Correspondence between all Things in Heaven, and all Things in Man.

87. What is meant by correspondence between heavenly and earthly things is scarcely known at this time, and that through various causes; but principally, because man has so far alienated himself from heaven by the love of self and the world; and they who give themselves up to these, direct all their views and pursuits to worldly things, as more agreeable to nature and their external senses, without attending to those that are spiritual, and suited to the entertainment of the mind and inward senses; wherefore they reject these, calling them abstruse, and too high for them: but the ancients were otherwise minded, for they accounted the knowledge of correspondences as the most exalted of all sciences, as the fountain from whence they drew their understanding and wisdom: and as to those who were of the church of God, it was by means hereof that they held communication with heaven; for the knowledge of correspondences is the knowledge of angels. The most ancient formed their minds by the doctrine and laws of correspondence, and thought according thereto, like the angels, and conversed with them; and hence it was that the Lord often vouchsafed to appear to them, and give them divine instructions: but this kind of knowledge is so far lost amongst us at this day, that it is scarcely any longer known what is meant by the term correspondence, as here used (72).

88. Now forasmuch as without some knowledge of what is meant by correspondence, nothing relating to the spiritual world can clearly be understood; neither concerning its influx into the natural world; nor of the distinction betwixt spiritual and

---

judged of use some time hereafter, to bring the substance of them together into the form of a distinct treatise on this subject. Tr.

(72) That the science of correspondences excels all other sciences, n. 4280. That herein consisted the principal wisdom of the ancients, but that it is now entirely lost, n. 3021, 3419, 4280—7729, 10252. That it flourished chiefly in the East, and in Egypt, n. 5702, 6092, 7097, 7779, 9391, 10407.

natural;

natural; nor yet any thing with clearness of the spirit of man called the soul, and its operation on the body; nor lastly, of the state of man after death; we shall therefore here shew what is meant by correspondence, by way of preparative to what follows.

89. And first, for what is meant by correspondence: Now the whole natural world corresponds to the spiritual world both in the whole, and likewise in its several parts; and what exists and subsists in the natural from the spiritual, is called correspondence; now the whole natural world exists and subsists from the spiritual, as an effect from its efficient cause; therefore there is a correspondent relation betwixt them. By the natural world is meant the whole expanse under the sun, and whatever therein receives light and heat from it belongs to that world: by the spiritual world is meant heaven, and all that is therein.

90. As man is an image both of heaven and of this world, in the least form (see above, n. 57.) therefore he stands here both in the spiritual and natural world: the things within (those of the mind and spirit) which respect the intellect and will, constitute his spiritual world; but those of the body, which respect his external senses and actions, constitute his natural world: whatever therefore in his natural world (or body, senses, and actions) derives its existence from his spiritual world (or mind, intellect, and will) that is called correspondent (*).

91. This doctrine is exemplified in the human countenance: Thus in the face of any one who is not practised in the art of dissimu-

(*) In this definition and distinction the intelligent reader will find a most admirable and important part of instruction, which will explain a man to himself, and point out to him all the good and evil in his life, without the help of that kind of sophistry commonly called Casuistical Divinity. It may be sufficient here, for a farther explanation of our author's meaning, to observe, that correspondence between things spiritual and natural, signifies the essence of a thing brought into form, or the principle manifested in act: thus benevolence shews itself in benefits, and malevolence in injuries: and thus throughout nature, the heavenly world or good principle realizes itself in beautiful and good productions; and the hellish, or evil principle, in all the various forms of monstrosity and evil: and so the rage and horrors of the dark world break forth in thunder and lightning, storm and tempest; but the meekness of paradise refreshes all nature with the genial warmth and soft blandishments of vernal delights. It is here to be noted, that the science of physiognomy is grounded in that of correspondences. Tr.

diffimulation, we may read the affections and paffions of his mind, as in their type or natural form: hence it is common to fay, that the face is the index of the mind; or in other words, the fpiritual world of fuch or fuch a one is confpicuous in his natural world: in like manner, the things of the intellect are reprefented in the fpeech; and thofe of the will, in the geftures and movements of the body: now all that is thus expreffed in the body, whether by the face, fpeech, or geftures, is called correfpondence.

92. Hence may be underftood what is meant by the internal, and what by the external man, and that the former is called the fpiritual, and the latter the natural man; and alfo that the one is as diftinct from the other, as heaven is from this world; and moreover, that all that is formed in or done by the latter is from the former.

93. So much for correfpondence between the inward or fpiritual, and the outward or natural man: we fhall now proceed to fpeak of that correfpondence which is between the whole of heaven, and the feveral parts of man.

94. It has been fhewed, that the univerfal heaven refembles one man, or is in a human form, and fo called the Grand (or greateft) Man; and alfo that the angelical focieties, of which heaven confifts, have accordingly their order and fituation like the members, organs, and vifcera in the human body, fo that fome of them occupy the place of the head, fome that of the breaft, others that of the arms, and others alfo different parts of thefe, fee n. 59 to 72: confequently fuch focieties as are in any particular member there, correfpond to the like member in man here; as for example, they who are in the head there, correfpond to the head in man here; they who are in the breaft, to the breaft; they who are in the arms, to the arms, and fo of the reft: it is from this correfpondence that man fubfifts, his fubfiftence or continued exiftence being from heaven only.

95. That heaven is diftinguifhed into two kingdoms, the one of which is called the cœleftial, the other the fpiritual kingdom, has been fhewed in its proper article: now the cœleftial kingdom in common correfponds to the heart, and what appertains to it in the whole body; and the fpiritual kingdom to

the

the lungs, and what appertains thereto in the whole body: the heart and lungs do also form two kingdoms; the former ruling therein by the arteries and veins; and the latter by the nervous and motive fibres, and both in every effort and action of the body. In the spiritual world or spiritual man of every one are also two kingdoms, the one is that of the will, the other that of the intellect: the will governs by the affections of good, and the intellect by the affections of truth; and these two kingdoms correspond to those of the heart and the lungs (*) in the body: so likewise in the heavens; the cœlestial kingdom is the will-part *(voluntarium cæli)* of heaven, and there the good of love has the ascendant or government; and the spiritual kingdom is the intellectual part *(intellectuale cæli)* of heaven; and there truth has the ascendant or government; and these two kingdoms correspond to the functions of the heart and lungs in man. From this correspondence it is, that the heart in the word signifies the will, and also the good of love; and also that the breath or pulmonary spirit signifies the understanding and true of faith: hence also it is, that the affections are ascribed to the heart, though in reality that is not the seat or cause of them (73).

(*) It is to be observed here, that though the word *lungs* is not mentioned in Scripture, as might be expected of so principal a correspondent in the human body, according to the doctrine and distinction of our author, yet the word *breath*, so frequently mentioned there, is used as its substitute, and answers to, or is the correspondent of spirit; and the same word in the Greek signifies both breath and spirit.

(73) Of the correspondence of the heart and lungs with the grand man or heaven, from experience, n. 3883 to 3896. That the heart corresponds to the angels in the cœlestial kingdom, and the lungs with those of the spiritual kingdom, n. 3685, 3886, 3887. That the angels have a pulse like that of the heart, and respiration like that of the lungs in men here, but more interior, n. 3884, 3885, 3887. That the pulse of the heart in angels varies according to their state of love; and their respiration according to their state of charity * and faith, n. 3886, 3887, 3889. That the heart in Scripture means the same with will, and therefore, *from the heart*, the same with *from the will*, n. 2930, 7542, 8910, 9113, 10336. That the heart in Scripture also signifies love, and therefore, *from the heart*, the same as, *from love*, n. 7542, 9050, 10336.

* The author here differences *love* from *charity* no otherwise, than as the former signifies love to the Lord, and the latter love to our neighbour.

96. The correspondence of the two kingdoms of heaven with the heart and lungs, is the correspondence of heaven with man in common, or of the whole of one with the whole of the other; the less common or particular, is with the several members, organs, and viscera of man, as shall be here specified: they who in the Grand Man or Heaven belong to the head, are the angels who excel all others in every species of good, as love, peace, innocence, wisdom, knowledge, &c. and consequently in joy and happiness; and from them proceeds the influx into the human head, and all that appertains to it here, for to these they correspond: those angels which in the Grand Man or Heaven belong to the region or province of the breast, excel in the good of charity and faith, and operate in their influence on the human breast here, inasmuch as they correspond thereto: but they who in the Grand Man or Heaven belong to the regions of the loins, and the organs appointed for generation, are they who chiefly excel in conjugal love: they who belong to the feet are in the lowest good of heaven, or that which is called spiritual-natural, or physico-spiritual good: they who belong to the arms and hands, are in the potency of that kind of truth which is derived from good: they who are in the eyes, excel in understanding: they who are in the ears, in attention and obedience: they who are in the nose, excel in the faculty of perception: they who are in the mouth and tongue, are eminent in speaking from clearness of intellect and perception: they who belong to the province of the reins, are more particularly in that kind of truth which illustrates, and distinguishes: they who are in the liver, pancreas, and spleen, excel in those faculties and powers which exalt the purity of the various kinds of good and truth, by separating them from mixtures with their contraries: and so in like manner with others respectively, by influx operating on the correspondent parts in man: now influx from heaven, is in order to the right end and use of all in man; and as uses are from the spiritual world, so they form themselves into effect by material instruments in the natural world; whence proceeds correspondence.

97. Hence

97. Hence it is, that the same members, organs, and viscera are used in the Scripture (according to the doctrine of correspondence) for the things represented by them: thus, by the head is there signified understanding and wisdom: by the breast, charity: by the loins, conjugal love: by the arms and hands, the power of truth: by the feet, that which is natural [in distinction from spiritual]: by the eyes, intellect: by the nose, perception: by the ears, obedience: by the reins, the purification [elucidation] of truth; and so on (74). Hence those customary expressions, when speaking of a man of deep knowledge, to say, that he has a head; of him who is true and faithful, that he is a bosom friend [*amicus pectoris*]; of any one of great sagacity, that he is ready at smelling a matter out; of a man that has a quick comprehension, that he is sharp-sighted; of one in great power, that he has long arms; and of him who says or does a thing with love, that he does it from his heart: these and many other sayings familiar to us, are from correspondence; for they are from the spiritual world, though we know it not.

98. That such is the correspondence between all things in heaven, and all things in man, has been manifested to me by long experience, and that in so full a measure, that my conviction herein is beyond all shadow of doubting; but to offer the whole of it here, is not only unnecessary, but, on account of its extent, beyond my power; but it has been given dispersedly in the *Arcana Cœlestia*, where I have treated of correspondences; of representations; of the influx of the spiritual into the natural world; and of the communication between soul and body (75).

---

(74) That the breast or bosom in Scripture signifies charity, n. 3934, 10081, 10087. That the loins and organs of generation signify conjugal love, n. 3021, 4280, 4462, 5050, 5051, 5052. That the arms and hands, the power of truth, n. 878, 3091, 4931 to 4937, 10017. That the feet signify external nature, or the inferior part of the human composition, n. 2162, 3147—4938 to 4952. That the eye signifies intellect, n. 2701, 4403, 4523 to 4534—10569. That the nose or nostrils signifies perception, n. 3577, 4624—10292. The ears, obedience, n. 2542, 3869—9396, 10061. The reins, purification, and separation of truth from error, n. 5380 to 5386, 10032.

(75) Of correspondence between all the members of the body and the Grand Man (*Maximus Homine*) or Heaven, both in general and particular, as from experience,

99. But though all things in man, even with refpect to his body, correfpond to all in heaven, yet he is not an image of heaven in his external, but in his internal form; for it is the interiour of man that receives the heavenly influx, whilft his exteriour or natural part is influenced by the things of this world; as far therefore as his interiour is receptive of the former, fo far only is he reputed a heaven in its leaft form after the likenefs of the greateft; but fo far as he is unreceptive of the heavenly influx in his interiour, or inner man, fo far is he not in the form of heaven; and yet his exteriour, or natural man, which communicates with this world, may be in order, according to the laws of this mundane fyftem, and confequently be of a beautiful form, for this originates from the parents, and his formation in the womb, and is preferved and nourifhed by the elements of this world; and therefore it is, that the natural form of a man often widely differs from the form of his fpiritual man. It has fometimes been given me to fee of what form the fpirit of a man was, and it plainly appeared to me, that in fome who were of a comely and beautiful countenance, it was ugly, black, and monftrous, and rather to be called the image of hell than of heaven; whereas in others, though uncomely in their exteriour, it was beautiful, fhining, and angelical: and it is to be noted, that the fpirit of a man after death appears fuch as it was before, whilft in the body.

100. But correfpondence is of much larger extent than in reference to man only; for there is a correfpondence of the heavens between one another: thus the fecond or middle heaven correfponds to the inmoft or third heaven; and the firft or loweft heaven correfponds to the fecond or middle heaven; and it is this firft or loweft heaven that more immediately correfponds to and communicates with the corporeal forms of men, their members, organs, and vifcera; and it is this corporeal part in man,

---

rience, n. 3021, 3624 to 3649, 3741 to 3751, 3883 to 3896, 4039 to 4051, 4218 to 4228, 4318 to 4331, 4403 to 4421—552 to 5573, 5711 to 5727, 10030. Of the influx of the fpiritual world or heaven, into this our natural world, and alfo of the influx of the foul into all parts of the body, from experience, n. 6053 to 6058, 6189 to 6215, 6307 to 6327, 6466 to 6495, 6598 to 6626. Of the communication *(de commercio)* between foul and body, from experience, n. 6053 to 6058, 6189 to 6215, 6307 to 6327, 6466 to 6495, 6598 to 6626.

in which the influence of heaven terminates, and refts as on its bafis: but this is a fecret which fhall be more fully opened in another place.

101. It is here to be noted, as a firft principle, that all correfpondence with heaven is through the Divine Humanity of the Lord, forafmuch as heaven originates from him as its effence, as has been fhewed before: for were not virtue flowing from his Divine Humanity to influence all in heaven, and by correfpondence all created nature here below, there would be neither angel nor man: and hence likewife it does appear why the Lord became man, and invefted his Deity with humanity, from its higheft to its loweft nature, and dwelt amongft us, viz. becaufe, through the degeneracy of man, all was brought into fuch diforder, that all communication with the Divine Humanity in heaven, on which his falvation depended, was cut off, and could only be reftored by the affumption of our natural humanity to his Divine, as a ground of communication between him and us. Concerning the Divine Humanity of the Lord, and the ftate of heaven before his advent in the flefh, fee the references mentioned at the end of the foregoing chapter.

102. The angels feem aftonifhed when they hear of men, who afcribe all to nature, and nothing to the Deity, and can believe that their own bodies, which confift of fo many wonderful correfpondences and reprefentations of heavenly things, fhould be formed and fafhioned by inanimate nature; and what is ftill more abfurd, that they fhould affign no higher origin to the rational principle; whereas the leaft exercife of reflection might fuffice to demonftrate this to be the effect of a divine formation; and that nature was created on purpofe to ferve for a covering or outward exhibition of what is fpiritual, and to yield a correfponding reprefentation of the fame in the loweft order of things. All fuch are compared by the angels to owls, which fee in the dark, but are blind in the light.

That

That there is a Correspondence between Heaven, and all Things on Earth.

103. We have already explained what is meant by correspondence; and also shewed, that the whole and every part of the human body is such: it now remains to make appear, that all things of the earth, nay, of this world in general, are correspondences in like manner.

104. All things belonging to the earth are distinguished into three kinds, which are called kingdoms, viz. the animal, the vegetable, and the mineral kingdoms: the things in the animal kingdom are correspondences in the first degree, as having life; those in the vegetable kingdom correspond in the second degree, as having growth, but no sensitive life; and those in the mineral kingdom correspond in the third degree, as having neither life nor growth. The correspondents of the first kingdom, are the animals of various kinds, which either walk or creep on the earth, or fly in the air; which being so well known, are not here enumerated, as neither those of the second or vegetable kingdom, which are all trees, herbs, plants, and flowers, which grow and flourish in the woods, gardens, fields, or elsewhere. The correspondents in the mineral kingdom, are the more noble, and also the inferior metals; precious and common stones; fossils, and earths of various kinds, and also waters. To these correspondences in the natural world, we are to add such things as are prepared and fabricated of them by human skill and industry for the general use of man, as food of different kinds, vestments, houses, temples, with many other things.

105. The things that are above the earth, as the sun, moon, stars, and also in the atmosphere, as clouds, rain, vapours, thunder, lightning, &c. are respectively correspondent; as also such as are occasioned by the presence or absence of the sun, as light and shade, heat and cold: in like manner those which are determined by its motions, distances, and variations, as the seasons of spring, summer, autumn, and winter, toge-

ther with the diurnal periods of morning, noon, evening, and night.

106. In a word, all things that exist in nature, from the least to the greatest, are correspondences (76); and that because this world, together with the whole of its furniture, exists and subsists from the spiritual world, and both from the Deity; it is said here to *subsist* also thence, as every thing subsists by that which is the cause of its existence, as its subsistence is no other than the continuation of its existence, and because it cannot subsist from itself, but from something prior to itself, and so on from its first cause, from which, if it be separated, it must perish, and be annihilated.

107. Every thing is said to correspond, which exists and subsists in nature according to the divine order; now divine good proceeding from the Lord, is that which constitutes divine order, for it begins and proceeds from him through the heavens to this world, where it terminates in its lowest form; and all things here, which are according to the laws of such order, are called correspondences, viz. all things that are good for use, for good and useful mean the same; whereas the form or distinction of a thing has relation to truth, forasmuch as truth is the form of good: hence it is, that all things in the universe, and in nature, as far as they subsist in the divine order, bear relation to goodness and truth (77).

108. That all things in the world are from God, and so invested by him with natural forms, as to give them correspondence and usefulness, manifestly appears from all things both in the animal and the vegetable kingdom, many of which display

---

(76) That all things in this world, and its three kingdoms, correspond to things in heaven, or, in other words, all things in the natural to things in the spiritual world, see n. 1632, 1881, 2758—2897 to 3003, 3213 to 3227, 3624 to 3649—5477, 9280. That the natural is joined to or communicates with the spiritual world by correspondences, n. 8615. That hence it comes to pass, that universal nature is one grand theatre representative of the kingdom of the Lord, n. 2758, 2999, 13000—8848, 9280.

(77) That all things in the universe, as well in heaven as on earth, which are in the divine order, have relation to goodness and truth under one denomination or another, see n. 2451, 3166, 4390—10122. And also have a tendency to conjunction, that they may have particular character and distinction, n. 10555.

evident

evident marks, to the thoughtful mind, of their divine original. To instance only in a few; and first in the animal kingdom: and here, what wonderful examples of science present themselves to the curious observer? What skill do the bees shew in collecting their honey from various flowers, and in forming their waxen cells wherein to deposite it for food for themselves and their offspring during the approaching winter? How do they wait upon the queen bee when she lays her eggs, dispose of them in proper apartments, and carefully provide for the safety of her future progeny? How excellent is their form of government, in which every one from an inward Teacher knows his proper place, and where, by a strict administration of justice, all the useful members of the society are protected, and the unprofitable ones expelled with the deprivation of their wings; not to mention many other wonderful particulars of knowledge derived to them from above, in order to the use and benefit of man: thus their wax, among other uses, being formed into candles, affords us light; and their honey supplies us with a grateful and salutary confection. How great is the sagacity of those worms, which extract their nourishment from the leaves of trees, and at a certain season invest themselves with a tegument of their own working, where, as in a womb, they deposite and nourish their tender young; whilst some taking the form of nymph or chrysalis, spin their slender threads, and after finishing their appointed task, assume another body, change their element, become volatile, and wing the soft air, chuse their mates, lay their eggs, and transmit their nature to a succeeding race. How wisely are all the birds of the air instructed where to seek and find the particular food that is proper for them; how to build their nests differently according to their kinds, to hatch their eggs, and to provide for their young till they are able to take care of themselves! And how early do they rightly distinguish between their enemies and friends, shunning the former, and associating with the latter! Not to mention here in particular the wonderful provision observable in their eggs, both for the formation and nutrition of their embryo young through the different stages of their growth, as also innumerable other wonderful particulars. Now who that has but

a spark

a spark of reason can deny these things to proceed from that wisdom which is from above, and to descend from the spiritual world, to which the natural is subservient, by clothing those things with material forms, which are spiritual in their several essences, or, in other words, to give effects to spiritual causes. The reason why this kind of knowledge is innate in the other living creatures, and not in man, though far more excellent than them, is because they stand in that order of life to which they were appointed; nor could they destroy that which is in them by influx from the spiritual world, as being destitute of reason; but it is otherwise with man, who, having perverted his more exalted powers by transgressing the order of his nature, was thenceforward to be born in mere ignorance, that so he might be reformed, and restored to the order in which he was created (which was the order of heaven) by the means appointed by God for that end.

109. As to correspondency in the vegetable kingdom; this might be illustrated by many considerations drawn from the growth of small seeds into trees, putting forth leaves, blossoms, and fruit, in which other seeds are contained, whereby propagation is carried on in a way of existence both simultaneous and successive, according to the laws of a wonderful order; to investigate all the uses of which would exceed the bounds of human science: and as these originate from the spiritual world or heaven, which is in the human form, as shewn before, so have they all relation to or correspondence with something in man, as is known to some few in the learned world. That all things in the vegetable kingdom are thus correspondent, I have had experimental evidence of; for oftentimes when walking in gardens I have inspected the trees, flowers, and plants therein, I have had a sight of their correspondents or correlatives in the spiritual world, and in conversation with those to whom these signatures belonged, have received the explanation of them from their particular descent, genius, and character (*).

110. As

(*) As this passage is somewhat obscure in the original, it necessarily renders the translation of it more difficult: however, the substance of it means, that the author had a satisfying knowledge of certain properties and qualities in some classes

of

110. As to those spiritual things in heaven, to which natural things in this world correspond, no one now can understand them, but by a particular illumination from above, forasmuch as the science of correspondences is at this time totally lost amongst us; however, I shall illustrate this doctrine of correspondence between natural and spiritual things by some few examples of the latter, as generally known here below. The beasts of the earth in general, not only the tame and useful ones, but also the wild and unprofitable, correspond to the affections of the human mind, the former to its good affections, the latter to its evil ones: in particular, oxen and calves correspond to the affections of the natural mind; but sheep and lambs to those of the spiritual mind; whereas the winged tribes, according to their respective kinds, correspond to the intellectual part in both (78): hence it was, that animals of various kinds, as oxen, calves, rams, sheep, goats, lambs, and also pigeons, and turtle doves, were appointed among the Israelites, who were a typical or representative church, for sacrifices

of the vegetable kingdom, as corresponding with and representative of certain characters, dispositions, or attributes in particular persons: now whether this be called analogy, correspondency, or emblematical similitude, it will amount nearly to the same. From this copious source of resemblances in nature to the microcosm, or little world of man, the art of poetry confessedly borrows its most striking beauties; and it formed a considerable part of the language of the ancient eastern nations: and it is also well known, that the sacred oracles of truth do instruct us by such similitudes (Hosea xii. 10.) in numberless places, and represent things, both divine and human, by images or resemblances thereof in the animal, mineral, and vegetable kingdoms of this our natural world: thus the wicked are described by thorns, to denote their oppressions and other pernicious qualities; whilst the candour, humility, and lovely simplicity of the true church and its members, are figured to us by their correspondent natural emblems in the lillies of the valley. But the doctrine of correspondency will be opened in a deeper ground, and more significant sense, under a variety of striking illustrations, in the following and other works of the author. Tr.

(78) That the beasts by correspondence signify the affections, good or bad, as the former are of the tame and profitable, or of the wild and unprofitable kinds, see n. 45, 46—3519, 9280. This also illustrated by experience from the spiritual world, n. 3218, 5198, 9090. Of influx from the spiritual world into the life of beasts, n. 1633, 3646. That oxen and calves by correspondence, the affections of the natural mind, n. 2180, 2566—10407. What sheep signify, n. 4169, 4809. What lambs, n. 3994, 10132. That the fowls signify intellectual things, n. 40, 745—5149, 7441. And that with difference according to their various kinds and tribes, by experience from the spiritual world, n. 3219.

and

and burnt offerings, as in such religious institutions they were representative of spiritual things, and accordingly were received in heaven according to correspondency. That animals, according to their difference as to *genus* and *species*, stand for the affections, is because they are endued with life; now the life of every creature is from the fire of love or affection, and according to the quality thereof; and such also is their innate knowledge respectively: man also, considered merely in the animal part of his nature, is constituted in like manner, and as such is compared to them; thus it is common to say of any one that is of a meek and gentle disposition, that he is sheepish, or lamb-like; to call a rugged or rapacious man, a bear or wolf; and to give the name of fox or serpent to the subtle and crafty, and so on.

111. Correspondency obtains in like manner in the vegetable kingdom: thus a garden in general corresponds to heaven in respect to understanding and wisdom; wherefore heaven is called the garden of God and paradise (79), and by man the heavenly paradise. Trees, according to their different kinds respectively, correspond to perceptions, and the cognitions of things good and true; and therefore the ancients, who were in the knowledge of correspondency, celebrated their religious worship in groves (80), and therefore it is that we have mention made in Scripture so often of trees, and that heaven, the church, and man, are in so many places compared to them, as to the vine, the olive, the cedar, and others, and our good works to fruit. The different kinds of food also, which are prepared from these, but more especially from the seeds of the field, correspond also to the affections of the good and the true, as these afford nourishment to the spiritual, as earthly foods do to the natural life (81).

(79) That garden and paradise by correspondence signify intellect and wisdom, n. 100, 108; from experience, n. 3220. That all things that mutually correspond have one and the same signification in Scripture, n. 2890, 2987—3002, 3225.
(80) That trees signify perceptions and knowledges *(cognitiones)* n. 103, 2163—2972, 7692. That therefore the ancients celebrated their religious worship in groves under trees, according to their correspondent kinds, n. 2722, 4552. Of the coelestial influx into the subjects of the vegetable kingdom, as trees and plants, n. 3648.
(81) That foods by correspondence signify such things as are for nourishment to the spiritual life, n. 3114, 4459—8562, 9003.

R   Hence

Hence it is that bread is the correspondent to affection respecting every particular good, as it is in a more eminent manner the support of life, and is used to signify the whole of food; and in this universal sense it is, that the Lord calls himself the bread of life; and likewise on this account bread was appointed for a sacred symbol in the Israelitish church, and was placed on a table in the tabernacle under the name of shew bread, or the bread of faces; and also that the whole of divine worship by sacrifices and burnt offerings was called bread: lastly, it is from correspondency, that bread and wine are used in the Holy Supper, as it is celebrated in the Christian church (82). These few instances may serve as a farther illustration of correspondency.

112. We shall here briefly shew how a conjunction is formed between heaven and this world by means of correspondences. The kingdom of the Lord is a kingdom of ends or uses, or, in other words, a kingdom, the administration whereof is to the end of uses; consequently the universe is so constituted by its Omnipotent Creator, that all things therein should be fitted with forms and powers to serve as means to produce and realize such uses, first in heaven, then in the general system of this world; and so on by a successive gradation to the least and lowest departments of nature; whence it follows, that the correspondence between natural and spiritual things, or of this world and heaven, subsists by uses as the means of their conjunction, and that the external forms of these uses do correspond and conjoin them, according to the degrees of their utility. All things in this natural world throughout its three kingdoms, as far as they stand in their established order, may be considered as so many forms of uses, or formed effects proceeding from use to use; and so circumstanced, are correspondences: with respect to man; as far forth as he lives according to the divine order, or in love towards the Lord, and in charity towards his neigh-

---

(82) That bread signifies every good that is for spiritual food to man, n. 2165, 2177—9545, 10686. That this was signified by the shew-bread of the tabernacle, n. 3478, 9545. That the sacrifices in general were called bread, n. 2165. That bread stands for all kinds of food, n. 2165: and therefore for all food cœlestial and spiritual, n. 276, 680—6118, 8410.

bour,

bour, so far his actions are forms of uses, and as such so many correspondents, whereby he communicates with and is joined to heaven; for to love the Lord and our neighbour, is, in a general sense of the expression, to perform uses (83): moreover, let it be remembered, that it is through man (as the proper medium of their connexion) that the conjunction is formed betwixt the natural and spiritual worlds, as he is the subject of both (see before n. 57.) and therefore as far forth as any man is spiritual, in such degree he is the medium of this conjunction; and as far forth as he is natural and not spiritual, he is not so; nevertheless, even in this latter case, the divine influx is continued to this world, and what belongs to it in man, though it be not received into his rational part.

113. As all things which continue in the divine order correspond with heaven, so all things which are contrary to the divine order correspond with hell: the former have relation to things good and true; the latter to such as are evil and false.

114. A word more as touching the science of correspondences, and its use. It has been said before, that heaven or the spiritual world is joined to the natural world by correspondences: hence it is that man here has the power of holding communication with heaven; for as the blessed angels form not their ideas like men from natural, but spiritual things; so when men are gifted with the knowledge of correspondences, they can think in like manner with the angels, and be joined with them

---

(83) That every kind of good has its delightful relish from and according to its uses, and also its particular distinction and quality, and therefore, as is the use, such is the good, n. 3049, 4984, 7038. That the angelical life consists in the goods of divine love and charity, and so in the exercise of uses, n. 453. That the Lord and his angels have respect only to the final causes or uses in human actions, n. 1317, 1645, 5844. That the kingdom of the Lord is the kingdom of uses or good ends, n. 453, 696—4054, 7038. That the service of good uses is to serve the Lord, n. 7038. That all in general, and every particular thing in man, are formed to the end of use, n. 3565, 4104, 5189, 9297: and that final causes or uses (as efficients to their effects) were prior to the formation of our bodily organs, by a divine influx through heaven, n. 4223, 4926. That also the interior faculties of the human mind, when attained to reason, are formed for a progression from use to use, n. 1964, 6815, 9297. That therefore man is to be estimated according to the uses that he fulfills, n. 1568, 3570—6938, 10284. That uses are the ends for which all things were created, n. 3565—6815. That use is the first and last, and so the whole end of man, 1964.

in

in the spiritual or inward man. The Holy Scriptures are written entirely according to the truth of correspondency (84), in order that we may thereby have communication with heaven; and therefore, were any one rightly possessed of the science of correspondences, such a man would thoroughly understand the Scriptures in their spiritual sense (as all things therein spoken of correspond) and would thereby come at the knowledge of such secrets as cannot be learned from their literal sense alone; for as in the written word there is a literal, so also is there a spiritual sense (85); the literal sense concerns the things of this world; the spiritual such as are heavenly; and as a conjunction is formed, by the relation of correspondences, between heaven and earth, therefore such a dispensation is vouchsafed to us, in which all things in both worlds do perfectly correspond, and answer the one to the other, as face to face in a glass.

115. I have learned from heaven, that among the most ancient inhabitants of our earth, there were certain heavenly men, who were in the true knowledge of correspondency, and whose conceptions and thoughts were according thereto, to whom the visible things of this world served as so many mediums of discerning spiritual things, and who as such associated and conversed with angels, and that through them was kept up a communication between heaven and earth; whence this was called the Golden Age; of which mention is made by ancient writers, who relate, that in those times the inhabitants of heaven became the visitors and guests of men, and familiarly conversed with them, as one friend with another; but that to these succeeded another race of men, who were not in the same intuitive knowledge of correspondences, but only understood them scientifically: that, however, there was a communication between heaven and earth in their days, but not so open and intimate as the former: this was called the Silver Age. In the next generation were those who retained some speculative know-

---

(84) That the Scriptures are to be understood according to the doctrine of correspondences, n. 8615. That hereby man has a communication with heaven, n. 2899, 6943—10375, 10457.

(85) Concerning the spiritual sense of the word, see a small Treatise concerning the White Horse [*De Equo Albo*] in the Apocalypse.

ledge

ledge of correspondences, but did not think and discern according thereto, as being only in natural, and not in spiritual good like the former; and their period was called the Copper Age. In the following times men became successively merely external, and at length corporeal or sensual, and without all knowledge of correspondency, and nearly so of all heavenly things. That the forementioned ages were denominated from gold, silver, and copper, was from the doctrine of correspondences (86), forasmuch as according thereto gold signifies cœlestial good, in which principle were the most ancient; silver, spiritual good, in which were the ancient that succeeded them; and copper, natural good, the signature or character of the following race; but iron, which gives denomination to the last times, signifies a sapless knowledge of ideal truth without any mixture of good in it.

Concerning the Sun in Heaven.

116. In heaven the sun of this world appears not, nor any thing that proceeds from it, as being natural, for nature takes its beginning or rise proximately from this our sun, and whatever so proceeds from it is termed natural; whereas that which is spiritual, as heaven, is above nature, and therefore entirely distinct from all that is called natural, neither is there any communication betwixt them, but by correspondency. This distinction will be understood by what has been said before in n. 38, concerning degrees; and what is here meant by communication, by what appears in the two preceding articles concerning correspondences.

117. But though neither the sun of this world, nor any thing proceeding from it, is seen in heaven, yet neither is heaven without its sun, light, and heat; nay, therein are all things that are in this world, with innumerable others, though of a different origin; for the things in heaven are spiritual, but those

(86) That gold according to correspondency signifies cœlestial good, n. 113, 1551—9881. That silver signifies spiritual good, or truth from cœlestial original, n. 1551, 1552, 2954, 5648. That copper signifies natural good, n. 425, 1551. That iron signifies truth in the lowest order, n. 425, 426.

on earth are natural. The sun of heaven is the Lord, the light of it is divine truth, and the heat of it divine love, proceeding from the Lord as a sun; and from him as their divine source do all heavenly things proceed: but concerning the light and heat in heaven, and whatever is produced by them, shall be treated of in the following articles; but here first as touching its sun. Now the Lord appears in heaven as a sun, forasmuch as he is that divine love from which all spiritual things derive their existence, and also, through the medium of this our mundane sun, all natural things likewise: he is that love whose brightness is as the sun.

118. That the Lord actually appears in heaven as a sun, has not only been told me by the angels, but also been granted me to see myself at certain times; and therefore I shall here briefly relate what I myself have so heard and seen of this wonderful appearance. The Lord appears in heaven as a sun, not as horizontally in heaven, but high above the heavens; not over head or vertical, but before the faces of the angels in a middle altitude: he appears in two places, in one before the right eye, in the other before the left eye, and that at a considerable distance: before the right eye he appears as a perfect sun, of a glow and magnitude similar to those of our mundane sun; but before the left eye he appears not a sun, but as a moon, of the like shine, but brighter, and of the like magnitude with our moon, and as surrounded with many lesser moons, each in like manner having its particular glittering lustre. That the Lord appears in two places so differently, is because that his appearance is to every one according to their quality and degree of their recipiency respectively, and therefore otherwise to those who receive him in the good principle of love, than to those who receive him in the good of faith; to the former his appearance is like that of a fiery refulgent sun, and they are the angels of his cœlestial kingdom; but to the latter as a pale but bright moon, and these are the angels of his spiritual kingdom (*); and to both in degrees respectively to their reci-

---

(*) The author, as observed before, distinguishes the third and second heavens by the names of cœlestial and spiritual; the third or cœlestial as the highest, the angels recipiency (87): the reason of which is, because the good of love corresponds to fire, and therefore fire in a spiritual sense signifies love: and the good of faith corresponds to light in a spiritual sense, and signifies faith (88). That he appears in the plane of or before the eyes, is because the interiour of the mind manifests itself by the eyes, the good of love through the right eye, and the good of faith through the left eye (89); for that which is on the right side of angels or men corresponds to that good, which is the source of truth; and that which is on the left, to that truth which issues from it (90). The good of faith, as to its essence, is that truth which proceeds from the good principle.

119. Hence it is, that in the Scriptures the Lord, with regard to love, is compared to the sun; and with regard to faith, to the moon; and also that our love to the Lord, as proceeding from him, is signified by the sun; and our faith in the Lord, as his gift, is signified by the moon, as in the following places: " Moreover, the light of the moon shall be as the light of the " sun, and the light of the sun shall be seven-fold, as the light " of seven days;" Isai. xxx. 26. " And when I shall put thee

---

angels of which excel in divine love; and the second or spiritual, the angels of which are more especially charactered by faith and love to their neighbour. Tr.

(87) That the Lord appears in heaven as a sun, and also is the sun of heaven, n. 1053, 3636, 3643, 4060. That he appears to the subjects of his cœlestial kingdom, which excel in love to him, as a sun; and to the subjects of his spiritual kingdom, whose more distinguishing character is that of faith and charity to their neighbour. n. 1521, 1529, 1530, 1531, 1837, 4696. That the Lord appears as a sun in the middle altitude before the right eye; and as a moon before the left eye, n. 1053, 1521, 1529—8812, 10809. That the Lord has been seen under this twofold appearance, n. 1531, 7173. That the real divinity of our Lord is far above his divine manifestations in heaven, n. 7270, 8760.

(88) That fire in the Scriptures signifies love in both senses, n. 934, 4906, 5215. That the sacred or cœlestial fire signifies divine love, n. 934, 6314, 6832. That the infernal fire signifies the love of self and of the world, and all concupiscence arising from those loves, n. 1861—7575, 10747. That love is the fire of life, and that life itself actually proceeds therefrom, n. 4096, 5071, 6032, 6314. That light signifies the true of faith, n. 3395, 3485—9548, 9684.

(89) That the sight of the left eye corresponds to the truths of faith, and the sight of the right eye to their good, n. 4410, 6923.

(90) That the parts or organs, which are on the right side of the human body, correspond to the good from which any truth proceeds, and those on the left to such kind of truth, n. 9495, 9604.

" out,

"out, I will cover the heaven, and make the stars thereof
"dark; I will cover the sun with a cloud, and the moon shall
"not give her light: all the bright lights of heaven will I
"make dark over thee, and set darkness upon thy land;" Ezek.
xxxii. 7, 8. "The stars of heaven, and the constellations
"thereof, shall not give their light: the sun shall be darkened
"in his going forth, and the moon shall not cause her light
"to shine;" Isai. xiii. 10. "The sun shall be turned into
"darkness, and the moon into blood; and the stars shall with‑
"draw their shining;" Joel ii. 31. iii. 15. "The sun be‑
"came black as sackcloth of hair, and the moon became as
"blood, and the stars of heaven fell into the earth;" Apoc.
vi. 12. "Immediately after the tribulation of those days shall
"the sun be darkened, and the moon shall not give her light,
"and the stars shall fall from heaven;" Matt. xxiv. 29, and
elsewhere: in which places, by the sun is signified love, and
by the moon faith, and by the stars the knowledges [*cognitiones*]
of good and truth (91), which are then said to be darkened, to
lose their light, and to fall from heaven, when the things signi‑
fied by them cease among men. That the Lord appears as a
sun in heaven, may also be gathered from his transformation
before Peter, James, and John, when "his faced shined as
"the sun;" Matt. xvii. 2. Such was his appearance to his
disciples, when they were out of the body, and in the light of
heaven. From some knowledge of this truth it was, that the
ancients, who formed a representative church, in their more
solemn adorations turned their faces to the east, where the sun
rises; and also gave a like aspect to their temples.

120. The greatness of divine love may in a sort be conceived
by us, from its being compared to the sun of our world, though
indeed it is far more ardent; and therefore the Lord, as under
the manifestation of his divinity by a sun, tempers the ardour
of it in the progression of its powers, according to certain de‑
grees, denoted by apparent radiant circles round the sun: the
angels, moreover, are surrounded by a kind of thin, transparent

---

(91) That the stars and constellations signify in the word the knowledges of
good and truth, n. 2495, 2849, 4697.

vapour,

vapour, to enable them to sustain the divine influx (92), according to their receptivity of which, is the nearer or greater distance of the angels; thus such of them as excel most in the good of love are nearest to this divine sun, whilst they who are charactered by the good of faith, are more remote from it: but as to those who are in no kind of good, of which sort are the infernal spirits, they are at an immense distance, and that in proportion to the degree of their opposition to all good (93).

121. When the Lord appears in heaven with the angels, as he often does, he appears not as clothed with the sun, but in an angelical form, though distinguished from the angels by a divine glory radiating from his countenance; not that this is properly his appearance in person, for that is always as clothed with the sun (Rev. xii. 1.) but it is his [apparent or] presence by aspect; for in heaven it is common for the blessed beings to appear in the termination of the beholder's view, though it be far distant from the place where they actually are; and this apparent presence is called the presence of the internal sight, of which hereafter. I also myself have seen the Lord without the sun, and in a lesser degree of altitude, in an angelical form; and also near, in a like form, with a splendid countenance; and once also in the midst of the angels as a flaming stream of light [*Jubar flammeum*].

122. The sun of this world appears to the angels as a dark spot, in opposition to the heavenly sun, and the moon in like manner, in opposition to the heavenly moon; and that because

(92) What and how great the divine love of the Lord is, illustrated by a comparison with the fire of this world's sun, n. 6834, 6844, 6849. That the divine love of the Lord is his love for all mankind, in order to their salvation, n. 1820, 1865, 2253, 6872. That the fire of divine love, in its full ardour, enters not heaven, but appears in the form of radiant circles round the sun, n. 7270. That the angels are, as it were, veiled with a kind of rare vapour, or diaphanous cloud, to moderate the ardour of the divine influx, n. 6849.

(93) That the divine presence with the holy angels is in proportion to their reception of the good of love and faith from the Lord, n. 904, 4198—10106, 10811. That the Lord's appearance to every one is according to his quality and disposition respectively, n. 1861, 2235, 4198, 4206. That the remote distance of the hells from the heavens, is because the infernals are not able to endure the influx of divine love, n. 4299, 7519—8266, 9327. Hence it is, that between heaven and hell there is so great a gulf, n. 9346, 10187.

the element of fire in this world corresponds to the love of self, and the light proceeding from it to falsehood the issue of that love: now the love of self is diametrically opposite to divine love, as falsehood is to divine truth; and all that is opposite to divine love and divine truth is as darkness to the angels: therefore it is, that to worship the sun and moon of this world, and to bow down to them, denotes in Scripture self-love, and falsehood, and error derived therefrom, and that all such should be cut off; Deut. iv. 19. xviii. 3, 4, 5. Jer. viii. 1, 2. Ezek. viii. 15, 16, 18. Apoc. xvi. 8. Matt. xiii. 6. (94).

123. As the Lord's appearance in heaven is as a sun from the divine love that is in him, and proceeds from him, therefore all the angels constantly turn their faces towards him; they in the cœlestial kingdom towards him as a sun, and the spiritual kingdom towards him as a moon; whereas the infernal spirits turn themselves to that blackness and darkness which are opposite thereto, having their backs towards the Lord, forasmuch as all that are in hell are in the love of self and of the world, and as such in opposition to his Divine Majesty. Such of them as face to that dark orb, which is representative of the sun of this world, are in the hells behind, and are called Genii; but they which face to that which is representative of the moon, are in the foremost hells, and are called Spirits: hence it is, that all who are in hell are said to be in darkness, and all who are in heaven to be in light: darkness corresponds to the false, as proceeding from evil, and light to the true, as proceeding from the good principle. That the inhabitants of the other worlds turn their faces as before-mentioned, is because all there direct their view to those things which correspond to their interiour, or what they love most; for the faces of angels and spirits manifest and are directed by their interior dispositions and

(94) That the sun of this world is not visible to the angels, it being as a dark orb behind them, opposite to the heavenly sun, n. 7078, 9755. That the sun, in an opposite sense, signifies the love of self, n. 2441; in which sense, to worship the sun, is to worship those things which are contrary to divine love, or to the Lord, n. 2441, 10584. That the heavenly sun is to those that are in the hells, as a blackness, n. 2441.

states; and, as observed before, in the spiritual world the four cardinal points are not fixed, as in the natural, but are determined by the aspect of the face: nor is it otherwise with the spirit of man in this world; for it turns its aspect to or from the Lord, according as it is in the love of him and its neighbour, or in the love of self and the world; but this man is ignorant of, while he continues in this natural world, where the four quarters are determined by the rising and setting of the sun: but as this is difficult of comprehension, it will be illustrated in the sequel of this work, where the four quarters, space, and time in heaven, will be treated of.

124. As the Lord is the sun of heaven (Rev. xxi. 23.) and all things there point to him as to their divine original, so consequently he is the common centre of all direction and determination (95): and hence it further follows, that all things both in the heavens above, and in the earth beneath, are present to him, and under his government.

125. From the things here laid down will more clearly appear what has been asserted and proved in some preceding articles concerning the Lord *as the God of Heaven*, n. 2 to 6. *That the Virtue of his Divinity constitutes Heaven*, n. 13 to 19. *That there is a Correspondence between all Things in this World and Heaven, and through Heaven with the Lord*, n. 87 to 115: *as also that the Sun and Moon of this World have their correspondent Relations*, n. 105.

Of Light and Heat in Heaven.

126. That there is light in heaven is not to be conceived by those, who form their idea of light only from our natural sun; whereas the heavenly light far exceeds the meridian light of this world: I have often seen it, and also at those times of its diminution, which answer to our times of evening and

---

(95) That the Lord is the common centre to whom all things in heaven tend, n. 3633.

night.

night (*). At first I was surprized to hear the angels affirm, that the light of this world was but as shade compared to that of heaven; but I can now assert the truth of it from ocular evidence, and that the splendour of it exceeds all description: the things which I have seen in heaven was by this light, and consequently with greater clearness and distinction than any which are seen on earth.

127. The light of heaven is not a natural light, like that of our world, but spiritual, for it proceeds from the Lord as a sun, and that sun is divine love, as was shewed in the preceding article. This emanation from the Lord, as a sun, is called in heaven by the name of Divine Truth, and is in its essence and source divine good united with divine truth; and hence the angels have their light and heat, the former from the divine truth, the latter from the divine good or love, which, like their divine original, are both spiritual, not natural (96).

128. That divine truth is the light of the angels, is because the angels are spiritual beings, and such see things by the light of their proper sun, as natural beings do by the light that is proper to them; and as divine truth is to the angels a source of intellectual sight, so this by influx produces their external vision; and thus the light of the divine sun illuminates all things in heaven, both inwardly and outwardly (97). And as such is the

---

(*) It is certain that the great Milton had some idea of such variation in heaven, by the following lines:

" ——————There is a cave
" Within the mount of God, fast by the throne,
" Where light and darkness in perpetual round
" Lodge and dislodge by turns, which makes through heav'n
" Grateful vicissitude, like day and night:
" ——————Though darkness there might well
" Seem twilight here."   PAR. LOST. B. VI.

The above quotation is not adduced by way of authority, but to shew that certain notices of heavenly things are impressed on some minds by a kind of heavenly irradiation or influx.

(96) That all light in the heavens is from the Lord, as a sun, n. 1053, 1521—9548, 9684, 10809. That divine truth proceeding from the Lord has its external appearance in heaven as light, and constitutes all the light of heaven, n. 3195, 3222—9684.

(97) That the light of heaven illuminates angels and spirits, both as to their intellectual and organical sight, n. 2776, 3138.

original

original of light in heaven, so does it likewise differ in degree, according to the different reception of divine truth from the Lord in the angels, or, in other words, according to their different qualities or measures, as to understanding and wisdom (*); for these are not the same in all, but different not only in the cœlestial and spiritual kingdoms, but also in the several societies in each of those kingdoms: thus, with respect to external vision, the light of the cœlestial kingdom appears of a flame colour, as the angels therein receive their light from the Lord as a sun; but in the spiritual kingdom it appears of a white or silver colour, as the angels of the latter receive it from the Lord as a moon. See above, n. 118. Nor is the light the same to one society as to another; thus, they who are in the centre have a larger measure of it than they who are in the circumference; and so in proportion according to their distances respectively, n. 43. In a word, according to the degree in which the angels are recipient of divine truth, or, in other words, according to the measure of their understanding and wisdom from the Lord, such is their light (98): however, all the angels of heaven are called angels of light.

129. As the Lord in the heavens is divine truth; and as divine truth there appears in the form of light, therefore he is called in Scripture, *The Light*; as likewise all truth that proceeds from him, as in the following places: " Jesus said, I am " the light of the world; he that followeth me shall not walk " in darkness, but shall have the light of life;" John viii. 12. " Whilst I am in the world, I am the light of the world;" John xix. 15. " Jesus said, Yet a little while, and the light " is with you: walk whilst ye have the light, lest darkness " come upon you: while ye have light, believe in the light, " that ye may be the children of light. I am come a light " into the world, that whosoever believeth in me should not

---

(*) According to that received maxim: *Quicquid recipitur, recipitur ad modum recipientis.*

(98) That light in heaven is according to the understanding and wisdom in the angels, n. 1524, 1529, 1530, 3339. That the differences in light there, are as many as angelical societies; and also in proportion to the successive variations in the degrees of goodness and truth, and so of wisdom and understanding, in those societies, n. 684, 690, 3241—7836.

" abide

"abide in darkness;" John xii. 35, 36, 46. "Light is come into the world, but men love darkness rather than light;" John iii. 19. And John, speaking of the Lord, says: "This is the true light, which lighteth every man that cometh into the world;" John i. 4, 9. "The people who sat in darkness shall see great light; and to those who sat in the shadow of death is light arisen;" Matt. vi. 16. "I will give thee for a covenant to the people, for a light to the Gentiles;" Isaiah xlii. 6. "I have given thee for a light to the Gentiles, that thou mayest be my salvation, even to the ends of the earth;" Isaiah xlix. 6. "The nations of them that are saved shall walk in his light;" Rev. xxi. 24. "Send forth thy light and thy truth: they shall lead me;" Psa. xliii. 3. In these and other places the Lord is called Light, as the fountain of that divine truth that proceeds from him, which also is called Light; and as he is the divine sun that gives light to the heavens, so when he was transformed before Peter, James, and John, "his face appeared as the sun, and his garments shining, and white as snow, so as no fuller on earth can white them;" Mark ix. 3. Matt. xvii. 2. That the Lord's garments appeared in this sort, was because they represented divine truth as proceeding from him in heaven, and as garments in the Scriptures signify truths (99); and to this purpose are those words of David: "O Lord, thou clothest thyself with light, as with a garment;" Psa. civ. 2.

130. That the light in heaven is spiritual, and the same with divine truth, may also be gathered from hence, viz. that there is also a spiritual light in man, which at times illustrates his mind with the knowledge of divine truth, according to his class in the school of wisdom. The spiritual light in man is the light of his understanding, as far as it has truths for its objects, which he disposes analytically in order, forms into reasons, and from thence draws conclusions (100): the natural

(99) That garments in the Scripture signify truths, as these are the clothing of good, n. 1073, 2576—9952, 10536. That the garments of the Lord, at his transfiguration, signified divine truth proceeding from his divine love, n. 9212, 9216.

(100) That the illumination of the human intellect by the light of heaven, is the cause of rationality in man, n. 1524, 3138—9399, 10569. That the mind has

man indeed knows not that this is a real light by which we so speculate, because he sees not either inwardly or outwardly; but nevertheless, many know it to be so, and have a distinct perception of its difference from that natural light which they are in, whose thoughts are not spiritual, but natural only; of which sort are all those who have regard only to things of this world, and ascribe all to nature; whereas they that think spiritually, think of heavenly things, and ascribe all to God: and that it is a real and true light which illuminates the minds, and totally distinct from that which we call natural light, has often been given me to discern, by a gradual ascent of the mind therein, and according to the degrees of such elevation, I have been given to perceive things, of which I had not the least perception before, and so on to higher things, which far exceeded my conception by any powers of the natural understanding; and sometimes I have been much disturbed and offended at my prior ignorance of things, which I saw with such convincing evidence by a spiritual light (101): and as light and vision are thus proper to the intellectual part, so by correspondence we apply to it the same terms that we make use of in speaking of corporeal sight; thus it is commonly said of the understanding, when it is in the perception of any truth, that it sees it, or is in the light of it; and so on the contrary, when it perceives it not, that it is in darkness concerning it, with many other like expressions.

---

has its capacity for divine illumination from its being receptive of truth, n. 6222, 6608, 10659. That its illumination is in proportion to its recipiency of truth in the good principle from the Lord, n. 3619. That the mind of man takes its particular distinction and character from the nature and quality of the truths it imbibes, and which form it, n. 10064. That the light of heaven is to the human intellect what the light of this world is to the eye, n. 1524, 5114, 6608, 9128. That heavenly light from the Lord is always present with man, but influences him no farther than as he is in that truth which is from good [*in vero ex bono*] n. 4060, 4213.

(101) When any one is raised up from a state of sensual darkness, he is first brought into a lower degree of light, and so on, till he is exalted to cœlestial light, n. 6313, 6315, 9407. That he is then exalted to heavenly light, when he attains to a right understanding of divine truth, n. 3190. How great the light I became percipient of, when I was raised above all thoughts relating to worldly things, n. 1526, 6608.

131. As the light of heaven is divine truth, or, in other words, divine wisdom and understanding; consequently, to be raised up to the light of heaven, and to have the illumination of divine understanding, mean the same thing; and therefore the light of the angels is in exact proportion to their understanding and wisdom: and as light in heaven [in its essence] is divine wisdom, so does it manifest the particular distinctions and qualities of the angels, for with those blessed beings the face is the index of the mind, and reveals all that is within; nay, the more interior angels love to have it so, as they harbour nothing but what is good in their intentions and wills: but the case is far otherwise with the infernal spirits; for as they are void of all good within, they dread being viewed in the manifesting light of heaven; and (which will be thought very strange) though they appear to one another in the regular human form, yet when viewed by the heavenly light, they appear as monsters, with ugly faces and hideous shapes, corresponding to the evil that is within them respectively (102): nor is it otherwise with man, as to his spiritual form, when viewed by the angels; for if he is in the good principle, he appears to them in a beautiful human form according to his good; but if in the evil principle, he appears to them deformed and ugly according to his evil; for all things are made manifest in the light of heaven, forasmuch as it is the same with divine truth.

132. As divine truth is the essence of the heavenly light, therefore all truths every where, whether within or without the angels, and within or without the heavens, have a lucid form, but the latter in a less degree; for truths without the heavens have a cold lucid aspect, like snow without heat, as not having their essence from good, like truths within the heavens; wherefore such kind of frigid light disappears upon the breaking in upon them of the heavenly light, and is turned into darkness, if evil be concealed under it: this I myself have sometimes seen, as also many other memorable things concerning shining truths, which I here pass over.

(102) That they who are in hell appear to one another like men by their own light, which resembles that from fiery coals, but as monsters in the light of heaven, n. 4532, 4533—6605, 6626.

133. I pro-

133. I proceed to say something concerning the heat of heaven, which in its essence is love, for it proceeds from the Lord as a sun, and that sun in its essence is divine love proceeding from the Lord, as has been shewed in a former article; so that the heat of heaven is equally spiritual with the light of heaven, seeing that the origin of both is the same (103). There are two things which proceed from the Lord as a sun, divine truth and divine good: the former has its manifestation in heaven as light, and the latter as heat, but both in such a state of union, as to form only one and the same thing; nevertheless in the angels they are distinct, as some angels receive more of the divine good, and some, on the other hand, more of the divine truth; they of the former class belong to the cœlestial kingdom of the Lord, and those of the latter to his spiritual kingdom; but such among them as receive of both in equal measure, are the most perfect of all.

134. The heat, as well as light of heaven, varies throughout the regions of bliss, not being the same in the cœlestial with that of the spiritual kingdom; nay, it differs in every society in both, as well in degree as quality; it is more intense and pure in the cœlestial kingdom, as the angels therein receive more of the divine good; but less intense and pure in the spiritual kingdom, as the angels therein receive less of divine good than of divine truth; nay, it varies in every particular society respectively, according to their difference of recipiency. The hells also have their heat, but of an impure nature (104): the heat in heaven, represented by the sacred and cœlestial fire, and the heat of hell, by the profane and infernal fire, are both correspondents of love; the former of love to the Lord and our neighbour, and of every particular affection proceeding there-

(103) That there is a twofold origin of heat and light, the one from the sun of this world, the other from the cœlestial sun, n. 3338, 5215, 7324. That heat from the Lord as a sun, is that spiritual affection which proceeds from love, n. 366, 3643. Hence, that spiritual heat in its essence is love, n. 2146, 3338, 3339, 6314.
(104) That the hells also have respectively their heat, but of an impure kind, n. 1773, 2757, 3340; and that it yields a fœtid, excrementitious smell; and in the lowest hells like that which proceeds from a putrid carcase, n. 814, 815—944, 5394.

X   from;

from; the latter of the love of self and the world, and of all their concomitant concupiscences. That love is heat from a spiritual source, is evident from its effects; for how does any one feel himself warmed by its influence, according to its degree and quality; nay, how hot when crossed in this passion? Hence those common forms of speaking; to take fire, to glow, to burn, and the like, when we would express the fervors of a lawful, or unlawful love.

135. That love proceeding from the Lord as a sun is felt in heaven as heat, is because the divine principle, or fire of love within the angels, excites that sensation in their external form, for love and heat mutually correspond both in kind and degree, as was observed before. The heat of this world finds no place in heaven, as being of a gross nature, and not spiritual; though it is otherwise with us men, as partaking of both worlds at the same time, the natural and the spiritual; and therefore have not only a spiritual heat adapted to spiritual affections, but also a corporeal sensation of heat derived by influx therefrom, as well as from the natural fire of this world. The correspondence between these different kinds of heat is manifest in the loves of the brute animals, the chief of which is that of propagating their species, and which operates in them according to its concurrence with our solar heat in the spring and summer seasons; but fundamental is the error of those, who suppose that the heat of this material world can, by any influxive power in itself, beget love [which is of a spiritual origin] for all influx is from spirit to matter, not from matter to spirit; the former being according to the established laws of divine order, but the latter contrary thereto (105).

136. Angels are endowed with intellect and free will, as well as men; the former they derive from the light of heaven, or, in other words, from divine truth and wisdom; and the latter from the heat of heaven, or that divine principle of goodness which produces divine love; however, the essence of the angelical life is from heat, or so far only from light, as light is

---

(105) That influx is spiritual, and not physical; consequently from the spiritual to the natural world, not *vice versa*, n. 3219, 5119—9110, 9111.

animated

animated by heat; and that this is so, appears evidently in that life entirely ceases upon a total extinction of heat. The case is exactly similar with respect to that kind of faith which is void of love, or that kind of truth which is void of good, as the true of faith [*verum fidei*] answers to light, and the good of love to heat (106). This may be illustrated from the heat and light of this world, to which those of heaven correspond, as from the conjunction of the light and heat of this world, which happens in spring-time and summer, all things on earth are animated and flourish; but from light without heat, as in winter, nothing thrives; but vegetables are torpid, and, as it were, without life. From correspondence herein, heaven is called Paradise or Garden, seeing that truth is there joined to good, or faith to love, in the same manner that light and heat are conjoined on earth in the spring-time. This may serve to illustrate what has been laid down before under its proper head, n. 13 to 19; viz. That the divine ruling principle with the angels, is love to the Lord, and charity or love towards their neighbour.

137. It is said in the Gospel (John i. 1, 3, 4, 10, 14.) " In " the beginning was the Word, and the Word was with God, " and the Word was God: all things were made by him, and " without him nothing was made that was made. In him was " the life, and the life was the light of men. He was in the " world, and the world was made by him. And the Word " was made flesh, and dwelt among us, and we saw his glory." It is evident, that by the *Word* is meant the Lord; for it is said, that the *Word* was made flesh; but what we are to understand by the *Word* in a more especial sense, has not as yet been explained, and therefore shall now be declared. By the *Word*,

---

(106) That truths (so called) without good as their root or essence, are not real truths, and therefore are said not to have life, for the life of truth is from the principle of good, n. 9603; and consequently are like a body without a soul, n. 3180, 9454; nor are such apparent truths acceptable to the Lord, n. 4368. As is truth without good, so is faith without love; and as according to the good, such is its truth; so according to the love, such is the quality of its faith, n. 1949, 1950—5830, 5951. That it comes to the same, whether we say truth or faith, and good or love, forasmuch as truth is the property of faith, and good is the property of love, n. 2839, 4353—7624, 10367.

in

in the places before cited, we are to underſtand divine truth as in the Lord, and from the Lord (107), and which there alſo is called *Light*, as ſignifying the ſame with divine truth, as has been ſhewed in the preceding numbers: and that all things were created and made by Divine Truth will appear from what follows. In heaven all power belongs to Divine Truth alone (108), and it is from thence that the angels are called Powers, and are ſuch according to the degree in which they are receptive of it: it is hereby that they prevail over the powers of darkneſs, and all oppoſition from every quarter, for a thouſand enemies are not able to withſtand a ſingle ray of divine light or truth (*): and as the angels derive their angelical nature from their being recipients of divine truth, ſo heaven muſt be from the ſame origin, inaſmuch as they conſtitute heaven. That there ſhould be ſuch a kind of Omnipotence in Divine Truth, muſt appear incredible to ſuch as hold the latter to conſiſt only in thoughts and ideas of the mind, or the agreement of certain propoſitions, which have no other power than what ariſes from the aſſent and obedience of thoſe that embrace them; whereas Divine Truth has power in itſelf, inſomuch that by it was created heaven and this world, and all things that are therein: this may be illuſtrated by two compariſons, viz. By the power of truth and good in man, and by the power of light and heat from the ſun of this world: with reſpect to the former, it is to be noted, that what-

(107) That *Word* in Scripture language has various ſignifications; as ſpeech, operation of the mind, real exiſtence, and in its higheſt ſenſe, divine truth, and the Lord, n. 9987. That *Word* ſignifies divine truth, n. 2803, 2884—7830, 9987. That it ſignifies the Lord, n. 2533, 2859.

(108) That to divine truth proceeding from the Lord belongs all power, n. 6948, 8200. That all power in heaven belongs to truth, as united to and proceeding from good, n. 3091, 3563—10019, 10182. That angels are called powers, and are powers from their reception of divine truth from the Lord, n. 9639. That hence, in ſome places in the Word they are called Gods, n. 4295, 4402, 8301, 8192, 9398.

(*) See in *Eſdras* the following characteriſticks of divine truth: "As for the "truth, it endureth, and is always ſtrong; it liveth, and conquereth for ever-"more. With her there is no accepting of perſons: ſhe is the ſtrength, king-"dom, power, and majeſty of all ages—Bleſſed be the God of truth." Eſdras, B. I. iv. 38, 40. Truth, under the character of wiſdom, is in many places of Scripture dignified with divine perſonality, and diſtinguiſhed by the attribute of Omnipotence: ſee in particular, Prov. *paſſim*, and the Book of Wiſdom. Tr.

ever

ever a man does, he performs it from his intellect and will; from his will by good, and from his intellect by truth; for all things in the will have some relation to good, and all things in the understanding some relation to truth (109): it is therefore by power derived from them, that he actuates his whole corporeal system, in which a thousand different parts concur to pay an obsequious obedience to their government, in conformity to the laws of that correspondency, according to which it is formed. As to the other instance respecting the power of heat and light, as proceeding from the sun of this world; it is to be observed, that all things that vegetate on earth, as trees, plants, flowers, grain, and seeds of all kinds, owe their vegetation thereto, and manifest the power of the solar influence; but how much greater must be the power of that divine light, which, in its essence, is divine truth; and of that divine heat, which, in its essence, is divine good, and from which the heavenly world derives its existence, and consequently this our world, as proceeding from the heavenly, as has been shewed before? Thus much may serve to illustrate this great truth; that by the Word all things were made, and that without him nothing was made that was made; and also that the world was made by him, viz. by divine truth from the Lord (110). Hence it is, that in the Book of the Creation mention is first made of light, and afterwards of those things that proceed from it,

(109) That the intellect is the recipient of truth and the will of good, n. 3623, 6125, 7503, 9300, 9930. That therefore all things in the understanding have relation to truths, whether really such, or only believed to be so; and that all things in the will have relation to good in like manner. n. 803, 10122.

(110) That divine truth proceeding from the Lord, is that which alone hath reality and existence in itself, n. 6880, 7004, 8200. That by divine truth all things were created and made, n. 2803, 2884, 5272, 7835.

N. B. The author, in the above note, speaks of the divine existence as distinguished, and proceeding from the divine essence from eternity to eternity, and as giving existence to all other things. Every thing has an essence and form, for without essence there could be no form; and without the form the essence would be unmanifested, and therefore unknowable: they are as soul and body to each other: the essence indeed is of prior consideration, yet in the divine nature they are coexistent and coequal, and differ only with respect to manifestation: but I dare not be confident that I express myself aright on this most awfully mysterious subject. Tr.

Y   Gen.

Gen. i. 3, 4; and also that all things both in heaven and earth have relation to good and truth, and to the conjunction of both, in the order of creation and use.

139. It is to be noted, that the divine good and the divine truth, which are in the heavens from the Lord as a sun (*), are not *in*, but *from* the Lord; for *in* him only is divine love, which is the essence [*esse*] from whence they exist: now to exist, and to proceed from an essence, mean the same thing, as may be illustrated by comparison with the sun of this world; as for instance, the heat and light in this world are not in the sun, but from the sun; for in the sun is only fire, and from it they derive their existence and procession.

140. Forasmuch as the Lord [under his manifestation and appearance in heaven] as a sun, is divine love; and as divine love constitutes the very essence of divine good, so the divine

---

(*) It will not be difficult for persons of an abstracted and philosophical turn of mind (and such will receive most benefit from our author's writings) to conceive that the most adorable Majesty of the Infinite Eternal God (unknowable in himself, as above the comprehension of all created intellect) should manifest himself in appearances, human or other, accommodated to the limited capacities of his creatures in all worlds: nor consequently will it be difficult for such to believe, that in a spiritual world there should be a spiritual sun, to represent visibly to the angels the invisible glory of the divine essence, and to serve as a medium or vehicle, under God, of communicating spiritual blessings to spiritual beings, both as to soul and body; especially as such a constitution in the heavenly world so aptly corresponds with the rule of analogy, and so fitly adapts itself to our familiar ideas concerning the divine wisdom, power, and goodness, as manifested in the constitution of this our solar system. That natural heat and natural light are the correspondent images of spiritual love and spiritual truth, is confirmed to us by the received use and application of these similitudes or emblems in all languages: now if natural heat and light are derived to us from a natural sun, where is room for doubting, that their spiritual correspondent relatives, love and truth, should in like manner proceed from a spiritual sun, though mediately from the Lord? It can only be from the newness of this representation of the subject before us, that it is of difficult admission to the mind of any reader; let it only be familiarized, and his objections will presently vanish. I shall conclude this note with observing, that this our natural sun, considered in all its animating and comforting influences, and in all its wonderful effects and productions in this world, exhibits such a striking display of the divine wisdom, power, and goodness, that it inclines one to suppose, that the religious veneration given to it by the unenlightened Eastern nations, was one of the most pardonable kinds of idolatry; if it may be allowed lawful to speak with the least degree of mitigation of any profane worship, whereby that honour is given to senseless matter, which is due only to the ever-living, life-giving God. Tr.

emanation

emanation from him in heaven is, for distinction sake, called Divine Truth, though, in reality, it is the divine good united with divine truth; and this, in quality of its divine operation and energy, is called the Holy Spirit [*Sanctum procedens*].

Of the Four Quarters in Heaven.

141. In heaven, as well as in this world, are the four quarters or cardinal points of the East, South, West, and North, and in both determined by their proper sun; in heaven by the cœlestial sun [representing] the Lord, and in this world, by our sun; but yet with much difference between them: first, in that the point of the sun's greatest altitude in our hemisphere, is by us called the South; the opposite thereto the North; the point where the sun rises at the times of the equinoxes, the East; and where it then sets, the West; so that in our world all the quarters are determined by the meridian sun. But in heaven that is called the East where the Lord appears as a sun; opposite thereto is the West; to the right hand is the South; and to the left hand is the North; and thus always the same to the angels, which way soever they turn their faces or bodies [as having the Lord always before them] so that in heaven all the four quarters are determined by the East, that being the quarter in which the Lord appears as a sun; from which he is called the origin (*) of all life; and agreeably thereto, in proportion to the heat and light, or love and understanding, received by the angels from him, in such degree the Lord is said to rise upon or in them: hence likewise it is, that the Lord in the Scriptures is called the East (111).

142. Another difference is, that the angels have the East always before them, the West behind them, the South on their right, and the North on their left hand: but as this is difficult

---

(*) This alludes to the signification of the words *Oriens* and *Origo*, from *oriri*, to *rise*.

(111) That the Lord, in the highest sense of the word, is the East or Orient, as being the sun of heaven, always risen, but never setting, n. 101, 5097, 9668.

to be underſtood by the inhabitants of our earth, who turn their faces indifferently to every one of the quarters, ſomething ſhall here be ſaid by way of explanation. The whole heaven has its aſpect towards the Lord, as to its common centre; conſequently that of the angels has the ſame direction. It is well known by us, that all things on earth have a direction to its centre, though this differs from the former, as in heaven the front or fore parts have this direction, but in our world, the lower parts, and this tendency is called centripetal, or otherwiſe gravitation. The whole interiour of the angels has its direction or tendency forward to the Lord; and as this influences and manifeſts itſelf in the face, ſo conſequently the face of the angel gives determination to the quarters (112).

143. But that the angels ſhould ever front to the Eaſt, which way ſoever they turn their faces or bodies, will appear ſtill more hard to be conceived by men, who view every quarter alike, accordingly as they turn their bodies: to this alſo a word. The angels move, and turn their faces and bodies every way like men on earth, and yet notwithſtanding, their aſpect is always to the Eaſt; but then it muſt be obſerved, that theſe their motions and turnings, though like to thoſe of men, are not the ſame, being from a different principle, viz. the love that prevails in them, which is the determining power, even in externals, both with angels and other ſpirits; for, as was ſaid before, their interiour is actually turned towards their common centre, and conſequently, in heaven, towards the Lord as a ſun; for love being the inward ruling principle of the angels, manifeſting itſelf in the face as its outward form; therefore the angels naturally turn their faces to him who is the great object of that love, or rather it is the Lord (as being in that love, and alſo the giver of it) that preſents himſelf to them which way ſoever they look (113). Theſe things cannot be farther eluci-

---

(112) That all the angels turn their faces to the Lord, n. 9828, 10130, 10189, 10219: not that the angels turn themſelves to the Lord, but that he turns them to himſelf, n. 10189. That the angels are not ſo properly ſaid to be preſent with the Lord, as the Lord to be preſent with them, n. 9415.

(113) That in the ſpiritual world all turn to the objects of their loves; and that the four quarters of the heavens have their names and determination from the aſpect

elucidated at prefent, but fhall be farther explained in the following articles, wherein reprefentations and appearances, time and fpace in heaven, will be treated of as their proper fubjects. That the angels have the Lord always before their faces, has been given me to know by full experience; for as often as I have been in company with them, I have been made fenfible of his being fo prefent, by light in my underftanding, when I had no ocular vifion of him; and the angels have often affirmed to me the truth of it; and indeed this is fo eftablifhed and confeffed a truth, that it is common among men, when fpeaking of fuch as truly believe in and love the Lord, to fay, they have the Lord always before them; that they walk in his fight; and the like: now it is from the fpiritual world that we are led fo to fpeak, for many forms of fpeech in the language of man exprefs ideas and truths derived from thence, though we know it not to be fo.

144. This feeing of the Lord by the angels, even where many of them look different ways from one another, and yet every one beholds him, notwithftanding their feveral different directions, is one of the wonders of the heavenly world; and however difficult to conceive, yet fo it is, that which way foever they turn themfelves, he is always before them, and they have the South on their right hand, the North on their left, and the Weft behind them (*). Among other wonderful things there are

afpect of the angels, n. 10130, 10189, 10420, 10702. That the face is formed fo as to correfpond with the mind or interiour, n. 4791 to 4805, 5695. That therefore the inward difpofition beams in the countenance, n. 3527, 4066, 4796. That the face and mind in the angels entirely correfpond, n. 4796, 4797, 4799, 5695, 8250. Of the influx of the mind into the face and its mufcles, n. 3631, 4800.

(*) The author's relation of the particulars before us, is undeniably furprizing; and yet I doubt not but many befides myfelf will not only give credit to, but alfo be able to form fome conception of them, would they but abftract their thoughts from the laws of vifion, place, and direction, as eftablifhed in this our natural world. Our cuftomary ideas are apt to tincture the mind with prejudices againft many truths even in nature; and were it not for mirrors and glaffes, how impoffible would it feem to many, that objects behind us fhould fo diftinctly be feen as before us; nay, how many deceptions are we liable to from appearances, and a falfe judgment concerning natural caufes and effects. It may truly be affirmed, that a great part of the infidelity that is in the world, proceeds from the immerfion

are likewife the two following, viz. First, Though the angels always front to the East, yet they have also a view of the other three quarters at the fame time, but of the latter by an inward kind of vifion like that of thought. Secondly, That no one in the heavenly world ftands behind another, fo as to look at the hinder part of his head, as this is contrary to the laws of influx of goodnefs and truth from the Lord.

145. The angels look at the eyes of the Lord [when he appears to them in perfon] but the Lord at the forehead of the angels, and that becaufe the forehead correfponds to love, through which the Lord influences their wills; as he enlightens their minds with the knowledge of him, to which intellectual light the eyes correfpond (114).

146. The quarters in the heavens, which conftitute the cœleftial kingdom of the Lord, differ from thofe which conftitute his fpiritual kingdom, and that becaufe the Lord appears to the angels of the former as a fun, and to the angels of the latter as a moon; and his appearance is in the Eaft: the diftance between the fun and moon there is thirty degrees, as alfo that of the quarters. That heaven is diftinguifhed into two kingdoms, the cœleftial and the fpiritual, fee in its proper article, n. 20 to 28: and that the Lord appears in the former as a fun, and in the latter as a moon, n. 118: but neverthelefs the quarters or cardinal points are not therefore indiftinct, becaufe the fpiritual angels cannot afcend to the cœleftial, nor thefe defcend to the former, fee n. 35 (*).

of mens minds into matter and fenfe, and their fetting up natural things as the ftandard of judgment in fpiritual things; or elfe from holding the former only to be realities. The conftitution and laws of things in all worlds (more efpecially between the natural and fpiritual worlds) are unqueftionably very different, fo as to exhibit, in endlefs variety, moft wonderful difplays of the infinite wifdom and power of the adorable Creator. Tr.

(114) That the forehead correfponds to heavenly love, and that therefore the latter is fignified by it in Scripture, n. 9936. That the eye correfponds to the underftanding as to the inward eye, n. 2701, 4410, 4526, 9051, 10569: wherefore to lift up the eyes and fee, fignifies to underftand, perceive, and animadvert, n. 2789, 2829, 3198—4339, 5684.

(*) I muft confefs that I underftand not the meaning of this laft fentence, as an inference from what goes before: there is much reafon to fufpect an error of the prefs here. Tr.

147. Hence

147. Hence it appears in what sense the Lord is present in the heavens; that he is every where, and with every one in that goodness and truth which proceed from him; and that he dwells with the angels in his own divine principle, as was mentioned before, n. 12. The perception of the presence of the Lord in the angels is primarily in their interior or intellectual part, from which their external sight proceeds, and whereby they behold him outwardly; for to them outward vision is a continuation of the inward; and thus we are to understand how the Lord is in them, and they in the Lord, according to those words: "Abide in me, and I in you," John xv. 4. "He who eateth "my flesh, and drinketh my blood, abideth in me, and I in "him," John vi. 56. The flesh of the Lord signifies divine good, and his blood, divine truth (115).

148. In the heavens all have their separate dwellings according to the several quarters. They who are in the good of love, in the East and West; they who are in the sensation of it, in a higher degree, dwell in the East; they who have it in a lower degree, have their dwellings in the West: they who are endowed with wisdom from that source of good, have their habitations in the South and in the North; such of them as partake of a clearer light of wisdom, in the South; and such as possess it in a lesser degree of clearness, in the North. In like manner are situated the angels of the spiritual kingdom, but with difference, according to their kind and degree of good, and of light from that good respectively; for as the prevailing love in the cœlestial kingdom is love to the Lord, and the light of truth from thence is wisdom; so in the spiritual kingdom, the prevailing love is that to their neighbour, which is called Charity; and the light of truth proceeding thence, is intellectual knowledge, which is called faith, see above, n. 23. There is a difference also betwixt them respecting the quarters, in the distance of thirty degrees, as mentioned before, n. 146.

(115) That the flesh of the Lord signifies his Divine Humanity, and also the divine good of his love, n. 3813, 7850, 9127, 10283: and that his blood signifies divine truth, and the holiness of faith [*Sanctum Fidei*] n. 4735, 4978, 7317, 7326—10152, 10204.

[92]

149. In like manner dwell the angels in their several societies: such of them as are in a greater degree of love and charity being situated to the East of their particular departments; they that possess a lesser degree, in the West: they who have more of wisdom and understanding, are to the South of their tribes; and they who have less, to the North: and this distinction takes place throughout the cœlestial regions, and that because every particular society is a representation of the whole heaven, nay, is a heaven in a lesser form, see n. 51 to 58. The same order is also observed when they meet in their assemblies, whilst every one knows and readily takes his proper place, as it were, by a heavenly instinct: it is likewise ordained, by an established law, that there should be some angels of all classes and degrees in every particular society, that there may be a conformity between the whole complex of heaven and its several parts, but yet with this difference, that the angelical societies in the East are of superior excellence to those of the West; and they who are stationed in the South to those of the North.

150. Hence it arises, that every quarter in the heavenly world points out or signifies the particular excellencies and qualities with their degrees, that appertain to their inhabitants respectively; thus the East signifies love and its good qualities in a higher degree; the West the same, but in a lower degree; the South signifies wisdom and understanding of eminent clarity; and the North the same, but with a degree of obscurity: and as the four quarters have such a signification, so the like things are represented to us in the internal or spiritual sense of the written Word (116), which exactly corresponds with the constitution of things in heaven.

151. The very reverse of what has here been related, is the case with the inhabitants of the infernal kingdoms, as they behold not the Lord as a sun, or as a moon; but, with their backs towards him, look at that black body which is to them in the room of what our sun is to us; and to that dark orb,

---

(116) That the East in Scripture language signifies love in clear perception, n. 1250, 3708: the West, love with a degree of obscurity, n. 3708, 9653: the South, a state of light with respect to wisdom and understanding, n. 1458, 3708, 5672: the north, the like state, but with some obscurity, n. 3708.

which

which is to them inſtead of a moon; thoſe which are called Genii to the former; and thoſe which are called Spirits to the latter (117). That the ſun of our world, and the moon belonging to our earth, are not ſeen in the ſpiritual world, but inſtead of the former a black diſk *(Caliginoſum quid)* oppoſite to the cœleſtial ſun; and inſtead of the latter a dark orb *(Tenebroſum quid)* oppoſite to the heavenly moon, ſee before, n. 122. Wherefore the four quarters with the infernals are oppoſite to thoſe in heaven, their Eaſt being where the black diſk, or the dark orb appears; their Weſt towards the cœleſtial ſun; the South to their right, and the North to their left hand; and thus, which way ſoever they turn; nor can it be otherwiſe, as blackneſs and darkneſs is the centre of all their motions. That all in the other worlds are determined in externals from their inward diſpoſitions and affections, ſee above, n. 143. That the love of ſelf, and the love of the world, are the prevailing principles that govern the inhabitants of the infernal regions; and that theſe two kinds of love are ſignified by the ſun and moon of our world, ſee n. 122. They are likewiſe oppoſite to the love of God and of our neighbour (118); and hence it is, that they who are actuated by them turn their backs to the Lord, and direct their faces to the dark orbs before mentioned. The infernals alſo have their habitations in the four quarters, according to their evil qualities and conditions reſpectively; they who are in the evil habits proceeding from ſelf love *(in malis ex amore ſui)* dwell from Eaſt to Weſt, according to the degrees of their malignity; and they who are in the depravity of error from an evil heart *(qui in falſis mali)* have their ſtations from South to North, according to their degrees in depravity: but more on this ſubject when we come to treat of the hells in particular.

152. When any evil ſpirit comes into the company of the good, it is wont to occaſion ſuch a confuſion in the four quar-

---

(117) Who and what they are which are called Genii, and who and what that are called Spirits, n. 947, 5035, 5977, 8593, 8622, 8625.

(118) That they who are in the loves of ſelf and of the world, turn their backs to the Lord, n. 10130, 10189, 10420, 10702. That love to the Lord, and charity towards our neighbour, conſtitute heaven; and that the love of ſelf and of the world conſtitutes hell, as being oppoſites to the former, n. 2041, 3610, 4225, 4726—10741 to 10745.

ters, that the latter are sometimes at a loss to know which is the East; and this I have sometimes been witness to, and have also heard the good spirits complain of the disorder occasioned thereby (*).

153. Evil spirits sometimes appear with their faces turned towards the quarters of heaven, at which times they become receptive of understanding, and perception of the truth, but not of any affection for good; and therefore, as soon as ever they turn back their faces to their own quarters, they become immediately deprived of such understanding and perception, denying that they have received or perceived any truths, nay, affirming them all to be lies, as having their wills and affections strongly bent for falsehood (*). As to such turnings to and from the truth, it has been given me to know, that the wicked and ungodly, even whilst they continue such, may be converted as to their intellectual, though not in their voluntary or will part; and that this is by a divine provision, to the end that all may come to the knowledge of the truth, though none can savingly receive it, unless they are principled in good, as what is good can alone effectually receive divine truth: and that likewise the case is the same with men, who can receive the truth intellectually, but are no farther the better for it, than as they are in the desire and affection for good, and so capable of true conversion; but if they are the willing servants of sin, they only get a speculative glimpse of truth, which leaves no impression, but through the evil in their wills, which rules in them, and perverts their judgment, they return to the side of error, and confirm themselves in it.

(*) Let it be observed here, that on particular and extraordinary occasions the general laws of œconomy in the heavens are suspended by divine permission, with respect to individuals, to answer certain purposes of the divine wisdom, many instances of which are given by our author, and some of them accounted for. Many such extraordinary cases, and particular exceptions to the rules of God's general government of this world, are productive of useful lessons and beneficial effects to us his poor creatures; and even the angels (who, as creatures, must be imperfect) may at times stand in need of extraordinary documents, to remind them of their dependence, and by way of preservatives to humility. Tr.

(*) The truth of this is exemplified to us by frequent instances of persons, who, on returning to their vices and sins, lose their former convictions, and become downright infidels. Tr.

Concerning

Concerning the Changes in the States of the Angels in Heaven.

154. By changes of states here, we are to understand such changes in the angels as have respect to their love and faith, and to their wisdom and understanding derived therefrom; for these constitute their states of life, and, which amounts to the same, are therefore called, their states of love and faith, and their states of wisdom and understanding: and these admit of variation or changes, as will here be shewed.

155. The angels are not always in the same state with respect to love, nor consequently in respect to wisdom; for their wisdom is derived from, and in quality according to their love: sometimes they are in a state of intense love, and sometimes in a state of it less intense; for it has its highest and lowest degrees: when their love is at the highest, their light and heat are then the greatest, and consequently their glory and joy; and when their love is at the lowest, then they may be said to be in the shade and in the cold, as their brightness is obscured, and their state unjoyous (*); but they return from the lowest up again to the highest, and from one degree to another by various successions, like to the changes in this world between day-light and twilight, heat and cold, morning, noon, and night; and also according to the various seasons of the year: and there is also a correspondence between them: thus morning answers to their state of love in clarity; noon to their meridian state of

---

(*) However strange it may appear in our author, that he should describe the states of the angels as bordering at certain times upon obscurity and dejection, yet it seems highly credible, even upon a rational view of the matter, that perfect bliss, without intermission or abatement, is not compatible with the nature of created beings, nay, perhaps without some vicissitudes, would cease to be bliss: besides, something of diversity herein, as it recommends and heightens enjoyment, may be of moral use even to the angels, as was observed in a preceding note. Let it be added, that probably those angels, which are most highly graduated in excellence and bliss, may, at certain short intervals, experience the greatest depressions, or deprivations of joy, as the most favoured servants of God are oft times most debased here, that they may be made meet to partake of a more exalted inheritance hereafter. Tr.

wisdom;

wifdom ; evening to their wifdom in a degree of obfcurity ; and night to a ſtate of deprivation as to both ; though it muſt be noted, that there is no correfpondence between night, and any ſtate of the angels in heaven, but only with the ſtate of thofe that are in hell (119), as the former never fuffer a total deprivation of their love and wifdom ; and therefore the twilight before day is the correfpondent to their loweſt ſtate. From this law of correfpondency it is, that *Day* and *Year* in the Word ſignify the ſtates of life in general, and *Heat* and *Light*, love and wifdom ; morning, the firſt and moſt intenfe degree of love ; noon, wifdom in its moſt luminous ſtate ; evening, wifdom in fome degree of obfcurity ; and night, a total deprivation of both love and wifdom (120).

156. Together with the interior ſtates of love and wifdom in the angels, is alfo changed the ſtate of various things without them that are the objects of fight, for thefe vary their appearance according to the inward ſtate of the angels (*) : but this will be treated of under the articles of *Reprefentatives* and *Appearances* in heaven.

157. Every angel is fubject to thefe changes, and alfo undergoes them, and alfo every angelical fociety in common, but one differently from another, and that becaufe of their difference as to love and wifdom ; for they who are in the centre of a fociety are in a more perfect ſtate than thofe who are nearer to its periphery, fee n. 23, 128 : but to dwell on the particular

(119) That in heaven there is no ſtate correfponding to night, but only to the morning twilight, n. 6110. That the morning twilight fignifies a middle ſtate between the higheſt and loweſt, n. 10134.

(120) That the viciffitudes of ſtates in heaven, in refpect to illumination and perception, anfwer to the times of day in this world, n. 5672, 5962, 6310, 8426, 9213, 10605. That *Day* and *Year* in the Word fignify all ſtates in general, n. 23, 487, 488—4850, 10656. That *Morning* fignifies the beginning of a new ſtate ; and alfo the ſtate of love, n. 7216, 8426, 8427, 10114, 10134. That *Evening* fignifies a ſtate of declining light and love, n. 10134, 10135. That *Night* fignifies a ſtate void of love and faith, n. 221, 709, 2353, 6000, 6110, 7870, 7947.

(*) This is imaged to us in this our natural world, in which things appear to us according to the frame and ſtate of mind that we are in : how dull, how ghaſtly do things appear to the view of the fpectator, when under trouble or melancholy ! Can we avoid obferving here on the folly of thofe who feek for happinefs in external things, whilſt they neglect to cultivate and cherifh that inward fenfe or ſtate, which alone can give good relifh to them ?

differences

differences would be too prolix, as the changes in every one are according to the quality of his love and faith, fo that one may be in his full fplendor and joy, whilft another may be eclipfed and in his joylefs ftate, and this even in the fame fociety; each fociety alfo has its refpective difference in this refpect, both in the cœleftial and the fpiritual kingdom. The difference in the changes of their ftates is in general like that of the days in the different climates here on earth, where it is morning to fome, whilft it is evening to others; fummer to one country, at the fame time that it is winter to another.

158. I have received light from heaven as touching thefe changes there, and been informed by the angels with refpect to the caufes of them, which are feveral. Firft, that the delights of life, and the joys of heaven, would by degrees fuffer diminution, if they were to continue always the fame, as happens to thofe who always go on in the fame round of pleafures. Another reafon is, that felf love is a property inherent in angels as well as men; that this is contrary to the laws of heaven, and that the angels excel in love and wifdom only fo far as they are kept from it by the Lord; and as otherwife, they would be carried away by this propenfity (121), therefore thefe viciffitudes of ftates are appointed for good to them. A third caufe is, that it may ferve as a means of their higher perfection, by keeping them habitually in the love of the Lord, and reftraining them from felf love; and alfo to increafe their relifh for the delights of good (122), by fuch occafional fufpenfions of them. They farther added, that the Lord does not produce thefe changes in their ftates from himfelf, feeing that, as a fun, he never withholds his heat and light, or love and wifdom; but that the hindrance is in themfelves, by giving way to that principle of felf, which renders them unreceptive of thofe bleflings; which

(121) That felf-love is a property inherent in man, n. 694, 731, 4317, 5660. That this muft be alienated, in order to the enjoyment of the Lord's prefence, n. 1023, 1044: and that accordingly it is actually alienated, fo long as any one perfeveres in the principle of good by prefervation from the Lord, n. 9334, 9335, 9336—945, 9938.
(122) That the angels advance in degrees of perfection eternally, n. 4803, 6648. That in the heavens no one ftate is exactly like another, whence a conftant progrefs in perfection, n. 10200.

they illuſtrated by a compariſon with our ſun and earth, obſerving that the ſucceſſive changes from heat to cold, and from light to darkneſs on this our globe, are not owing to the ſun, which continues always the ſame, but to the form, ſituation, and revolutions of the earth.

159. It has been given me to behold, how the Lord appears as a ſun to the angels of the cœleſtial kingdom, in their firſt ſtate, how in their ſecond, and how in their third ſtate: and firſt, his appearance was as that of a ſun of a bright red colour, and glittering with a ſplendor ſurpaſſing all deſcription. It was told me, that ſuch was the appearance of the divine glory to thoſe angels in their firſt ſtate [of higheſt love]: afterwards there appeared a large duſky circle or belt round the ſun, whereby its bright redneſs and ſplendor were much abated; I was informed, that ſuch was its appearance to the angels in their ſecond ſtate. After this, the circle or belt before mentioned appeared of a ſtill darker complexion, which ſtill farther diminiſhed the ſun's ſplendor, and ſo on gradually, till at length its glittering redneſs was changed to a pale colour; ſuch was the appearance of the ſun to the angels in their third ſtate. After theſe mutations, this pale ſun ſeemed to paſs on the left towards the moon of heaven, and to join itſelf to her, whereby her ſplendor was exceedingly augmented; I was told, that hereby was repreſented the fourth ſtate of the cœleſtial angels, and the firſt or higheſt of the ſpiritual angels; and that theſe changes take place in both kingdoms ſucceſſively, but not in every ſociety therein at the ſame time: nor are theſe changes at any fixed periods, but befall the angels ſooner or later, without any knowledge of their approach. Moreover, they ſaid, that theſe were not real changes in the ſun itſelf, but only ſo many appearances depending on the ſucceſſive changes in the ſtates of the angels, foraſmuch as the Lord, as repreſented by the ſun, appears to every one according to the quality of his ſtate; as for example, bright and ruddy to thoſe that are in the degree of intenſe love; leſs ſo to ſuch as are in an inferior degree of it, and ſo on to quite pale, as their love departs; and that the quality and degree of their ſtates is repreſented by that dim circle, which apparently ſuperinduces theſe variations in the luſtre and light of the ſun.

160. When

160\. When the angels are in their lowest state, or property of self love, they decline into sadness: I have conversed with some of them in this state, and was witness to their dejection; but they told me, that they hoped to be soon restored to their heavenly state; for it is heaven to them to be delivered from propriety or self love.

161\. The infernal spirits also have their change of states; but of this hereafter, where we shall treat of Hell.

Of Time in Heaven.

162\. However all things go on in heaven according to succession and progression, as in this world; nevertheless, the angels have no idea of time or space, nor any notion concerning them: we shall here treat of time in heaven, and hereafter of space, under its proper article.

163\. That the angels have no idea of time, though all things go on successively with them in like manner as with us, is owing to there not being years and days in heaven, but only changes of condition; now as the former constitute times, so the latter are called States.

164\. By times on earth, we mean the sun's apparent progress from one degree of its annual orbit to another, so constituting that period of time which we call a year; and also its apparent diurnal revolution round the earth, which we call a day; and these according to stated vicissitudes: but it is otherwise with the sun in heaven, which makes no such progressions and revolutions, to constitute years and days, but only apparent changes of states in the angels, and these according to no stated rules, as was observed in a preceding article; hence it is, that the angels can have no idea of time, but only of state in room thereof, see *State* above, n. 154.

165\. As the angels derive no idea from time, after the manner of men, so neither have they any conception of its divisions, as of years, months, weeks, days, hours, to-day, to-morrow, yesterday, &c. insomuch, that when they hear of these distinctions by men (to whom they are always present by divine appoint-

appointment) in the room thereof they substitute states, and such things as appertain thereto; thus changing the natural idea of a man into the spiritual idea of an angel: hence it is, that times in the written Word signify states, and the distinctions of time, as mentioned above, such spiritual things as correspond thereto (123).

166. It is the same with all things that owe their existence to time, as the four seasons of the year, called Spring, Summer, Autumn, and Winter; the four times of the day, morning, noon, evening, and night; also with the four ages of man, as infancy, youth, manhood, and old age; and in like manner with other things, which derive their being from time, or succeed according to it: when any of these are present to the mind of man, his thoughts thereon are regulated by time, but those of an angel by state; thus the latter changes the idea of spring and morning into the idea of love and wisdom, as in their first state with the angels; summer and noon into the idea of love and wisdom, as they are in the second state; autumn and evening, as they are in their third state; and night and winter into the idea of the absence of love and wisdom, and so constituting a hellish state; and hence it is, that such states are signified by such times in the written Word, see above, n. 155. Thus we see how the ideas of natural things in the mind of a man are converted into corresponding spiritual ideas in the mind of an angel present with man.

167. As the angels have no notion of time, so do they form a very different idea of eternity from that of men: by *Eternal*, the angels conceive a state without end, but not a time without end (124). As I was once thinking on the subject of eternity, I found, that by my ideas of time, I could form a conception of what might be to eternity, or without end, but not of what

(123) That *Times*, in the Word, signify *States*, n. 2788, 2837, 3254—10133, 10605. That the angels never think of time or space, n. 3404. The causes why, 1274, 1382—7218, 7381. What *Year* signifies in the Word, n. 487, 488—10209. What, *Month*, n. 3814. What, *Week*, n. 2044, 3845. What, *Day*, n. 23, 487, 488, 10605. What, *To-day*, n. 2838, 3998—6984, 9939. What, *To-morrow*, n. 3998, 10497. What, *Yesterday*, n. 6983, 7124, 7140.

(124) That men think of eternity from time, but the angels not from time, n. 1382, 3404, 8325.

has

has been from eternity, nor consequently of what God did from eternity before the creation: and being troubled in my mind at this, I found myself exalted to angelical illumination concerning eternity, and given to know, that as to things eternal, we are not to take our measure of thinking from time, but from state; and that by this means we may form a conception of what has been from eternity; which I experienced to be the case.

168. When the angels converse with men, they never speak to them from those natural ideas which are common and proper to man, as these are all derived from time, space, materiality, and things analogous thereto; but from their own spiritual ideas derived from states, and their various mutations within and without the angels: however, these ideas of the angels, though spiritual, yet when they enter the minds of men instantaneously, and as of themselves, convert into such natural ideas as are proper to men, and correspond to the spiritual ones, though imperceptibly both to the angels and men; and the case is the same with the heavenly influx in man. On a certain time there were some angels who had access to my mind, in which were many natural thoughts borrowed from time and space; but, as they could form no conception of them, they immediately withdrew; on which I heard them say, that they were darkened and confused. I had also the following convincing experiment how far the angels are strangers to every idea of time: one of them, who was more receptive of natural knowledge, and with whom, on that account, I was by degrees able to converse as one man with another, at first did not know what I meant by time; and so was obliged to explain to him how our sun, by its apparent revolutions round the earth, constituted what we call days and years; how the year was divided into four seasons, and also into months and weeks, and the days into twenty-four hours; and that these divisions took place regularly at stated periods, from whence the idea of times originates; on hearing which he wondered, saying, that he had no other notion of these, but as states. In the course of our conversation, I said, that we men shewed our assent to the truth of there not being time in heaven, by our familiar forms of expression concerning the deceased, as

that temporal things were over with them; that they had passed through time, or left this world, and the like. I told him, moreover, that some seemed conscious that times in their origin were no other than states, inasmuch as they so nearly corresponded to the state of their affections and feelings, seeming short to those who are in pleasing and joyous frames; tedious to those that are sorrow and sadness; and different according to the state of our hope, or expectation: and therefore hence it is, that the learned are so much puzzled in their investigations concerning the nature and essence of time and space, and that some among them are agreed, that they are only relative to man during his existence in this natural world.

169. The mere natural man may here be led to fancy, that if he were deprived of his ideas of time, space, and material things, he should in that case be stript of the faculty of thinking, forasmuch as they are the fundamentals of all his thoughts (125): but, on the contrary, let him know, that so far as his thoughts are confined to time, space, and material things, in such proportion are they limited and narrowed; and only so far at liberty and enlarged, as they are disengaged from these subjects, as hereby soaring above the contracted regions of corporeal and earthly things: hence proceeds the sublime wisdom of angels, which is incomprehensible by ideas of so low an extraction.

Of Representatives and Appearances in Heaven.

170. The man who thinks only from natural light, cannot comprehend that there should be any resemblance between things in heaven and in this world, and that because from such light he has accustomed himself to think, and confirmed himself in the notion, that angels are only mere minds, or a kind of æthereal spirits, and as such have not senses like men, nor

(125) 'That man cannot think, without having some idea of time; but that it is otherwise with the angels, n. 3404.

eyes;

eyes; and if not eyes, consequently not objects of sight; whereas they have all the senses that men are gifted with, and those in a more exquisite degree of perfection; and the light in which they see is far brighter than ours. That angels are men in a perfect form, and endowed with every sense, see above, n. 73 to 77; and that the light in heaven is far more splendid than any light in this world, n. 126 to 132.

171. It is hard to describe the various kinds of things that are seen by the angels in the heavens: let it suffice to say, that in the main they resemble those on earth, though in form more perfect; and far excelling in abundance. That such things are in the heavens is given us to understand by those which are recorded as seen by the prophets, and in particular by Ezekiel, concerning the new temple and the new earth, as described from ch. xl. to xlviii: by Daniel, from ch. vii. to xii: by John, from the beginning to the end of the Apocalypse; and by others as recorded in the prophetical and historical parts of the written Word. Such things were seen by them when heaven was opened to them, or, which is the same thing, when their inward sight, which is the sight of the spirit of a man, was opened to see things in heaven, for these are not to be seen by the bodily, but spiritual eye only; and this is opened, according to the good pleasure of the Lord, when a man is withdrawn from the natural light, which is the light of his bodily senses, and exalted to the spiritual light, which is the proper light of his spirit; and in this light have I beheld things that are in the heavens.

172. However, the visible things in the heavens, though, in respect to a great part of them, they resemble the things on earth, yet they differ from them in regard to their essence, inasmuch as the former derive their existence from the cœlestial sun, but things on earth [*proximately*] from the sun of this world: the former are called spiritual, and the latter are called natural.

173. Things in the heavens exist not in like manner with things on earth; in the former, all things are formed by the Lord according to correspondency with the interiour [*cum interioribus*] of the angels; for with the angels are things interior and

and exterior; the former have relation to love and faith, and consequently to will and intellect as the receptacles of them, and their exterior things correspond to those that are interior, see above, n. 87 to 115. This may be illustrated by what has been said before of the heat and light of heaven, viz. that the angels possess a heat according to the quality and degree of their love, and a light according to the quality and degree of their wisdom, see n. 128 to 134; and so other things in like manner, which are the objects of their senses.

174. When I have had the privilege to be in company with the angels, all things about them appeared to me in the same manner as things do on earth, and that with such clearness of perception, that I seemed to be in some royal palace in this world, conversing with them, as one man converses with another.

175. As all things that outwardly correspond to things that are inward do also represent them, therefore they are called REPRESENTATIVES; and as they vary according to the variation of such interior things, therefore they are called APPEARANCES, though the things which present themselves to the sight of the angels, and are perceived by their senses, make as distinct and clear impressions as things on earth, and more so, for they have a real and substantial existence, though there are some which are mere appearances without substance, viz. such as have no relation or correspondence to things interior (126); but of these hereafter.

176. One instance, by way of illustration, shall here be given, to explain what is meant by corresponding appearances.

(126) That all things that appear among the angels are representatives, n. 1971, 3213 to 3226—9576, 9577. That the heavens abound with representatives, n. 1521, 1532, 1619. That the nearer to the centre, the more beautiful they are, n. 3475. That they are realities, as being from the light of heaven, n. 3485. That the divine influx assumes the form of representatives in the superior heavens, and descends thence to the inferior, n. 2179, 3213—9577. They are called representatives, which appear to the sight of angels in such forms as are known in nature or this world, n. 9574. That things internal are thus changed into external, n. 1632, 2987 to 3002. What kinds of representatives in heaven, illustrated by various examples, n. 1521, 1532, 1619—9090, 10278. That all things which appear in heaven are according to correspondency, and called representatives, n. 3213 to 3226—9576, 9577. That all things which correspond, do also represent and signify their archetypes, n. 2890, 2987, 2971, 2989, 2990, 3002, 3225.

To

To such of the angels as excel in knowledge do appear delightful plantations and gardens, abounding in all kinds of trees and flowers, where beautiful rows of trees form arched vistos, and other pleasing walks, diversified with exquisite skill, not to be described. Here the highly intellectual angels take their walks amidst various kinds of trees and flowers not known in this world, sometimes gathering the flowers, and dressing up garlands for the children of Paradise, whilst the spreading branches, decorated and enriched with fruit, emblematically represent the interior good qualities of these intellectual happy beings; for such plantations, gardens, fruit-bearing trees, and flowers, are correspondent to their high understanding and wisdom (127). That there are such delightful scenes as these in the heavenly world, some good people here, who have not obscured their cœlestial notices of these things by their fallacious natural reason, are fully convinced of; and accordingly are not only used to think, but to say, as concerning heaven, that many more things are there than " ear hath heard, or eye hath seen" on earth.

Of the Garments in which the Angels appear to be clothed.

177. As the angels are heavenly men, and live together as men do on earth, so also have they garments, dwellings, and many other like things in common with us men, but with this difference, that as they themselves are in a more perfect state, so likewise are all things that belong to them : thus, for instance, as the angelical wisdom excels the human beyond expression, so do all things about them, and that are perceived by them, for

---

(127) That Garden and Paradise signify understanding and wisdom, n. 100, 108, 3220. What the Garden of Eden, and Garden of Jehovah signify, n. 99, 100, 1588. How magnificent paradisiacal things appear in the other world, n. 1122, 1622, 2296, 4528, 4529. That trees signify the perceptions and cognitions from which understanding and wisdom originate, n. 103, 2163, 2682, 2722, 2972, 7692. That fruits signify the goods of love and charity, n. 3146, 7690, 9337.

these are correspondent to the wisdom that is within them, see above, n. 173.

178. The garments with which the angels are invested have, like other things, a corresponding relation to their interior perfections, and consequently a real existence, see above, n. 175. Now their vestments correspond to their degrees of understanding and wisdom, and therefore they appear arrayed accordingly; and as some excel others in intellectual endowments, (n. 43, and 128) their garments are suitably adapted to their different distinctions therein: such as are most highly intellectual appear in glistering flame-coloured robes, and some in shining vestments; they who are intellectual in a lower degree are in white, or pale-coloured, but not shining garments; and those who are so in the lowest degree wear raiment of different colours respectively: but the angels of the third or inmost heaven appear naked (*).

179. As the garments of the angels correspond to their understanding, so do they also correspond to truth, as all right understanding is from divine truth, and therefore it amounts to the same thing, whether you say, their clothing is according to the one or the other. That the vestments of some glister as from flame, and those of others are of a shining light, is because flame corresponds to good, and light to truth from good (128):

(*) From this last particular given us by the author, it seems, that Adam and Eve, before the fall, represented the state of the angels of the third heaven; for they were naked, and were not ashamed. To the pure all things are pure, and with respect to such no part of the human body wants a covering; for perfect innocence knows no shame, as it needs none; whilst consummate guilt, that can even glory in its shame, knows no modesty to conceal that shame. Little children, who have a relative or comparative purity, as free from actual sin, may serve to image to us the truth of the foregoing remark, and to indicate how consciousness of guilt, producing shame, is the fruit of that tree, by which comes the knowledge of good and evil. If then garments only became necessary to us by the loss of innocence, how great must appear the folly of those, who turn that into an occasion of pride, which first took its rise from sin, and continues to be the badge and evidence of their shame. Tr.

(128) That garments in the Word signify truths from correspondence, n. 1073, 2576—7692; and that because good is invested with truth, n. 5248. That a covering also signifies the intellectual part, as this is the recipient of truth, n. 6378. That white linen garments signify truths from a divine origin, n. 5319, 9469. That flame signifies spiritual good, and the light of it truth from that good, n. 3222, 6832.

that

that the garments of others are white and pale without splendor, and some of different colours, is because divine good and divine truth are less splendid, and also differently received in those, whose intellectual faculties are of the lower degrees (129). White and pale do also correspond to simple truth (130), and colours to the different kinds and measures of it (131). That the angels of the inmost or third heaven appear unclothed, is because they are in perfect innocence, and innocence is the correspondent to nakedness (132).

180. As the angels are clothed with garments in heaven, therefore did they appear in like manner to the prophets, and also at our Lord's sepulchre, with " raiment white as snow," Matt. xxviii. 3. Mark xvi. 5. Luke xxii. 4. John xx. 11, 13. as likewise those who were seen in heaven by John, Apoc. iv. 4. And as all wisdom is from divine truth, therefore our Lord's raiment, at his transfiguration, was " shining, and exceeding " white as snow," Mark ix. 3. That light corresponds to divine truth proceeding from the Lord, see above, n. 129. Therefore it is, that *Garments* in the Word signify *Truths*, and hence understanding; thus in John, " They which have not " defiled their garments shall walk with me in white, for they " are worthy: he that overcometh, the same shall be clothed " in white raiment: blessed is he that watcheth and keepeth his " garments," Rev. iii. 4, 5. xvi. 15. And of Jerusalem, by

(129) That angels and spirits appear clothed according to their truths, or intellectual powers, n. 165, 5248—10536. That the garments of angels are shining, or otherwise, n. 5248.
(130) That white in the Word signifies truth, because from a heavenly light, n. 3301, 3993—4922.
(131) That colours in heaven are variegations of light of heaven, n. 1042, 1043, 1053—4922. That colour signify various things relating to understanding and wisdom, n. 4530, 4922, 4677, 9466. That the precious stones in Urim and Thummim, according to their colours respectively, signified the whole of divine truth from divine good, n. 9865, 9868, 9905. That colours, so far as they partake of red, signify good; and so far as they partake of white, they signify truth, n. 9476.
(132) That all in the inmost heaven are innocences, or perfect in innocence, and therefore appear naked, n. 154, 165, 297—9960. That innocence is represented in heaven by nakedness, n. 165, 8375, 9960. That to the innocent and chaste nakedness gives no shame, because they are free from all offence, n. 165, 213, 8375.

which

which is meant the true church (133), is said in Isaiah, "Awake, Awake, put on thy strength, O Zion, put on thy beautiful garments, O Jerusalem," lii. 1. And in Ezekiel, "I girded thee about with fine linen, and covered thee with silk: and thy raiment was of fine linen and silk," xvi. 10, 13. not to mention many other places: but he that is not in the truth, is said, not to be "clothed with a wedding garment: and when the king came in to see the guests, he saw there a man which had not on a wedding garment: and he said unto him, Friend, how camest thou in hither, not having a wedding garment? Wherefore he was cast into outer darkness," Mat. xxii. 12, 13. By the marriage house is to be understood heaven and the church, from the union of the Lord therewith by his divine truth; and therefore the Lord is called in the Word, the Bridegroom and Husband, and heaven with the church, the Spouse and the Wife.

181. That the garments of the angels not only appear such, but really are what they appear to be, is evident both from their sight and feeling: and also they have change of raiment, which they put on and off, and lay by for future use, as occasion may require: and that they appear clothed differently at different times, I have been eye-witness to a thousand times: I also asked them whence they had them; they answered, by the gift of the Lord, and that sometimes they found themselves clothed therewith without their knowledge. Moreover, they said, that their garments were varied according to the variation of their states; that in their first and second state they were of a shining white, but in their third and fourth something darker, and that according to the rules of correspondency, as the changes happened in respect to their understanding and wisdom, of which see above, n. 154 to 161.

182. As in the spiritual world every angel has garments adapted to and representative of his intellectual gifts, or according to the particular truths which form his understanding; so likewise the infernal spirits, who are destitute of all truth, appear also in their garments, but such only as are ragged and

---

(133) That Jerusalem signifies the church, wherein the true doctrine is taught, n. 402, 3654, 9166.

filthy,

filthy, each according to the kind and degree of his folly and madnefs, nor can any others fuit them; however, the Lord allows them clothing, that their nakednefs and deformity may not appear.

Of the Habitations and Manfions of the Angels.

183. As the angels live in focieties, as men do on earth, fo in like manner they have their particular dwellings, and thefe different according to their ftates of life refpectively, magnificent to thofe who are worthy of greater honour; and lefs fo to thofe of inferior degree. I have fometimes difcourfed with the angels concerning their dwellings, and told them, that among us at this time fcarcely any believed that they were fo accommodated, fome becaufe they are not vifible to them; fome becaufe they have no notion of angels being men; fome becaufe they fuppofe the angelical heavens to be the fame that they behold with their eyes; and as thefe appear to them no other than void fpace, and fancying at the fame time that the angels are only thin ætherial forms, therefore they conclude that they hover in the æther: befides, as they have not the leaft notion of any thing fpiritual, fo neither can they conceive how there can poffibly be in the fpiritual world things like to thofe in the natural. The angels replied, that they knew that fuch ignorance prevailed on earth at this time, and wondered at it, more efpecially in the Chriftian church, and therein more among the learned, than among thofe whom they called the illiterate and fimple; adding moreover, that they might gather from the written Word that angels are men, as having appeared of old always as men, and from the Lord's having rifen again, and afcended with his entire humanity; and if the angels are men, that they muft of confequence have habitations or dwellings, and not as fome foolifhly (madly they termed it) fuppofe, hover in the air, or becaufe they are called fpirits, are therefore no other than a breath of wind. They likewife faid, that fuch might emerge from their prefent ignorance as touching thefe matters, would they but drop their

E e   prejudices,

prejudices, and not bewilder themselves by starting questions and doubtful disputations, whether these things be so or not, since there are in the mind of every man certain plain, common notices or impressions concerning the truth of angels being men, and dwelling in heavenly mansions, far excelling any structures here on earth; but that these common notices or impressions (which are from above) are obliterated when men exercise themselves in vain reasonings, and bring the subject into question with their logical ambiguities and subtle reasonings; which is principally the case with the learned, who, by their *oppositions of science falsely so called*, darken divine truths, and render their minds inaccessible to the light of heaven. And just so it is with respect to their belief of the state of the soul after death: he that is conversant on this subject without puzzling his head with the curious disquisitions of the learned concerning the nature of the soul, and its reunion with the body, readily takes for granted, that man enters upon a new life after death, and passes into the society of angels, if he has lived well, where he is entertained with ravishing scenes, and feels joy unspeakable; but no sooner does he bend his mind to philosophical reasonings upon the subject, or to consider it by some learned hypothesis concerning soul and body, and their mutual relations and communications, but he loses his former faith, and falls into doubting.

184. But it will bring the matter more home, to alledge instances drawn from experience: as often as I have conversed with the angels face to face, it was in their habitations, which are like to our houses on earth, but far more beautiful and magnificent, having rooms, chambers, and apartments in great variety, as also spacious courts belonging to them, together with gardens, parterres of flowers, fields, &c. Where the angels are formed into societies, they dwell in contiguous habitations, disposed after the manner of our cities in streets, walks, and squares: I have had the privilege to walk through them, to examine all round about me, and to enter their houses; and this when I was fully awake, having my inward eyes opened (134).

(134) The angels have their cities, palaces, and houses, n. 940, 941, 942, 1116, 1626, 1627, 1628, 1630, 1631, 4622.

185. I have

185. I have seen also the palaces in heaven, the magnificence of which exceeds description, the roofs glittering as with pure gold, and the floors as with precious stones; but some more splendid than others; the inner apartments likewise were ornamented beyond all human conception. On the south side were gardens, where all things appeared with radiant lustre, certain trees bearing leaves of a silver hue, and fruit that glittered like burnished gold, whilst flowers in the borders, by a beautiful arrangement of their colours, presented, as it were, rainbows to the eye of the spectator: at the end of the walks fresh palaces rose to the view, and terminated the prospect. Such is the architecture and beautiful scenery in heaven, insomuch that it may well be said, that the very principle of art appears there in its effects, and no wonder, when we consider such art is heavenly: and yet the angels said, that not only like things, but others beyond number of still higher degrees of perfection, were at times exhibited to their view by the goodness of the Lord, for their recreation and entertainment; and yet that the intellectual pleasure they received therefrom was greater than the sensible, and that, because in all and singular of those objects they discerned correspondency, and through their correspondents the divine things which they represented.

186. As touching correspondences I learned, that not only palaces and houses, but likewise all things within and without them were relative to the interior divine gifts and qualities in the angels; that house in general corresponded to the principle of good in them, and the particular things therein, to the different species or kinds of good (135); as the things without their houses, to the truths relative to and proceeding from such good respectively, and also to perceptions and knowledge of different kinds; and as they correspond to the principles and different species of goodness and truth [*bonis et veris*] which are in them by influx from the Lord, so also do they correspond to

---

(135) That a house, with the things in it, signify things pertaining to the mind, or interior state of man, n. 710, 2233—7929, 9150, and consequently his state as to things good and true, n. 2233, 2234—7929. That chambers and inner apartments signify such of them as are more interior, n. 3900, 5994, 7353. That the roof of a house signifies what is inmost in his mind, n. 3652, 10184. That a house of wood signifies things of the quality of good, and a house of stone, things of truth, n. 3720.

the prevailing principle of love in them, and to their understanding and wisdom originating thence, for love originates in good, wisdom in goodness and truth [*Sapientia est boni et simul veri*] and intellectual knowledge proceeds from that truth which is the offspring of good [*veri ex bono*]. The sight of the forementioned corresponding objects excites in the minds of the angels these perceptions, which yield more delight to their intellectual faculties, than the objects themselves to their exterior senses.

187. Hence it appears why the Lord applied to himself the name of the temple at Jerusalem, John ii. 19, 21. (136); and why the New Jerusalem appeared to be of pure gold, its gates of pearls, and its foundations of precious stones, Apoc. xxi. viz. because the temple represented the Divine Humanity of the Lord; the New Jerusalem signifies the church hereafter to be established on earth; the twelve gates, the truths which lead to goodness; and the foundations, those essential truths on which the new church is to be built (137).

188. The angels which constitute the cœlestial kingdom, or third heaven, dwell mostly in lofty places, which appear as mountains; those of the spiritual kingdom or middle heaven, in places of less eminence; and those of the lowest or first heaven in rocky situations, and all this from correspondency; for the more interior states correspond to visible eminences, and the more exterior to inferior places (138); and therefore it is that mountains in Scripture-language signify cœlestial love; hills, spiritual love; and rocks, faith (139).

(136) That the house of God, in its highest sense, signifies the Divine Humanity of the Lord with respect to divine good; the temple the same, in respect to divine truth; and in a comparative sense, heaven and the true church, in respect to goodness and truth, n. 3720.

(137) That Jerusalem signifies the church, in which is true doctrine, n. 402, 3654, 9166. That gates signify introduction into, or initiation in the doctrine of the church, and through the doctrine into the church, n. 2043, 4478. That foundation signifies truth, on which heaven, the church, and its doctrine are founded, n. 9643.

(138) That in Scripture-language things of a more interior kind are expressed by outward things of a superior kind, and signified by them, n. 2148, 3084, 4599, 5146, 8325. That *high* signifies *inward*, and also heaven, n. 1735, 2148, 4210, 4599, 8153.

(139) That in heaven there appears to be mountains, hills, rocks, valleys, and different kinds of earth, altogether like what we see here, n. 10608. That on the mountains

189. There are likewise angels which live not in societies, but dispersed in separate houses: such dwell in the middle parts of heaven, as being the best of the angels.

190. The mansions inhabited by the angels are not built by them, as we build ours, but are the gift of the Lord to them, to each according to his recipiency of goodness and truth; and they also are subject to some changes, accordingly as variations happen in the inward state of the angels, concerning which above, n. 154 to 160. The angels live in a constant sense of their dependence on, and gratitude to the Lord for all that they possess, and all that they stand in need of he freely gives them.

Of Space in Heaven.

191. Though all things in heaven appear to exist in place and space after the manner of this world, nevertheless the angels have no idea of either: now as this cannot but appear a paradox, and is a subject of great importance, I proceed to the explanation of it.

192. All progressions and advances in the spiritual world are caused by change of states in the interiour, nor are they any otherwise (140); accordingly I have been taken up by the Lord

mountains dwell the angels, who excel in the good of love; on the hills those that excel in charity or love of their neighbour; on the rocks those that walk by faith, n. 10438. That therefore by mountains in Scripture is signified the good of love, n. 795, 4210—10438, 10608. By *hills*, the good of charity, n. 6435, 10438. By *rocks*, the good and truth of faith [*bonum et verum fidei*] n. 8581, 10580. That *stone*, from whence comes rock, in like manner signifies the truth of faith, n. 114, 643, 1298—10376. Hence that by *mountains* is signified heaven, n. 8327, 8805, 9420. And by the top of a mountain, the supreme part of heaven, n. 9422, 9434, 10608. That therefore the angels celebrated their religious worship on mountains, n. 796, 2722.

(140) That places and spaces in the Word signify states, n. 2625, 2837, 3356, 3387, 7381, 10578. Proved from experience, n. 1274, 1277, 1376 to 1381—10578. That distance signifies difference in the states of life, n. 9104, 9967. That movements and changes of place in the spiritual world are from changes in the life's states, n. 1273, 1274, 1275, 1377, 3356, 9440; as also progressive motion, n. 9440, 10734; illustrated from experience, n. 1273 to 1277, 5606; that hence it is, that in the Word, *to walk*, signifies to live, and also the progress of life, as also does journeying, n. 3335, 4554, 4585—8557. To walk with the Lord means the same as living agreeably to his will, n. 10567.

into heaven, and have been in different worlds in the universe as to my spirit, whilst my body was all the while here on earth in the same place (141): and so it is with the angels, for to them distances are nothing, and if nothing, so neither is space any thing, but instead thereof are their states and changes, and changes therein.

193. As progressions are effected this way, it is evident that the approximation to, and elongation from persons reciprocally, consists in the similarity or dissimilarity of their interior states respectively, they who are in the former approaching near to one another, and such as are in the latter separating from each other; and that spaces in heaven are nothing more than their external states corresponding to their internal ones: so also it is that the heavens are distinct from one another, as also the societies in each heaven, and every individual of a society: hence likewise that the different hells are totally separated, and in opposition to the heavens, as being by conditions and qualities diametrically contrary to one another.

194. From the same cause it comes to pass, that in the spiritual world one becomes immediately present to another, who intensely desires his company, for by that means he sees him in thought, and enters into the same state with his; and, on the contrary, that one is separated from another in proportion to his aversion to him: and as all aversion proceeds from contrariety of affections, and dissent of minds, hence it appears oftentimes, that many who continue together whilst they agree, immediately disappear on the first quarrel.

195. So likewise when any one takes a walk from one place to another, whether in the city he belongs to, in the squares, gardens, or on a visit to any of another society, he reaches the end of his walk sooner or later, according to the greater or lesser earnestness of his desire to be there, the way, though the same in itself, appearing shorter or longer in proportion to such desire: this I have often seen and wondered at. Hence it is plain, that distance, and consequently space in heaven, are alto-

---

(141) That man, in spirit, may be conveyed to a great distance by change of states, his body remaining in the same place: this from experience, n. 9440, 9967, 10734. What it means to be led by the spirit to another place, n. 1884.

gether

gether relative to the interior states of the angels, and therefore that the idea of space enters not into their thoughts (142).

196. This may be illustrated from what passes in the mind of man, in which there is no space, but every thing that he intensely thinks of appears present to him: in like manner, every one that reflects on the matter must know, that space is no object of sight, any farther than he borrows the idea of it from intermediate objects, and from what he has learned of distance by experience: now this proceeds from the following cause, viz. that in what is continuous we have no precise idea of distance, but from things that are not continuous (*): and this is still more strongly the case with the angels, as their seeing is corresponding to and one with their thinking, and their thinking with their affections, and as things appear to them near or remote, and in all their variations, according to their inward states, as has been shewed before.

197. Hence, that in Scripture-language, by places, spaces, and all things that carry in them any idea of space, we are to understand things pertaining to states; thus by distances, as near, far off, ways, journeys, wandrings; by miles, furlong, fields, gardens, cities, streets, and going from one place to another; also by measures of various kinds, as long, broad, high, and deep, and innumerable other things, as most of the ideas

---

(142) That places and spaces appear according to the interior states of angels and spirits, n. 5604, 9440, 10146.

(*) It will be somewhat difficult for the reader, that is not of a philosophical turn of mind, to take the author's meaning in this place. It may appear something clearer, if expressed thus: Were any one surrounded only by space, as it consists of no distinct visible parts, but is all one continued sameness, he would not be able to form any notion of distance therein; but were bodies of visible dimensions introduced into it, they would interrupt the continuity, and serve as so many measures of space, by having a relative distance one from another: thus place, which arises from the different situation of bodies, becomes the measure of space, by giving to it distinction. Eternity also is of like consideration, as having no division or distinction in itself, but borrows them from time, as time has its measures only from the successions of bodies and sounds, according to their impressions on the senses. Thus do things discontinuous and finite give us some, though inadequate, notions of things continous and infinite, whilst they leave us utterly incapable of forming any positive idea of them as they are in themselves: so full of inconceivable mystery is every thing infinite and eternal, and abundantly sufficient to humble the pride of man, when he turns his thoughts to such subjects. Tr.

in

in the human mind borrow something from space and time: to instance only in what is meant in Scripture by length, breadth, and height; in this world what is called long, broad, or high, is so denominated from space; but in heaven, where they have no ideas of space, by length is meant a state of good, by breadth a state of truth, and by height their respective difference as to degrees, of which in n. 38; and the reason of understanding these dimensions in such senses, is because that there *Long* is from East to West, where dwell the angels who excel in the good of love; and *Broad* in heaven is from South to North, where the angels, whose chief eminence and distinction is in truth proceeding from good, have their habitations, see above, n. 148: and *High* in heaven signifies both, according to their degrees respectively; whence it is that length, breadth, and height have such significations in Scripture-language. Thus in Ezekiel, from ch. xl. to xlviii. where the measures assigned to the new temple and the new earth, together with their courts, doors, gates, chambers, windows, &c. are denominated according to length, breadth, and height: all which signify and typify the New Church, and the various species of good and truth therein; and to what else can such measures be applicable? And in like manner the New Jerusalem, as described by St. John in the following words: " And the city lieth four square, " and the length is as large as the breadth. And he measured " the city with the reed, twelve thousand furlongs: the length, " and the breadth, and the height of it are equal," Rev. xxi. 16. Now, as by the New Jerusalem is here signified the New Church, so by those measures are signified the things pertaining to this Church: by length there is signified its good of love; by breadth its truth, as the offspring of that love, and by height the degrees of both respectively; as by the twelve thousand furlongs, the whole of its good and truth in their complex (*): what other meaning can belong to, *the length, and the breadth,*

(*) As it appears from many parts of our author's writings, that numbers in Scripture signify things, so that the number twelve signifies the complex or aggregate of all the things of the kind mentioned; thus, if *Good* be the predicament, the number twelve added to it makes it to signify all sorts of good; if *Truth*, the same number added makes it to signify all truths. Tr.

and

and *the height of it* being *equal?* That by *Breadth* in the Word is signified truth, appears from those words of David, Pf. xxxi. 8. "Thou hast not shut me up into the hand of the enemy: thou hast set my feet in a large room [*in latitude*]. I called upon the Lord in distress [*in straitness*]; the Lord answered me, and set me in a large place" [*in breadth*], Pf. cxviii. 5. So in If. ch. viii. 8. and Hab. i. 6. and also in other places.

198. From what has been said it may appear, that though there be space in heaven, as well as here, yet no account is made of it there, but only of states; and that it is not measured there by distances, as in this world, but from and according to the interior state of the angels (143).

199. The true and principal cause hereof is, that the Lord is present to every one according to his faith and love (144), and that all things appear near or far off according to his presence, for this gives determination to all things in the heavens; on this depends the wisdom of the angels, and the extent of their mental powers; to this is owing the communication of all heavenly things; and hence it is that the angels think spiritually, and not naturally after the manner of men.

Of the Form of Heaven, according to which are regulated the Angelical Consociations and Communications.

200. As concerning the form of heaven, what has already been said on that subject may serve to give the reader some idea of it; as that it is uniform and similar to itself in all its parts, both great and small, n. 72; whence it is, that every society therein is a heaven in a lesser form, and every individual angel

---

(143) That in the Word, *Length* signifies *Good*, n. 1613, 9487. That *Breadth* signifies *Truth*, n. 1613, 3433, 3434, 4482, 9487, 10179. That *Height* signifies *Good* and *Truth*, according to their degrees respectively, n. 9489, 9773, 10181.
(144) That the Lord is adjoined to and present with the angels, in proportion to their recipiency of love and charity from him, n. 290, 681, 1954, 2658, 2886, 2888—4524, 7211, 9128.

a heaven in the smallest form, n. 51 to 58; and that as heaven in its whole or complex resembles one man, so does every society in a lesser, and every angel in the least form, n. 59 to 77: that in the middle are the wisest of the angels, and round about them towards the circumference those who less excel in wisdom respectively; the like regulation also takes place in every particular society, n. 43: that from East to West dwell the angels who are eminent in the good of love, and from the South to the North those who are eminent in truths derived from that good, all according to their degrees, and the same in every particular society, n. 148, 149. All these regulations are according to the form of heaven, and may serve to give us a general idea of it (145).

201. It concerns us the more to have some apprehension of the form of heaven, not only as all the societies of the angels are regulated by it, but also as it determines the method of their communications with one another; and if so, the extent of their thoughts and affections also, and consequently their understanding and wisdom, receive their determinations herefrom, insomuch that the nearer any one approaches in himself to the perfect form of heaven, the higher is the degree of his wisdom: now whether we say of any one, that he is in the form of heaven, or in the order of heaven, it comes to the same, as the form of every thing is from the law of its order, and according to it (146).

202. It will be proper in this place to explain briefly what is meant by being in the form of heaven. Man was created after the image of heaven, and after the image of this world; as to the former internally, and as to the latter externally, see above, n. 57. (Now after the image, and after the form, mean the same). But forasmuch as man, by the evil in his will, and the false in his thoughts [*per falsa cogitationis inde*] in conse-

---

(145) That the universal heaven, with regard to all the angelical societies, is disposed or regulated by the Lord according to his own divine order, forasmuch as the divine presence in the angels constitutes heaven, n. 3038, 7211, 9128—10157. Of the heavenly form, n. 4040, 4041—9877.

(146) That the form of heaven is according to the divine order, n. 4040 to 4043, 6607, 9877.

quence

quence of the former, destroyed in himself the image or form of heaven, and in the room of it introduced the image or form of hell; therefore it is that man is born into the world in greater ignorance than any other animals, and to the end that the image or form of heaven may be restored in him again, it is become necessary for him to be instructed in things pertaining to the divine order, for, as was said before, the form of any thing is according to its order. The Word of God contains all the laws of divine order in the precepts therein delivered, and therefore as far as any one knows and keeps them, so far is his internal, or inward man, opened, and the order or image of heaven formed therein: hence appears what is meant by being in the form of heaven, viz. a life according to the divine laws (147) and order, as laid down in the Word of God.

203. As far as one is in the form of heaven, so far is he in heaven, nay, so far is a heaven in its lowest form, n. 57, and consequently in divine understanding and wisdom; for, as was said before, the thoughts of his mind, and the affections of his heart, extend themselves every way according to his form, and wonderfully communicate with the angelical societies there, and they with him (148). Some suppose that their thoughts and affections have no actual extent around them, but are shut up within them, because they view what they think of as within their own minds, and not at a distance; but this is a great

---

(147) That divine truths are the laws of order, n. 2247, 7995. That as far as any one lives according to order, consequently in good according to divine truths, so far only is he to be esteemed a man, n. 4839, 6605, 6626. That man is the proper subject of all things pertaining to divine order, and that by original creation he was a form of divine order, n. 4219, 4220, 4223, 4523—10156, 10472. That man is not now born in the principles of goodness and truth, but in the evil and the false, and consequently in contrariety to the divine order, and of consequence in mere ignorance, and therefore must of necessity be born again, or regenerated by the power of divine truth from the Lord, before he can enter again into the divine order, n. 1047, 2307, 2308—10286, 10731. That when the Lord forms man anew, or regenerates him, he disposes all things in him according to divine order, or fashions him to be a form of heaven, n. 5700, 6690, 9931, 10303.

(148) That every one in heaven partakes in a communication of life (which may be called an extension of it) with the angelical societies around him, in proportion to his quantity and quality of good, n. 8794, 8797. That thoughts and affections have the like extension, n. 2475, 6598 to 6613. That the angels are associated or separated according to their ruling affections respectively, n. 4111.

mistake,

miſtake, for, as the ſight of the eye extends to very diſtant objects, and is affected by them according to their nature, though at a great diſtance, ſo the interior ſight of the underſtanding extends to the ſpiritual world, though it perceives it not, for the reaſon mentioned above, n. 196: the only difference is, that the ſight of the bodily eye is affected naturally, as from things in the natural world, and the intellectual ſight is affected ſpiritually, as from things in the ſpiritual world, all which latter have relation to goodneſs and truth. That man is not conſcious of its being thus with him, is becauſe he does not apprehend that it is a real light which gives him underſtanding, and that without ſuch light in his underſtanding he would not be able to think at all: concerning this light, ſee above, n. 126 to 132. There was a certain ſpirit, who believed that the power of thinking was from and within himſelf only, without any extenſion beyond himſelf, and conſequently without communication with any ſociety; and to convince him of his error, all communication was cut off betwixt him and the ſocieties next to him, on which he was not only immediately deprived of the power of thinking, but alſo fell down as dead, except that he flung about his arms like a child newly born: in a little time after, the communication was again opened, and according to its return he was gradually reſtored to the uſe of his underſtanding: hereupon, certain angels that were witneſſes to this tranſaction, confeſſed that all thought and affection were by influx from communication, and conſequently the whole of life, as the whole of the life of man conſiſts in his thinking and being affected, or, in other words, that he can underſtand and will (149).

204. But

(149) That there is only one original life, from which all lives exiſt both in heaven and this world, n. 1954, 2021, 2536—5847, 6467. That the Lord is the ſole fountain of that life, n. 2886 to 2889, 334—9276, 10196. That it is derived by influx to angels, ſpirits, and men, after a wonderful manner, n. 2886 to 2889, 3337, 3338, 3484, 3742. That this influx is from divine love, whoſe nature it is to communicate of its own, n. 3472, 4320: and from thence it is, that life appears to man as properly his own, and not by influx, n. 3742, 4320. Of the joy which the angels receive (and whereof they aſſured me) from knowing that their life is by continual influx from the Lord, n. 6469. That evil people will not receive this truth concerning influx, n. 3743. That life even in evil men,

is

204. But we are to take with us, that understanding and wisdom vary in all according to the kind of communication; they in whom these are formed from genuine and pure species of goodness and truth [*ex genuinis veris et bonis*] communicate with the angelical societies according to the form of heaven; but they whose understanding and wisdom are not formed of such goods and truths, but of such only as may consist with them, here the communication is in a sort broken and incoherent, as not being rightly conformable to the order of heaven: but as to those who have no true understanding and wisdom, but are absorbed in the false of evil [*in falsis ex malo*] their communication is only with the infernal societies. It must be observed, that the degree of extension before-mentioned is according to the degree of confirmation in the state of the parties respectively, and that such communication with the societies is not attended with any perception of what they do, or passes among them, but only a communication of their qualities and influence (150).

205. All are consociated in heaven according to their spiritual affinities of good and true, in their several ranks and degrees, whether in the universal heaven, in the several societies, or in particular families, insomuch that the angels, who are in the same kinds and degrees of good and truth, know one another like kindred here on earth, who have been educated together; and there is the like affinity and agreement between the several truths and species of good that constitute their understanding and wisdom, in every particular angel, and productive of the same harmony (151): whence it comes to pass, that they in whom goods and truths are united after the form of heaven,

is by influx from the Lord, n. 2706, 3743, 4417, 10196; but that such change good into evil, and true into false; for as the man is, such is his recipiency of life —this illustrated, n. 4319, 4320, 4417.

(150) That thought diffuses itself to the societies of spirits and angels around us, n. 6600 to 6605, and that without affecting or disturbing their course of thinking.

(151) That every good knows its own proper truth, and every truth its own proper good, n. 2429, 3101, 3102—5835, 9637. Hence the conjunction of good and truth, n. 3834, 4096, 4097—7623 to 7627—9258, 10555: and that this is the effect of heavenly influx, n. 9079.

see things in their various combinations and distant consequences all around them; but it is otherwise where goods and truths are not so combined in a heavenly form.

206. There is a like form belonging to each of the heavens, according to which the communication and extension of the thoughts and affections of the angels are effected, and consequently their understanding and wisdom; and yet there is a difference in the communication between one heaven and another, viz. of the third or inmost with the second or middle heaven, and of both these with the first or lowest heaven; though the communication between heaven and heaven is not properly called communication, but influx, of which we proceed to speak. That there are three heavens, and these distinct from one another, see above in its proper article, n. 29 to 40.

207. That, properly speaking, it is not communication, but influx, that subsists between heaven and heaven, as may appear from the order of the heavens: the third or inmost heaven is the supreme; the second or middle heaven is beneath it; and the first heaven is the lowest of all. All the societies in each of the heavens are distinguished in like manner; as for example, those societies which are stationed in places of the highest eminence, having the appearance of mountains, (see n. 188.) are thus distinguished: they who are of the greatest excellence, and of the quality of the angels of the third heaven, have their dwelling on the summits; they who resemble more the angels of the second heaven, are ranked beneath them; and they who come nearer to the angels of the first heaven are classed still lower; and the same regulations are observed both in the superior and the inferior situations. A society of a superior heaven has its communication with that of an inferior heaven only by correspondency, see above, n. 100; and communication by correspondency is that which we call influx.

208. It is the Lord only that conjoins heaven with heaven, or the society of one heaven with that of another, and this by influx immediate or mediate; immediate from himself, and mediate through the superior to the inferior heavens (152). As

---

(152) That influx is twofold, immediate from the Lord, and mediate through heaven, n. 6063, 6307, 6472, 9682, 9683. That immediate influx from the Lord

the conjunction of the heavens is from the Lord only, so it is carefully provided, that no angel of a superior heaven look into any society of an inferior heaven, or converse with any there; for no sooner should he do this, than he would be deprived of his understanding and wisdom, and that through the following cause: every angel has three degrees of life, answering to the three degrees of heaven; they who are in the inmost heaven have the third or inmost degree of life open, and the second and first shut: they who are in the middle heaven, have the second degree open, and the first and third shut: and they who are in the lowest heaven, have the first degree open, and the second and third shut: as soon therefore as an angel of the third heaven looks down upon any society in the second, and converses with any therein, his third degree of life is shut, whereby he is deprived of his wisdom, which lies only in the third degree of life, for he has none in the second or first; according to which meaning are those words of our Lord, Matth. xxiv. 17, 18. " Let not him which is on the house top come down to take " any thing out of his house; neither let him which is in the " field return back to take his cloaths:" and also in Luke xvii. 31, 32. " In that day he which shall be on the house top, and " his stuff in the house, let him not come down to take it " away: and he that is in the field, let him likewise not return " back: remember Lot's wife."

209. There is no influx from the inferior heavens to the superior, this being contrary to the laws of order, but only from the superior to the inferior; for the wisdom of the angels of a superior heaven, as far exceeds that of an angel of an inferior heaven, as a myriad exceeds a unit, which is the reason why the angels of an inferior cannot converse with those of a superior heaven, nor can they see them when they look up, their heaven being, with respect to them, veiled as it were with a dark mist; but the angels of a superior heaven can see those beneath them, but not converse with them, but at the peril of being deprived of their wisdom, as was said before.

Lord extends to the most minute particulars of all things, n. 6058, 6474 to 6478, 8717, 8728. Of the mediate influx of the Lord through the heavens, n. 4067, 6982, 6985, 6996.

210. The

210. The thoughts, affections, and discourse of the angels of the inmost heaven, come not within the apprehension of those of the middle heaven, as far transcending their capacities; but at times, as the Lord sees fit, there appears thence in the inferior heavens a kind of flame-coloured phænomenon; and from the middle heaven into the lowest, a lucid form, and sometimes a white or party-coloured cloud, from the ascent, descent, or shape of which they are able to form some judgment concerning what they are discoursing of above.

211. What has been said on this subject may serve to give the reader an idea of the form of heaven, and how that of the inmost heaven is the most perfect; that of the middle heaven, less perfect; and that of the first or lowest heaven, the least perfect of all; and that the form of one heaven owes its subsistence to that of another, under the efficiency of the divine influx; but what communication by influx is, cannot be comprehended without having an idea of the degrees of altitude, and knowing the difference between them, and those of longitude and latitude, concerning which, see n. 38.

212. As concerning the form of heaven in particular, together with its several changes and fluctuations; this is a subject passing the comprehension even of the angels, though some conception of it may be borrowed from the structure of the human body, as viewed and examined by a skilful anatomist, it having been shewed before in its proper place, that the whole of heaven resembles one man, see n. 59 to 72; and how all things in man correspond to the heavens, n. 87 to 102. Now, how inexplicable and past comprehension this wonderful structure of man is, may appear even from a general view of the nervous fibres whereof its several parts are compacted, and which are so extremely small, as to escape the notice of the sharpest sight in their several meanders and transits in the brain, which assumes its soft, medullary, and almost fluid substance from their innumerable complications; and yet, through their mediate instrumentality, all the operations of the will and intellect pass into their respective distinct acts and forms: and how they meet again, to form admirable complications in different parts of the body, appears from their various plexus or folds in the heart,

mesentery,

mesentery, and other regions of the body; and also from those nodes or network called ganglions, where many fibres from different provinces of the human microcosm meet to form their proper combinations, and thence proceed in their various intertextures to discharge other functions in their progress, and that by sundry repetitions; besides other like offices in every bowel, member, organ, and muscle in the body. The artist, who, with a discerning eye and a reflecting mind, views all this and many other admirable contrivances in the human structure, must stand astonished at the skill of the divine artificer; and yet the things which are discoverable therein by the eye, though assisted by the best glasses, are but few in comparison of those still more wonderful things concealed from us in the deep of interior nature. That the human form corresponds to the form of heaven, is evident from the operations of the understanding and will therein and according to it, for whatever any one determines in his will, the same spontaneously influences the body, and passes into act (*); and so what he thinks of, that instantaneously affects the fibres from their beginning to their terminations, and produces sense: now that which is the form of

(*) This doctrine laid down by our author effectually solves that knotty point so much controverted by the learned, concerning muscular motion, as it accounts for it, in a satisfactory manner from the instantaneous operation of the will, by influx, on the correspondent parts of the body: and at the same time it totally annihilates that objection of the materialists against the immortality of the soul, drawn from the disorder occasioned in the understanding through a distempered state of the brain, or any injury sustained by it; for beginning at the wrong end, and tracing the intellectual operations from organized matter, as the source and cause of them, they infer, that the cause being vitiated or taken away, the effect must necessarily cease; whereas perception, thought, and memory, do not flow from the brain, but from the mind into it, as the proper recipient thereof, for the manifestation of these powers in outward nature: the defect or destruction of the organ occasions no annihilation or loss of the intellect, for that remains still the same in its own spiritual principle or world; but only hinders its influx into another condition of existence, and so from manifesting its operations in this outward natural world. The soul and its mind are absolutely independent on this mortal body, they communicate to it, but receive nothing from it, though they reach to natural things by means of and through it: they live, even during their union with the body, in the spiritual world in their own spiritual body, and here only by communication with this organized natural body: so much depends on assigning to influx its proper source and progress, even the whole of the difference between infidelity and believing rightly. See *Theosophic Lucubration*, p. 23, 24.

thought and will, is also the form of understanding and wisdom. Such is the human form as corresponding to the form of heaven, and may serve to give us some idea of the extension appertaining to the affections and thoughts of angels, and how their understanding and wisdom are in proportion to their degree of perfection as to that form. That the form of heaven is from the Divine Humanity of our Lord, see above, n. 78 to 86. These things are offered to the reader, with a design to shew, that the form of heaven is a subject of such vast extent as not to be exhausted, even with respect to generals, and consequently, not to be comprehended even by the minds of angels, as was before observed.

Of the Governments in Heaven.

213. As heaven is distinguished into societies, the greater of which consist of some hundred thousands of angels, n. 50: and as all in the same society are in the like good, but not alike in wisdom, n. 43; it therefore necessarily follows, that there must be governments there, for order in every society is of necessary observation and use; however, governments in the heavens are of various kinds, some respecting the societies which constitute the Lord's cœlestial kingdom, and others respecting those which constitute his spiritual kingdom: and they also differ with regard to the difference of office and ministry appointed to societies in particular: but then it must be noted, that in the heavens there is no kind of government differing from that of mutual love, for this is universally the heavenly government.

214. The government in the Lord's cœlestial kingdom, or third heaven, is called JUSTICE [Righteousness] as all there are in the good of love to the Lord, from the Lord; and all that proceeds from that principle is called Just [Righteous]. Here the Lord is the sole governor, guiding the angels himself, and teaching them the ways of life they should walk in, and writing on their hearts those truths, which are called the Truths of Judgment; insomuch that every one there sees and knows them,

them (153), and therefore there is no controverfy on thefe fubjects among them, but their thoughts and converfation turn chiefly on things pertaining to righteoufnefs and holinefs of life: they who are lefs wife confult thofe who excel in wifdom, and the latter afk counfel of the Lord, who vouchfafes to give them anfwers: upon the whole, it is their heaven and higheft joy to live righteoufly and holily under the influence and government of the Lord.

215. The government in the Lord's fpiritual kingdom is called Judgment, the fubjects of it being in fpiritual good, which is the good of charity towards our neighbour, and in its effence is truth (154); for truth relates to judgment, and good to righteoufnefs (155). Thefe alfo are under the Lord's guidance, but mediately by others, n. 208; and accordingly they have rulers, more or fewer, according to the exigences of that particular fociety to which they belong: they live together under laws which are well underftood and obferved by their rulers in the adminiftration of their office, and when any difficulty or doubt arifes, they receive light from the Lord.

216. As that government which is from good (*), as in the Lord's cœleftial kingdom, is called Righteoufnefs; and that which

---

(153) That the cœleftial angels do not think and reafon of truths like the fpiritual angels, feeing that they are in the perception or immediate intuition of all things relating to truth, by the gift of the Lord, n. 202, 597, 607, 784—8780, 9277, 10336. That the cœleftials, where truths are the fubject of converfation, only fay concerning fuch fubjects, The matter is fo, or is not fo; whereas the fpiritual angels reafon concerning them, as whether the matter be fo, or not, n. 2715, 3246, 4446, 9166, 10786; where is given the explication of thofe words of our Lord: "Let your communication be, yea, yea; nay, nay; for whatfoever is more than thefe cometh of evil." Matt. v. 37.

(154) That the angels of the fpiritual kingdom are more for intellectuals, or the knowledge of truths; and thofe of the cœleftial are more in good, n. 863, 875, 927—5113, 9596.

(155) That juftice or righteoufnefs, in the Word, is predicated of good, and judgment of truth; and therefore to exercife righteoufnefs and judgment fignifies to practife both goodnefs and truth, n. 2235, 9857. That great judgments fignify the laws of divine order, or divine truths, n. 7206.

(*) Let it be obferved here, by way of caution againft miftake, that our author never ufes the terms good and truth in the way of contradiftinction, or as though either could fubfift entirely feparate from the other; and therefore where he fpeaks of fome angels being in [the principle of] good, and others in the [principle of] truth,

which is from truth, as in his spiritual kingdom, is called Judgment; therefore the terms justice or righteousness, and judgment, are so often in Scripture-language, where heaven and the church are the subjects treated of, and there, by justice or righteousness is signified cœlestial good, and by judgment spiritual good, which latter, as was said before, in its essence is truth: thus in the following texts: " Of the increase of his govern-
" ment and peace there shall be no end, upon the throne of David
" and upon his kingdom, to order and to establish it with judg-
" ment and with justice, from henceforth even for ever," Isai. ix. 7. By David in this place is meant the Lord (156), and by his kingdom, heaven, as appears from the following words:
" I will raise unto David a righteous branch, and a king shall
" reign and prosper, and shall execute judgment and justice in
" the earth," Jer. xxiii. 5. " The Lord is exalted, for he
" dwelleth on high: he hath filled Zion with JUDGMENT and
" RIGHTEOUSNESS," Isai. xxxiii. 5. By Zion here is meant heaven and the church (157). " I am the Lord exercising
" loving-kindness, JUDGMENT, and RIGHTEOUSNESS in the
" earth; for in these things I delight, saith the Lord," Jer. ix. 24. " I will betroth thee unto me for ever, yea, I will
" betroth thee unto me in RIGHTEOUSNESS and in JUDG-
" MENT," Hosea ii. 19. " Thy RIGHTEOUSNESS is like the
" great mountains; thy JUDGMENTS are a great deep," Psal. xxxvi. 6, 7. " They ask of me the ordinances [the judgments]
" of JUSTICE; they take delight in approaching to God," Isai. lviii. 2: and also in other places.

217. In the Lord's spiritual kingdom are different forms of government in different societies, according to the various offices

truth, it means only that the former were more eminent for love in the affectionate part, than for knowledge in the intellectual, and so *vice versâ:* but no angel can be destitute of either, however they may differ in the degrees of the one or the other. In like manner, when we mean to distinguish any one more particularly by the name of a good man; this does not imply that he is deficient in the intellectual part or knowledge of truth, but only that goodness forms the more distinguishing part of his character.

(156) That by David in the prophetic parts of the Word is meant the Lord, n. 1888, 9954.

(157) That by Zion in the Word is meant the Church, and particularly the Cœlestial Church, n. 7362, 9055.

and

and miniftrations of thofe focieties, and thofe anfwer to the functions of the feveral parts in man, which every one knows are manifold: thus one function belongs to the heart, another to the lungs; and fo in like manner, the liver, the pancreas, the fpleen, and every organ of fenfe, &c. have each their feveral offices; and according to their different miniftrations in the body are thofe of the angelical focieties correfponding thereto; for that there is a correfpondence between all things in heaven, and all things in man, has been fhewed before, fee n. 87 to 102. Now thefe feveral forms of government agree in this, that they are all calculated to promote the good of the whole, and of every member in particular (158); and this, becaufe all throughout the univerfal heaven are under the care and guidance of the Lord, who loves them all, and has therefore fo conftituted the good of the community, that every individual finds his own private good connected with it, and receives of it in proportion to his love for the community; for in loving the whole he loves every one, and according to the extent of his love (which is a divine gift) he is beloved of the Lord, and is bleffed in the fame degree.

218. Hence we may form a judgment of the character of their rulers, viz. that they are fuch as excel in love and wifdom, and confequently affectionately wifh the good of all, and are endowed with knowledge fufficient to effect it: now they who are of this character, are not given to behave lordly and imperioufly over thofe that are fubject to them, but minifter to and ferve them; for to do good to others from love, is to ferve them, and to provide the means of their receiving it, is to minifter to them: nor do they efteem themfelves greater, but lefs than

---

(158) That every man, and alfo the community, as likewife our country, the church, and, in a univerfal fenfe, the kingdom of the Lord, is our neighbour; and that, to do them good from love, according to their quality and condition, is charity or love to our neighbour: fo their good and benefit, collectively confidered, is our neighbour, n. 6818 to 6824, 8123. That alfo civil good or juftice, abftractedly confidered, is our neighbour, n. 2915, 4730, 8120, 8123. Hence it is, that charity towards our neighbour extends to all the particulars of the life of man, and that to do good from the love of good and truth; and to do juftice from the love of juftice in all the offices and relations of life, is the fum and complex of charity to our neighbour, n. 2417, 8121, 8124.

K k   others,

others, for they have respect to the good of the community and of their neighbour in the first place, and of their own but subsequently; now that which is first is greater than that which follows: however, honour and preeminence are assigned them, for they are situated in the centre of their society, in places somewhat exalted above their brethren, and dwell in magnificent palaces; and they accept of these honourable distinctions, not for their own sakes, but for the sake of obedience, to the end all may know, that as they are appointed for them of the Lord, so they are to pay them obedience as governors instituted by him: alluding to what has been said are those words of our Lord to his disciples: " Whosoever will be great among you, " let him be your minister; and whosoever will be chief among " you, let him be your servant, even as the Son of man came " not to be ministered unto, but to minister," Matt. xx. 26, 27, 28. " He that is greatest among you, let him be as the " younger, and he that is chief as he that doth serve," Luke xxii. 26.

219. Every family also is a government in a lower form; for there is master and servants, and the master loves his servants, and the servants their master, and so serve each other from love; whilst the master instructs them how they are to live, and what they are to do; and the servants, on their part, discharge the duties belonging to them: and let it be noted, that to be useful is their highest delight; for the Lord's kingdom is the kingdom of uses.

220. There are governments also in the hells, for otherwise the infernals could not be kept within bounds; but the governments there are of an opposite nature to those in the heavens, as being founded in self-love, every one striving to be the greatest, and domineering over others, and pursuing all that refuse to be subject to them, with hatred and revenge, such being the nature of self-love: therefore they have the most fierce and malignant for their rulers, that they may obey through fear (159): but of this hereafter, where we shall treat of the hells.

(159) That there are two kinds of government, the one founded in love to our neighbour, and the other in self love, n. 10814. That from the former proceed all things good and delightful, n. 10160, 10814. That in heaven no one desires
to

Of Divine Worship in Heaven.

221. Divine worship in heaven is not unlike that on earth, as to the external part, though with regard to the internal there is a difference: they have their doctrines, their preachings, and their temples, as we have, and their doctrines in all essential points perfectly agree together, but of more interior wisdom in the superior heavens than in the inferior, and their preachings are according to their doctrines: and as they have houses and palaces, n. 183 to 190, so likewise have they temples to preach in. That these things are so in the heavens, is because the angels continually advance to higher degrees of perfection in wisdom and love, for they have understanding and will like men, and those are capable of such proficiency, the understanding in intellectual truths, and the will in the various species of good arising from love (160).

222. But the true divine worship is not considered in the heavens as consisting in frequenting the temples, and hearing preachings, but in a life of love, charity, and faith, according to the doctrines received, preaching serving only as the means of instruction in things pertaining to life. I have conversed with the angels on this subject, and told them, that it is the general belief in this world, that divine worship consists only in frequenting the churches, hearing sermons, receiving the sacrament of the supper three or four times a year, and observing other rites instituted by the church, together with attending at the publick prayers with reverence and devotion: to

---

to govern from the love of self, but that all chuse to minister to others, and that this is to govern from love to our neighbour, and the cause of their great power, n. 5732. That from government founded in the love of self proceed all kinds of evil, n. 10038. That from the time that the love of self and the love of the world began to prevail in the earth, men found themselves obliged to have recourse to civil government for their safety, n. 7364, 10160, 10814.

(160) That the intellect is the recipient of truth, and the will of good, n. 3623, 6125, 7503, 9300, 9930. As all things have some relation to good and truth, so all things in the life of man to the understanding and will, n. 803, 10122. That the angels advance in degrees of perfection eternally, n. 4803, 6648.

which

which the angels replied, that these external things ought to be observed, but that they availed nothing, if they did not proceed from an inward good principle, and that this consisted in a life according to sound doctrine.

223. That I might be an eye-witness to the manner of their assemblies in their temples, I have been indulged with permission to enter them, and hear the preachings. The preacher stands in a pulpit on the East side; before him sit those who are most eminent for wisdom, and on each hand such as are inferior in this respect: they sit in something of a circular form, so that all can see the face of the preacher, but no one so as to be out of his sight: at the gate which is on the East side of the temple, to the left of the pulpit, stand those who are in the degree of the newly initiated; but no one is allowed to stand behind the pulpit, for should any one do so, it would confuse the preacher, as would also be the case, should any one present dissent from his doctrine; and if this were to happen, such a one would be obliged to turn away his face from the minister. The preachings there are fraught with such sublime instruction, as is not to be equalled in this world, so greatly superior is their wisdom. Their temples in the spiritual kingdom appear to be constructed of stone, and of wood in the cœlestial, and that because stone corresponds to truth, for the investigation of which the angels of the former are more distinguished; and wood to the principle of good, which is more eminently the characteristick of the angels in the latter (161); nor are they called Temples in the latter, but the House of God. In the cœlestial kingdom their structures are without magnificence, but in the spiritual, not without a greater or lesser degree of it.

224. I had some discourse with one of their preachers concerning the pious disposition of their hearers during their assemblies, who said, that the degree of piety, devotion, and holiness in every one was in proportion to his love and faith within, as all sanctity is from the internal presence and grace of the Lord, and that without these he could not see what an

(161) That *Stone* signifies *Truth*, n. 114, 643, 1298, 3720, 6426, 8609, 10376. That *Wood* signifies *Good*, n. 643, 3720, 8354: that therefore the most ancient of our ancestors, as being of cœlestial good, dwelt in houses of wood, n. 3720.

apparent

apparent external sanctity availed; and then reflecting a little on the latter, he farther added, that there might be something like sanctity in the outward practice and behaviour, either acquired artificially, or assumed in hypocrisy, but that without the internal of holiness in the heart, all was no better than a false fire kindled by the love of self, and to catch the praise of men.

225. All the preachers are of the Lord's spiritual kingdom, for none belong to his cœlestial; and the reason of this is, because in the former they are in the province of truths from good, and all preaching must be from truths; whereas in the cœlestial kingdom, they are all in the province of the good of love, which principle gives them an intuitive perception of all truths, so that they have no occasion to discourse of them; however, notwithstanding, they are not without their publick instructions, as well for illustration of the truths they already know, as to enrich them with a farther increase, which, as soon as offered, they own and perceive, without speculating or reasoning upon them; and what they so perceive they graft in their hearts, and bring forth in their lives, it being usual with them to say, that, to live according to his truths, is to love the Lord (162).

226. All the preachers are of the Lord's appointment, and accordingly endowed with the gift of preaching, nor are any others allowed to teach in their temples: they are called preachers, and not priests, and that because the cœlestial kingdom is the priesthood of heaven, forasmuch as priesthood signifies the good of love to the Lord, in which are all the angels of that kingdom; whereas the spiritual kingdom is called the Royalty of Heaven, for the royal or kingly office signifies truth as proceeding from good, see above, n. 24. (163).

227. The doctrines on which their preaching is grounded have, all of them, respect to life and practice, and none to

---

(162) That to keep the divine precepts is to love the Lord and our neighbour, n. 143, 10153, 10310, 10578, 10645, 10648.
(163) That the priests represented the Lord as to divine good, and kings, as to his divine truth, n. 2015, 6148. Hence, that the title *Priest* in the Word signifies such as are in the good of love to the Lord, and priesthood the good itself, n. 9806, 9809. That *King* in the Word signifies divine truth, and *Royalty* the same truth as proceeding from good, n. 1672, 2015, 2069, 4575, 4581, 4966, 5044.

believing only, as separate from life: the doctrine taught in the third or inmost heaven is more replete with wisdom than that of the middle heaven; and the latter more highly intellectual than that of the lowest heaven; for the doctrines in each are adapted to the perception and capacities of the angels therein respectively; and it is an essential point in all their doctrines to inculcate the belief of the Lord's Divine Humanity.

Of the Power of the Angels.

228. Such as have no notion of the spiritual world, and its influx into the natural, will not be able to form an idea of the power of the angels, supposing, because they are spiritual, and not visible to us, that such pure, immaterial beings must be destitute of power; but they who think deeper have different sentiments of this matter, as knowing that all power in man is from his intellect and will, which constitute his spiritual man, and without which he could not give motion to any part of his body, it being therefrom that his whole corporeal frame receives direction in all its movements; thus, what the mind thinks, the mouth and tongue utter; and that which the will commands, the body and its members obey, the intellect and will being subject to the government of the Lord, through the ministry of angels and spirits, and consequently all the bodily functions depending thereon; and, however incredible it may seem, man would not be able to move a single step without influx from the heavenly world. Of this truth I have had full experience at such times as it has been given to the angels [without my concurrence] to govern my actions, and to move my steps, tongue, and speech at their pleasure, and that by [sensible] influx into my mind and will, insomuch that I perceived myself incapable of doing any thing as of myself: after which they told me, that every one was actuated in like manner, as he might learn from the doctrine of the church, and from the Scriptures, being therein taught to pray, that God would send his angels to guide him, and direct his steps, to teach and inspire him what to think, and what to speak, and the like,

though

though at other times, when this doctrine is out of his mind, he believes and speaks differently. This instance is given, to shew the power and influence of the angels with man.

229. The power of the angels in the spiritual world is so exceeding great, that were I to relate the proofs of it which I have seen, they would exceed belief. If at any time ought should happen there to obstruct the established laws of government and peace, and therefore to be removed as contrary to divine order, they subdue and banish it with a mere effort of their will, or even with a forbidding countenance; so have I seen mountains, that had been occupied by evil spirits, cast down and overturned, or shaken from top to bottom, as by an earthquake; rocks also rent asunder to their very foundations, and the evil spirits upon them swallowed up; nay, I have seen some hundred thousands of such scattered before them, and by their power cast into their proper hells; for neither numbers, policy, nor confederacies, avail ought against them; for they discover their most subtle devices in the twinkling of an eye, and discomfit all their adversaries in a moment (*): see more on this subject in the account of *Babylon destroyed.* Such power have

---

(*) However contrary the foregoing testimony of our author may appear to the general preconceived opinions concerning the heavenly worlds, and the established laws of harmony, peace, and bliss therein; it is far from incredible (setting aside his authority) that the settled course of things in those blessed regions may admit of some variation on certain occasions, and for wise purposes, by divine permission and appointment: thus, for example, the admission of evil spirits into the heavenly kingdoms at particular times may answer the following good ends, viz. to confound and mortify their pride, and the vain conceits of their own sufficiency as to strength, subtlety, and numbers, and to humble them the more under their disappointments and defeats; and secondly, to convince them, that it is not in change of place, but in condition of existence, that happiness or misery consists, and that therefore, as evil spirits, they are and must be impotent and miserable, and carry their hell within them. On the other hand, to the good angels it may serve as a salutary memento (and what created beings are without all need of it) of due gratitude to him, who hath so made them to differ from others once of the same species with themselves; to confirm them in pious humility, adoration, and love to their Divine Benefactor; and prompt them with greater alacrity to praise and glorify him for their victory and triumph over all that might otherwise offend or hurt them: and we may add to the foregoing considerations the following one, viz. that certain interruptions, even in bliss, may serve to give a higher relish to the returns of it; and that perfect happiness, without some degrees of abatement at times, may be incompatible with the nature of created beings: and it may

farther

have the holy angels in the spiritual world; nor have they less in the natural world, when the Lord sees fit to make use of them there, as appears from the Scripture, of their destroying whole armies, and of causing a plague, of which no less than twenty thousand died; concerning which angel we read, that, " When the angel stretched out his hand upon Jerusalem to " destroy it, the Lord repented him of the evil, and said to " the angel that destroyed; It is enough: stay now thine hand: " and David saw the angel that smote the people," 2 Sam. xxiv. 16, 17: not to mention other instances. From the angels being invested with such powers, they are sometimes called Powers; and in David: " Bless the Lord, ye his angels that excel in " strength," Pf. ciii. 20.

230. But we must take with us, that the angels have not this power from themselves, but wholly from the Lord, and that they are only so far powers, as they acknowledge it; for should any of them believe that such power belonged to himself, he would instantly become so weak, as not to be able to contend with one evil spirit: wherefore the angels absolutely renounce all merit as belonging to them, and ascribe the praise of what they do to God only.

231. All power in the heavens is from divine truth proceeding from the Lord, as he is essentially divine truth united with divine good, see n. 126 to 140, and as far forth as the angels are recipients thereof, so far are they powers (164), and in the same measure each is true and good, or endued with understanding and will, their correlatives; or, in other words, according to their degree of divine goodness and truth from the

---

farther be remarked, that were an invariable administration of government in heaven and earth to take place, all proof of the divine liberty and interposition, together with the uses arising from the belief of them, would be removed, and the notion of fatality be substituted in their stead: some vicissitudes and interruptions may therefore be appointed to obviate such errors, as also to keep dependent creatures under a constant sense of their dependence, and to answer many purposes of good both to men and angels that they know not. Tr.

(164) That the angels are called *Powers*, and are really such from their reception of divine truth from the Lord, n. 9639. That the angels are recipients of divine truth from the Lord, and as such called in Scripture *Gods*, n. 4295, 4402, 8301, 8192, 9398.

Lord,

Lord, fo far is each his own good and truth (165), and fo far excels in power; and as there is the like variety in heaven as in earth, fo no two angels are exactly equal in the above refpects, nor confequently in power: they who conftitute the province of the arms are invefted with the greateft power, as they moft excel in truths, which are replenifhed with good from the univerfal heaven, like as the ftrength of the whole body transfers itfelf to and exerts itfelf in the arms; hence it is that power is expreffed and fignified in Scripture by the arms and hands (166). In heaven is fometimes the emblematical appearance of a naked arm, apparently of ftrength fufficient to break in pieces the hardeft rock; it once came very near me, and feemed as if it could bruife my bones to powder.

232. That all power is from divine truth as proceeding from the Lord, and that the angels are fo far in power as they are recipients of it, fee above, n. 137: neverthelefs, their reception of divine truth is in proportion to their reception of divine good, for truths have all their power from good, and none without it, as good exerts all its power through truths, and none without them; it is from the conjunction of both that power exifts: and the cafe is the fame with faith and love; for whether we call it faith or truth, it is all one, becaufe the whole of faith is truth; fo, whether we fay good or love, it means the fame, as the whole of love is good (167). How great the power of the

(165) That the proper good and truth [by derivation from the Lord] of every angel and man, and confequently his love and faith, is that which conftitutes his identity, n. 10298, 10367; or, in other words, his underftanding and will give him that diftinction, as being the effences of his life; the life of his good confifting in his will, and that of his truth in his underftanding, n. 10076, 10177, 10264, 10284.
(166) Of the correfpondence of the hands, arms, and fhoulders with heaven, or grand man, n. 4931 to 4937. That by the arms and hands in Scripture is fignified power, n. 878, 3091, 4931, 6947, 10017.
(167) That all power in the heavens is through truth from good, and confequently through faith from love, n. 3191, 3563—10019, 10182. That all power is from the Lord, as from him proceeds all the truth appertaining to faith, and all the good appertaining to love, n. 9327, 9410. That this power is meant by the keys delivered to Peter, n. 6344. That to divine truth, as proceeding from the Lord, appertains all power, n. 6948, 8200. That this power of the Lord is meant by his fitting at the right hand of Jehovah, n. 3387, 4592—8281, 9133. That the right hand fignifies power, n. 10019.

angels

angels is through truths from good [*per vera ex bono*] may be gathered from this, that an evil spirit, when viewed intently by the angels, presently falls, as it were, into a swoon, and loses the appearance of a human form till the angel turns away his eyes; the cause of which is, that the sight of the angels is from the light of heaven, which is the same with divine truth, see above, n. 126 to 132: the eyes also correspond to truths proceeding from good [*veris ex bono*] (168).

233. Forasmuch as all power belongs to truths from good, so none belongs to false from evil [*falsis ex malo*] (169): in the latter are all the infernal spirits, and therefore they have no power over truth and good; but what kind of power belongs to them amongst themselves, and what before they are cast into hell, shall be spoken to hereafter.

Of the Speech of the Angels.

234. The angels converse together as we do on earth, and in like manner, on various subjects, whether of a domestick, civil, moral, or spiritual nature, nor is there any other difference between them and us in this respect, than that their conversation is more intellectual, as coming from a deeper ground. I have been permitted to be often in their company, and to converse with them as a friend with friends, and sometimes as a stranger with strangers; and at such times, from the similarity of our states, it appeared to me as if I were conversing with men on earth.

235. The speech of angels is equally divided into words with ours, and alike sonorous and audible, for they have mouths, tongues, and ears, as we have, and also an atmosphere to give articulation to their speech; but then that atmosphere is spiritual, accommodated to their nature, and they make the same use

---

(168) That the eyes correspond to truths from good, n. 4403 to 4421, 4523 to 4534, 6923.
(169) That no power belongs to false from evil, but all to truth from good, n. 6784, 10481.

of it for respiration and enunciation, as we do of our atmosphere (170).

236. There is but one language used throughout heaven, so that all of every society, however distant, understand one another; nor is that language learnt, but natural to every one, flowing spontaneously from their affections and thoughts, whilst the sound of the voice corresponds to the affection, and the articulations of that sound, or the words, to the ideas of the thoughts proceeding from that affection; and as their language corresponds thereto, it is also spiritual, and may be called a sounding affection, and a speaking thought. Whoever considers the matter attentively, may know that all thought proceeds from some affection of love, and that the ideas of the mind are so many different forms into which the common affection diffuses itself, for every idea which is the object of thought owes its existence to some affection. Hence it is that the angels know the disposition and qualities of another from his speech, his affection from the sound of his voice, and his intellectual quality from the articulations of that sound in his words; and such of the angels as are eminent in wisdom can tell from a sentence or two what is the ruling passion in another, which is a thing they principally attend to. That every one is sensible of various affections by turns, is very well known, as of one when merry, of another when sad, of another under the prevailing influence of mercy and pity, of another when in sincerity and truth, of another in love and charity, of another when in deceit and guile, of another when actuated by zeal or anger, and of another in the pursuit of honour and fame, and so on; but yet the principal or ruling love is more or less in all of these different affections, insomuch that the more eminently wise among the angels, who have a quick discernment in this matter, can judge of the state of another by his speech: and that this is so, it has been given me to know from full experience: I

---

(170) That the angels in the heavens are not without respiration, though in a more interior way, n. 3884, 3885: this from experience, n. 3884, 3885, 3891, 3893. That their respiration varies according to the difference of their states, n. 1119, 3886, 3887, 3889, 3892, 3893. That the evil spirits are incapable of respiration in heaven, and when admitted there suffer a kind of suffocation, n. 3893.

have

have heard the angels declare what life another person has led from only hearing him speak; nay, that they could discern all the particulars of the life of another from certain ideas in his mind, as knowing thereby his ruling passion, which enters into all the divisions of it, and exhibits a register or book of the life.

237. The language of the angels has nothing in it common with that of men, except in certain words which express an affection, and that, not with the words themselves, but only with the sound of them, of which hereafter; and that this is so, appeared to me from the angels not being able to utter one word in any human language, after repeated trials, it being impossible for them to utter any thing which does not correspond with their affection, for what is not so, is contrary to their principle of life, which is from affection, and from which they speak: they informed me, that the first language of the human race here on earth was of the like kind, as being of heavenly extraction; and that the Hebrew language in some words is conformable thereto.

238. As the speech of the angels corresponds to some affection of their love, and as the love of heaven is love to the Lord and to their neighbour, see n. 13 to 19, we may hence gather how harmonious and delightful their speech must be, for it not only pleases the ear, but also exhilarates the minds of those that hear it. A certain hard-hearted spirit being once on a time in conversation with an angel (*), he was so charmed with his speech, that he shed tears, owning that he could not refrain, though he had never done the like before, saying, that it seemed to him as if love itself had spoken with a tongue.

(*) Though this seemingly contradicts what has been said before by the author, viz. that no bad spirit (as every hard-hearted one must needs be) can stand before an angel, or bear the efflux or virtue proceeding from him, as a surrounding sphere, without the greatest confusion and dismay; yet it is to be noted, that on particular occasions, and to answer certain purposes, according to the Lord's good pleasure, the laws and properties of the heavenly world are suspended, or so qualified, as to admit of conferences between the angels and evil spirits, frequent instances of which are to be met with in our author's writings. The reader is here cautioned against being stumbled upon his meeting with some few things that he cannot easily reconcile, as in the farther course of his reading, or in the Translator's notes, he probably will find matters cleared up to his satisfaction. Tr.

239. The discourse of the angels is full of wisdom, as proceeding from a deep ground, and as their interior thoughts are wisdom, so their interior affection is love, which both unite in their expression. Hence it is, that they possess so copious a wisdom, as to be able to express more in one word than we can do in a thousand, and that they comprehend in their ideas such things as the mind of man is not capable to receive, much less to express; wherefore it is said of the things heard and seen in heaven, that they are unutterable, and such as ear hath not heard, nor eye seen: and the truth of this has been given me to know by experience; for having been sometimes translated into the angelical state, and given to converse with the angels in that state, I at such times understood all that I heard from them; but when, upon being restored to my former state and natural way of conceiving things, I endeavoured to recollect what I had so heard and understood, I was by no means able to do it, there having been a thousand things incommensurate to the natural mind, and therefore not to be communicated by human words, but by the variegations of heavenly light only. The ideas in the thoughts of the angels, which form their words, are likewise modifications of the light of heaven, and their affections, which produce the sound of their words, are so many variations of the heat of heaven; for as the light of heaven is divine truth or wisdom, so the heat of heaven is divine good or love, see above, n. 126 to 140; and as the angels derive their affections from divine love, so do they think from divine wisdom (171).

240. As the speech of the angels proceeds immediately from their affection (for, as was said before, n. 236, their ideas in thinking are so many different forms, into which the common affection is distributed) so they can express in a minute, things which a man could not do in less than half an hour, and also the contents of several pages in a few words, as I have often experienced (172). The ideas in the thinking of the angels,

(171) That the ideas from which the angels speak are formed by wonderful variegations of the heavenly light, n. 1646, 3343, 3693.
(172) That the angels can express more in their language in a moment, than we can in ours in half an hour, and also such things as cannot be accommodated to human language, n. 1641, 1642, 1643, 1645, 4602, 7089.

and their words in speaking, are one, as cause and effect, the former being the producer, and the latter the product; whence it is, that every word comprehends so much: when the flow of thoughts and words of the angels is at any time represented under a visible appearance, it resembles a thin undulating fluid; or a circumfluent atmosphere, in which appear innumerable things in wonderful order flowing from the fountain of their wisdom, which make delightful impressions on the mind of the spectator; for it is to be observed here, that the ideas in the minds both of angels and men are capable of being represented under visible forms, as viewed in the light of heaven, according to divine permission (173).

241. The angels of the Lord's cœlestial kingdom speak in like manner as do the angels of his spiritual kingdom [the middle heaven], but the former from a deeper ground than the latter; for as the cœlestial angels are in the good of love to the Lord, they speak from wisdom; and the spiritual angels, who are more distinguished for their good of love to their neighbour (which in its essence is truth, n. 215.) they speak from intellectual knowledge; for as wisdom is from good, so the latter is from truth. Hence it is, that the speech of the cœlestials may be compared to a smooth, gently flowing water; but that of the spiritual angels to a current somewhat interrupted and broken: the speech of the former sounds much from the vowels *U* and *O*, and that of the latter from the vowels *E* and *I*; for as the sound is in the vowels, so the affection is in the sound; for, as was said above, n. 236, the sound in the speech of the angels corresponds to affection, and the articulations of the sound, which are the words, correspond to their ideas derived from such affection: and forasmuch as the vowels do not properly constitute any part of the language, but only serve to give

(173) That there are innumerable things in every single idea, n. 1008, 1869, 4946—6618. That the ideas of the human mind are laid open in the other life, and rendered visible, n. 1869, 3310, 5510. How they appear, n. 6201, 8885. That the ideas of the angels of the inmost heaven appear like flaming lights, n. 6615. That the ideas of the angels of the lowest heaven appear as small, thin, white clouds, n. 6614. The idea of an angel as seen, from which streamed a ray of light towards the Lord, n. 6620. That the ideas of the thoughts extend themselves wide to the circumjacent societies of angels, n. 6598 to 6613.

sound

found to the words according to the various affections of every one's state; therefore it is, that in the Hebrew language the vowels are not written, and also are differently pronounced; and from the difference in founding the vowels, the angels can diftinguifh the particular affection and love of the fpeaker. The fpeech of the cœleſtial angels is without hard confonants, and they feldom utter two words together, where the former ends and the latter begins with a confonant, but interpofe a third beginning with a vowel; whence it comes to pafs, that the little word *and* is fo often met with in the Hebrew Bible, as that word in the Hebrew language has a foft found, and both begins and ends with a vowel: by the Scripture words alfo in that language may partly be known, whether they belong to the cœleſtial or fpiritual clafs, and fo relate to *Good* or to *Truth*, the former founding mostly from U and O, and partly from A, and the latter from E and I: and as the affections principally diftinguifh themfelves by founds, therefore in the human language, when any thing of an exalted nature is the fubject, as *Heaven* and *God*, we give the preference to fuch words, whereby to exprefs them, as have U or O in them: and alfo, when we would exprefs any thing fublime in mufick, we naturally fwell thofe notes which come neareft to the found of thofe vowels, but not fo, when things of an inferior nature are the fubject. Hence it is, that the art of mufick is fo aptly fuited to exprefs the affections and paffions of the human mind.

242. In the fpeech and converfation of the angels there is an expreffible kind of harmony (174) arifing from this caufe, viz. That their affections and thinking, from which they fpeak, are according to the laws and form of heaven, which are the bond of their union and communications. That the angels are confociated according to the form of heaven, and that their thoughts and affections are regulated thereby, fee n. 200 to 212.

243. There is an innate language in man, fimilar to that in the fpiritual world, but in his interior intellectual part; but as it does not manifeft itfelf in man in words analogous to the affection, as it does in the angels, therefore he knows not that

---

(174) That the fpeech of angels refembles the flowing harmony in a tune or concert, n. 1648, 1649, 7191.

it is in him; yet from hence it is, that when he enters into the other life, his language is the same with that of the spirits and angels there, without any occasion of learning it (175). But more on this subject hereafter.

244. They have all one and the same language in heaven, as was said before, though with this difference, that the speech of the angels, who are most eminent for wisdom, is more inward, and abounds with greater variety in the affections, and also in the ideas, than that of the inferior angels; and as to such of them as are more in simplicity, their conversation is still more exterior and in words, to be understood after the manner of men: there is also a kind of conversing by the face, terminating in sound, which is modified by the ideas: there is also a kind of conversing together, wherein representations of heavenly things are mixed with their ideas, and the latter exhibit themselves in visible forms: there is another by gestures corresponding to affections, and representative of things in like manner as words are: there is, moreover, among them, a manner of conversing by general affections and general thoughts; and also a rumbling way of speaking like the rolling of thunder: and others besides.

245. The language and speech of the bad and infernal spirits is likewise natural to them, as proceeding from their affections also, but such affections as are evil, and from such impure ideas as originate from those affections, and which the angels are highly averse to, so great is the contrariety between infernal and heavenly things, insomuch that they cannot endure one another; the speech of the infernals being as a stink in the nostrils of the angels. The language of those hypocrites, who are used to counterfeit angels of light, in words resembles that of the angels, but with respect to the affections and ideas that are concealed under it, it is quite contrary thereto; and therefore,

(175) That there is a spiritual or angelical speech belonging to man, though he knows it not, n. 4914. That the ideas of the inward man are spiritual, but that in this life he perceives them naturally, forasmuch as his thoughts here have their exercise in his natural part, or man, n. 10236, 10240, 10550. That man after death enters into his interior ideas, n. 3226, 3342, 3343, 10568, 10604. That then his ideas form themselves into his proper spiritual language, n. 2470, 2478, 2479.

when their interiour is difcovered, as it is by the wifer angels, the found of their voice feems like the gnafhing of teeth, exciting horror.

Of the Converfation of the Angels with Men.

246. When angels converfe with any man, they do not fpeak their own language, but that of the man, or any other that he is acquainted with, but never in an unknown tongue; and that becaufe the angels at fuch times turn and join themfelves to him, and from fuch conjunction they both come to be in a like mode of thinking; and as man's thinking coheres with his memory, and his fpeaking proceeds from both, therefore they are both in one language: befides, an angel, or fpirit, when he comes to any man, and fronts him fo as to be joined to him, he enters into the whole of his memory fo far as that, in a manner, it becomes his own, infomuch that he can hardly difcern between the man's knowledge and his own, and the fame with regard to his language. I have converfed with the angels on this fubject, and told them, that perhaps they might imagine, according to appearance, that they fpake with me in my own native language, whereas it was not they, but I who fpake it; and that this might be evidenced, in that angels were not able to utter a fingle word of any human language, fee n. 237, for that being natural, and they fpiritual, they could not poffibly effect that which was of a nature different from themfelves: to which they replied, that they well knew that their communion with any man they converfed with was with his fpiritual thinking part, but as this paffed by influx into his natural thoughts, and thefe cohered with his memory; it muft therefore appear to them as if his human language and fcience were theirs, and that this was by divine appointment, to the end that fuch union and communion between heaven and man might be effected; but that the condition of the human nature was at this time fo altered, that fuch communion between man

and angels could no longer take place, but only between him and other ſpirits. I have alſo converſed with ſpirits on the ſame ſubject, who would not be convinced, that it was man that ſpake, not they in him; nor yet that the knowledge in the mind of man (during their communion with him) was not their own: I endeavoured to prove the contrary to them by many arguments, but all to no purpoſe. Who are meant by ſpirits, and who by angels, ſhall be ſhewed when we come to treat of the world of ſpirits.

247. That angels and ſpirits are ſo cloſely united to man, that they miſtake what belongs to him for their own, is becauſe the ſpiritual and natural worlds are ſo nearly connected in man, that they in a manner make but one: now as man had ſeparated himſelf from heaven, proviſion was made in mercy by the Lord, that there ſhould be angels and ſpirits with every man, that he ſhould be governed by him through their miniſtry, for which reaſon there is ſo ſtrict a communion between them: but had man not cut off the communication between himſelf and heaven, the matter had been otherwiſe, as in that caſe he might have been directed and governed by the Lord through a general influx from heaven, without the adjunction and inſtrumentality of ſpirits and angels: but more particularly of this when we come to treat of the conjunction of heaven with man.

248. When an angel or ſpirit converſes with a man, he is heard as plainly as one man is by another, but by himſelf only, and not by any of the by-ſtanders: and the reaſon is, becauſe the ſpeech of the angel or ſpirit firſt inſinuates itſelf into the thinking faculty of a man, and ſo by a ſecret paſſage ſtrikes his organ of hearing from within; whereas the voice of one man talking with another paſſes into the atmoſphere, and ſtrikes the organ of hearing from without; hence it comes to paſs, that the ſpeaking of the former is equally audible in many, as the organ is affected in like manner, though it be by impulſe from within: and that the ſpeaking of an angel or ſpirit has this operation on the ear, was evidenced to me by its having a like effect on the tongue, by its influx on that member, in which it cauſed ſome gentle vibrations, though not the ſame ſenſible motions, as when we therewith articulate our words.

249. To

249. To hold converse with spirits is rarely permitted at this day, as being dangerous (176), for in such cases the spirits are given to know that they are in company with a man, which they would not know otherwise; and so great is the malignity of evil spirits, that they bear a mortal hatred to man, and wish for nothing more than to injure him in soul and body, in which they too well succeed with those who abandon themselves to melancholy phantasies and rigorous mortifications: some also, who lead solitary lives, hear spirits talking to them, and that without any danger, such spirits being removed from them at proper intervals by divine appointment, that they may not know that they are in company with men; for the greater part of spirits have no knowledge of any other world but their own, nor consequently of men; and therefore no one ought to enter into converse with them, and thereby give them light in this matter. They who so addict themselves to musing on religious things, as to work their minds into superstitious reveries concerning them, come in time to hear spirits talking to them; for such religious reveries, where any one wilfully gives himself up to them [*illis ex inhæret*] to the neglect of relative duties and usefulness in his station, enter deep, and gain a form in the interior part of man, and so taking full possession of him, communicate with the spiritual world, and excite certain spirits there to associate with him: such are properly visionaries and enthusiasts, who believe every spirit they hear to be the Holy Spirit, whereas they are no other than enthusiastick spirits, who, being under delusion themselves, delude those whom they have access to and influence over; but these also are generally removed upon their instigating to evil. The enthusiastick spirits are distinguished from others by their imagining themselves to be the Holy Ghost, and what they deliver to be divinely oracular: these spirits offer no injury to the persons they are asso-

---

(176) That a man is capable of conversing with spirits and angels, and that the ancients frequently conversed with them, n. 67, 68, 69, 784, 1634, 1636, 7802. That in some worlds spirits and angels appear in a human form, and converse with the inhabitants therein, n. 10751, 10752; but that in our world it would be dangerous at this time to have communication with spirits, unless a man were in true faith, and under the guidance and defence of the Lord, n. 784, 9438, 10751.

ciated

ciated with, because they receive divine honour from them: with these also I have sometimes conversed, and so have had opportunity of detecting the delusions which they instill into their votaries: their situation is to the left hand in a desart region.

250. To converse with angels is granted to none but those who are in truths from the source of good, and in particular to such as are in the faith of the Lord, and of the divinity as in his humanity, for on this truth the heavens are founded, the Lord being the God of heaven, as was said before, n. 2 to 6. The divinity of the Lord constitutes heaven, n. 7 to 12. The divine influx from the Lord in the angels is love to him, and charity to their neighbour, n. 13 to 19. The universal heaven in its complex resembles a man; in like manner every society in heaven, and every angel in particular, is in a perfect human form, and this from the Divine Humanity of the Lord, n. 59 to 86; whence we may gather why to converse with angels is only granted to those whose interiour is open to the Lord, through the influence of divine truths, as it is through these that the Lord communicates with man, and if the Lord, so heaven. That divine truth opens the interiour of man, so as to render it receptive of heavenly communications, is because man is so created, as to be the image of heaven, as to his inward man, and the image of this world, as to his outward man, n. 57: and the inward man is only opened by divine truth proceeding from the Lord, as this is both the light and life of heaven, n. 126 to 140.

251. Divine influx passes from the Lord to man through the forehead, and so into his whole face; for the forehead of a man corresponds to love, and the face to the interiour of his mind (177). The influx from the spiritual angels to man is all round from his forehead and temples to every part under which lies the brain, as that region of the head corresponds to intel-

---

(177) That the forehead corresponds to heavenly love, and accordingly signifies it in Scripture, n. 9936. That the face corresponds to the interior things of thought and affection in man, n. 1568, 2988, 2989—5695, 9306. That the face also is formed in correspondency with the interiour of man, n. 4791 to 4805, 5695. That hence the face in Scripture signifies the inward man, n. 1999, 2434, 3527, 4066, 4796.

lect: but the influx of the cœleſtial angels is on that part of the head which covers the cerebellum, and is called the occiput, or back part of the head round from the ears to the neck, for that region correſponds to wiſdom: when angels converſe with man, their ſpeech enters by theſe ways into his thoughts; hereby I could perceive who the angels were that ſpake with me.

252. They who ſee and converſe with the angels, behold alſo the things that are in heaven, for they ſee by that heavenly light which illuminates their interiour; the angels alſo through them behold the things on earth (178); becauſe through their union heaven and earth are conjoined, for, as was ſaid above, n. 246, when the angels turn themſelves to the front of a man, they are, as it were, ſo united to him, that they cannot diſtinguiſh between the things of a man and their own, and this not only with reſpect to ſpeaking, but alſo to ſeeing and hearing; and man, on the other hand, is apt to think that what he receives from the angels by influx is from himſelf. In this kind of union with the angels of heaven were the moſt ancient of our race on earth, and therefore the times in which they lived were called the Golden Age; and becauſe the Divine Nature under a human form, and conſequently the Lord, therefore they had the privilege of converſing with angels, as with their familiar friends, and the angels converſed with them in like manner, and ſo heaven and this world became in them as one. But man ſince that time cut himſelf off ſucceſſively more and more from theſe heavenly communications, by transferring his affections from the Lord and from heaven, to himſelf and the world, and ſo brought himſelf to reliſh no other delights, but what proceeded from the love of ſelf and of the world, upon which his internal faculties, before open to heaven, became ſhut, and his external faculties wide open to the world; and where this is the caſe, man is in light with regard to the things of this world, and in darkneſs with regard to the things of heaven.

(178) That ſpirits can ſee nothing in this ſolar world through man now o'days, but that they have ſeen things therein through my eyes, together with the reaſon of this difference, n. 1880.

253. Since

253. Since thofe times it has rarely happened for any one to fpeak with the angels of heaven, though fome have with fpirits that are not in heaven; for the interior and exterior parts in man are fo conftituted, that they are either turned to the Lord as their common center, n. 124, or to felf, and fo reverfely from the Lord: in the former cafe, they are turned towards heaven; in the latter, towards the world; and where they have this latter direction, it is difficult to elevate them to things above; yet, as far as fuch elevation is poffible, it is effected by the Lord through the converfion of their love, which is wrought by the inftrumentality of truths from the Word.

254. I have received information in what manner the Lord fpake to the prophets, through whom the Word was revealed, and that it was not by influx into their interiour, according to the manner of his communication with the antients, but by emiffary fpirits, whom the Lord filled with his afpect, and fo infpired the words which they dictated to the prophets; and therefore the revelation was not by influx, but by dictation; and as the words came immediately from the Lord, therefore they were replete with divine truth, and contain an inward meaning, fo that the fame words which men underftand in a natural fenfe, the angels receive in a cœleftial and fpiritual fenfe; fo hath the Lord joined together heaven and this world by the Word. It has alfo been fhewed to me how fpirits are filled with divine truth from the Lord by afpect: the fpirit that is fo filled knows no other than that he himfelf is the Lord, and the fountain of what he utters, till he has finifhed his meffage, and then he perceives and owns that he is only a fpirit, and that he fpake not from himfelf, but from the Lord. From this being the ftate of the fpirits that fpake with the prophets, it is faid by them, that Jehovah [the Lord] fpake; and even thofe very fpirits called themfelves Jehovah, as appears both from the prophetical and hiftorical parts of the Scriptures.

255. That the reader may be informed as to the manner of the union of angels and fpirits with man, I find myfelf at liberty to declare the following remarkable particulars, for the elucidation of that matter. When angels and fpirits turn their faces to a man, fo as to be in communion with him, at fuch times

times they know no other than that they and the man are of one and the same language, and this, because they are then in his, and not in their own, of which they have no remembrance; but as soon as they turn themselves from him, they immediately enter again into their own angelical, spiritual language, and know nothing of his. The same thing happened to me when in company with some angels, at a time when I was in a similar state with them, for then I conversed with them in their own language, having no knowledge or remembrance of mine; but I was no sooner disengaged from their company, than I was in my own again. It is also worthy of remarking, that when angels or spirits turn their faces to a man, they can converse with him at any distance; and have spoken with me as audibly when far off, as when near to me; but when they turn away their faces from a man, and converse together by themselves, the man hears nothing that they say, though they speak close to his ear; whence it was evident to me, that all communion [*omnis conjunctio*] in the spiritual world, is according to the direction of the face. It is also a memorable particular, that several of them can converse with a man at the same time, and the man with them: the manner is thus: When they would hold conversation with any man, they send a spirit to him from their company, which emissary spirit turns to the man, and they to their spirit, by which means they concentrate their thoughts, which the emissary delivers, he not knowing at the time but that he utters them from himself, nor they that sent him, but that they are the speakers: thus a communication of many with one is conducted by conversion or direction of the faces (179). But of these emissary spirits, which are also called subjects, more shall be spoken hereafter.

256. No angel or spirit is allowed to converse with man from his own memory, but from that of the man only, for angels and spirits have memory as well as men: if an angel or

---

(179) That the spirits which are sent by one society to another, are called Subjects, n. 4403, 5856. That communications in the spiritual world are conducted by such emissary spirits, n. 4403, 5856, 5983. That a spirit sent on these occasions, is a mere subject, and does not think from himself, but from them that send him, n. 5985, 5986, 5987.

spirit were from his own memory to converse with any man, the latter would in that case know no other than that the things mentioned were his own, though they really were the spirit's, and consequently it would be like the remembrance of what he never saw nor heard of; and that this is so has been given me to know by experience: hence some of the ancients were of opinion, that at the expiration of some thousands of years, they should return to their former life on earth, and live over again all the particulars of it; and that they had actually so returned; and this they inferred from hence, viz. that sometimes there occurred to their minds a recollection of things which they had never seen nor heard of during their present life: now this happened to them, because some spirits had, by influx into their minds, excited therein ideas from their own (the spirit's) memory.

257. There are also some spirits, which are called natural and corporeal spirits, which, when they come to a man, do not join themselves to his thinking part, like other spirits, but enter into his body, take possession of his senses, and speak through his mouth, actuating likewise his corporeal members, not knowing any other at the time, than that all things in the man are their own: these are the spirits that obsess (*) a man: but these spirits are remanded to hell by divine appointment, and so entirely removed from us; and therefore it is, that such obsessions are no longer known amongst us (180).

(*) Where the body only is under the influence and power of evil spirits, it is called *Obsession*; where the mind and affections, *Possession*.

(180) That external obsessions of the body are not now permitted as formerly, n. 1983: but that internal obsessions [possessions] of the mind are more common than formerly, n. 1983, 4793. That any one is inwardly possessed, when he entertains impure and dishonourable thoughts of God, and is only restrained from making them known, by outward considerations, as fear of the law, the loss of honour, gain, and the like, n. 5990. Of those diabolical spirits which possess the minds and affections [*interiora*] of men, n. 4793. Of such diabolical spirits as have a longing to possess the bodies [*exteriora*] of men, but are now confined to their proper hells, n. 2752, 5990.

Of

Of Writings in Heaven.

258. As speech is a property belonging to angels, and as their speech consists of words, so also have they writing among them, whereby they express their thoughts, as well as by words: sometimes I have had sent to me papers accurately written, exactly resembling our manuscripts, and some appeared as if printed; I was able to read them, but could seldom pick out any meaning from them, as it is not according to the divine order that man should receive instruction from heaven by any other writings than the sacred Scriptures, as these are the instituted means of communication between heaven and earth, and therefore between the Lord and man. That the prophets saw writings in heaven, appears from Ezekiel ii. 9, 10. "And when I looked, behold, an hand was sent unto me; and lo a roll of a book was therein; and he spread it before me; and it was written within and without: and there was written lamentations, and mourning, and woe." As also from John, Apoc. v. 1. "And I saw in the right hand of him that sat on the throne a book written within, and on the back side, sealed with seven seals."

259. It is appointed of the Lord, that there should be writings in heaven, for the sake of the Word, as this is, in its essence, that divine truth from which both men and angels receive cœlestial wisdom, as being dictated by the Lord; and what is dictated by him, passes successively through all the heavens, and terminates in man, and therefore is accommodated to the wisdom of angels, as well as to the understanding of men. Hence it is, that the Word [the Holy Scriptures] is committed to the angels, who read it as well as we, and therefrom deduce their doctrinals, and the subjects of their preaching, n. 221: the Word is the same to both; but the natural sense of it, which is to us the literal sense, is not known in heaven, but its spiritual or internal sense only; and what this is, may be seen in a little work concerning the *White Horse*, mentioned in the Revelations.

260. On a certain time a little paper was sent me from heaven, on which were written some words in Hebrew characters, and it was told me that every letter contained some secrets of wisdom, nay, the very flexures and curvatures of the letters, and the founding of them from thence; which gave me to understand the meaning of those words of the Lord: "Verily I say unto you, till heaven and earth pass, one jot or one tittle shall in no wise pass from the law," Matt. v. 18. Now that the Word is divine, as to every tittle of it, is allowed in the church; but in what sense it is thus divine in every apex and point, being at present unknown, it shall here be declared: The Scripture in the inmost heaven consists of various characters inflexed and circumflexed; all which inflexions and circumflexions are according to the form of heaven, and by them the angels express the secrets of their wisdom, and also many other things which they cannot utter by words; and, which is wonderful, the angels know how to write thus without study and instruction, it being in them from divine instinct, as well as their speech, see n. 236, which evidences that they write from cœlestial skill; and that it is thus natural to them is, because the progression of their thoughts and affections, and the whole communication of their understanding and wisdom, is regulated by the form and constitution of heaven by influx, n. 201, and so is their writing. I have been informed, that such also was the manner of writing by the most ancient inhabitants of our earth, before the invention of letters; and that it was afterwards translated into Hebrew characters, which were all inflexed formerly, and not terminated by spaces, as at present: hence it is, that the Word contains divine and heavenly secrets, even in its jots, tittles, and points.

261. This manner of writing in characters of a cœlestial form is used by the angels of the inmost heaven, who excel the others in wisdom, and by them they express the very affections from whence their thoughts originate, and proceed in order, according to the subject treated of, replete with wisdom not to be conceived by the human mind: these writings I myself have seen: but this kind of writing is not known in the lower heavens, but others of a similar kind, and of like letters with those

that

that are used by us in this world, though not intelligible by us, as being in the language of angels, which has nothing in it that agrees with human languages, n. 237; for they express affections by the vowels, and the particular ideas of their thoughts proceeding from those affections, by the consonants; and by the words derived from thence, the whole sense of the matter; see above, n. 236, 241: this kind of writing contains more in a few words than any man can express in some pages: these also I have been gratified with a sight of. Thus it appears, that they have the written Word in the lower heavens as well as in the highest heaven, though in the latter, in a cœlestial form.

262. It is worthy of remark, that writing by the angels flows naturally from their thoughts, and with the same ease, as if thought cast itself upon paper; nor do they experience any hesitation as to the choice of words, as both the words which they speak and write correspond to their thoughts; and all correspondency is natural and spontaneous. There is also in the heavens a kind of writing without the use of the hand, as being solely from correspondence with the thoughts; but this is not permanent.

263. I have also seen writings from heaven that consisted merely of numbers [figures] placed in order and sequence with the same regularity as letters and words, and was informed that they were from the inmost heaven; and that their cœlestial Scripture, of which see above, n. 260, 261, presents itself in numbers by influx to the angels of the next heaven, and also contains a depth of wisdom not to be fathomed by thought, nor consequently to be expressed by words; for all numbers are in correspondency, and according to their correspondence respectively, signify things equally with words (181), only with this difference, that numbers express things in the general, and

(181) That all numbers in the Word [the Scriptures] signify things, n. 482, 487, 647, 648, 755, 813—9659, 10217, 10253. This revealed from heaven, n. 4495, 5265. That multiplied numbers signify the same things [in substance] with the simple numbers whence they arise in multiplication, n. 5291, 5335, 5708, 7973. That the most ancient of the human race preserved their heavenly secrets in numbers, in manner like an Ecclesiastical Kalendar [*Computum Ecclesiasticum*] n. 575.

words

words in their particulars; and as one general includes in it numberless particulars, therefore this way of writing in numerals is far more comprehensive than the literal way of writing: hence it appeared evident to me, that numbers in the Holy Scriptures signify things as much as words. What is therein signified by the simple numbers, as 2, 3, 4, 5, 6, 7, 8, 9, 10, 11, 12; and what by the compounded ones, as 20, 30, 50, 70, 100, 144, 1000, 10000, 12000, and many others, may be seen in the *Arcana Cælestia*, in the places where they are mentioned. In the Scripture in heaven before-mentioned, the radical number from which the others proceed in sequence, and on which they depend as their principal, is prefixed to the following ones, and is, as it were, the index of the subject treated on, and from which the rest receive their determinate signification with regard to the particulars of that subject.

264. They who know nothing of heavenly things, and reject every other idea of heaven than that of its being a mere atmosphere, in which the angels hover about as in the air, like so many intellectual minds, or thinking spirits, but without any sense of sight or hearing; such can have no notion of their being able to speak or write, inasmuch as they confine these and numberless other acts to material substances; whereas the things in heaven [though not material] have really as substantial an existence as the natural things of this world; and the angels have there all things as means conducive to life, increase of wisdom, and happiness.

Concerning the Wisdom of the Angels of Heaven.

265. It is very difficult to form any moderate conception of the wisdom of the heavenly angels, as it so far transcends all human wisdom, as not to admit of any comparison with it; now what exceeds the reach of the latter must appear as nothing to it: however, it may be described by some things, which, though at present unknown to us, yet are knowable, if the
mind

mind takes delight therein; for delight, as proceeding from love, carries light with it; and on such as are affectionately disposed to become acquainted with divine and heavenly wisdom, light shines from heaven, and illuminates their understanding.

266. The greatness of the angelical wisdom may be gathered from their being in the light of heaven: now the light of heaven is, in its essence, the same with divine truth or wisdom; and this light enlightens the eyes of their understanding, as well as gives them external sight: that the light of heaven is divine truth or wisdom, see above, n. 126 to 133. The angels also are in the heat of heaven, which is, in its essence, divine good or divine love, from which they derive their affectionate desire of wisdom: that the heat of heaven is, in its essence, divine good or divine love, see above, n. 133 to 140: that the angels are so highly advanced in wisdom, that they may even be called Wisdoms, may be gathered from hence, that all their thoughts and affections are congruous to the form and constitution of heaven, which is the form and display of the divine wisdom, and that their interiour, which is the recipient of it, is according thereto: that their thoughts and affections flow in such direction, and consequently their understanding and wisdom, see above, n. 201 to 212: that the wisdom of the angels is highly eminent, may also appear from this, that their speech or conversation is the language of wisdom, for it flows immediately and spontaneously from their thoughts, as these do from their affections, insomuch that it may be said, that their speech is thought and affection in an external form: hence it comes, that nothing interrupts or disturbs the divine influx into them, nor any of those foreign things or thoughts which in man so often break in upon and clash with his communications: that the language of angels is the language of their thoughts and affections, see n. 234 to 245. To this wisdom of the angels also conspires not a little, that all which they see with their eyes, and perceive by their senses, is congruous to their wisdom, as being correspondences, and accordingly so many representative forms of things appertaining or relating to wisdom: that all things visible in heaven correspond to things internal in the angels, and are representatives of their wisdom, see above, n.

170 to 182. Moreover, the thoughts of angels are not limited and straitened by ideas from space and time, as the human thoughts are; for space and time are peculiar to nature, and what is peculiar to nature withdraws the mind from spiritual things, and fetters the understanding: that the ideas of angels have no relation to space and time, and are therefore less confined than ours, see above n. 162 to 169, and 191 to 199. The thoughts of angels are neither drawn down to earthly and material things, nor interrupted by any cares or necessities of life, and therefore are not detained from the sweet relish of wisdom after the manner of men; their food, their raiment, their habitations, and all things being freely given them of the Lord, n. 181, 190: and they have also many pleasures and delights bestowed on them in proportion to their reception of wisdom from the Lord. Thus much has been said, to shew from what causes the angels are so eminent for their wisdom (182).

267. That the angels are in a capacity of receiving so high a measure of wisdom is, because their interior faculties are open, and wisdom, like every other perfection, has its increase inward, according to the opening of the interiour (183). There are three degrees of life corresponding to the three heavens in every angel, see n. 29 to 40: they in whom the first degree is open, are in the first or lowest heaven; they in whom the second degree is open, are in the second or middle heaven; and they in whom the third degree is opened, are in the third or inmost heaven; and in proportion to these degrees is the wisdom of the angels in the heavens: hence it is, that the wisdom of the angels of the third or inmost heaven immensely transcends that of the

---

(182) That the wisdom of angels is both ineffable and incomprehensible, n. 2795, 2796, 2802—9094, 9176.

(183) That as far as man is elevated from external to internal things, so far he enters into light and true understanding, n. 6183, 6313. That this is a real elevation, n. 7816, 10330. That elevation from externals to internals, is, as it were, from a mist into a clear day, n. 4598. That what is external in man is proportionably remote from what is divine, and by consequence respectively obscure, n. 6451; and also respectively inordinate, n. 996, 3855. That interior things are more perfect, as being nearer to what is divine, n. 5146, 5147. That in the interiour are thousands of particulars, which in the exteriour appear only in the light of one general truth or subject [ut commune unum] n. 5707: and therefore the more inward the thought and perception, the clearer it is, n. 5920.

angels

angels of the middle heaven; and the wisdom of these, that of the angels of the lowest heaven, see above, n. 209, 210; and what these degrees are, n. 38. The reason of these differences is, because those things which are of a superior degree are more particular and distinct; and those of an inferior degree, of a general and common predicament, in which precision and distinction lie concealed; now the former are to the latter as thousands or myriads to one, and in such proportion is the wisdom of the superior to that of the inferior angels respectively (*); and yet the wisdom of the latter exceeds human wisdom in as high a proportion; for man in his present condition being chained to a natural body and its senses, and as what is corporeal and sensual is lowest in degree, it is evident what sort of wisdom theirs must be, who think only from sense, and therefore are properly denominated sensual men; but indeed it cannot be called wisdom, for it is nothing more than science at best (184): but it is otherwise with those who have their thoughts

(*) This distinction of our author may be illustrated by the following instance in historical knowledge, thus: To know only so much of the history of this our island, before the conquest of it by Will. I. as that in the time of the ancient Britons it was conquered by Julius Cæsar, became subject to the power of the Romans, and afterwards passed successively into the possession of the Saxons, Danes, and Normans: to know the times when these revolutions happened, together with the names of its several kings, and the most remarkable battles and events of their reigns: such a general and common knowledge of the English history falls within the compass of a low capacity: but to enter minutely into the particular genius and character of those several nations respectively; their manners, customs, laws, tenures, forms of government, and various connections; their state of religion, learning, and traffick; the rise and progress, or decay of arts and sciences in these several periods; the distinguishing characters of their princes, statesmen, and men of eminence in all professions, together with their maxims and rules of policy in conducting matters both ecclesiastical and civil; and to trace back important changes and events from remote beginnings, and causes seemingly of little consequence, making judicious observations and reflections on the whole: these, and a thousand other particulars respecting legislation, government, and publick weal, constitute the province of a sage historian, and shew us, by comparison and in miniature, the distinction of our author between the wisdom of the superior, and that of the inferior angels, under the two predicaments of general and particular wisdom. Tr.

(184) That the sensual part of man is his lowest degree of life, as properly belonging to and inherent in his earthly, corporeal frame, n. 5077, 5767, 9212, 9216, 9331, 9730. That this is called the sensual man, who judges and draws conclusions of things by his bodily senses, and believes nothing but what he can

thoughts elevated above matter and sense; and still more so with such as have their minds open to the heavenly light.

268. We may also form an idea of the exalted wisdom of angels from their mutual communication of all things without reserve, insomuch that the understanding and wisdom of one is communicated to another; for heaven is a communion of goods of every kind, it being of the nature of heavenly love to impart of its own to others, and accordingly no one there considers any thing he has as good, unless others partake of it: this principle of love constitutes the essential happiness of heaven, and is derived to the angels from the Lord, whose divine love is infinitely communicative. It has been granted me to have an experimental knowledge of such communication in the heavens from being present with some spirits of great simplicity, which, upon their exaltation thither, were illuminated with angelical wisdom, and understood and spake things which were inconceivable and ineffable by them before.

269. The wisdom of the angels is not to be described in words, but may in a sort be conceived by some general instances; thus, the angels can express more in one word than a man can in a thousand; and moreover, every word of theirs is replete with numberless senses not to be expressed in human language, and containing secrets of wisdom beyond the reach of our faculties; and farther, where words fail to utter the copiousness of their meaning, the angels supply that defect in the sound of them, which expresses the affections therein; for, as was said before, n. 236, 241, they express their affections by sounds, as they do their ideas and thoughts by words; whence it is said,

see with his eyes, and feel with his hands, n. 5094, 7693. That such a one thinks as a mere animal [*in externis*], and not in his spiritual part [*interius in se*], n. 5089, 5094, 6564, 7693. That the interior faculties of such a one are shut, so that he is incapable of discerning spiritual truth, n. 6564, 6844, 6845. That such a one is in the dimness of mere nature, and so perceives nothing by the light of heaven, n. 6201, 6310, 6564, 6844, 6845, 6598, 6612, 6614, 6622, 6624. That, inwardly, he is in opposition to things that are heavenly, and such as be of the church of God, n. 6201, 6316, 6844, 6845, 6948, 6949. That sensual men are crafty and malicious above others, n. 7693, 10236. That they are acute and subtle in reasoning, but so only from their natural faculties and memory, in which lies all the strength of their understanding, n. 195, 196, 5700, 10236; and that this is from the fallacy of their senses, n. 5084, 6948, 6949, 7693.

that

that in heaven are heard things that cannot be uttered. The angels also can express in a few words the contents of a whole volume, and likewise insinuate into every word a power of raising the subject to a more interior sense; for their language is so constructed, as to be consonant to the affections, at the same time that the words communicate the ideas of the speaker; and what is still more extraordinary, their words admit of infinite variations, whereby to express in exact order and sequence all the combinations and connexion of parts that form the most complicated subjects. The more interior angels can discover by the sound, and certain words of him that speaks, the whole course of his life, perceiving by the variegations in the voice, occasioned by the ideas in his mind, what is his ruling passion, as herein are recorded, as in a register, all the particulars of his life (185). Hence we may form some idea of the superior excellence of the wisdom of the angels, it being respectively to man's wisdom as a myriad (ten thousand) to one, and comparatively as all the moving instruments and powers in the body, which are innumerable, to the act produced by them, which appears to our senses; or like the thousand minute parts of an object, when examined by a good microscope, which, when viewed by the naked eye, appears but as an atom. To illustrate this by example: A certain angel, in describing the work of regeneration from the high wisdom he possessed, discovered a hundred secret things in the chain of his discourse on the subject, every one of which abounded with still more mysterious secrets, and so on from the beginning to the end of his exposition; shewing how the spiritual man is conceived anew, passes, as it were, through a kind of gestation, is born, grows up, and

(185) That the prevailing or ruling passion in man influences all the particulars of his life, and all and singular his thoughts and affections, n. 4459, 5949, 6159, 6571, 7648, 8067, 8853 to 8858. That as is the prevailing love, such is the man, n. 918, 1040, 8858. This illustrated by examples, n. 8854, 8857. That the passion which has dominion over a man, forms the life of his spirit, n. 7648. That it constitutes his will, his love, and the direction of his whole life; and this, because that which he chuses and wills, that he loves, and what he loves most, to that tend all his pursuits, n. 1317, 1568, 1571, 1909, 3796, 5949, 6936. That therefore, as the will, or the ruling love, or the proposed end of living is, such is the man, n. 1568, 1571, 3570—10109, 10110, 10284.

is succeſſively perfected: he alſo ſaid, that he could ſwell the number of myſterious diſcoveries on this ſubject to ſome thouſands; and that what he had delivered thereupon concerned the regeneration of the outward man only; and that unſpeakably more belonged to the regeneration of the inward man. Theſe and other like things told me by the angels evinced the ſublimity of their wiſdom, and how that of man may be ſtiled ignorance, if compared to it; as he ſcarcely knows what regeneration means, and ſees not any one ſtep he takes in his progreſs through it.

270. We ſhall now ſpeak of the wiſdom of the angels of the third or inmoſt heaven, and how far this exceeds that of the angels of the firſt or loweſt heaven: now the wiſdom of the former is incomprehenſible by the latter, and that becauſe the interior faculties of the former are open in the third or higheſt degree, and thoſe of the latter only in the firſt or loweſt degree: now all wiſdom increaſes in proportion to its progreſs inward, and is perfected according to the opening of the interiour, n. 208, 267; and as the interiour of the angels of the third heaven is open in the third degree, therefore divine truths are moſt intimately written in their hearts, this degree being more near to the form of heaven than thoſe of the inferior angels, and becauſe the form or conſtitution of heaven is from divine truth, and therefore according to divine wiſdom, therefore divine truths appear to the higheſt angels as innate or congenial to them, and therefore as ſoon as they are propoſed, they immediately aſſent to and own them, and preſently after perceive, and, as it were, read them in themſelves. Such being the ſtate of the angels of the inmoſt heaven, they have no need to reaſon concerning divine truths, much leſs have they controverſies about any truth, to know whether it be a truth or not; nor do they underſtand what it is to believe, or have faith in this or that thing, ſaying, What is faith, when I perceive and know the matter to be ſo? uſing moreover the following compariſons, viz. That it would be as abſurd in them to talk of believing, as if any one were to view a houſe, and all things in and about it, and were to ſay to one in company with him, that he muſt needs believe that to be a houſe with ſuch and ſuch furniture:

or

or as if any one saw a garden with its trees and fruit, and were to tell his companion, that he could not but believe that to be a garden with trees and fruit in it, whilst at the same time his own eyes beheld them. Hence it is, that the angels beforementioned never name the word faith, nor have any idea of it, and consequently never reason nor dispute about the reality of any divine truth (186): but the angels of the first or lowest heaven have not divine truths so implanted within them, as having only their first degree of life open; and therefore they reason concerning them: now they who reason on any subject speculate it, as it were, without themselves, and go no farther, using arguments only for confirmation, and when they have confirmed the matter to others, they require their belief in it. I have discoursed with the angels on this subject, who told me, that there was as great a difference between the wisdom of the angels of the third, and that of the angels of the lowest heaven, as between the twilight and noon day; and compared that of the former to a magnificent palace richly furnished with all things for use, and surrounded with spacious gardens splendidly ornamented, into which the angels of wisdom enter, and enjoy the variegated delights of the whole in their full extent: but that it is very different with those that are in reasonings, and more especially if in controversies concerning truths; for such persons not seeing them in the light of truth, but either receiving them from others, or from the literal sense of the Scriptures without the spiritual-understanding of them, they cry out, You must believe or have faith, without allowing any farther demonstration, or inward manifestation of them: as touching

(186) That the cœlestial angels (*) very far excel the spiritual angels in knowledge and wisdom, n. 2718. That the former do not think and speak of faith like the latter, as having received of the Lord to be in the clear perception of all things pertaining to faith, n. 202, 597, 607—9277, 10336. That they only affirm or deny with regard to the truths of faith; whereas the spiritual angels reason much whether these things be so or not, n. 2715, 3246, 4448, 9166, 10786; where an explanation is given of those words of our Lord: " Let your commu- " nication be, yea, yea; nay, nay;" Matt. v. 37.

(*) It is judged proper to remind the reader under the above note, that the author distinguishes the angels of the third or highest heaven by the addition of *cælestial*, and those of the middle heaven by that of *spiritual*.

these,

these, they said, that they come not even up to the gate of the palace of wisdom, much less enter in, and walk in its paradisiacal gardens; whilst they who are in the very truths themselves, not only do this, but also make free excursions into wisdom's wide domains, passing by sight from truth to truth, the extent and connexions whereof know no bounds. They said farther, that the wisdom of the angels of the third or inmost heaven, more especially consisted in their beholding divine and cœlestial things in every particular object, and still more wonderful things in an assemblage of many; for all that they see with their eyes correspond to interior things; thus for example, when they view palaces and gardens, their view does not terminate in the objects themselves, but extends to the contemplation of their causes and correspondences, and that in all the variety represented by the different forms and appearances of the corresponding visible objects, besides innumerable things answering to their order, series, and connexions respectively, which delight even to extacy their intellectual faculties. That all visible things in the heavens correspond to divine things derived from the Lord to the holy angels, see before, n. 170 to 176.

271. That the angels of the third heaven are thus constituted, is from their being in the element of love to the Lord, and this love opens the interior faculties of their minds to the third degree, which renders it the receptacle of all things appertaining to wisdom; and we are moreover to understand, that the angels of this heaven are continually advancing to still higher degrees in wisdom, and this in a different manner from the angels of the lowest heaven, as not committing divine truths to their memory, and so forming them into a science; but, from a clear perception of them as soon as offered, ingrafting them into their very life, whereby they become a principle, and written, as it were, upon their hearts: but the case is otherwise with the angels of the lowest heaven; for they first commit them to memory, and then digest them scientifically, calling them forth occasionally for their intellectual improvement, but without an interior perception of their truth, so that they see them but obscurely in comparison with the former angels; however, they constantly use them for the direction of the will,

and

and the government of life. It is worthy of being noticed here, that the angels of the third heaven advance in wifdom by hearing, and not by fight; for what they hear from preaching enters not into the memory, but immediately into their perception and will, and fo into the form of their life: but what the other angels behold with their eyes, they commit to their memory, and reafon and difcourfe therefrom; whence it plainly appears, that their way of increafing wifdom is by hearing, and that by correfpondence, for the ear correfponds to obedience, and obedience relates to life; but the eye correfponds to the intellect, and intellect relates to doctrine (187). The ftate of the cœleftial angels is defcribed in many places of the Scriptures, and particularly by Jeremiah, as follows: " I will put " my law in their inward parts, and write it in their hearts: " and they fhall teach no more every man his neighbour, and " every man his brother, faying, Know the Lord; for they " fhall all know me, from the leaft of them unto the greateft " of them," xxxi. 33, 34. And in Matt. v. 37. " Let your " communication be, yea, yea; nay, nay; for whatfoever is " more than thefe cometh of evil." By *cometh of evil*, is meant comparatively and refpectively fo, as not coming from the Lord; for the truths poffeffed by the angels of the third heaven are from the Lord, as proceeding from love towards him. Love to the Lord in this heaven is to will and act from divine truth, for divine truth is effentially one with the Lord in heaven.

272. To the reafons already given in proof of the angels being receptive of fuch exalted wifdom, this farther one (which is of primary confideration in heaven) may be added, viz. That they are without felf-love; for fo far as any one is free from this, in fuch proportion he is capable of receiving wifdom in divine things; for that kind of love fhuts the inward eye and faculties to the Lord and heavenly things, whilft it opens thofe

---

(187) Of the correfpondence of the ear and of the hearing, n. 4652. That the ear correfponds both to perception and obedience, and therefore fignifies them, n. 2542, 3869, 4653, 5017, 7216, 8361, 9311, 9397, 10065. That it alfo fignifies the reception of truths, n. 5471, 5475, 9926. Of the correfpondence of the eye and its light, n. 4403 to 4421, 4523 to 4534; that therefore the eyes fignify the underftanding that cometh of faith, and alfo faith itfelf, n. 2701, 4410, 4526, 6923, 9951, 10569.

that are external, and gives them a direction to itself; and therefore all thofe, over whom this paſſion gains the dominion, are in darkneſs with regard to heavenly things, however quick-ſighted they may be in thoſe of this world: and on the other hand, the angels, as not being infected with it, are in the pure light of wiſdom; for the cœleſtial loves with which they are principled, viz. to the Lord, and to their neighbour, open their hearts to the divine influx, and ſo the Lord is in them. That theſe two loves conſtitute heaven as its common, eſſential principles, and alſo form a heaven in every one in particular, ſee above, n. 13 to 19. As theſe cœleſtial loves open the inward man to the Lord, ſo all the angels turn their faces towards him, n. 142; for in the ſpiritual world it is the divine principle of love that turns the heart of every one to itſelf, and whither it turns the heart, it alſo turns the face, for there the face acts in conſent with the heart, as its expreſſion: and as love, together with the object of it, turns both the heart and the face to itſelf, therefore it joins itſelf thereto (for it is the bond of ſpiritual union) and communicates of its own to them; and from this converſion, and conſequent conjunction and communication, the angels derive their wiſdom. That all conjunction or union (or fellowſhip) in the ſpiritual world, is according to this converſion or turning, may be ſeen above, n. 255.

273. The angels continually advance to higher degrees of perfection in wiſdom (188); and yet attain not in eternity to ſuch perfection therein, as bears any proportion to the divine wiſdom; for this is infinite, and theirs only finite, and between finite and infinite there is no proportion.

274. As wiſdom conſtitutes the perfection of angels, and alſo the very form of their life; and as heaven, with all the good things therein, communicates with every angel in proportion to his wiſdom, ſo all there deſire and hunger after it, even as a hungry man after his food; for knowledge, underſtanding, and wiſdom, are as truly ſpiritual nouriſhment, as earthly food is natural nouriſhment, and they alſo mutually correſpond.

(188) That the angels advance eternally in degrees of perfection, n. 4803, 6648.

275. The

275. The angels of the fame heaven, though of one and the fame fociety, differ in degrees of wifdom; they being in the higheft who are fituated in the center, and the reft in lower degrees of it, in proportion to their diftance from the center, decreafing gradually like light verging to fhade, fee above, n. 43, 128. They have alfo light in the fame degree; for the light of heaven and divine wifdom agree in one, and every one has fo much of the former as he receives of the latter. Concerning the light of heaven, and the various receptions of it, fee above, n. 126 to 132.

Of the State of Innocence in the Angels.

276. Few in this world have any tolerable notion concerning innocence, and they who are in the evil principle, none at all: they fee indeed fomething that carries in it the appearance, efpecially in the faces, language, and actions of little children; but yet they underftand not the true nature of it, much lefs that it is the receptacle of heaven in man: that the reader therefore may be the better inftructed in this matter, I fhall proceed in the following order to fhew, firft, what is the innocence of little children; then, what is the innocence of wifdom; and laftly, what is the ftate of angels with refpect to wifdom.

277. The innocence of infancy, or of little children, is not genuine innocence, as being only in their exterior, not interior form; and yet we may conceive fomething of innocence by what appears in their looks, in fome of their actions, and their prattle, which affects us the more, as they have no defign nor reflexion, know neither good nor evil, nor what is true or falfe, from whence reflexion proceeds; and confequently they have no prudence of their own, no deliberation, purpofe, nor ill intention: neither have they as yet attained to any notion of property from the love of felf and the world; but look on themfelves as obliged to their parents for all that is given them, with which they are pleafed and content, not being folicitous about food or raiment, or what may befall them, neither regarding
the

the world, nor the things of it, but confining their affections to their parents, nurses, and little companions, and shewing a ductile obedience to their governors: such being their state, all that they are capable of receiving enters into the form of their life, and constitutes (without their knowledge) the whole of their winning behaviour, and serves for the rudiments of their language, memory, and thinking, according to their state of innocence respectively: but yet this kind of innocence, as was said before, is only external, as being animal, and not mental (189), their minds being not yet formed; for mind consists of intellect and will, and as such only becomes the fountain of reflexion and true affection. I have been taught from heaven, that little children are in a particular manner under the Lord's care and protection, and that they are the subjects of an influx from the inmost heaven, which is the state of perfect innocence, which influx pervades their interiour, and operates in them by the effects of innocence, exhibiting appearances of it in their faces and certain of their actions, thereby exciting in their parents that natural affection, which we call by the name of Storge [στοργη].

278. But the innocence of wisdom is the true and genuine wisdom, as being internal in the mind, and consequently in the will and understanding; and where innocence is in these, there also is wisdom, for they are wisdom's dwelling; and therefore it is a common saying in heaven, that " Innocence " dwells in wisdom;" and that every angel has so much of the latter as he possesses of the former; and they confirm it by this argument, viz. because they who are in innocence assume nothing to themselves, but ascribe all they have to the goodness of the Lord as his free gift; that it is their desire to be led and governed by him, and not by themselves; that they love every thing that is good, and delight in all truth, inasmuch as

---

(189) That the innocence of infants is not the true innocence, but that the true innocence dwells in wisdom, n. 1616, 2305, 2306, 3495, 4563, 4797, 5608, 9301, 10021. That the good of childhood is not spiritual good, but becomes so by the sowing of truth into their minds, n. 3504; and that their good of relative innocence is the medium of effecting this, n. 1616, 3183, 9301, 10110. That man, without this good of innocence in childhood, would be a savage, n. 3494. That whatever the mind imbibes in childhood appears natural, n. 3494.

they

as they know and perceive, that to love good (that is, to will and do it) is to love the Lord; and to love truth is to love their neighbour; that they are content with what they have, be it little or much, as knowing that to all is given what is needful for them, little to those that need little, and much to them that need much, and that they know not what that fit measure is, but the Lord only, who possesses all things, and provideth all things for all; and therefore they are not solicitous about what shall befall them, calling this, the "taking thought "for the morrow," and being anxious about what does not belong to them, nor is needful for them. They never deal deceitfully by their fellows, but uprightly and in sincerity, calling every other way by the name of subtlety, which they avoid as poison, and contrary to all innocence: and as they delight to be under the tuition and guidance of the Lord, above all things, ascribing whatever they have to his free bounty, therefore they are far removed from selfishness, and so far enriched with divine communications from the Lord. Hence it is, that whatever they hear immediately from himself, or through the means of the word, or of preaching, they do not lay by in their memory, but apply it to practical use, that is, will it and do it, their will serving them instead of memory. The external aspect of these is, for the most part, that of great simplicity, though within they are full of wisdom and prudence, being such as are meant in those words of our Lord: " Be ye wise as serpents, " and harmless as doves," Matt. x. 16. Such is the nature of that innocence, which is called the innocence of wisdom. Now as innocence takes no merit to itself, but gives the praise of all good to the Lord only; and as it delights to depend upon him for all that goodness and truth which constitute genuine wisdom; therefore it is so appointed, that man, during the time of his infancy, should have the external form of innocence, and when old, its internal form, that so through the former he may pass on to the latter, and in the latter to a resemblance of the former: and accordingly it comes to pass, that man in his old age decreases in bulk, and in many particulars puts on, as it were, the child again; but this in order to be as a wise child, as an angel; for a wise child, in an eminent sense of the word,

U u   is is an angel: therefore it is, that in the written Word, a child signifies one that is innocent; and an old man, one that is wise, in whom dwelleth innocence (190).

279. It happens in like manner to every one that is regenerated, for regeneration is a new birth as to the spiritual man: and here he is first brought into that innocence of childhood, to be sensible that he cannot attain to the knowledge of good and truth from himself, but from the Lord only, and to desire and hunger after them as his true nourishment; and these are given to him according to his growth in the spiritual life: first, he is given to know them scientifically, then intellectually, and after this, he is brought into wisdom; seeing and confessing all the way, from the innocence and humility within him, that his sufficiency herein is only from the Lord, without which faith and conviction no one is capable of heavenly communications, in which chiefly consists the innocence of wisdom.

280. As it is the property of innocence to chuse the Lord only for our guide, therefore all in heaven are in innocence, as this is the choice of all that are there, as knowing well, that to set up for our own directors, is to abandon ourselves to self-love, and to renounce the Lord's government over us: as far therefore as any angel is in innocence, so far is he under the divine leadings and influence, and so far in heaven, or, in other words, so far is he principled in goodness and truth, which constitute the bliss of heaven; and therefore the heavens are distinguished according to the different degrees of innocence: thus they who are in the lowest or first heaven, are in innocence of the first or lowest degree; they who are in the second or middle heaven, are in innocence of the second degree; and they who are in the third or inmost heaven, are in innocence of the third or highest degree, and may be titled the very innocences of heaven, as they are more particularly distinguished for their love of being

---

(190) 'That by infants or little children in the Word is signified innocence, n. 5608; and also by sucklings, n. 3183. That by an old man is signified a wise man, and in the abstract, wisdom, n. 3183, 6523. That man is so created, that as he verges towards old age, he becomes as a child, and that then innocence is in wisdom; as also that in this state he may pass the better qualified into heaven, and become an angel, n. 3183, 5608.

guided

guided and governed by the Lord, as little children by their common Father; and therefore, whatever divine truth is communicated to them, either immediately from the Fountain of all Truth, or by means of the Word, or preaching, they inſtantly receive it into their will, and ſo conſign it to life and practical uſe; and hence it is, that they ſo far excel the angels of the inferior heavens in wiſdom, ſee n. 270, 271. Such being the nature of theſe angels, they are next in honour to the Lord, who is the author of their innocence; and they are ſo far removed from all propriety, and every thing that borders upon ſelf, that they may be ſaid to live in him. Their external form expreſſes great ſimplicity, and they appear in the ſight of the inferior angels as little children with little ſhow of wiſdom, whilſt they are in reality the wiſeſt of all the angels, yet knowing at the ſame time, that they are only receivers of all they have, and that it is a part of wiſdom to be ſenſible of it, and alſo that what they do know is nothing in compariſon with the things they are ignorant of: to be thoroughly convinced of this truth they call the firſt ſtep to wiſdom. Theſe angels are without any garment or covering, for nakedneſs correſponds to innocence (191).

281. I have difcourſed much with the angels concerning innocence, and been informed by them, that innocence is the eſſence of all good, and that the latter cannot ſubſiſt without it, conſequently that wiſdom is only ſo far wiſdom, as it leads to innocence; and that the ſame may be ſaid of divine love, charity towards our neighbour, and faith ((192); from whence it will follow, that without innocence no man can be qualified for heaven, according to thoſe words of our Lord; " Suffer the " little children to come unto me, and forbid them not, for of " ſuch is the kingdom of heaven: Verily I ſay unto you, that " whoſoever ſhall not receive the kingdom of heaven as a little

(191) That all in the inmoſt heaven are innocences, n. 154, 2736, 3887: and that therefore they appear to others as children, n. 154: alſo that they are naked, n. 165, 8375. That it is cuſtomary with ſpirits, in teſtimony of their innocence; to throw off their garments, and appear naked, n. 8375, 9960.

(192) That innocence is eſſential to every good of love, and every truth of faith, n. 2526, 2780, 311, 3994, 6013, 7840, 9262, 10134. That no one deſtitute of innocence is admitted into heaven, n. 4797.

" child,

"child, shall not enter therein," Mark x. 14, 15. Luke xviii. 16, 17. where, as well as in other parts of the Word, by *little children* we are to understand *innocent persons*. The state of innocence is also described by our Lord, Matt. vi. 24, &c. but merely by correspondences. The reason why good is only so far good as innocence is in it, is because all good is from the Lord, and innocence consists in a disposition to be led and governed by him. I was also informed, that good and truth can only be mutually conjoined by the medium of innocence; and that therefore any angel is only so far an angel of heaven, as he partakes of innocence, for heaven is not in any one till truth be joined to good within him: therefore it is, that this conjunction of truth and good is called the heavenly marriage, for this constitutes heaven. I was also informed, that true conjugal love derives its nature from innocence, as proceeding from the union of good and truth in two minds, viz. of husband and wife, which union, in its descent from above, is represented under the form of conjugal love; for where two such persons are joined together, they necessarily love each other, and in them the conjugal state may be called a display of the delights of infancy and innocence (193).

282. As innocence (*) is the very essence of good in the angels of heaven, it follows, that divine good proceeding from the Lord must include it in its principle, for it is that very

---

(193) That true conjugal love is innocence, n. 2736. That conjugal love is a mutual consent of wills in both parties, n. 2731. That they who are in the inward principle of conjugal love dwell together in heaven, n. 2732. That they become one through union of minds, n. 10168, 10169. That true conjugal love derives its origin and essence from the union of good and truth, n. 2728, 2729. Of the angelical spirits, who have a true perception of the conjugal state from the idea of good and truth in conjunction, n. 10756. That conjugal love entirely corresponds to such conjunction, n. 1094, 2173, 2429—9495, 9637. That for this reason by *Marriage* in the Word, we are to understand the marriage or conjunction of good and truth, as it subsists in heaven, and shall do in the new church, n. 3132, 4434, 4834.

(*) Innocence throughout this chapter is not to be taken in a mere negative sense, or freedom from evil, for so our author does not mean it; but as a positive good from the Lord, consisting in that heavenly congruity and disposition in all the powers and properties of the soul, which render it as a well tuned instrument of divine harmony, or as the substratum or subject of every divine virtue, gift, and grace. Tr.

principle

principle in the angels that difpofes and qualifies them for all the bleffednefs of heaven. The cafe is fimilar with regard to little children, whofe interiour is not only formed by a transflux of innocence from the Lord, but alfo difpofed and adapted to receive the good of cœleftial love, forafmuch as the good of innocence acts from their inmoft faculties, and is, as was faid before, the effence of every good: and as all innocence is from the Lord, therefore he is called in the Word, *The Lamb*, for Lamb fignifies innocence (194); and as innocence is the effence of all cœleftial good, fo it affects the minds of others with fo much fweetnefs and delight, that he who is fenfible of its influence (as happens on the approach of any angel from the inmoft heaven) is, as it were, ravifhed from himfelf, and feels a joy which far furpaffes any that this world can yield—I fpeak this from experience.

283. All who are in the good of innocence are, in proportion thereto, cordially affected with the fame in others; but it is far otherwife with thofe that are not in a fimilar ftate; and therefore all the infernals are utter enemies to innocence, though they have no idea of what it is, nay, their evil nature is fo oppofite to it, that they burn with a defire to injure every innocent perfon, and therefore cannot bear with little children, but are feized with a rage at the fight of them, and long to do them a mifchief: hence it appeared evident to me, that a contracted fpirit, filled with the love of felf, is contrary to innocence, as is the cafe of all in hell (*).

(194) That Lamb in the Word fignifies innocence, and the good thereof, n. 3994, 10132.

(*) This defcription of infernal fpirits by our author, as to their enmity to all innocence and goodnefs, exhibits likewife a melancholy, but too true a reprefentation of that malignity, which the human nature is capable of in its greateft degree of depravity and corruption; as when men, felf-alienated from divine grace, and abandoned to evil, inftead of being the temple of the living God, through the effectual operation of his fpirit, become the habitation of evil fpirits, and, as fuch, haters of their brethren, and defpifers of them that are good: fo true it is, that man even in this life may be as an angel or a devil, according to the fpirit that governs him; for his fervants we are to whom we obey, and become like unto the mafter that rules over us. Tr.

Concerning the State of Peace in Heaven.

284. He that has not been in the peace of heaven, can have no true perception of that peace which the angels enjoy, forasmuch as the perceptions of man, during his close connexion with this mortal body, are in nature, and hinder such experience; and therefore, in order to be capable of it, he must be brought into such a state of elevation above nature, by an abstraction of his spirit from the body, that he may be with the angels: now as by this means I have been favoured with the privilege of experiencing this heavenly peace, I am qualified to give some account of it; not as though human language were equal to the description, but in such words as may express it comparatively with that rest or tranquillity [commonly called peace] of mind, which is the common privilege of godly persons.

285. There are two most inward principles in heaven, viz. innocence and peace; and they are called most inward or inmost, as proceeding immediately from the Lord. Innocence is that from which springs every good in heaven; and peace is that which constitutes the delightful sense or relish [*jucundum boni*] of such good; for every good has its delightful sensation [*suum jucundum*]: now both the good, and its delightful favour or relish, are in the love property [*sunt amoris*], for what we love we call good, and take delight therein; and consequently these two inmost principles of innocence and peace proceed from divine love, and constitute the central joy of angels. That innocence is the fundamental ground of good, see the preceding article; and that peace is the ground of delight, arising from the good of innocence, will appear from what follows.

286. And first for the origin of peace: and this has its source in the Lord from the union of his Divinity with his Divine Humanity, and so giving birth to the divine peace in heaven by his communication with the angels, and more particularly by the conjunction of good with truth in every angel: and as such is the origin of peace in heaven, it must necessarily be

be a divine principle communicating bleſſedneſs to every good therein, and be the ſpring of a joyous life in all the cœleſtial inhabitants, it being nothing leſs than the joy of divine love flowing from the Lord into every one of them. Such is that peace which conſtitutes the joys and happineſs of the bleſſed above (195).

287. From this divine original of peace the Lord is named the Prince of Peace, and ſpeaks of himſelf as the author and giver of it: hence likewiſe the angels are called the Angels of Peace, and heaven the Habitation of Peace, as in the following places: " Unto us a child is born, unto us a ſon is given, and " the government ſhall be upon his ſhoulder; and his name " ſhall be called, Wonderful, Counſellor, The mighty God, " The everlaſting Father, The Prince of Peace: Of the in- " creaſe of his government and peace there ſhall be no end," Iſai. ix. 6, 7. Jeſus ſaid, " Peace I leave with you, my peace " I give unto you: not as the world giveth, give I unto you," John xiv. 27. " Theſe things I have ſpoken unto you, that " in me ye might have peace," John xvi. 33. " The Lord lift " up his countenance upon thee, and give thee peace," Numb. vi. 26. " The ambaſſadors of peace ſhall weep bitterly; the " highways lie waſte," Iſai. xxxiii. 7, 8. " The work of " righteouſneſs ſhall be peace; and my people ſhall dwell in " a peaceable habitation," Iſai. xxxii. 17, 18. And that by peace in the Word we are to underſtand a divine and heavenly peace, will appear from other places wherein it is mentioned, as Iſai. lii. 7. liv. 10. lix. 8. Jer. xvi. 5. xxv. 37. xxix. 11. Hag. xi. 9. Zech. xviii. 12. Pſa. xxxvii. 37. and elſewhere. Foraſ- much as peace ſtands alſo for the Lord its author, for heaven, for heavenly joy, and the bleſſing of every good; therefore the uſual ſalutation in old times, from whence we alſo derive the cuſtom, was, " Peace be with you!" And this received divine

---

(195) That by peace, in the higheſt ſenſe of the word, is meant the Lord, as being the fountain of peace, and in the inward ſenſe, heaven, as the ſeat of peace, n. 3780, 4681. That peace in the heavens is a divine influx, conſtituting eſſen- tially the bleſſedneſs of every good and truth therein; and that the nature of it is incomprehenſible by man, n. 92, 3780, 5662, 8455, 8665. That divine peace is in every good, but not in truth void of good, n. 8722.

ſanction

function from our Lord, when he sent out his disciples, saying: "Into whatsoever house ye enter, first say, Peace be to this house; and if the son of peace be there, your peace shall rest upon it," Luke x. 5, 6. And likewise, when our Lord appeared to the apostles, he said, "Peace be unto you," John xx. 19, 21, 26. The state of peace is also signified in the Word by, "A sweet favour unto the Lord," as in Exod. xxix. 18, 25, 41. Lev. i. 9, 13, 17. ii. 2, 9. vi. 8, 14. xxiii. 12, 13, 18. Numb. xv. 3, 7, 13. xxviii. 6, 8, 13. xxix. 2, 6, 8, 13, 36. A sweet favour, or a favour of rest, signifying, in a heavenly sense of the word, the perception of peace (196). And because peace signifies the union of the Divinity with the Divine Humanity in the person of the Lord, and his conjunction with heaven and his church, and with all that receive in both, accordingly was the sabbath instituted in remembrance thereof, and had its name from rest or peace, being a holy representative of the church; and therefore the Lord called himself Lord of the Sabbath, Matt. xii. 8. Mark ii. 27, 28. Luke vi. 5. (197).

288. As the peace of heaven is that inward divine principle which gives blessing to all the good in the angels, so it only manifests itself to them perceivably by a heart-felt joy, when in their happiest frames; as also by a sweet relish of the truth which is concordant with their particular good, when they hear it; and by an exhilarating delight on the union of both, diffusing a joyous influence in all they do, and all they think, and manifesting itself in all their looks. However, this peace, as

(196) That odour or favour in the Word, signifies the perceptivity of what is well pleasing, or otherwise, according to the kind or quality of good and faith predicated of, n. 3577, 4626, 4628, 4748, 5021, 10292. That odour of rest, when spoken of Jehovah, signifies perception of peace, n. 925, 10054. That therefore incense, perfumes, and the odours in oils and ointments, become representatives, n. 925, 4748, 5621, 10177.

(197) That the sabbath, in the highest sense of the word, signifies the union of the Divinity and Divine Humanity in the person of the Lord; in the inward sense, the conjunction of his Divine Humanity with heaven and with his church; and in general, the conjunction of good with truth, or the heavenly marriage, n. 8495, 10356, 10730. Hence, that rest on the sabbath day is significant of the state of that union, and, in a relative sense, of the conjunction of the Lord with man, as the efficient cause of his peace and salvation, n. 8494, 8510, 10360, 10367, 10370, 10668, 10730.

to

to its specifick quality and degree, differs in the different heavens, according to the innocence of their inhabitants respectively; for innocence and peace, as was said before, go hand in hand with one accord, innocence being the source of heavenly good, and peace the delightful sensation of that good [*jucundum illius boni*] so that nearly the same that was said in the preceding article, of the state of innocence in heaven, may be said of peace in this, as they are conjoined in like manner with good, and its pleasant fruit; for good is known by the delight it yields, and the particular delight distinguishes the kind of its proper good, and is owned by it. Hence it appears, that the angels of the inmost or third heaven are in the third or inmost degree of peace, as being in the third or inmost [highest] degree of innocence; and that the angels of the inferior heavens are in a lower degree of peace, as being in a lower degree of innocence, see above, n. 280. That innocence and peace go together, like good, and the pleasing sensation of it, may be known by little children, which are in peace, because in innocence; and because in peace, there all things serve to them as matter of play and harmless delight: however, the peace of infants is only external, for internal peace, like internal innocence, is only to be found in wisdom, and consequently where good and truth are conjoined, for hence comes wisdom. There is also an heavenly or angelical peace in such men as are possessed of wisdom from a conjunction of good with truth, and thereby find themselves resigned to the will of God; but this peace, during their abode here, lies concealed in their inner man, but is manifested when they quit the body, and enter into their heavenly rest, for then the things that were hidden will be revealed.

289. As divine peace originates from the conjunction of the Lord with heaven, and particularly in every angel, from the conjunction of good and truth, therefore the angels, when in their highest state of love, are in their most perfect state of peace, for then good and truth are in their most perfect conjunction with them (*). That alternate changes of states take

---

(*) The reader, for the better understanding of our author's meaning, is to take with him all along, that as the two chief constituent principles of man's spiritual

place in the angels, fee above, n. 154 to 160. Similar to this is the regeneration of man, when the conjunction of good and truth is formed within him; which more especially is effected after temptations, when he enters into the delightful state of heavenly peace (198). This peace may be compared to a lovely morning in the spring season, when nature appears revived, as well as beautified, by the warmth and splendor of the newly risen sun, whilst grateful odours, exhaling from the vegetable world, mix their rich sweets with the descending dew of heaven, and at the same time that they add fertility to the earth, regale the senses, and exhilarate the minds of men: and this comparison must appear the more apt, as the morning redness in the spring time corresponds to the state of peace in the heavenly angels, see n. 155 (199).

290. I have also conversed with the angels on the subject of peace, and told them, that the men of our world call that peace, when wars and hostilities cease between nations, and enmity and discord between neighbours; and have no other notion of internal peace, than of that which consists in a freedom from anxious cares about things future, and especially in a pleasing tranquillity of mind arising from the success of their temporal affairs: to which the angels replied, that however such ease and tranquillity might, in their opinion, carry in them the appearance of peace, yet they had nothing of the true nature of it, except with those who were in the principle of cœlestial good, as in that good only the true peace was to be found, seeing that it was a pure influence emaning from the Lord into their inmost or superior faculties, and thence descending into their inferior ones, and so producing true rest and tranquillity of

spiritual nature are the will, and the understanding or intellect, so the divine good of love is the perfection of the former, and the divine light of truth that of the latter; and that when these two principles or faculties in man are thus dignified and exalted, he is then in his most perfect state, as having the highest good and truth conjoined or united in him: hence proceeds, derivatively from the Lord, the relative perfection both of men and angels.

(198) That the conjunction of good and truth in a regenerate person is effected when in a state of peace, n. 3696, 8517.

(199) That the state of peace in heaven is comparatively as a delightful spring morning on earth, n. 1726, 2780, 5662.

mind,

mind, and the joy that proceeded thence: but as to those who are in the evil principle, they know not what peace is (200); for as to that apparent tranquillity and pleasure which they have, when things go according to their wishes, it is all external and superficial only, whilst enmity, hatred, revenge, and wrath, with other evil passions, remain unmortified within, and are ready to break out on the first provocation or incitement, when unrestrained by fear; and that therefore what pleasure they are capable of is founded on insanity; but that of those who are principled with good, on wisdom, the difference between them being nothing less than that which is betwixt hell and heaven.

Of the Conjunction of Heaven with Men.

291. It is a received doctrine in the church, that all good is from God, and none originally from man, and that therefore no one ought to assume any merit to himself on that account: and it is equally confessed, that evil is from the Devil; and accordingly it is common for those, who speak from doctrine, to say of such as live well, preach the truth, and are of a godly conversation, that they have God for their guide, and the contrary of such as are of bad life and conversation; but this could not be so were there no communication between heaven and hell and men, and that with their wills and intellects, as from these the body is actuated, and the mouth speaks. What kind of communication or conjunction this is, shall now be shewed.

292. There are good spirits and evil spirits present with every man; by the former he has communication with heaven, by the latter with hell; now both these kinds of spirits belong to that intermediate state or world of spirits which is betwixt heaven and hell, of which we shall particularly treat hereafter. When these spirits come to any man, they enter into the whole of his memory, and the whole of his thinking; the evil spirits

---

(200) That the lust arising from the love of self, and the love of the world, hinder all true peace, n. 3170, 5662. That some place peace in dissipation, and things contrary to the nature of peace, n. 5662. That there can be no true peace till evil lusts be first eliminated, n. 5662.

into

into all the evil that is in his memory and thoughts, and the good spirits into all the good therein: now these spirits know nothing of their being in the person, but all the time they are with him, suppose that his memory and thoughts are their own; neither do they see him, for the things in our solar world are not objects of their sight (201). The Lord has in a particular manner provided, that the spirits should not know that they are present with the person, for were they to know this, they would converse with him, and so the evil spirits would have power to destroy him; for as they are conjoined with hell, they covet nothing more earnestly than his destruction, not only as to his soul, or which is the same, his faith and love, but also as to his body: but it is far otherwise when they converse not with him, for in that case they know not that they think his thoughts, nor communicate them to their fellow spirits, for they converse together from man, as it were by proxy, whilst at the same time they believe that they think and speak from themselves; now as it is natural for every one to esteem and love himself, so these spirits are allured to esteem and love the man [for their own sakes] without knowing that they do so. That spirits are thus conjoined with man, I can and do certify from many years full experience.

293. That spirits which communicate with hell are also joined to man, is because that man is born into all kinds of evil, which are, as it were, the elements of his natural life; and therefore, unless spirits similar to himself were joined to him, he could not live, nor consequently be reformed and regenerated; so that he is continued in life by means of his communication with evil spirits, and attracted to good by the good spirits, and so stands in a kind of equilibrium between both, and in this equilibrium consists his liberty or free will, whereby he is in a capacity of eschewing the evil, and chusing the good,

---

(201) That angels and spirits are present to every man, and that through them he has communication with the spiritual world, n. 697, 2796, 2886, 2887, 4047, 4048, 5846 to 5866, 5976 to 5993. That man cannot live without the association of spirits, n. 5993. That man does not see those spirits, nor is seen by them, n. 5885. That spirits can see nothing in this solar world belonging to man, unless they are permitted to converse with him, n. 1880.

and

and also of being principled with the latter, which could not be effected, were he not in the power of free will; nor could he be thus free, did he not stand in the exact medium between the equal influence of evil spirits on the one hand, and the counter influence of good spirits from heaven on the other (*). It has likewise been made known to me, that if man, as now born and constituted in his present fallen state, had not the power of being in the evil that he chuses, and was destitute of free will, he could not continue in life; as also that he cannot be compelled to good, forasmuch as what he does by constraint makes no part of his proper life, nor continues with him; but that the good which he receives freely, takes root in his will, and so becomes, as it were, his own property: and hence it is, that man may have communication with hell, and also with heaven.

294. What kind of communication subsists betwixt heaven and good spirits, and what betwixt hell and evil spirits, and consequently what kind of conjunction is formed thereby respectively, shall here be mentioned. All spirits in the world of spirits have communication with heaven or hell, the good with the former, the evil with the latter; and both heaven and

(*) It must be owned, that the discoveries held forth to us in this article or section, are no less wonderful than important, as explaining man's relation to good and evil spirits; his communication with heaven or hell through them; and the origin of free will. Surely, I think, that human reason on invention could never have hit on these discoveries, nor that cool unbiassed reason can easily reject them when offered, especially as they so well consent with what is recorded in the sacred writings concerning the agency and influence of spirits on the human intellect and will: nor is it any new point of belief in the church, that the influence and operations of the Holy Spirit on the hearts and minds of pious Christians are conducted by the instrumentality of the good angels, who are stiled " ministring spirits sent forth to minister for them who shall be heirs of salvation:" and by like authority we may conclude, that Satan advances the dominion of sin, and " worketh in the hearts of the children of disobedience" by the ministry of his evil angels. And as the holy angels are represented in Scripture as ministring in spiritual things from God to man, so are they likewise there represented as the mediums or conveyancers through which spiritual sacrifices ascend from man to God; thus Rev. viii. 3, 4. " And another angel came, and stood at the altar, " having a golden censer; and there was given unto him much incense, that he " should offer it with the prayers of all saints upon the golden altar which was " before the throne: and the smoke of the incense, with the prayers of the saints, " ascended up before God out of the angel's hand." Tr.

hell are distinguished into separate societies, to one of which every particular angel belongs, and as he subsists by influx from it, so he co-operates in all things with it: hence it is, that accordingly as a man is joined to spirits good or bad, so is he joined to heaven or hell, and also to that particular society in either, which he resembles most in his affections or prevailing love; for all the heavenly societies are classed according to their affections of good and truth; and all the infernal societies according to their affections of evil and false. Concerning the societies of heaven, see above, n. 41 to 45, as also, n. 148 to 151.

295. As man is with regard to his affections or love, accordingly similar spirits are joined to him, the good spirits by appointment from the Lord; but the evil spirits are attracted to him by man's ownself, however the spirits that are for his companions are changed according as his affections vary; thus one sort attends him in his infancy, another in childhood, a third sort in youth and manhood, and another in old age: in infancy he is attended by such spirits as are more particularly distinguished for their innocence, and as such communicate with the inmost or third heaven; in early youth by those who are in the affection of knowledge, or such as communicate with the lowest or first heaven; in riper age by those who are in the affection of truth and good, and so on to intellectual attainments, and as such communicate with the second or middle heaven; and in old age they have for their associated spirits such as excel in wisdom and innocence, and have communication with the inmost or third heaven: but this association or adjunction is effected by the Lord in those who are in a capacity of being reformed and regenerated, and not in any else, it being otherwise with such; for though persons, who are in no such capacity, have good spirits attending them to keep them from evil, as far as it is possible to be done, yet their close connexion [*conjunctio*] is with evil spirits that communicate with hell, from whence they are supplied with associates of like disposition with themselves: thus, if they are addicted to self-love, given to filthy lucre, revengeful, or adulterers; in this case similar spirits become present to them, and unite with their evil affections; and where

such

such a one cannot be kept from evil by the good spirits, they inflame his evil passions, and enter in and dwell with him. In this manner bad men are joined to hell, and good men to heaven.

296. That man is thus under the government of spirits by divine appointment, is because he is not constituted, in his present state, according to the laws and order of heaven; but subject, by the depravity of his nature, to the evils which originate from hell, and as such contrary to the order of heaven, to which he must be restored, which can only be by the ministry of spirits, whereas the matter would be otherwise were man born perfect according to the order of heaven: for in such case he would not have been under the mediate government of spirits, but under that of divine instinct, and subject to the general laws of influx; and by influx man is now governed as to those things which proceed from his thoughts and will into act: as for example, his words and actions; for these flow spontaneously, according to the established laws of order in this natural world, with which the spirits that are joined to him have nothing in common. The inferior animals also are governed by a general instinct, or influx from the spiritual world, for they are in the appointed order of their nature, which they could not corrupt or destroy, as being without rationality (202). As to the difference between men and them, see above, n. 39.

297. With respect to the conjunction of heaven with man, we are moreover to know, that the Lord acts upon him according to the established laws of order, both inwardly and out-

(202) That the difference between the human and the bestial nature consists in the capacity of the former to be exalted to a participation of the divine: that men are qualified by grace to think of God, to love him, and to be joined to the Lord, and consequently to become heirs of eternal life, of which the brute beasts are in no wise capable, n. 4525, 6323, 9231. That the brutes come into the world in the appointed order of their nature, and therefore in a condition every way suitable thereto; but that it is otherwise with man, who is to be introduced again into the primitive order and condition of his nature by instruction, and the improvement of his intellectual faculties, n. 637, 5850, 6323. That according to the general law of influx in human nature, thought spontaneously forms itself into speech, and the will into bodily gestures and acts, n. 5862, 5990, 6192, 6211. Concerning the general laws of influx from the spiritual world into the life of brutes, n. 1633, 3646.

wardly,

wardly, and difpofes him to receive the heavenly influence, that fo both parts of his conftitution, viz. the outward and inner man, may mutually co-operate in an uniform obedience to his government. This influx from the Lord is called immediate, and the former by angels, which depends on this, is called mediate influx: immediate influx is from the Lord's Divine Humanity into the will of man, and through the will into the underftanding; or, in other words, into his good, and through the good into his truth; or, which amounts to the fame, into his love, and through the love into his faith, but not alternately, or *vice verfâ*, much lefs into a faith without love; or into a truth without good; or into underftanding not influenced by the will. This immediate kind of divine influx never ceafes, and is received in the good principle by the good, but not by the evil, for thefe reject, ftifle, or pervert it; and therefore they continue in that kind of evil life, which in a fpiritual fenfe is called death (203).

298. The fpirits that are affociated to a man, whether they be fuch as communicate with heaven, or with hell, never operate on him by influx from their memory and thoughts; for in that cafe he would be led to miftake their memory and thoughts for his own, fee above, n. 256; but the influence which he receives from heaven through them is affection principled with the love of good and truth, and that which he receives from hell through them is affection principled with the love of what is evil and falfe; and as the man's affection is concordant with the influx, fo far he receives it into his mind and thoughts, for

(203) That influx is twofold, immediate from the Lord, and mediate through the fpiritual world, n. 6063, 6307, 6472, 9682, 9683. That there is an immediate influx from the Lord into the moft minute particular things [*in omnium fingulariffima*] n. 6058, 6474 to 6478, 8717, 8728. That the divine influence extends to the firft and laft in all things, and how, n. 5147, 5150, 6473, 7004, 7007, 7270. That the divine influx is into the good property in man, and through good into truth, and not *vice verfâ*, n. 5482, 5649, 6027—10153. That the vital principle flowing from the Lord is varied according to the ftate of man, and his reception of it, n. 2069, 5986, 6472, 7343. That in the wicked, the good influx from the Lord is changed into evil, and truth into falfhood; this from experience, n. 3643, 4632. That fo much of good and truth is received by influx from the Lord, as is not obftructed by the contrary properties in man, n. 2411, 3142, 3147, 5828.

man's

man's inward thoughts keep pace with his affection or love; but in proportion to their disagreement the influx is rejected. Hence it appears, that as man receives not his thoughts through the spirits, but only the affection of good, or of evil, that he is endowed with election, or is free to receive good or evil, concerning which he is instructed in the written Word; now which of these he receives into his mind with affection and desire, that becomes his own, or a principle within him; but what he does not so receive, that makes no part of himself, or is not appropriated to him. Thus much may suffice to shew the nature of influx of good from heaven, and of evil from hell in man.

299. It has also been given me to know whence anxiety, grief, and that sadness of mind, which we call melancholy in man, proceed: there are certain spirits which are not yet joined to hell, as being newly departed from the body (of which hereafter when we come to treat of the world of spirits) which take delight in things indigested and putrid, such as meats corrupted in the stomach, and hold their confabulations in such sinks of uncleanness in man, as suitable to their impure affections; now if these their affections are contrary to those in man, they become in him the occasion of sadness and melancholy; but on the contrary, if they correspond to his own affections, he is pleased and delighted therewith. These spirits appear near to the stomach, some to the right, some to the left of it, some higher, some lower, some nearer, some more distant, according to their different kinds of affection; and that they cause uneasiness of mind, I am fully convinced by much experience: I have seen and heard them, and felt the uneasiness caused by them, and I have also conversed with them: upon their removal the uneasiness has ceased, and returned upon their return; and I have also been sensible of its increase and decrease, according to the degrees of their approach or removal respectively: and hence I have learnt whence it comes, that they who have no notion of conscience, from not having any themselves, ascribe the anguish of it to disorders in the stomach or bowels (204).

300. The

---

(204) That they who are without conscience themselves, have no notion of what conscience is, n. 7490, 9121. That there are some, who, when they hear mention

300. The communication [*conjunctio*] of heaven with man, is with the interiour of his mind, that is, with his fpiritual or inner man, and with his natural or external man by correfpondences, of which more particularly in the following article, wherein we fhall treat of the conjunction of heaven with man through the Word.

301. That the conjunction of heaven with man is of fuch a nature, that they have a mutual dependence on each other, fhall be fpoken to in the following article.

302. I have converfed with the angels on this fubject, and told them, that fuch as are members of the church on earth do indeed doctrinally hold, that all good is from God, and that angels are prefent with men; but that few inwardly and truly believe that they are joined to them, much lefs in their thoughts and affections. To which the angels replied, that they knew there was fuch a contradiction betwixt profeffion and actual belief among men in this matter, and efpecially in the church, which they wondered at the more in thofe who were in poffeffion of the Holy Scripture, which inftructed them in the things of heaven, and man's communication therewith, efpecially as his power of thinking, and the whole of his fpiritual life, depended on fuch communication and conjunction with fpirits: moreover they faid, that the caufe of this ignorance in man was his belief, that he lived wholly from himfelf, without any connexion with the Author and Fountain of Life; and that his connexion was through the medium of the heavens, and that were this broken or interrupted man would inftantly die. Did man firmly believe, as is the very truth, that all good is only from the Lord, and all evil from hell; in that cafe he would not affume any merit to himfelf on account of the former,

mention made of confcience, turn it into ridicule, n. 7217. That fome believe there is no fuch thing; others, that it is nothing more than fome natural melancholy or diforder, occafioned by bodily indifpofition, or difappointment in worldly matters; and fome, that it is only fuperftition in vulgar minds, n. 950. That there is a true confcience, a fpurious confcience, and a falfe confcience, n. 1033. That remorfe of confcience is an uneafinefs of mind for fomething unjuft, deceitful, or evil, that a man has done, which he confiders as contrary to his duty to God or his neighbour, n. 7217. That they, and they only have confcience, who love God and their neighbour, n. 831, 965, 2380, 7490.

nor would the latter be imputed to him; but in all the good he thinks or does, he would look up to, and afcribe the praife of it to the Lord, and all the evil wherewith he is tempted he would give back to hell from whence it came; whereas by difbelieving all influx, either from heaven or hell, and by fuppofing that all he thinks and wills is in and of himfelf alone, he appropriates to himfelf the evil, and corrupts the good by a vain conceit of felf-righteoufnefs.

Of the Conjunction of Heaven with Man by the Word.

303. All who reafon from any depth of thinking know well, that there is a connexion between all things and their firft caufe through intermediate caufes, and that whatever is not fo connected muft immediately ceafe to be, as nothing can fubfift from itfelf, but from fomething prior to itfelf, and all things from that which is original, or firft; and that this connexion, with what is prior to itfelf, is an effect from its efficient caufe, which caufe being removed, the effect neceffarily ceafes. Hence it is become a maxim among the learned, that fubfiftence is no other than a continuation of exiftence; and that therefore all things fubfift from that firft caufe to which they owe their exiftence: but as to the particular connexion of every thing with its prior caufe, and fo back to the firft caufe or origin of all things, this is fo multifarious, as not eafily to be defcribed; and therefore let it fuffice to obferve in general, that there is fuch a connexion betwixt the fpiritual and natural worlds, that all things in the latter correfpond to thofe in the former, concerning which correfpondence, fee n. 103 to 115; as alfo that there is a connexion, and confequently a correfpondence between all things in man, and all things in heaven, of which, fee above, n. 87 to 102.

304. Man is fo formed by his nature, as to be capable of connexion and conjunction with the Lord, but only confociation with the angels of heaven; and why not conjunction, is becaufe he

he is by creation fimilar to an angel with refpect to his inward man, having a like will and a like underftanding, and therefore after death, if his life had been according to the divine order and laws, becomes an angel, and of like wifdom with the angels; and therefore by man's conjunction with heaven is meant his conjunction with the Lord, and his confociation with the angels; for heaven is not conftituted from any thing proper or peculiar to the angels, but from the Divinity of the Lord; and that this is fo, fee above, n. 7 to 22. But man has, moreover, this privilege above the angels, that he not only belongs to the fpiritual world with refpect to his interior part, but is alfo an inhabitant of this natural world in refpect to his exterior or outward man. Now to this latter part of his compofition appertain all things belonging to his natural or external memory, together with his thoughts and imaginations from thence, as in general is his knowledge of arts and fciences, and the natural delights thefe yield him; as likewife his natural fenfes, fpeech, and actions, which conftitute the loweft part of his nature, and are the ultimate things in which the divine influx terminates; for it paffes through what is intermediate in man to the moft inferior parts of his compofition: whence it will appear, that in man is the laft and loweft difplay of the divine influx and order, and, as it were, the bafis and foundation of it. Now, as fuch is the tranfit of the divine influx through its medium (the angelical heaven) to its ultimatum or termination in man; and as nothing is unconnected or independent, fo the conjunction of heaven and mankind forms fo clofe and neceffary a relation between them, that neither can fubfift without the other; infomuch that men without heaven would be as a chain without a faftening [*catena ablato unco*] and heaven without mankind, as a houfe without a foundation (205).

305. But

(205) That nothing exifts from itfelf, but from a prior caufe, and all things from a firft caufe: that they owe their fubfiftence to that from which they derive their exiftence, as fubfiftence is a continuation of exiftence, n. 2886, 2888, 3627—6056. That divine order terminates not fhort of man, but in man as its ultimatum, n. 634, 2853, 3632—10329, 10335, 10548. That internal and fpiritual things pafs by fucceffive order of influx into external and natural things, as into their extreme or limit, where they exift and fubfift, n. 634, 6239, 6465, 9216, 9217.

305. But forasmuch as man has broken his connexion with heaven, by that which has estranged his affections from heavenly things, and turned them to self and the world by the love thereof, and so withdrawn himself from good, that he was no longer in a capacity to serve for a basis and foundation to heaven; therefore the Lord has graciously provided a substitute in the room thereof by the medium of the Word, for his conjunction with heaven; and how this serves for such a medium has been shewed in many places of the work intitled *Arcana Cælestia*, or *Heavenly Secrets*, which are to be found collected together in a little treatise on the *White Horse*, spoken of in the Apocalypse; as also in the appendix to the *Heavenly Doctrine*, from which some articles are adduced in the notes underneath (206).

306. I have been informed, that the most ancient church on earth had immediate revelations, as their minds and affections were turned towards heaven, and therefore, that then there was

---

9217. That interior things exist and subsist in their last state in simultaneous order, n. 5897, 6451, 8603, 10099. That all things are continued in a chain of connexion from first to last, n. 9828. That therefore the first and last signify the whole of any thing, n. 10044, 10329, 10335; and that the strength and power of the preceding efficient causes are continued to the last effect, n. 9836.

(206) That the Word in its literal sense is in a natural form, n. 8783: and that because things natural are the last and lowest form of manifestation belonging to things inward and spiritual, and therefore serve as a foundation in nature for the latter to rest on, n. 9430, 9433, 9824, 10044, 10436. That the Scripture may serve to this end, it is formed by correspondences in nature, n. 1404, 1408, 1409—8615, 10687. That the Word being such in the literal sense, it is as the containing vessel of the inward and spiritual sense, n. 9407: and that it is accommodated to the use both of men and angels, n. 1769 to 1772, 1887, 2143—7381, 8862, 10322: and also the connecting medium between heaven and earth, n. 2310, 2495, 9212, 9216, 9357, 9396, 10375. That the conjunction of the Lord with man is by the Word through the medium of its interior sense, n. 10375. That this conjunction is by the Word throughout, and therefore that it is of wonderful virtue and excellence above all other writings, n. 10632, 10633, 10634. That since the Word was committed to writing, the Lord communicates himself to man thereby, n. 10290. That the church in which the Word, and by it the Lord, is known, is to those who are without the church, and know them not, as the heart and lungs in man respectively to those parts of the body which derive their vital powers from them, n. 637, 931, 2054, 2853. That the universal church on earth is before the Lord as one man, n. 7395, 9276. Hence it is, that were there no church on earth where the Word, and by it the Lord, was known, there would be an end of the human race on this globe, n. 468, 637, 931, 4545, 10452.

a conjunction of the Lord with men; but that after that time there was no such immediate revelation, but a mediate one by correspondences, and that their divine worship consisted in these; whence the churches of those days were called Representative Churches, for they then understood the nature of correspondences and representations, and that all things on earth corresponded to spiritual things in heaven and in the church, or, which signifies the same, represented them; wherefore those natural things, in which their outward worship consisted, served them as means to their thinking spiritually, and so with the angels. After the science of correspondences and representations was lost, then the Word was committed to writing, all the words and senses of which are according to the rules of correspondency, and so containing that spiritual or inward sense in which the angels understand them; for when a man reads the Word, and understands it in its literal or external meaning, the angels receive it according to its internal or spiritual sense; for the angels think spiritually, as men think naturally; and though these two ways of thinking appear widely different, yet they come to the same by correspondency. Thus it came to pass, that after man had broken off his connexion with heaven, the Lord substituted the Word as a medium, whereby to restore that connexion.

307. In what manner heaven is joined with man by the Word, shall here be illustrated by some passages taken from it. The New Jerusalem is described in the Apocalypse as follows: "I saw a new heaven and a new earth; for the first heaven and "the first earth were passed away: and I saw the Holy City, "the New Jerusalem coming down from God out of heaven: "and the city lieth four square, and the length is as large as "the breadth: and the angel measured the city with the reed "twelve thousand furlongs: the length, and the breadth, and "the height of it are equal: and he measured the wall thereof, "an hundred and forty and four cubits, according to the mea- "sure of a man, that is, of an angel: and the building of it "was of jasper; and the city was pure gold, like unto clear "glass: and the foundations of the wall of the city were gar- "nished with all manner of precious stones: and the twelve
"gates

" gates were twelve pearls; and the ftreet of the city was pure
" gold, as it were tranfparent glafs," ch. xxi. 1, 2, 17, 18, 21.
When man reads the above defcription, he takes it only in the
literal fenfe, as that the vifible heaven and earth fhall perifh,
and be fucceeded by a new heaven and earth, and that on the
latter fhall defcend the holy city Jerufalem, of the above given
dimenfions: but the angels take it in a very different fenfe, underftanding all thofe things fpiritually, which man underftands
naturally. Thus, by the new heaven and the new earth they
underftand the new church, and by the city Jerufalem coming
down from God out of heaven, its heavenly doctrine as revealed
by the Lord: by the length, breadth, and height thereof as
equal, and by 12000 furlongs they underftand every good and
truth contained in that doctrine in their complex or total: by
the wall thereof they underftand the truths which guard and
defend that doctrine, and by the meafure of the wall, viz. 144
cubits, which is the meafure of a man, i. e. of an angel, all its
auxiliar truths in their complex, and their feveral kinds: by its
twelve gates of pearls, they underftand initiatory or introductory
truths, fuch being meant thereby; and by the foundations of
the wall of the city, as garnifhed with all manner of precious
ftones, the knowledges [*cognitiones*] upon which its doctrine is
founded; and by pure gold like unto tranfparent glafs, of which
the city and its ftreet confifted, they underftand the good of love,
from which the heavenly doctrine of the new church originates,
together with all its clear, convincing truths. Such are the
perceptions of the angels as touching thefe things, and fo different from thofe of men; and in this manner the natural ideas
of men are converted and changed into fpiritual ideas in the
minds of the angels, without the latter knowing any thing of
the literal fenfe of the word, as of a new heaven and earth, of
a new city called Jerufalem, of a wall and its foundations, and
of meafures: however, the thoughts of the angels coincide with
the thoughts of men by correfpondency, and meet together like
the words of the fpeaker, and the fenfe of thofe words in the
mind of the hearer, who attends not to the found, but to the
fenfe of the words. From what has been faid, it may appear
how heaven is joined with man through the medium of the
Word.

Word. But to illustrate the matter by another example from the written Word: "In that day shall there be a highway out of "Egypt to Assyria; and the Assyrian shall come into Egypt, "and the Egyptian into Assyria, and the Egyptians shall serve "with the Assyrians. In that day shall Israel be the third with "Egypt and with Assyria, even a blessing in the midst of the "land, whom the Lord of hosts shall bless, saying: Blessed be "Egypt my people, and Assyria the work of my hands, and "and Israel mine inheritance," Isai. xix. 23, 24, 25. The difference in thinking and understanding between angels and men, on reading the above passage, will appear by giving both the literal and the spiritual sense of it. Now, according to the former, men understand, as meant thereby, that the Egyptians and Assyrians are to be converted, and find acceptance with God, and to make one church in conjunction with the people of Israel: but the angels interpret it spiritually, of the man of the spiritual church, who is there meant, according to the inward sense; and whose spiritual part is signified by Israel, his natural part by the Egyptian, and his rational part (which is the medium between the two former) by the Assyrian (207): and yet both these senses meet in one by correspondence; and therefore, at the same time that the angels think and understand in a spiritual, and men in a natural manner, they are conjoined like body and soul, the internal sense of the word being, as it were, the soul, and the literal sense its body. Such is the Word throughout, and consequently a fit medium of conjunction between heaven and man, to which the literal sense serves for the basis or foundation.

308. There is also a conjunction of heaven, through the Word, with those that are without the church, and have not the Word; for the church of the Lord is catholick or universal, consisting of all who believe in a God, and live in charity one with another, for such after death are instructed by the angels,

(207) That Egypt and Egyptian in the Word signifies natural [*naturale*], and thence scientifick, n. 4967, 5079, 5080—9340, 9319. That Ashur or Assyrian signifies rational [*rationale*], n. 119, 1186. That Israel signifies spiritual [*spirituale*], n. 5414, 5801, 5803, 5812, 5806, 5817, 5826, 5951—6868, 7201, 8805, 9340.

and become partakers of divine truth (208); of which hereafter in its proper place, when we come to treat of the Heathens. The univerſal church in the ſight of the Lord is as one man, as was ſaid before of heaven, n. 59 to 72: but the church where the Word is, and whereby the Lord is known, is as the heart and lungs in that man. It is well known that all the viſcera and members of the body derive life from the heart and lungs through various channels and conveyances; ſo that part of mankind which is without the church where the Word is, yet derive virtue from it, as members of the ſame body: the conjunction of heaven, through the Word, with thoſe that are at a diſtance from the church, and therefore have it not, may alſo be compared to light propagated from its center to the circumference; now in the Word is divine light, and therein the Lord is preſent, and diffuſes light, in a meaſure, from thence to all that are afar off; which would not be ſo but for the Word. This may be farther elucidated by what has been ſaid before concerning the form of heaven, according to which the conſociations and communications therein are regulated: but this is among thoſe ſecrets of wiſdom, which are to be underſtood by ſpiritual minds only; for as to thoſe who are poſſeſſed of natural light, it will be too hard for them, as the former diſcover innumerable things, which the latter ſee not, or ſee but very obſcurely.

309. Unleſs ſuch a Divine Word had been diſpenſed to the inhabitants of this world, they would have been ſeparated from heaven, and in that caſe would have ceaſed to be rational creatures; for the rationality of our nature proceeds from the influx of heavenly light: beſides, men here are ſo conſtituted, as not to be capable of immediate revelation, and ſo to be inſtructed

(208) That the church, in a more eſpecial ſenſe of the word, means that church which is in poſſeſſion of the Word, and where the Lord is known by means thereof, and conſequently where divine truths are revealed from heaven, n. 3857, 10761. That in a larger ſenſe of the word, the church of the Lord conſiſts of all throughout the whole world, who lead a good life according to that religion which they profeſs, n. 3263, 6637, 10765. That all who do ſo, wherever they are, and believe in God, are accepted of the Lord, n. 2589 to 2604, 2861, 2863, 3263, 4190, 4197, 6700, 9256: and alſo all infants whereſoever they are born, n. 2289 to 2309, 4792.

in divine truths, like the inhabitants of other worlds (of whom I have treated in a diſtinct ſmall piece) as being more in earthly affections than them, and conſequently more outward, whereas they are the inward and ſpiritual only, who are receptive of ſuch revelation; for if they who are otherwiſe ſhould receive it, yet divine truths would not enter into their intellectual faculties: and that ſuch is the nature of men now o'days on earth, is evident from many within the church, who, although they have been inſtructed from the Word concerning heaven and hell, and a life after this, yet remain unbelievers in their hearts; among whom are ſome who have ſhewed an ambition of being thought more learned than their neighbours, and conſequently from whom might have been expected greater proofs of wiſdom than from many others.

310. I have ſometimes diſcourſed with the angels concerning the Word, and told them, that ſome held it in contempt on account of the ſimplicity of its ſtyle; and that as its internal ſenſe was no longer underſtood, therefore few believed that it contained ſuch a rich treaſure of wiſdom: to which the angels replied, that though the ſtyle of the Word in the ſenſe of the latter appeared ſo ſimple, yet nothing was comparable to it for excellence, as it contained divine wiſdom, not only in every ſenſe, but in every word, and that the illumination therefrom was manifeſt in heaven, meaning thereby that it was the light of heaven, as being divine truth; for divine truth has a viſible ſplendor in heaven, ſee above, n. 132. Moreover they ſaid, that without ſuch a Divine Word men on earth would have no divine light, nor any conjunction with heaven; for in proportion to the former is the latter, and alſo every one's meaſure of revealed truth: that man's ignorance as to ſuch conjunction through the ſpiritual ſenſe of the Word, in correſpondence with its natural ſenſe, is the cauſe of his ignorance likewiſe as touching the ſpiritual perception and language of the angels, and the difference between theirs and thoſe of us poor mortals in this our natural ſtate; without underſtanding ſomething of which, he can form no judgment concerning the ſpiritual ſenſe of the Word, and how thereby man may be conjoined with heaven. They moreover ſaid, that if man believed that ſuch an inward

and

and spiritual sense belonged to the Word, and in some sort framed his mind according thereto on reading it, he would advance in wisdom's school, and to a nearer conjunction with heaven, through a greater conformity to the angels in spiritual conceptions.

That Heaven and Hell are from Mankind.

311. That heaven and hell are from mankind, is a doctrine entirely unknown in the Christian world, it being therein believed by all, that the angels were first created such, and so heaven became their dwelling; and that the Devil or Satan was an angel of light, but on revolting from his obedience was cast down from heaven, together with his rebellious crew, and that so hell came from them. That such a belief should prevail among Christians is matter of astonishment to the angels, and a still greater, that they should be under a total ignorance as to heaven, though it ought to be so fundamental a doctrine in the church: as men have been so long in darkness touching these important points, the angels expressed great joy that the Lord was pleased now at last to vouchsafe to them farther discoveries concerning heaven and hell, in order, as far as possible, to dispel that darkness which has continued to increase upon them, and that the rather, as the church [with respect to its present dispensation] has now entered upon its last period, and is near to the end of it: therefore it is their desire that I would declare upon assurance from them, that there is not a single angel in the universal heaven that was created such at first, nor a single devil in all hell that had been an angel of light, and afterwards cast out from heaven; but that all, both in heaven and in hell, are of the human race; in the former, such as had lived in the world in heavenly love and faith, and in the latter, such as had lived in hellish affections and dispositions; and that the whole of hell taken collectively, or in its complex, is called the Devil and Satan, as well that hell which is behind (*), in which are

(*) Here the author is to be understood as speaking of the situation of things and places as they appear to the spectator in the spiritual world, and which always
have

the evil genii called the Devil, and that hell which appears in front, in which are the evil spirits called Satan (209); of which shall be spoken more distinctly hereafter. They moreover said, that the erroneous belief of the Christian world on these subjects proceeded from certain passages in the Word taken according to their literal sense, and not illustrated by the light of genuine doctrine, as delivered in the same Word; and that the letter of Scripture, if not understood and explained by the rule of the latter, often misleads the mind into mistakes and erroneous opinions, from which have arisen heresies in the church (210).

312. The forementioned error in Christian men has given occasion to that other in believing, that no one goes to heaven or hell before the time of the last judgment, when they suppose that the present visible frame of things shall perish, and be succeeded by a new creation, and that our souls shall then be reunited to our bodies, and so we shall live again as men; and this belief is connected with that of the angels having been created angels from the beginning, as it cannot be thought that heaven and hell are inhabited by the human race, if none of them go to either before the end of the world: but that the matter may appear from evidence to be otherwise, the privilege of being in company with angels has been granted to me, and also of conversing with some that are in hell, and that now for

---

have the same aspect with respect to his body, as to right and left, behind and before, above and beneath, &c. wheresoever he is, or which way soever he turns, see before, n. 123, 124. Tr.

(209) That the hells in their complex, or the infernals collectively, are called the Devil and Satan, n. 694. That they who were devils in this world become devils after their death, n. 968.

(210) That the doctrine of the church must be taken from the Word, n. 3464, 5402, 6832, 10763, 10765. That the Word, as to particulars, is only to be understood by the general tenor of its doctrine, n. 9021, 9409, 9424, 9430, 10324, 10431, 10582. That true doctrine is a light to those who read the Word, n. 10401. That genuine doctrine must come from those who are in illustration from the Lord, n. 2510, 2516, 2519, 10105. That they who rest in the letter, without any knowledge of doctrine, attain not to the understanding of divine truths, n. 9409, 9410, 10582; and also fall into many errors, n. 10431. The difference between those who teach and learn from the doctrine of the church, as taken from the Word, and those who go by the sense of the letter only, n. 9025.

several

several years together, sometimes from morning till evening, and so to receive information concerning both kingdoms; and this to the end that Christian men may no longer continue in their mistaken notions concerning the resurrection at the final judgment, the state of souls in the mean time, and also concerning angels and the devil; which notions, being founded on a false belief, introduce darkness into the mind, and in those who are led entirely by their own reasonings, engender doubtings, and at length a total denial of the truth itself, whilst they argue thus with themselves: How can it be that such a glorious heaven, with all its rich furniture of stars, together with sun and moon, should be destroyed and perish; and how can the stars fall down from heaven to the earth, which are so much bigger than it? How can bodies, after they have been devoured by worms, passed through corruption, and been scattered by winds to the four corners of the heavens, be restored to their proper forms for the use of their respective souls; and what, in the mean time, becomes of the soul, and what sort of a being is it without all sense? With many such like difficulties, which, being unintelligible, fall not within the province of faith, and, with respect to many, beget infidelity concerning the immortality of the soul, heaven and hell, and other articles of faith as held by the church; and that they have been productive of such effect we have a proof in all those who say, Who ever came from heaven to tell us what sort of a place it is? or who from the other world to tell us whether there be such a place as hell? What means being tormented for ever in fire? and what the day of judgment? Have not men looked for it many ages in vain? with many such like speeches, shewing rank disbelief of all the articles of the Christian faith: lest therefore such like infidels (among whom are too many of the wise of this world, who pass for great scholars) should any longer confound and seduce the simple-hearted, and such as are weak in the faith, spreading darkness over the minds of men in relation to the belief of a God, of heaven, of eternal life, and of such truths as depend thereon, therefore the Lord has been pleased to open my spiritual eyes and senses, and given me to converse with all whom I knew in the body after their departure from it, with some for days, some for months, and some for a year together; and also with so many others, that I should come short of the truth were I to reckon the number of them all at a hundred thousand, many of whom were in heaven, and many in hell. I also spake with some two days after their decease, and told them that their friends were at that time preparing for their funeral; to which they replied, that they did well to remove out of the way what was no longer of use to them, as it had been, and bade me to tell them, that they were not dead, but were as truly living men as before; having only passed out of one world into another, and did not know that they had lost any thing by the change, having a body and senses as before, with understanding and will, as also like thoughts, affections, and desires, as when they lived in this world. Most of those who were newly departed, on finding themselves living men as before, and in a similar state of mind (for immediately after death every one's state of life is the same as when he left this world, but is successively and gradually changed either for heaven or hell) they were affected with a new kind of joy at their being alive, and said that they could scarce believe their senses; and yet wondered at their former hebetude and blindness with respect to a future state, and more particularly, that professing members of the Christian church should remain in darkness as to these points of faith, who have opportunities, above all persons in the world, of being thoroughly instructed in them (211); and that they then for the first time saw the true cause of this

---

(211) That at this day few in the Christian world believe that man shall rise again immediately after death, Pref. to ch. xvi. of Gen. and n. 4622, 10758; but not till the time of the last judgment, upon the dissolution of this visible world, n. 10594. The cause of this belief, n. 10594, 10758. That notwithstanding, man will rise again immediately after death, and will be a living man in all respects, n. 4527, 5006, 5078, 8939, 8991, 10594, 10758. That the soul which lives after death is the spirit of a man, which is, properly speaking, his true man, and has a perfect human form in the next life, n. 322, 1880, 1881, 3633, 4622, 4735, 5883, 6054, 6605, 6626, 7021, 10594, from experience, n. 4527, 5006, 8939; from the Word, n. 10597. An explanation of what is meant by the dead being seen in the holy city, Matt. xxvii. 53. n. 9229. How a man is raised from the dead, by experience, n. 168 to 189. Concerning his state after his resuscitation, n. 317, 318, 319, 2119, 5079, 10596. False opinions concerning the soul and its resurrection, n. 444, 445, 4527, 4622, 4658.

ignorance,

ignorance, which is, that external things, such as mundane and corporeal, have so captivated and filled their minds, as to render them unreceptive of the light of heaven, and of the truths maintained in the church, any farther, than as to doctrinal knowledge [not as principles of life] and that from such earthly and sensual affections arises a darkness with respect to any thing farther than mere speculative belief.

313. Many of the learned from the Christian world, when they find themselves, after death, in a body, in garments, and in houses, are in amazement; and when they recollect their former thoughts concerning a future state, the soul, spirits, heaven, and hell, they are covered with shame, own their past infatuation, and that the simple, illiterate believer was far wiser than themselves. On scrutinizing into some of these learned sophisters, who had confirmed themselves in their errors, and particularly in ascribing all to nature, it was found that their interior or spiritual part was shut against all influx from heaven, and their exterior or natural open and expanded, shewing that they had not turned their thoughts and affections to heavenly things, but to things earthly, sensual, and devilish: for according to the opening or shutting of the spiritual or natural part in man respectively, so are his thoughts and affections directed to things above, or things beneath; and as his interiour is formed for the reception of heavenly things, and his exteriour for the things of this world, so if he receives only the latter, without any thing of heaven at the same time, he receives likewise an evil influx from the kingdom of darkness along with them (212).

314. That the inhabitants of heaven are of the human race, may also be gathered from hence, that the minds of angels and men are alike, both possess the same faculties of understanding, perceiving, and willing, and both are equally formed to receive the heavenly virtue and powers; for the human mind is capable of like wisdom with the angelical, and the only reason why men are not as wise in this world as the angels, is because they

---

(212) That in man are conjoined the spiritual and natural worlds, n. 6057. That the internal or spiritual part of man is formed after the image of heaven, and his external or natural part after the image of this world, n. 3628, 4523, 4524, 6057, 6314, 9706, 10156, 10472.

are

are here confined to earthly bodies, and in such a prison the spiritual mind can only think naturally, or according to the nature it is joined to; but when it is set at liberty therefrom, it no longer performs its operations naturally, but spiritually, stretches itself beyond the reach of mortal ken, comprehends things inconceivable by the natural man, and possesses the wisdom of an angel; from whence we may gather, that the interior part in man, called his Spirit, is, in its essence, angelical, see above, n. 57 (213); and when delivered from its earthly prison, appears in the same perfect human form with the angels: that such is their form, see above, n. 73 to 77: but when man's internal principle is not open in its superior part, but only in its inferior, then, after his separation from the body, he continues indeed to appear in a human form, but in such a one as is deformed and diabolical; nor can he look up to heaven, but only down to hell.

315. He that is instructed in the nature of the divine order, may also know, that man was created so as to become an angel, forasmuch as the divine order terminates in him, n. 304, and makes a part of his original composition; consequently, heavenly or angelical wisdom may be formed, renewed, and augmented in him. Divine order does not stop short of its utmost possible progress, for if so, it would not be full and perfect; but it proceeds to its ultimatum or limit; and when it has attained thereto, it proceeds afresh (according to the divine fecundity therein, and by the use of appointed means) to new formations; and these it effects by the means of procreation, which so becomes a new seminary and display of the divine wisdom and wonders.

316. That our Lord rose again, not only as to his spirit, but also as to his body, was because, when in the world, he glorified, that is, divinized his whole Humanity; for the soul which he received from the Father was the Divinity itself [*ex se ipsum*

---

(213) That there are as many degrees of life in man as there are heavens, and that they are opened in him after death, according as his life has been, n. 3747, 9594. That heaven is in man, n. 3884. That men, who live in love and charity, have in themselves angelical wisdom, but hidden here; and that they enter upon it after this life, n. 2494. That the man, who is recipient of the good of love and faith from the Lord, is called angel in the Word, n. 10528.

Divinum

Divinum fuit] and the body was formed after the similitude of the soul, that is, of the Father, and so also was made divine; and therefore he rose again as to both (214), differently from all other men; which he also declared to his disciples when they took him for a spirit, saying, "Behold my hands and my "feet, that it is I myself: handle me, and see; for a spirit "hath not flesh and bones, as ye see me have," Luke xxiv. 39. By which he made it appear, that he was man, not only as to his spirit, but also as to his body.

317. That it might be made known, by sensible evidence, that man lives after death, and goes to heaven or hell, according to the life which he lived in the body; therefore many things have been manifested to me concerning the state of man after death, of which hereafter, when we come to treat of the world of spirits.

Concerning the Gentiles, or People without the Church, in Heaven.

318. It is a common opinion, that all who are born and die without the pale of the church, such as are called Heathens or Gentiles, are not in a way of salvation, as being without the Word, and so remaining ignorant of the Lord, without whom none can be saved; and yet we may better conclude on the other hand, that they are in a salvable state, because the " Lord's " mercy is over all his works," and therefore he is merciful to every man, they being men as well as those who are born within the pale of the church, and by far the greater number; and also because it is not their fault that they know not the Lord: besides, every one that is in any good degree rational will conclude, that the Lord made none of set purpose for hell, as he is love itself, and that it must be a property of divine love to will the salvation of all men; to which end he has provided, that all should have some religion, and consequently some sense of

(214) That man rises again only in spirit, n. 10593, 10594. That the Lord alone rose again also with his body, n. 1729, 2083, 5078, 10825.

a God,

a God, and of an inward spiritual life, for that all religion teaches, inasmuch as it respects God, and so far it turns the thoughts from the world, and from outward things (215).

319. That the Heathens are in a salvable state, as well as Christians, is easy for such to know, as know what constitutes heaven in man; for heaven, strictly speaking, is within him, and they who have the heavenly principle within them, and cherish it, may go to heaven. Heaven is said to be in man, when he owns a God, and conforms to his will: this is a fundamental in all religion, without which it cannot subsist; and all religion teaches, that God is to be worshipped in some manner, so as to render the worshipper acceptable to him. This is an acknowledged principle in the mind of man, and so far as he is led by it, so far he acts conformably to the will of God and his conscience. It is well known that the Heathens lead as moral lives as Christians, and many of them excel professing Christians in this particular: now morality is that which we practise either in respect to God, or in respect to men; and the former is called the spiritual life: both outwardly appear alike, but inwardly and in principle they are very different: the one is profitable to salvation; the other is not; for he who lives a moral life, as commanded by God, such a one is actuated by a divine principle; but he who does the same only from human respects, is actuated by a selfish principle. To illustrate this by an example: He that forbears to injure his neighbour, because it would be acting contrary to religion, and consequently to the divine will, such forbearance is from a spiritual origin; but he that refrains from doing the like only through fear of the law, of loss of character, honour, or advantage; such a one's re-

(215) That the Gentiles are saved as well as the Christians, n. 932, 1032, 1059, 2284, 2589, 2590, 3778, 4190, 4197. Of the lot of the Gentiles, and of people without the church in the other world, n. 2589 to 2604. That the church, in a more special sense of the word, is that which is in possession of the Divine Word, and where the Lord is thereby known, n. 3857, 10761: yet not so to be understood, as if all who had these advantages were of the true church, but only such therein as live in faith and charity, n. 6637, 10143, 10153, 10578, 10645, 10829. That the catholick church of the Lord consists of all throughout the whole world that lead good lives according to the religion they know, and acknowledge a Supreme Being; and that such are accepted of the Lord, and go to heaven, n. 2589 to 2604, 2861—6700, 9256.

straint

straint from evil being only from selfish and worldly respects, it has nothing of virtue or religion in it; and as the former is a spiritual, so the latter is a mere natural man; in the one a heavenly influence opens his interior, and so proceeds to operate in his exterior life; in the other a worldly principle from beneath influences his external man, but not his internal; for no influx is from the natural to the spiritual world, but *vice versâ:* wherefore, if the good principle from above is not received at the same time, the interior gate in man becomes shut, and such a one altogether a man of this world: hereby we may know who they are who receive heaven into themselves, and who do not. But heaven, or the heavenly principle, is not the same in one as in another, but differs in every one according to his affection of good and its truth: thus, they who are in the affection of good from love to God, they also love divine truth, for good and truths of the same kind love one another by sympathy, and tend to union (216); and therefore the Heathens, though they be not in genuine truths in this world, yet in the love-principle receive them in the next.

320. A certain spirit from the Heathen world, who had lived in all good charity in his life here, being in company with some Christian spirits, heard them disputing on the articles of their belief (for spirits reason, especially on the nature of good and truth, more fully and acutely than men) upon which, expressing some surprize at the warmth of their controversy, he said, that he could not endure to hear any more of it, for that their dispute was merely from appearances and fallacies, saying to them thus: If I am in the good principle, I can easily know the truths that proceed from it, and those which I see not at present may be given me hereafter.

321. I have been fully taught, that the Heathens, who have led a good moral life, in becoming obedience and subordination, and in mutual charity, according to the religion they knew,

---

(216) That there is a conjunction, like that of marriage, between good and truth [*bonum et verum*] n. 1094, 2173, 2503. That good and truth have a perpetual tendency to union, and that every good desires its proper truth, and to be united to it, n. 9206, 9207, 9495. How good and truth are joined together, and in whom, n. 3834, 3843, 4096, 4097—7623 to 7627, 9258.

and thence derived a principle of conscience, are accepted in the other life, and are there diligently instructed by the angels in all things of good and truth respecting faith, and readily receive truths so as to be principled with them, behaving with great modesty, and shewing a teachable disposition ; and that they receive instruction the more readily, as not having been tinctured with erroneous doctrines or prejudices against the truths of faith, and as such to be first purged from their minds, much less with heretical doctrines concerning our Lord's divine person, like many professing Christians, who entertain no other conception of him than as of another man ; whereas the Gentiles, on the contrary, as soon as they are informed that God became man, and manifested himself to the world in our nature, they presently acknowledge and adore the Lord, saying ; " It " must needs be true, that God did so manifest himself, as he " is the God of heaven and earth, and as the human race are " his offspring" (217). It is indeed a divine truth, that without the Lord there is no salvation ; but then it is to be understood thus, viz. that there is no salvation, but from the Lord. There are many worlds in the universe, and those full of inhabitants ; and yet very few among them know any thing of our Lord's having assumed the human nature in this our world ; but nevertheless, as they worship the Deity under a human form, they are accepted of the Lord, and taken under his guidance. Concerning which subject, see a little piece intitled, *De Telluribus in Universo, Of the Worlds in the Universe.*

322. There are among the Heathens, as well as Christians, both wife and simple ; and that I might know the difference,

(217) The difference between the good of the Gentiles, and the good of the Christians, n. 4189, 4197. Of truths among the Gentiles, n. 3263, 3778, 4190. That the inner gate of the mind in the Gentiles cannot be so shut against the divine influx as in Christians, n. 9256 : nor can truth be vailed from the sight of the former by so thick a cloud, if they live up to the religion they have, as in the case of Christians who live without charity, and the causes of this, n. 1059, 9256. That the Gentiles cannot profane holy things like the Christians, as the former are in ignorance concerning them, n. 1327, 1328, 2051. That the Heathens are afraid of the Christians on account of their bad lives, n. 2596, 2597. That such among the Heathens as have lived good lives according to the light they had, are instructed by the angels, and readily receive the truths of faith, and acknowledge the Lord's Divinity, n. 2049, 2595, 2598, 2600, 2601, 2603, 2661, 2863, 3263.

I was

I was allowed to converse with both, sometimes for hours, at others for days together; but of the wise, few such are to be found now as in former times, particularly in the ancient church, which spread over a great part of Asia, and from whence religion was propagated in many other countries: that I might judge of their abilities, it was allowed me to have familiar conversation with some of them; and accordingly I was in company with one, who was formerly in high reputation for his wisdom, and as such well known in the learned world, with whom I discoursed on various subjects, and it was impressed upon my mind that he was Cicero; and knowing him to be a man of understanding, I reasoned with him on wisdom, on intellectual knowledge, on order, on the Word, and, lastly, on the Lord: concerning wisdom he said, that nothing deserved that name, but what related to the conduct of life; and as to true intellectual knowledge, that it was the offspring of wisdom: with respect to order, he said, that it proceeded from the most high God, and that to live according to it was the best wisdom and understanding: in regard to the Word; when I read to him a portion from the prophetick writings, he appeared highly delighted, and in particular, that all the names and words therein had an inward and spiritual meaning, expressing his wonder at the same time, that the learned now o'days did not take delight in the study of it; whereby I could plainly perceive that his mind was inwardly enlightened. Moreover, he said, that he was not able to attend farther to my reading, as the sacred influence that flowed in upon him was too much for his faculties to bear: at last we entered into discourse concerning the Lord; of his being born man, but conceived by the Deity; and how he put off the human part received from his mother, and put on the Divine Humanity; and that he is the Great Governor of the universe. To which he answered, that he knew many things concerning the Lord, which he understood according to the measure of his capacity; and that mankind could not have been saved by any other means. At this time certain heretical professing Christians present suggested some scandalous things on what had been said, which he seemed not to regard in the least, saying, no wonder if they, who had cor-

rupted

rupted their minds in their bodily life-time with such irreverent notions on these subjects, were harder to be convinced than the ignorant, who were not tainted in like manner.

323. It was also allowed me to converse with others who lived in old times, who were diſtinguiſhed for wiſdom: at firſt they appeared in front at a diſtance, and could even there diſcover my ſecret thoughts with ſuch ſagacity, as to know from a ſingle idea the whole train to which it belonged, and alſo how to fill my mind with pleaſing images and inſtructive emblems of wiſdom; from which it was eaſy to judge, that they were ſages of an eminent claſs; and it was told me, that they were ancients of renown: they then drew nearer, and as I read to them a portion of the Word, they appeared greatly delighted; and I could perceive, that it gave them a more particular pleaſure to find that all and ſingular the things I read to them out of the Word, were repreſentative and deſcriptive of cœleſtial and ſpiritual things: they told me, that when they lived upon earth, their manner of thinking, ſpeaking, and writing, was of the ſame kind, and therein conſiſted their ſtudy of wiſdom.

324. As to the modern Heathens, they come ſhort of the ancient in wiſdom, but moſt of them are men of great ſimplicity; and ſuch among them as lived in mutual charity on earth readily receive wiſdom from their inſtructors in the other world, of which I ſhall here give an example or two. As I was reading the hiſtory of Micah, Judg. ch. xvii and xviii; how the Danites took away his graven image, his Teraphim, and his Levite; a certain ſpirit from the Gentile world was preſent, who, in the time of his living in the body, had been a worſhipper of a graven image; and upon hearing of the injury done to Micah, he was ſo affected with it, as to be overwhelmed with grief, ſhewing unqueſtionable marks of his innocent and tender affections; which ſome Chriſtian ſpirits preſent taking notice of, they wondered that an idolater could be affected with ſuch tenderneſs of compaſſion on the occaſion: preſently after this, two good ſpirits joined him, and told him that no image was to be worſhipped, and that he might know ſo much, as a rational creature, or man; and therefore, that he ought to extend and direct his thoughts and worſhip beyond ſuch ſenſeleſs objects to
the

the Great God, the Creator and Governor of heaven and earth, and that God is the Lord. Upon uttering thefe words, it was given me to perceive (by communication with his fpirit) an affecting fenfe of interior, devout adoration within him, beyond that of many Chriftians; from which we may gather, that many from the Heathen world gain a more eafy admiffion into the kingdom of heaven than many modern profeffing Chriftians, according to thofe words of our Lord: "And they fhall come "from the Eaft, and from the Weft, and from the North, and "from the South, and fhall fit down in the kingdom of God: "and behold, there are laft which fhall be firft, and there are "firft which fhall be laft," Luke xiii. 29, 30; for in the ftate in which he was, he was capable of being imbued with all things pertaining to a true faith, and of receiving them into his affections; in him was compaffion from the love-principle, and in his ignorance was innocence; and where thefe are conjoined, true faith gains a fpontaneous and welcome admiffion: after this he was received into the fociety of angels (*).

325. One morning I heard a company [chorus] at a diftance, which by their badge of diftinction (reprefenting a kind of woolly goat, a cake of millet, an ebony fpoon, and a floating city) appeared to be Chinefe: on their nearer approach fome of them defired to be alone with me for the fake of private converfation; but they received for anfwer, that their companions refented the propofal, as having a right to be prefent alfo; upon which, perceiving anger rifing in their minds, they began to queftion with themfelves, whether they had not fome how given juft caufe of offence to their brethren; and fhewed marks of trouble and fhame, as though they had done them wrong, giving proof hereby of a tender confcience, and of their being in the principle of charity. Soon after, I entered into converfation with them, and turned the fubject of it to our Lord, under the

(*) It is to be noted, that this and the foregoing tranfactions in the two preceding articles, are to be underftood as having paffed in the world of fpirits, or that intermediate ftate betwixt heaven and hell, in which fpirits receive their laft preparation for the one or the other, accordingly as they have been principled with good or evil in this life, of which our author diftinctly treats in the following part of this work. Tr.

name of Christ; on which I perceived them to shew some repugnance when I mentioned the name of Christ, and found that it proceeded from some prejudice they had been tinctured with in this life from seeing the Christians lead worse lives, and to shew less of charity than their own countrymen; but when I only used the name of the Lord, they gave tokens of a devout reverence: they were then informed by the angels, that the Christian doctrine recommended and enjoined love and charity beyond all other religions in the world, but that few of its professors lived according thereto. There are some Gentile spirits, who in their life-time here, knowing from character and conversation with them, how Christians, many of them, lived in adultery, hatred, strife, drunkenness, and other vices, which the Gentiles held in abhorrence, they become thereby more timid in the other world in embracing the truths of the Christian faith, till instructed by the angels, that the Christian religion teaches the very contrary to such practices, though the generality of its professors walk less by its rules and precepts than the Heathens themselves; upon which, though after some delay, they embrace the faith, and worship the Lord.

326. It is customary for such of the Gentiles, as were wont to worship any supposed god under the form of an image or statue, to be introduced, on their entrance into the other world, to some spirits who were to represent such gods or idols, and that, in order to expose and cure them of such vain and foolish phantasies; and after staying with them some days they are dismissed: and they who have been given to worship men, are introduced to those very men, or some appointed to represent them; as many of the Jews are to Abraham, Jacob, Moses, or David, and when they find that they have no divine power to help them, they are put to confusion, and remanded to their proper stations. Of all the Gentiles, the Africans meet with the kindest reception in heaven, as they shew the readiest disposition to receive all the good things and truths of that kingdom: they chuse to be called the obedient, and not the faithful, saying, that the latter character belongs to the Christians, as being in the faith, and not to them, unless they had received it, or are, as they term it, capable of receiving it.

327. I have conversed with some who were of the ancient church (that is here called the ancient church which was next after the deluge, and which spread over many kingdoms, viz. Assyria, Mesopotamia, Syria, Ethiopia, Lybia, Arabia, Egypt, Philistia to Tyre and Sidon, through the land of Canaan on both sides of Jordan (218): and they who at that time were instructed in the doctrine of our Lord's Advent upon earth, and received the faith, but afterwards departed from it to idolatry, had their station in front to the left, in a dark place, and were in a miserable condition; the sound of their voice was a piping monotony, and they scarce talked rationally: they said, that they had been there many ages, but were at times set at liberty to do drudgery and servile offices for others. By their condition was given me what to think of many professing Christians, and of their state in the other world; I mean such as, though not outward idolaters, yet are so inwardly, worshipping themselves and the world with an affectionate service, and denying the Lord in their hearts.

328. That the church of the Lord consists of members dispersed over the face of the earth, and therefore it is denominated catholick or universal, including all of whatsoever religion that live conscientiously according thereto; and that the church, which is in possession of the Word, and has attained to the knowledge of the Lord thereby, is to all that are without the pale of it, as the heart and lungs in man, from which all the

---

(218) That the first and most ancient church on earth was that which we read of in the first chapters of Genesis, and that it was cœlestial, and the chief of all churches, n. 607, 895, 920, 1121, 1122, 1123, 1124, 2896, 4493, 8891, 9942, 10545. Concerning the quality and state of its members in heaven, n. 1114 to 1125. That there were diverse churches soon after the deluge, called the ancient churches, n. 1125, 1126, 1127, 1327, 10355. Men of the ancient church, of what condition, n. 609, 895. That the ancient churches were representative churches, n. 519, 521, 2896. That the ancient church had a revealed Word, but that it was long since lost, n. 2897. Of the ancient church when it began to apostatize, n. 1128. The difference between the most ancient and the ancient church, n. 597, 607, 640, 641, 765, 784, 895, 4493. That the statutes, judgments, and laws, commanded to be observed in the Jewish church, are in part like those that were in force in the ancient church, n. 4288, 4449, 10149. That the Lord was the God of the most ancient, and also of the ancient church, and that he was called therein Jehovah, n. 1348, 6846.

viscera and members of the body derive life, according to their different forms, situations and conjunctions, see above, n. 308.

Of Infants, or Little Children, in Heaven.

329. According to the belief of some, no other infants go to heaven than those which are born in the church, and the reason they assign is, because such are baptized, and by baptism initiated into the faith of the church : but such persons are to be told, that baptism is not the procuring cause either of heaven or of faith to any one, but serves only for a sign or memorial that such person is to be regenerated; and that they who are born in the church have the means of being so, as therein is the Word, which contains those divine truths by which regeneration is effected, and whereby the Lord is known, who is the author of regeneration (219) : and they are also to know, that every infant, dying such, whether he be born in the church, or out of the church, whether of godly or ungodly parents, is accepted of the Lord, and educated by angels, according to divine order; and thus being formed to good affections, and through them to the knowledge of truth, when advanced in understanding and wisdom, he is introduced into heaven, and becomes an angel. Every one that thinks rationally may know of a truth, that none were ever designedly born for hell, but, on the contrary, all for heaven; and consequently, that whoever goes to the former, must owe it to his own fault, which cannot be the case of infants.

330. All who die infants are equally such in the other world, of like infantile minds, of like innocence in ignorance, and a like tenderness in all things, being only as the young plants

---

(219) That baptism is a sign of regeneration from the Lord through the truths of faith revealed in the Word, n. 4255, 5120, 9089, 10239, 10386, 10387, 10388, 10392. That baptism is a sign of our belonging to that church, where the Lord, who is the Author of Regeneration, is acknowledged, and in which is the revealed Word, from which we derive those truths of faith, by means of which regeneration is effected, n. 10386, 10387, 10388. That the outward baptism neither gives faith nor salvation, but is a sign and pledge of their being received by the regenerate, n. 10391.

that

that are to grow up to angels; for infants are not angels as yet, but only in the way of becoming such, seeing that every one appears, upon his entrance into the other world, in the same state in which he departed this, whether infant, child, youth, adult, or aged, but, in some time after, every one's state is changed; but it is to be observed, that the state of infants has this advantage over others, that being in innocence, actual evil by consent of will has not taken root in them, so that they are easily receptive of all heavenly good; for innocence is the proper receptacle of the truth of faith and the good of love.

331. The state of infants in the other world is much higher than in this, as there they are not invested with an earthly body, but with one like to that of the angels; for the earthly body being gross, does not receive its first sensations and movements from the interior or spiritual, but from the exterior or natural world, and therefore infants here must learn to walk, behave, and speak, nay, their very senses, as seeing and hearing, must be formed by use; but not so in heaven, for then, being spirits, they are actuated by an interior impulse, walk spontaneously of themselves; they also speak, but at first only confusedly from the impulse of affection in general, without any distinct arrangement of ideas; but this they soon come to, as their exterior part is conformable to their interior. That the discourse of angels flows spontaneously from their affections modified by their ideas, and therefore speak as they think, see above, n. 234 to 245.

332. Infants, as soon as raised from death, which is immediately after their decease, are taken up into heaven, and are delivered to such of the female angels as, when in this world, were more particularly fond of children, and who also loved God: now as such, from a certain maternal tenderness in their nature above common, loved all little children, so they receive them as their own, and the children in return love them as their own mothers, each of which takes as many of them under her care as her tenderness for them prompts her to take. This particular heaven appears full in front in the same direction of view wherein the angels behold the Lord, and that because all little children are under the immediate tuition of the Lord; and
their

their influx is from the heaven of innocence, which is the third heaven.

333. Little children are of different difpofitions, fome like the fpiritual, fome like the cœleftial angels: fuch as are of the former clafs appear in heaven ftationed to the left hand; thofe of the latter clafs, to the right hand: and all little children in the Grand Man or heaven, are in the province of the eyes; fuch as refemble the fpiritual angels, in the province of the left eye; and fuch as refemble the cœleftials, in the province of the right eye; and that becaufe the Lord appears to the angels of his fpiritual kingdom, fronting the left eye; and to the angels of cœleftial kingdom, fronting the right eye, fee above, n. 118. Little children being thus in the province of the eyes, denotes them to be under the immediate guardianfhip and protection of the Lord.

334. How infants are educated in heaven fhall here briefly be told. They are firft taught to fpeak by thofe that have the care of them: their firft utterance is only a kind of affectionate found, which, by degrees, grows more diftinct, as their minds become furnifhed with ideas; for the ideas of the mind fpringing from the affectionate part, immediately give birth and form to the fpeech of the angels, as mentioned above, n. 234 to 245. Into their affections, which all proceed from innocence, the delectable things, which are the objects before them, firft infinuate themfelves; and as thefe are of a fpiritual origin, they ferve as receptacles of fuch heavenly things as are of ufe to open their minds, and enlarge their faculties in the way of intellectual attainments: after completing this their firft age, they are tranflated to another heaven, where they are inftructed by angelical mafters, and fo pafs on to further improvements.

335. Little children are firft taught by beautiful fimilitudes and inftructive emblems, adequate to their genius and capacity, containing leffons of wifdom beyond imagination: thus they are gradually formed to that wifdom, which has goodnefs for its effence. To mention here only two fimilitudes or reprefentatives that I was witnefs to, whereby to judge of the reft: and firft, they reprefented our Lord as rifing from the fepulchre, and alfo the uniting of his humanity with the divinity, and that with

fuch

such divine skill, as far exceeded all human wisdom, and, at the same time, with infantile simplicity: they represented likewise the form of a sepulchre, and also of our Lord, but in so delicate and refined a manner, as scarcely to be perceived; and that because there is something so affectingly mournful and sad in that image of mortality, which they thus prudently softened: they then caused to pass into the sepulchre, as it were, a thin lucid vapour, remotely to represent the spiritual life signified in baptism. After this I saw a representation of our Lord's descent to the spirits in prison (1 Pet. iii. 19, 20.) and his ascent with them into heaven, conducted with incomparable skill and pious reverence; and in order to accommodate the representation to their childish minds, they let down, as it were, small cords of the finest texture, to aid in the elevation of his body; guarding at the same time, with religious caution, against admitting any thing into the representation that did not image and lead their tender thoughts to something spiritual and heavenly; not to mention other kinds of emblematical scenery made use of, in order to instil into them good affections, and to form their minds to truth, by entertainments adapted to their faculties.

336. I had also a proof of the delicacy of their sentiments once, as I was praying the Lord's prayer, when they joined their ideas with mine; and I became sensible of an influx proceeding from their intellectual part, as that of tender affection; and that their minds were open to the Lord, so that I could perceive, that what at first seemed an influx from them, was a transflux through them; for there is a near communication from the Lord to the minds of little children, as not being shut against the divine influx like those of adults, and neither opposing the entrance of truth through the resistance of error, nor hindering the admission of good, and so of wisdom, by any wilful and acquired evil. Hence we may learn, that infants do not enter upon the angelical state immediately after death, but are gradually prepared for it by the knowledge of good and truth, according to heavenly order; the Lord providing means suited to their capacities and dispositions, to fit them as recipients for all the truths pertaining to good [*vera boni*] and all the good things pertaining to truth [*bona veri*].

337. It has alſo been ſhewed to me, how things inward and ſpiritual inſinuate themſelves into their tender minds, through ſuch external delights as are accommodated to their genius reſpectively. I have ſeen them beautifully dreſſed, and adorned on their little arms and breaſts with flowers of cœleſtial colours; and thus I ſaw them once walking with their angelical inſtructors and virgins in one of the gardens of paradiſe: the garden was not ſo much adorned with trees, as with what may be compared in a ſort to our laurel eſpaliers and arched walks, with alleys leading to ſweet receſſes; and as the little children drew near, the borders of flowers ſeemed to glow with freſh and more lively luſtre; from whence we may gather what pleaſure they muſt receive from ſuch exhilarating ſcenes, miniſtering to the increaſe as well as delights of innocence and charity, through the bounty and influence of the Lord.

338. It has been ſhewed to me by a manner of communication common in the other world, what kind of ideas infants have of the objects they ſee; and it was found, that they all appeared to them as having life, from whence the idea of life became joined with all their thoughts. It appeared alſo to me, that children here on earth have much the ſame ideas in all their little diverſions, as not having yet attained, like thoſe of a more advanced age, to know by reflexion what it is to want life.

339. It has been ſaid above, that all little children are by diſpoſition and genius diſtinguiſhed into cœleſtial and ſpiritual reſpectively: now they of the former claſs are eaſily known by this, viz. that there is ſomething ſoft and gentle in all they think, ſay, and do, as if it ſpontaneouſly flowed from a principle of good within, of love to the Lord, and to other little children; whereas the latter ſhew not the like ſoftneſs, but ſomething quick and ſmart [*alatum et vibratile*] in all their behaviour (*). The like alſo appears in their reſentment, and other ways.

340. Many may think that little children keep their ſtate in heaven, and ſo continue children among the angels; and they who know nothing of the nature of angels may be confirmed

(*) See n. 241.

in this mistake, by seeing angels painted and carved in the churches: but the matter is quite otherwise; for as understanding and wisdom are essential to an angel, so children, being destitute of these, though among the angels, yet are not of their number; but as soon as they have attained thereto, they then first become angels; and then, which was matter of wonder to me, they no longer appear as children, but as adults, having, through wisdom, changed the infantile genius and character for that which is angelical. That children in heaven, when perfected in understanding and wisdom, appear in the form of adults, or as youths, is because understanding and wisdom is their true spiritual food (220); and what is nourishment to their minds, serves for the same to their bodies also, and this by correspondency; for the form of the body [with respect to all in the other worlds] is the form of the spirit within. It is here to be noted, that in heaven children advance not in their external form and appearance beyond youth, or the flower of their age, but stop there for ever: that I might know this for certain, it was permitted me to converse with some that were educated in heaven as children, and grown up; and also with some others whilst they were children, and with the same afterwards, when they had attained to their flower of youth; and from both I received information concerning their progression in life from state to state.

341. That innocence is the receptacle of all heavenly good things, and therefore that the innocence of little children is the plane or ground of all their affections for good and truth, may appear from what has been said before, n. 276 to 283, concerning the innocence of the angels in heaven; that it consists in a resigned submission to the government of the Lord, and a renunciation of man's own will, who is only so far in innocence

---

(220) That spiritual food is the same with knowledge, understanding, and wisdom, and also constitutes the good and truth from which they proceed, n. 3114, 4459, 4792, 5147—5656, 8562, 9003. Hence that food, in a spiritual sense of the word, signifies all that proceedeth out of the mouth of God, Matt. iv. 4. n. 681. As bread signifies all kinds of food in general, consequently so does it signify all coelestial and spiritual good, n. 276, 680, 2165, 2177, 3478, 6118, 8410; and that because the latter nourishes the mind, which is the inner man, n. 4459, 5293, 5576, 6277, 8418.

as

as he is remote from felf, and fo far only is he in the Lord, or partakes of his righteoufnefs and merits: but the innocence of little children, as obferved before, is not genuine innocence, becaufe void of wifdom; for genuine innocence is wifdom, and fo far only is any one to be reputed wife, as he is refigned to the will of the Lord, or is content to be under his guidance: and therefore children are conducted from their primary external innocence of infancy to that internal innocence of wifdom, which crowns their education and progrefs; and when they have attained to this, their formal external innocence, which was the ground of the latter, is joined with it, and fo they become perfect children or angels. The innocence of children was imaged to me by the reprefentation of a child in wood with fcarce any thing of life in it, but which was vivified gradually, anfwerably to the progrefs of children in their knowledge of truth, and their affection for good: and afterwards I had a reprefentation of genuine innocence in a very beautiful child quite lively and naked; for the innocents which are in the inmoft heaven, and as fuch neareft to the Lord, appear as little children, and fome of them naked; for innocence is reprefented by nakednefs without fhame, as we read of the firft man and his wife in paradife, Gen. ii. 25; but when they loft their innocence, they were afhamed, becaufe of their nakednefs, and hid themfelves, ch. iii. 7, 10, 11. In a word, the more the angels excel in wifdom, the higher is their degree of innocence; and the higher their degree of innocence, the more do they appear to one another as little children: hence it is, that infancy in the Word fignifies innocence, fee above, n. 278.

342. I have converfed with the angels concerning infants, and afked them, if they were pure from all evil, feeing they had not committed actual evil, like adults; to which they anfwered, that they were in evil as well as the latter; nay, that of themfelves they were nothing but evil (221); but were kept from evil, like as were the angels, and preferved in good by the Lord,
and

---

(221) That all men, without exception, are by nature born to all kinds of evil, fo that as to their proper felves, they are nothing but evil, n. 210, 215, 731, 874, 875, 876—10284, 10286, 10731. That therefore man muft be born again, that is, regenerated, n. 3701. That it is an hereditary evil in man to love himfelf
more

and that in a way so little perceived by them, that it appeared to them as if they were good of themselves; and therefore all infants, after they are grown up in heaven, in order to cure them of such a false conceit of themselves, as though they possessed any good but from the Lord, are sometimes left to their own hereditary evils for a while, to convince them of the truth of the matter: one such, who was a certain king's son, and had died an infant, but was grown up in heaven, had conceived the foregoing erroneous opinion, and was therefore suffered to be possessed of his own hereditary innate evils; upon which I perceived from his sphere, that he was of an imperious mind, and made light of adultery, having inherited these propensities from his parents: but after seeing what he was by nature, and being humbled at the sight, he was received again into the society of angels to which he belonged. No one suffers punishment in the other world merely for hereditary evil, as that was not contracted by his own fault, but only for that actual evil which proceeded from himself; and consequently, only for so much of hereditary evil as he adopted and appropriated to himself by his own will and deed: nor are infants, when grown up to adults in heaven, consigned for a time to their proper natural state of hereditary evil merely for the sake of punishment, but in order to their conviction, that of themselves they are only evil, and therefore delivered from hell, which belongs to an evil nature, by the mere mercy of the Lord; consequently, that their heavenly inheritance is from his free gift, and not from any merit in themselves; and therefore they have nothing to glory in, or whereof to esteem themselves above others, on account of any self-assumed good; for that in so doing, they would as much transgress the law of mutual love, as the true doctrine of faith.

more than God, and this world more than heaven, and to esteem his neighbour as nothing in comparison of himself, or only for himself, so that he may be said to be love of self and of the world in the very abstract, n. 694, 731, 4317, 5660. That the prevailing love of self and of the world is the root of all evil, n. 1307, 1308, 1321, 1594, 1691—10038, 10742, such as contempt of others, enmity, hatred, revenge, cruelty, deceit, &c. n. 6667, 7372, 7373, 7374, 9348, 10038, 10742: and that from these evils proceeds every false [*omne falsum*] n. 1047, 10283, 10284, 10286.

343. Oft times when companies [*Chori*] (*) of little children have been with me, and their speech sounded in a soft confused manner, as not having yet attained to speak in concert as when grown up, I observed with something of surprize, that certain spirits present could not refrain from urging them to speak in another manner, on which the infant chorus shewed a repugnance, denoting something like resentment, saying, when given them to speak, *that it should not be so*. This I have often perceived, and was told, that it was for their trial, and to accustom them to resist any temptation to what is false or evil, as also not to suffer themselves to be compelled to think, speak, or act by direction from any other than the Lord only.

344. Thus much may serve to shew in what manner infants are educated in heaven, that so through the knowledge of truth, and the wisdom of good, they may be qualified for the angelical life, consisting in that love to the Lord, and one another, which has its ground in innocence: but how contrary is the education of children with many on earth! To give only the following instance. As I was one day walking in the street of a certain great city, I saw some boys fighting, which presently drew a great croud round them, which seemed much pleased with the fight; and I was told, that the parents of the young warriors were among them, encouraging their sons to the combat: certain good spirits and angels then present with me saw all that passed, through my eyes, and were affected, even to horror, at the fight, more especially at the encouragement given to the fray by the parents; saying, that all such ways of inciting children to hatred and revenge, tended to extinguish in them all mutual love and innocence implanting in them by the Lord; consequently, that they did all in their power to disqualify their own children for heaven, where all is love. May such parents as wish well to their children take warning hereby.

345. And here for a word concerning the difference between those who die in their infant state, and those who die adults.

(*) By the word *Chori* in this place, the author means such companies of spirits or angels as think in unity, and speak in symphony, so concentrating, as it were, their thoughts and words, as if they constituted but one person: but this is hard to describe, see above, n. 242, 255. Tr.

Now

Now the latter have in this life acquired a ground or plane [*planum*] which they take with them to the other world, and which confifts of their memory and prevailing natural affection; this remains fixed, and though quiefcent after death as to any activity, yet it ferves as an ultimate ground or bafis to the thoughts; and hence it follows, that according to the quality of this ground or plane, and the correfpondence of the rational part therewith, fo is the man after death (*): but fuch as die infants have no fuch plane, but one that is natural-fpiritual [*planum naturale spirituale*] as not having contracted any impurity from this material world and earthly body, and therefore not being infected with the like grofs affections and cogitations, but having imbibed all they have from heavenly influence: befides, infants know nothing of their having been born in this world, but look upon themfelves as natives of heaven, being ignorant of every other kind of nativity than what is fpiritual, and effected by knowledges of good and truth, and that underftanding and wifdom from which man is only properly denominated man; and as thefe are only from the Lord, fo it is their belief, and their rejoicing therein, that they are the Lord's. But notwithftanding this, the condition of men, who have had their time in this world, may be equally perfect with that of infants in the next, if they put away from them their corporeal and earthly affections, which are the love of felf and of the world, and in the room thereof become receptive of fpiritual loves.

(*) As it is very difficult to give a clearer tranflation of the foregoing paffage; fo probably, few of our readers, befides thofe who have been accuftomed to thinking abftractedly, will readily enter into the author's meaning: let it fuffice here to obferve in general, that by the acquired ground or plane (or fund) here fpoken of, we are to underftand fuch an habitual difpofition or tendency to the things of this world as remains with us after death, and by a kind of fecret influence of habit withholds the thoughts and affections from heavenly things; and yet not fo to be underftood, as if this tendency were not to be done away by the methods appointed for our purification in the intermediate ftate, where it was not by free choice and determination of the will become radical and effential in the conftitution of the foul. Let it be obferved, that the leffon here held forth to the reader is of infinite importance, as it denotes, that grace may be fo extinguifhed, and the habitual love of fin fo confirmed in this life, as to place us beyond the poffibility of help in the next, according to thofe words of the prophet: " Can the Ethiopian change " his fkin? or the leopard his fpots? then may ye alfo do good that are accuftomed " to do evil," Jer. xiii. 23. Tr.

Of the Wife and the Simple in Heaven.

346. It is commonly believed, that wife men will be exalted in heaven above the simple in honour and dignity, because we read in Daniel xii. 3. that " they that be wife shall shine as the " brightness of the firmament, and they that turn many to " righteousness, as the stars for ever and ever;" but few seem to know who are meant here by the wife, and by those that turn many to righteousness; it being generally thought, that this is spoken of the learned and the wife doctors in the church, who excel in doctrinal knowledge and preaching, and more especially such among them as have converted many to the faith; these are called men of wifdom and understanding in this world, but they are not so in a spiritual sense, unless their wifdom be of a heavenly quality, which shall here be spoken to.

347. True understanding, in a heavenly sense of the word, is interior understanding, springing from the love of truth, and not from any motive of glory either here or hereafter, but from a pure regard to truth itself in minds intimately affected and delighted with it; and all such love the light of heaven or divine truth, and consequently the Lord himself, who is the truth itself, see above, n. 126 to 140. Now this heavenly light of truth only enters the interior recesses of the mind, as being its proper receptacle; and as it enters and is received there, it gives delight, as is the property of all influx from heaven to do; such is the origin of genuine affection for truth, for its own sake; and they who are in this affection or love, they are in the true heavenly understanding, and " shine as the brightness of the " firmament:" they are said to shine, because divine truth in heaven appears splendent, see above, n. 132 : and the firmament or expanse of heaven signifies by correspondency that interior intellectual part both in angels and men, which is in the light of heaven : but as to those who love truth only for the sake of honour here, or glory hereafter, such shine not in heaven, forasmuch as their delight is not in the light of heaven, but of this world, which of itself, without the former, is mere

darkness;

darkness (222); for all such consider self only as the end, and truth but as the means subservient to that end; and therefore as their view is directed, not to heaven, but to this world, not to the Lord, but to themselves, consequently, they are not in the light of heaven, but in that of this world only: these, indeed, to outward appearance, and before men, seem as knowing and wise as the children of light, nay, and sometimes wiser, as being more warmed with the fire of self-love, and having learned to speak the same language with them, and also to make a shew of heavenly affections; but inwardly and in the sight of the angels they appear very different. Let this suffice to shew, who are meant in Scripture by the wise, who shall " shine in " heaven like the brightness of the firmament:" and now for a word as to such as are meant by those " that turn many to " righteousness, who shall shine as the stars."

348. By such as turn many to righteousness are meant the truly wise, and they only are called such in heaven, who are in the good of life, or who apply divine truths immediately to practical use; for divine truth, when so applied, becomes good, as being animated with free will and love, which constitutes the very essence of wisdom; whereas they who are called intellectual or understanding men, live not from truth as a principle, but commit it first to their memory, and from thence as a storehouse draw occasionally the documents of truth, whereby to regulate their life (*). In what particulars these two classes differ

---

(222) That the light of this world is for the outward, and the light of heaven for the inner man, n. 3222, 3223, 3337. That the light of heaven is in the natural light by influx, and that the natural man becomes wise only so far as he receives of the light of heaven, n. 4302, 4408. That the things of heaven are not visible by the light of this world, n. 9754, 3108. That the light of this world is as darkness to the angels, n. 1521, 1783, 1880.

(*) The difference between wise and intellectual men, according to our author's definition, appears to be this, viz. that the former receive divine truths into their affections (and not speculatively only) and are led thereby spontaneously, as from a divine principle or instinct into all good; whereas the latter treasure up truth in the memory, and so fit the external life thereto by a kind of reflex operation of mind; so that the good life of the former seems, as it were, natural, and the good life of the latter, as it were, studied and artificial. I wish that I may have so expressed myself here, as to render the matter more clear to the reader. Let it be remembered, that the author does not always use these two words, understanding and wisdom

differ in the heavens may be seen in the article concerning the two kingdoms of heaven, the cœlestial and the spiritual, n. 20 to 28; and also in the article concerning the three heavens, n. 29 to 40. They who are in the cœlestial kingdom of the Lord, which is the third or inmost heaven, are called Righteous, and that because they ascribe no righteousness to themselves, but all to the Lord only. Now righteousness in heaven signifies good proceeding from the Lord (223), and they who receive the same, and minister therefrom to the conversion of others, are such as the Lord speaks of, Matt. xiii. 43. " Then shall the " righteous shine forth as the sun in the kingdom of my Fa- " ther." Their shining as the sun, is from their being in love to the Lord from the Lord, as that love is signified by the sun, see above, n. 116 to 125: their light also partakes of the brightness of flame; and their ideas are vivacious and corresponding thereto, inasmuch as they receive the good of love immediately from the Lord as the heavenly sun.

349. All who have acquired true understanding and wisdom in this world are received into heaven, and become angels, every one according to the measure and quality thereof; for whatsoever principle any one has acquired and fixed in himself in this world, that remains with him after death, and is also augmented to fulness, but that within the degree of his affection and desire of good and truth, and not beyond it; they who have little affection and desire, receive but little, but yet as much as they can contain; and they who have much affection and desire, receive increase accordingly; the degree of affection and desire in every one being the measure that is to be filled: the reason of this is, because love, the properties of which are

---

wisdom [*intelligentia et sapientia*] precisely according to these definitions; but where they are spoken of in distinction, they are to be understood according thereto. Tr.

(223) That the merit and righteousness of the Lord is properly that good which prevails and reigns in heaven, n. 9486, 9986. That the righteous or justified person is he to whom is imparted that merit and righteousness; and he the unrighteous and unjustified person, who builds upon his own fancied righteousness and merit, n. 5069, 9263. The condition of the self-righteous in the other life, n. 942, 2027. That righteousness or justice in the Word is spoken of good, and judgment of truth; and therefore, to do justice and judgment means there, to act according to good and truth, n. 2235, 9857.

affection

affection and desire, receives what is answerable or suitable to itself according to its measure, as signified by those words of our Lord, " Whosoever hath, to him shall be given, and he " shall have more abundantly." " Good measure shall be given " unto you, pressed down, and shaken together, and running " over," Matt. xiii. 12. xxv. 29. Luke vi. 38.

350. All are received into heaven, who have loved good and truth as such; and they who have loved them much are called wise, and they who have loved them little are called simple; the former enjoy much light in heaven, the latter less; each according to the degree of his love: to love good and truth as such, or for their own sake, is to will and to do them from choice, for such only can be said to love them; and they are the people who love the Lord, and are loved by him; for good and truth are from the Lord, and consequently the Lord is in them as proceeding from him, and also in all such as receive them into their life's principle by willing and doing them. Man also, considered in himself, is no other than his measure of good and truth from the Lord, the former constituting his will, and the latter his understanding; and as the will and understanding are, such is the man: hence it follows, that so far any is loved of the Lord, as his will is formed by good, and his understanding by truth: to be loved of the Lord is inseparable from love to him, for love is reciprocal, and to him whom the Lord loveth he giveth to love him again.

351. It is commonly believed in the world, that they who are men of learning and skill in the doctrines of the church and the letter of Scripture, or in the sciences, are more acute discerners of truths than other men, and consequently excel them in true understanding and wisdom; and such form the like judgment as touching themselves; and therefore we shall proceed to shew what true understanding and wisdom is, what is the spurious, and what the false. True understanding and wisdom consists in seeing and perceiving what is good and what is true, and thereby what is false and evil, and in accurately distinguishing betwixt them, and that from an interior intuition and discernment. There is in every one an interiour and an exteriour, the former belonging to the inward or spiritual, and the

the latter to the outward or natural man; and accordingly as the interiour is formed and co-operates with the exteriour, so a man sees and perceives. The interiour of man can only be formed in heaven; but the exteriour is formed in this world. When the interiour is formed in heaven, then heavenly things pass by influx into the exteriour, which is from this world, and form it to a correspondence with the former, that so both may co-operate or act as one; and when this is effected, then the man sees and perceives from an inward sight. In order to the formation of the interiour, this one medium is requisite, viz. that man look up to a Divine Supreme Being, and to heaven; for, as was said before, the interiour is formed in heaven; and a man is then said to look up to the Divine Being, when he believes in him, and that he is the fountain of all good and truth, and consequently of all understanding and wisdom; and is willing to be led and governed by him: so, and so only, the interiour of man is opened to divine things. A man in this belief, and living according thereto, is in the power and capacity of becoming intellectual and wise; but in order to his being really so, he has many things to learn, both concerning heaven and this world; as touching the former, from the Word and the doctrines of the church; and as touching the latter, from scientifick knowledge; and is also to take along with him, that in the same proportion that he applies knowledge to the purposes of good life, so far only is he worthy of being reputed an understanding and wise man, as in that degree and no farther, his interior sight, which is the property of his intellect, and his interior affection, which is that of his will, derive their progress to perfection. The simple are of the following class, viz. such as have their interiour open to divine things, but their understanding not so well cultivated by truths, spiritual, moral, civil, or natural; such have indeed a sight of truths, and receive them when heard, but have no inward clear perception of them: but they who are denominated wise, are as follows, viz. such who have not only their interior affections open to divine good, but also their intellectual faculties so cultivated and enlarged, that they see divine truths by an internal evidence.

Thus

Thus much may serve to shew what is meant by true understanding and wisdom.

352. A spurious understanding and wisdom is, not to see what is true and good, and from thence what is false and evil, from any interior sight, but only to believe it so on the authority of others, and then to study to confirm ourselves in that belief. Now as such persons receive not truth by the light of truth, but on the credit given to another, they are equally liable to embrace falsehood as well as truth, and to confirm themselves in the former by reasonings and arguments adapted thereto, so as to give it the appearance of truth, for whatever is so confirmed puts on that appearance; and there is nothing but what is capable of such kind of confirmation. Now the interior faculties of such persons are only open from beneath, but their exterior in proportion to the degree of such confirmation; and therefore the light they see by is not the light of heaven, but the light of this world, or natural light, in which light what is false may appear as true, and when confirmed by a specious kind of arguments, may carry in them an apparent lustre of evidence, but not so when viewed in a heavenly light. Of this class such are least intelligent and wise, who have dealt most in this way of confirmation; and they come nearest to wisdom, who have practised it the least. Hence may be gathered what is meant by spurious understanding and wisdom; however, we range not under this class what has been received by children on the authority of their teachers, if when grown up to the use of reason they do not implicitly enslave themselves to their documents, but study to find out the truth, and cherish it when found: as such are led by a sincere affection for truth for its own sake, they see it in the light of its own evidence before they set themselves to confirm it by arguments (224). To illustrate this by an example: Certain spirits were reasoning together, how

(224) That it is the part of a wise man to see and perceive the truth of a doctrine before he goes about to confirm it by arguments, and not because it is held for truth by others, n. 1017, 4741, 7012, 7680, 7950. To see and perceive the truth by its own native evidence without the aid of argument, is the privilege of those only who love truth for its own sake, and as a rule of life, n. 8521. That the evidence arising from confirmation by argument is a natural, not a spiritual light,

how it came to pafs that the brute animals were born to all knowledge congruous to their nature refpectively, but not man; upon which they were told, that the former ftood in the primitive order of their nature, but man not fo, and therefore he is to be led back into it by inftruction and difcipline; whereas if man had preferved his original perfection, confifting in loving God above all things, and his neighbour as himfelf; in that cafe he would have been born with innate underftanding and wifdom, and to the belief of all truth, according to the enlargement of his faculties. Now the good fpirits immediately perceived the evidence of this argument by the light of truth; but the fpirits, who had confirmed themfelves in folifidianifm, and thereby had caft afide divine love and charity, could not receive it, as their confirmation in error had obfcured in them the light of truth.

353. Falfe underftanding and wifdom is that which is feparate from the acknowledgment of a Divine Being in all thofe who place nature in the room of God : all fuch think as mere animals, and are no other than fenfualifts, whatever character they may have in the world for erudition (225); for their learning reaches no farther than to the objects of fenfe laid up in their memory, and viewed in the light of material nature, though the fame natural fciences are of fubfervient ufe to form the minds of perfons truly intellectual : by the fciences we underftand experimental knowledge of various kinds, phy-

light, and fuch as fenfual and bad men may have, n. 8780. That all things, even fuch as are falfe, may be fo confirmed by fpecious arguments, as to put on the appearance of truth, n. 2482, 2490, 5033, 6865, 8521.
(225) That the fenfual part is the loweft degree of the life of man, as appertaining to his corporeal nature, n. 5077, 5767, 9212, 9216, 9331, 9730. That he is called a fenfual man, who forms all his judgment and conclufions from his bodily fenfes, and believes nothing but what he can fee with his eyes, or touch with his hands, n. 5094, 7693. That fuch a one thinks in his extremities, and not in his interiour, n. 5089, 5094, 6564, 7693. That his interior or fpiritual part is fhut againft all light of divine truth, n. 6564, 6844, 6845. That he is in the dim light of nature, and can fee nothing that is difcoverable only by the light of heaven, n. 6201, 6310, 6564—6622, 6624. That he is therefore inwardly in a ftate of oppofition to all things that relate to heaven and the true church, n. 6201, 6316, 6844, 6845, 6948, 6949. That even the learned, who have confirmed themfelves againft the truths of the latter, are no better than fenfual men, n. 6316. A defcription of the fenfual man, n. 10236.

ficks,

ficks, aftronomy, chymiftry, mechanicks, geometry, anatomy, metaphyficks, philofophy, the hiftory of kingdoms, and of the learned world, criticifm, and languages. Now as to thofe who prefide in ecclefiaftical matters, who at the fame time difbelieve the operations of a divine principle, and have no higher fentiments of religion than what relate to the outward man; such fee nothing farther in the Scriptures than others do in their fciences, nor confider them as containing matters that are to be underftood only by a reafon enlightened from above; and this becaufe the inner gate of their minds, and the faculties next to them, are fhut againft divine illumination; and this becaufe they have turned away their affections and underftanding from heavenly to earthly things; and therefore it is that truth and good are to them as darknefs, and falfe and evil as light: but, notwithftanding, mere fenfual men can play their part at reafoning, and fome of them very acutely, but then it is from the fallacies of fenfe in which they have confirmed themfelves by the fubtleties of fcience, and becaufe of their adroitnefs herein they conceit themfelves to be wifer than others (226); and their love of felf and the world is the fire that gives earneftnefs and warmth to their reafonings: fuch are they who are in falfe underftanding and wifdom, and are meant by thofe words of our Lord, Matt. xiii. 13, 14, 15. " Seeing they fee not, and hearing they hear not, neither do they underftand, &c." xi. 25. " Thou haft hid thefe things from the wife and prudent, and " revealed them unto babes."

354. I have had the privilege of converfing with many learned men after their deceafe, fome of them of great fame, and celebrated in the learned world for their writings; and with others of lefs note, but of deep underftanding: now fuch of them as inwardly difbelieved a Divine Being, though they outwardly profeffed one, became fo ftupid in the other world, as

(226) That fenfual men often reafon with great fubtlety and acutenefs, from an inferior underftanding joined to a prompt corporeal memory, n. 195, 196, 5700, 10236: but this from the fallacies of the fenfes, n. 5084, 6948, 7693. That the fenfual are fubtle and knavifh above others, n. 7693, 10236. That fuch were called by the ancients, ferpents of the tree of knowledge, n. 195, 196, 197, 6398, 6949, 10313.

not to be able to comprehend truths relating even to civil matters, much less such as are spiritual: and I could also perceive, nay, behold (for in the spiritual world such things are represented in a visible manner) that their interiour was so darkened, even to blackness, and so shut against every thing spiritual, as to be inaccessible to all heavenly light and influx: and that inward blackness appeared more particularly intense in those who had confirmed themselves in unbelief by their scientifical reasonings. All such in the other world greedily imbibe falsehood and error, as a sponge does water, and reject all truth, as rain is repelled from the tile of an house; nay, I have been informed, that the interiour of those, who have exalted nature in the room of God, appears, as it were, ossified; and their heads, even to the nostrils, have the resemblance of ebony, in token of their being destitute of all spiritual and intellectual perception: they who are of this class are plunged into a kind of gulphs or bogs, where they are disquieted and terrified with phantasies produced by the falsities they had adopted and cherished: the infernal fire of their life is a thirst of glory and the pride of distinction, by which they are incited to exasperate one another, and to torment all they can such as refuse to worship them as deities; and this they do by turns. Such is the end of all the learning and wisdom of this world, which, not having its foundation in the faith of Almighty God, is utterly destitute of heavenly light.

355. That such is the lot of the persons before mentioned, in the other world, may be gathered from hence; viz. that all things in their natural memory, and immediately connected with their bodily senses (as are the scientifical acquisitions spoken of above) are then totally quiescent, and only the conclusions or principles formed from thence remain as a fund for to supply them with thoughts and matter for conversation; for though a man carries his natural memory along with him, yet what he had laid up therein falls not under his intuition as before, as not being concordant with the light of a different world, and therefore he cannot call them forth to use; whereas things of a rational and intellectual nature, grounded on scientifick principles, quadrate with the light of the spiritual world; consequently,

quently, so far as any one has attained to rationality by the use of the sciences in this world, so far he is rational after he is set free from the body, it being the same spirit that thinks in both worlds (227).

356. But as to those, who, by the cultivation of their minds, by the sciences and different kinds of knowledge, have acquired true understanding and wisdom, as is the case with those who apply all their attainments to the purposes of good life, walk in the fear of God, reverence his Word, and adhere to spiritual morality *(spiritualem moralem vitam,* see above, n. 319). To such the sciences serve, as the means of attaining to wisdom, and of strengthening the things appertaining to faith: it was given me to perceive the interiour of their minds, wherein all appeared transparent from the light within them, and representing the sparkling colours and brightness of the diamond, the ruby, and the sapphire, in degree of lustre, according as they had employed their knowledge of the sciences in proof and confirmation of divine truths: such is the appearance which true understanding and wisdom exhibit, when represented as visible in the spiritual world (*), and this answerably to the nature of

---

(227) That things scientifical appertain to man's natural memory whilst in the body, n. 5212, 9922. That man carries with him his whole natural memory after death, n. 2475. This from experience, n. 2481 to 2486: but that he cannot draw from that memory in the other world, as he did in this, and that for many reasons, n. 2476, 2477, 2479.

(*) It is by no means incredible, that things spiritual and intellectual should be represented under visible appearances in the other world, as nature in this abounds with such significant emblems and expressions far beyond what is generally supposed: how do the passions and affections, the virtues and vices, and even the intellectual powers, figure themselves in the countenance and gestures of the body! and how do many of the flowers readily excite in us the ideas of mental properties and qualities, as of modesty, innocence, and purity, &c. inducing us, by consent, to denominate them by such epithets respectively! and thus heavenly things are pictured to us by such as are natural, according to an ancient doctrine alluded to by the sublime Milton in the following lines:

> " I shall delineate so,
> " By lik'ning spiritual to corporeal forms,
> " As may express them best, though what if earth
> " Be but the shadow of heav'n, and things therein
> " Each to other like more than on earth is thought."
> Par. Lost. Book V.

heavenly light, which is divine truth from the Lord, who is the original fource of all true underftanding and wifdom, fee above, n. 126 to 133. The grounds [*plana*] of that light in its feveral variegations of colours, are the interior receffes of the mind; and the illuftrations and confirmations of divine truths by fuch things as are in nature, and therefore in the fciences, produce thofe variegations (228); for the more interior and fpiritual part in man contemplates what is laid up in the natural memory, and whatever is therein employed for the confirmation of divine truth, it fublimates, as it were, by the fire of cœleftial love, takes it to itfelf, and fpiritualizes it: whilft man is in the body, he continues a ftranger to this procedure of the mind, and that becaufe during his abode therein he thinks in a double capacity, both fpiritually and naturally, but has no perception of the former, but only of what paffes in his natural thoughts; but when he enters upon the fpiritual world, he has then no longer any perception of what he thought naturally in this world, but only of what he thought fpiritually (*); and this by change of ftate. Hence it may appear, that men through knowledge and inftruction in the fciences, as the means of wifdom, may become fpiritual, if this obfervation be confined to fuch as live in the faith and fear of God: nay, fuch meet with a more particular acceptance in heaven, and obtain a place in the center of their refpective focieties, n. 43, as being more illuminated than their fellows. Thefe are the underftanding and wife ones, who are faid to fhine as the brightnefs of the firmament, and as the ftars in the heavens: but they are denominated fimple, who indeed had faith in God, reverenced his Word, and

---

(228) That there are moft beautiful colours in heaven, n. 1053, 1624. That thofe colours are the modifications or variegations of the light of heaven, n. 1042, 1043—4922, 4742, and confequently fo many appearances of truth from good, and fignify things appertaining to underftanding and wifdom, n. 4530, 4922, 4677, 9466.

(¹) Let it be noted here, that the author does indeed, in many parts of his writings, fpeak of departed fpirits as recollecting and referring to paft tranfactions in the body from their natural memory; but then this is not to be underftood according to the ftated laws of the other world, but as a particular privilege, permiffion, or ftate, to anfwer certain purpofes; and accordingly he generally premifes on thefe occafions, that they were placed in fuch a ftate as when in the body, or the like. Tr.

lived

lived spiritual and moral lives, but had not much improved their intellectual part; for the mind of man, like any soil, rises in value according to the degree of its cultivation.

Of the Rich and the Poor in Heaven.

357. Various are the opinions concerning admission into the kingdom of heaven, whilst some suppose that the poor only, not the rich, meet with a reception there; others hold, that both rich and poor are admitted alike; and a third sort, that the former can gain no admittance without first divesting themselves of their wealth, and entering into a voluntary poverty: and all these support their different opinions by passages from the Scriptures: but they who make such distinctions between the rich and the poor, in respect to their qualification for heaven, shew themselves strangers to the right meaning of the Scriptures, which have both a recondite or spiritual, and also a literal or natural sense; and they who interpret them only according to the latter, must mistake their true meaning in many places, particularly in what is spoken therein concerning the rich and the poor in relation to this subject; as for instance, that it is as impossible for the rich to enter into the kingdom of heaven, as for a camel to pass through the eye of a needle; but that it is easy for the poor, as we are therein told, that " theirs is the " kingdom of heaven," Luke vi. 20, 21; whereas they who know any thing of the spiritual sense of the Word, understand these sayings very differently, being convinced on the authority thereof, that the kingdom of heaven is appointed for all who live the life of faith and love, whether they be rich or poor; and who they are that are meant by this distinction in Scripture shall be explained in what follows. From much conversation and long abode with the angels, I know of a truth that the rich find as ready admission into heaven as the poor, and that no one is excluded merely on account of his wealth, or received because of his poverty in this world; both classes are there alike, and more of the rich in the higher stations of bliss and glory than of the poor.

358. I shall

358. I shall enter upon this subject with observing, that a man may lawfully acquire riches, and increase his store, according to the opportunity afforded him, provided he keep free from subtle devices, and every evil art; may eat and drink of the best, if he place no part of his happiness therein; may dwell magnificently, if according to his rank in life; converse like others upon common worldly topicks, and share in the publick diversions; that there is no need of severity of behaviour, downcast looks, and other appearances of mortification; but he may be pleasant and chearful; nor is under any other obligation of divesting himself of his goods to bestow them on the poor, than what his own particular impulse or choice may lay upon him: in a word, that as to externals, he may live in a common way like other orderly people, without any bar to his admission into heaven, provided that he inwardly cherishes a due reverence and fear of the Lord, and acts justly and with all good conscience towards his neighbour; for every one's real character is to be estimated according to his internal sentiments and affections, or by his faith and love; for these are the principles that give life and character to all that proceeds from him, as the life of the act is in the will, and the life of the speech is in the sentiment; for as we act from the will, so we speak from the thought; and, therefore, where it is said in Scripture, that every one shall be judged according to his deeds, and recompensed according to his works, we are to understand it, as if it were said, according to his thoughts and affections, from which his works proceed, or which are in his works; for without the former, the latter are of no consideration, and therefore receive their quality and character from them (229). Hence we see, that it is not the exteriour,

(229) That it often occurs in Scripture, that man shall be judged and recompensed according to his deeds or works, n. 3934. By deeds and works there, we are not to understand them as they appear in their external form, but as they are in their root or inward principle; for even bad men do works apparently good in their external form, but only good men such as are both outwardly and inwardly good, n. 3934, 6073. That all moral deeds, as well as bodily acts, proceed from man's inward faculties and powers, as his thinking and willing, and owe their essence and qualities thereto; and, therefore, according to the internal principle is the external production, n. 3934, 8911, 10331; consequently, according to a man's love and faith, n. 3934, 6073, 10331, 10333: that therefore the works contain
their

exteriour, but the interiour, which commands the exteriour, that does all in man. To illustrate this by the following instance: He that refrains from defrauding another only through fear of the laws, and of the loss he might otherwise suffer in his reputation or interest, and who but for such restraints would not scruple to take all advantages of him in his power; such a one, however honest his dealings may appear outwardly, yet he is guilty of deceit and fraud in his thoughts and will, and is governed by a principle from beneath [*infernum in se habet*]. On the other hand, the upright man, who refrains from taking all undue advantages of another, though secure from discovery, and that because it would be contrary to his duty to God and his neighbour; such a one makes a conscience of his willing and thinking, and is under a heavenly influence: their dealings outwardly are the same in both, but inwardly and in principle they are widely different.

359. As then a man may pursue an ordinary course of life in externals, may acquire riches, and live elegantly according to his rank, as to good cheer, dress, and dwelling; carry on his worldly business like other men, and take pleasure in the good things of this life, to the comforting both of his body and mind, provided that he lives in the true fear of God, and in love towards his neighbour. As this is the case, it will not appear so difficult a matter to get to heaven, as some imagine (*): the main difficulty lies in resisting the love of self and of the world, that they gain not the victory over us; as from this quarter all our danger proceeds (230): and that otherwise our way

---

their principle, or are the principle itself in effect and operation, n. 10331. Therefore, to be judged and recompensed according to our deeds and works, is the same as if spoken of our principles, n. 3147, 3934, 6073, 8911, 10331, 10333. That those works which have respect to self, and the world, are not good works, but only such as respect the Lord, and the good of our neighbour, n. 3147.

(*) It must be owned, that our author here is far from shewing any thing of the precisian, or of monastick rigour; and yet his doctrine, when taken along with the applied restrictions, is as far from giving countenance to carelessness, or over-indulgence; and the danger he subjoins that we are in from the love of self and of the world, and whatever wrong habits we may have contracted thereby, will be found to minister to the best of us abundant matter for repentance, self-denial, and watchfulness. Tr.

(230) That all evils originate from the love of self and of the world, n. 1307, 1308.

way is not fo hard to make, as fome fuppofe, we may learn from thofe words of our Lord; " Learn of me, for I am meek " and lowly in heart, and ye fhall find reft unto your fouls; " for my yoke is eafy, and my burden is light," Matt. xi. 29, 30. Now the yoke of the Lord is eafy, and his burden light, fo far as man renounces the evils flowing from the love of felf and of the world, for fo far the Lord is his guide, and gives him the maftery over them.

360. I have converfed with fome after their deceafe, who had in this life abdicated the world, and betook themfelves to folitude, that they might be the more at leifure for devout exercifes, as the fafer way to heaven: but fuch moftly appear of a melancholy caft in the other world, lightly efteem thofe that are not like themfelves, and are diffatisfied, through a fuppofed merit in themfelves, that they are not exalted to a higher ftate than others; they have little affection for others, and therefore are backward to exercife thofe offices of love, which is the bond of a heavenly conjunction (*): they exceed, it is true, in an ardent defire for heaven, but when they are exalted to be with the angels, they carry with them a certain fadnefs that damps the joys of the former; wherefore they are disjoined from them, and betake themfelves to a kind of lonely fituations, where they lead a reclufe life, as they did in this world. Man can only be formed for heaven in this world, where his affections have their beginning objects, but vanifh and come to nothing, if not exercifed in focial connexions, or rather are fwallowed up folely in felf, to a total neglect of his neighbour; fo that a life of charity towards our neighbour, confifting in a confcientious difcharge of every relative and focial duty, is the path-way to heaven, and not a mere fpeculative piety feparated therefrom (231); now action, and not inaction, is the vital fupport

---

1308, 1321, 1594—9348, 10038, 10742; fuch as contempt of others, enmity, hatred, revenge, cruelty, deceit, &c. n. 6667, 7372, 7373—10038, 10742. That man is born with a natural propenfity to thefe two loves, and that his hereditary evils are from thence, n. 694, 4317, 5660.

(*) Hitherto we are to underftand them as in the intermediate ftate. Tr.

(231) That charity towards our neighbour confifts in doing every thing that is good, juft, and right, in all our acts and relations refpecting him, n. 8120, 8121, 8122;

port of charity. I shall here give an instance of this from experience: I have known more in the regions of bliss among those that had acquired riches in trade by an honest industry, than among such as had become wealthy through the emoluments of high and honourable offices in the state; as the latter are so liable to be infected, on account of their honours and importance, with the pride of life and love of the world, which have a natural tendency to beget self-love, and consequently to alienate the affections from heavenly things.

361. The lot of the good rich, when translated to heaven, is that of being in a condition of greater apparent splendor than others; some of them dwell in stately palaces, richly furnished and ornamented as with gold and silver, together with abundance of all things ministering to the delights of life; however, they place no part of their affections on these things, but only on their uses; of these they take good notice, but the mere ornamental part, as gold and silver, this they regard with little attention, and that because when in this world their minds were set on uses, and they considered gold and silver only as means subservient thereto. Now uses in the other world appear in splendid forms, the good of use as gold, and the true of use as silver (232); and according to their practical uses in this life, such is the splendor and such the delights of their state in the following. Among the good uses, are those of providing things needful for ourselves and dependants suitably to our rank; to seek the means of promoting the publick good; and also to have

8122; and therefore it extends to all that a man thinks, wills, and does, n. 8124. That a life of piety without charity avails nothing, but joined with charity leads to every good, n. 8252, 8253.

(232) That every good has its particular delight from use, and according to its use respectively, n. 3049, 4984, 7038; and also its specifick quality, consequently as is the use such is the good, n. 3049. That all the delight and comfort of life is from uses, n. 997. That, generally speaking, life consists in uses, n. 1964. That the angelical life consists in the goods of love and charity, consequently in the exercise of uses, n. 453. That the Lord, and consequently the angels derivatively from him, has principally only regard to final causes, which answer to uses among men, n. 1317, 1645, 5844. That the kingdom of the Lord is the kingdom of uses, n. 453, 696, 1103, 3645, 4054, 7038. That the service of the Lord consists in the performance of uses, n. 7038. That all have their distinguishing character from the uses they perform, n. 4054, 6815. This illustrated, n. 7038.

where-

wherewith to help our neighbour, which he that abounds, can better do than he that does not; besides, that such a diligence to procure what may be for the good of them that lack, preserves us from idleness, that pernicious kind of life which gives our innate evil the power to take possession of us. These are among the good uses, as far as they are invigorated by a divine principle, or so far as man is actuated therein by motives of duty to God, and regards worldly means only as subordinate thereto.

362. But quite contrary is the lot of such rich persons in the other world, as lived without religious faith in this, nay, hardened themselves in unbelief: all such are in hell, where filth, misery, and want of every comfort, is their portion; for into these are riches changed, when loved for their own sake; and not only their riches, but also the uses to which they applied them, such as their luxury and self-indulgence for the gratification of their other corrupt passions, or to evidence their pride and contempt of others: riches in such hands, having nothing but what is earthly and vile in their use, become changed into vileness at last. A spiritual use and application of riches is, as it were, a seasoning and preservative to them, and may be compared to the soul in the body, or to the light and heat of the sun in their effects on a humid soil; but in the other case, riches may be considered as a body without a soul to preserve it from putrefaction; or to a swampy ground in a deep valley shaded from the light of the sun: such are the men who suffer riches to alienate their hearts from God.

363. Every one's darling affection or ruling passion continues with him after his departure from this world, nor is it extinguished in eternity (*); for the spirit of a man is as the love that prevails in and possesses him; and, moreover, (which has hitherto been a secret on earth) the body of every spirit and angel is the external form of the love that presides in him, and

---

(*) It must here be observed to the reader, that a more concerning doctrine (and highly credible it appears from scriptural authority) or one that infers more important caution as to what affections and habits we contract, cannot present itself to the mind of man; and therefore the subject of this particular number is warmly recommended to his serious attention. Tr.

corresponds

corresponds to the internal form of his mind and will, insomuch that spirits know one another by their countenances, gestures, and speech; and by the same correspondent marks it would be known what spirit a man is of in this world, were he not accustomed to act the counterfeit in these particulars; the ruling passion would equally manifest itself in time, as it does in eternity. I have conversed with some that lived seventeen centuries ago, whose lives are recorded in the writings of those days; and they appeared to be governed by the same affections and dispositions by which they are charactered therein; from which we may gather, that the same love of riches, and for the same ends, continues with every one hereafter, though with this difference, that the riches which had been applied here to good purposes are changed into heavenly pleasures to the owners in the other world according to their uses respectively; and that the riches, which had been applied here to bad purposes, become changed to the owners into filth and corruption hereafter, answerably to the evil uses they had made of them; nay, such nastiness they take pleasure in, as corresponding to those filthy lusts to which they had made their riches subservient, or to that sordid avarice which consists in the love of riches for their own sake; for such passions are a spiritual filthiness defiling the soul.

364. The poor are not qualified for heaven by their poverty, but by their principles and life, for these follow every one, be he rich or poor, nor is there any distinguishing mercy for the one more than the other (233); but he is received whose life has been good, and he is rejected whose life has been evil: besides, poverty may be turned into as great a snare and hinderance to a man in his way to heaven, as riches themselves, seeing that many of the poorer sort fall into discontent at their condition, covet many things above their rank, and looking upon riches as the greatest of blessings (234), grudge if they be not satisfied, and

---

(233) That mercy is not arbitrary and immediate, but respective and mediate; and that all they, who live in the fear of the Lord, are under his merciful protection and guidance both here and for ever; n. 8700, 10659.

(234) That riches and honour are not real blessings in themselves, and therefore are given alike both to the good and the evil, n. 8939, 10775, 10776. That the true blessing is love and faith from the Lord, effecting a union with him, and thereby

and indulge murmurings against God's providence; add to these, their envyings against others, their fraudulent practices, and gross sensual indulgences: how different will be the lot of these from that of the contented industrious poor, who pass the time of their sojourning in all godliness and honesty? I have sometimes conversed in the other world with certain departed peasants, who had lived here in the fear of God and all good conscience, who, having an affectionate desire to know the truth, sought to be more particularly instructed as to faith and charity, having heard much concerning the former in this world, and more concerning the latter in the other; on which it was told them, that charity has respect to every thing belonging to life, and faith to every thing belonging to doctrine; consequently, that the former consists in willing and doing every thing that is just and right, and the latter in thinking and believing according thereto; and that when any one wills and does what he thinks and believes to be right and good, then faith and charity are no longer two but one, just as thought and will unite in forming a determinate act of the mind: this they well understood and received with pleasure, saying, that when in this world they did not look upon believing as a thing different or separate from living.

365. From what has been offered on this head, it will appear, that the rich may find as easy an admission into heaven as the poor; and the notion of its being more difficult to the former is from a wrong understanding of those places in Scripture, where both are mentioned. By the rich there, in a spiritual sense, we are to understand such as abound in the knowledge of good and truth, and accordingly those who are within the church where the Word is known; and by the poor, such as are destitute of that knowledge, but desire it, consequently those who are without the church, and strangers to the Scriptures. By the rich man cloathed in purple and fine linen, who was cast into hell, is meant the Jewish nation, which being in possession of the Word, and through that abounding in the knowledge of good and truth, is represented by the rich man;

by becoming the procuring cause of man's eternal happiness, n. 1420, 1422, 2846. —4981, 8939, 10495.

by

by purple clothing, is meant the knowledge of good; and by fine linen, the knowledge of truth. By the poor man, who lay at his gate, and defired to be fed with the crumbs that fell from the rich man's table, and was carried into heaven by the angels, we are to underſtand the Gentiles, who had not the forementioned knowledge, but defired to have it, Luke xvi. 19, 31. By the rich, who were invited to the great fupper, and excuſed themſelves, is alſo to be underſtood the Jewiſh nation; and by the poor, who were called to fupply their place, are underſtood the Gentiles, or fuch as were without the pale of the church, Luke xii. 16, 24; and as to the rich man, concerning whom the Lord faith, that " it is eaſier for a camel to go through the " eye of a needle, than for fuch a one to enter into the king- " dom of heaven," Matt. xxix. 24. we are to underſtand as mean rich men both in a literal and figurative fenſe; in the former, fuch as abound in riches, and fet their hearts upon them; in the latter, fuch as abound in natural knowledge and the fciences; for theſe are their fpiritual riches, by which, through the effort of their own underſtanding, they prefumptuouſly think to poſſeſs themſelves of the knowledge of divine things, which method being contrary to the divine order, it is faid to be harder, than for a camel to paſs through the eye of a needle; for in this fenſe *camel* fignifies fcientifical knowledge in general, and by *the eye of a needle* is fignified fpiritual truth (235). That theſe are fignified by *camel*, and the *eye of a needle*, is not underſtood at this day, becauſe the key to that knowledge, which

(235) That by *camel* in the Word is fignified, in general, fcientifical knowledge, or what paſſes through the fenſes, n. 3048, 3071, 3143, 3145. What is fignified by embroidery and needle-work, and confequently by needle, n. 9688. That to enter into the truths of faith by fuch kind of knowledge is contrary to the divine order, n. 10236. That they who attempt this are infane with reſpect to things pertaining to heaven and the true church, n. 128, 129, 130, 232, 233, 6047; and appear as intoxicated in the other world when they think of fpiritual things, n. 1072. Their particular difpoſition, n. 196. Illuſtration by examples, that fpiritual things are not to be comprehended by fuch natural knowledge, n. 233, 2094, 2196, 2203, 2209. That by means of fpiritual light we may fearch out the fcientifical knowledge of the natural man, but not *vice verſa*, becauſe fpiritual influx defcends into nature, but nature afcends not up to fpirit, n. 3219, 5119—9110, 9111. That divine truths are firſt to be admitted and received into the mind, and then we may apply to things of fcientifical knowledge for illuſtration, but not *vice verſa*, n. 6047.

explains

explains how spiritual things are signified by the literal sense of the word, is not in the hands of the church; for there is both a spiritual and a natural sense throughout the Word, it being written according to correspondency between things natural and spiritual, to the end that there might be an alliance between heaven and earth, and between angels and men, since the time of their immediate communication ceased. Thus we have shewed who are meant in particular by the rich in the Word, viz. such as abound in the knowledge of good and truth, and that by the several kinds of this knowledge are meant the riches there spoken of, as may be seen in the passages here referred to, Isai. x. 12, 13, 14. ch. xxx. 6, 7. xlv. 3. Jer. xvii. 3. xlvii. 7. l. 36, 37. li. 13. Dan. v. 2, 3, 4. Ezek. xxvi. 7, 12. xxvii. 1. to the end. Zech. ix. 3, 4. Psal. xl. 13. Hos. xii. 9. Apoc. iii. 17, 18. Luke xiv. 33. *et alibi:* and that by the poor are meant those who have not the same means of knowledge, but are desirous of them, see Matt. xi. 5. Luke vi. 20, 21. xiv. 21. Isai. xiv. 30. xxix. 19. xli. 17, 18. Zeph. iii. 12, 18. All these passages referred to may be seen explained according to their spiritual sense in ARCANA COELESTIA, n. 10227.

Of Marriage in Heaven.

366. As heaven is inhabited by the human race, and the angels there are of both sexes; and as by the order of creation the woman is for the man, and the man for the woman, and the love of each for the other innate in both, it follows, that there are marriages in heaven as well as on earth, though very different in kind. Now wherein they differ, and wherein they resemble each other, shall be the subject of the following chapter (*).

(*) The reader will have no reason to be offended at the title of this chapter, when he is told, that the spiritual union here treated of under the name of marriage, is quite of a different kind, both as to means and end, from that marriage which our Lord declares to have no place at the resurrection, as will evidently appear to him as he proceeds. Tr.

367. Mar-

367. Marriage in heaven is the conjunction of two in unity of mind, the nature of which shall here be explained. The mind consists of two parts, one of which is called the intellect or understanding, and the other the will, and where both these co-operate or act in union, they form one mind. Now the husband there represents and exercises the intellectual part, and the wife the province of the will; and when the interior union of both manifests itself in the exterior or sensitive part, it is called conjugal love; whence it appears, that conjugal love derives its origin from the conjunction of two in unity of mind, and this is called in heaven cohabitation, without the idea of distinction of parties; and, therefore, where two are so united in spiritual marriage, they are not called two, but one angel (236).

368. That such is the proper conjunction and intimate union of minds between husband and wife, is indicated by their very formation, the man being formed more for intellectual purposes, and of deeper thought; but the woman naturally to be led and actuated more by the motions of the will. The like also seems denoted by the particular genius and form of each respectively; *by the genius*, in that the talent of the man consists more in the exercise of reason; that of the woman in the display of affection: and by the difference of *form*, in that man has a rougher and less comely aspect, a harsher speech, and a more robust body; whilst a lovely countenance, a soft voice, and a tender frame, recommend the female: nor is the difference less between the understanding and will, or thought and affection; and so also between truth and good, and faith and love; for truth and faith respect the understanding, as good and love respect the will. Hence it is, that in the Word, by *youth* and *man*, in a spiritual sense, are meant the understanding of truth; and by *virgin* and *woman*, the affection of good; and likewise, that the church, from its affection to good and truth, is represented and denominated woman, and also virgin; as likewise,

(236) That men little know now o'days what and whence true conjugal love is, n. 2727. That true conjugal love consists in unity of will, n. 2731. That such as are in it have, as it were, but one mind, n. 2732, 10168, 10169. From this conjunction of minds proceeds spiritual love or union, n. 1594, 2057, 3939—7081 to 7086, 7501, 10130.

that all, who are in the affection of good, are ſtiled virgins; thus in Apoc. xiv. 4. (237).

369. What has been ſaid above is not ſo to be underſtood, as if huſband and wife were not each ſeparately endowed with underſtanding and will, but only that the intellectual part has the aſcendant in the former, and the will part in the latter, and each is denominated from the predominant property, though, ſtrictly ſpeaking, there is no predominancy in the heavenly marriages, becauſe the will of the wife is that of the huſband, and the intellect of the huſband is that of the wife, both willing and thinking the ſame, and conſequently of one mind: and this union is the more cloſe and intimate, as the will of the wife joins itſelf to the intellect of the huſband, and the intellect of the huſband to the will of the wife, and that more eſpecially when they face each other; for, as has been ſaid more than once, there is then a mutual communication of thoughts and affections in the heavens, and more eſpecially between huſband and wife through greater mutual affection. Thus much may ſuffice to explain that conjunction of minds, which is the bond of ſpiritual marriage in the heavens, and is the ſource of conjugal love, viz. when each freely communicates their ſpiritual good things to the other.

370. I have been told by the angels, that as far forth as any two are conjoined in this bond of mental union, ſo far are they advanced in conjugal love, and alſo in underſtanding, wiſdom, and happineſs, and that becauſe divine truth and good, from whence proceed all true underſtanding, wiſdom, and happineſs, have their ingreſs into conjugal love, as their proper plane or ground, wherein truth and good unite; for as there is

---

(237) That by *young men* in the Word is meant the underſtanding of truth, or the perſons that underſtand it, n. 7668. That *men* ſignifies the ſame, n. 158, 265, 749, 915, 1007—9007. That by *woman* is ſignified the affection of good and truth, n. 568, 3160, 6014, 7337, 8994. The church by the ſame, as alſo by *wife*, n. 252, 253, 749, 770—252, 253, 409, 749, 770: under what difference, n. 915, 2517, 3236, 4510, 4822. That *huſband* and *wife*, taken in their moſt exalted ſenſe, are ſpoken of the Lord, and his conjunction with heaven and the church, n. 722. That *virgin* ſignifies the affection of good, n. 3067, 3110, 3179, 3189, 6731, 6742: and alſo the church, n. 2362, 3081, 3963, 4638, 6729, 6775, 6778.

a cona conjunction of intellect and will, so is there also of truth and good, becaufe the intellect is that which receives divine truths, and is formed thereby; and the will is that which receives divine good, and alfo receives its form from it; for what a man wills, that is his good; and what he receives into his underftanding, that appears to him as truth; and, therefore, it comes to the fame, whether you call it a conjunction of the intellect and will, or a conjunction of truth and good. The conjunction of truth and good conftitutes an angel, and alfo his underftanding, wifdom, and happinefs; for according to fuch conjunction is the degree of angelical perfection; and, therefore, as far as truth and good, or, which comes to the fame, as far as faith and love, are conjoined in any angel, fuch is his angelical character and excellence.

371. That a divine virtue proceeding from the Lord is the influencing principle in true conjugal love, is becaufe the latter is derived from the conjunction of good and truth; for, as was faid above, it is all the fame, whether we call it the conjunction of intellect and will, or the conjunction of good and truth: now this conjunction of good and truth derives its origin from the divine love of the Lord towards all in heaven and earth. From this divine love proceeds divine good, and divine good is received both by angels and men in divine truth as its proper receptacle; and, therefore, he, who is in no degree of divine truth, can receive nothing from the Lord and from heaven; but as far forth as good and truth are conjoined in any one, fo far is he joined to the Lord and heaven. Such is the origin of true conjugal love, and accordingly a fit plane or ground for the reception of the divine influx; and hence it is, that the conjunction of good and truth is called in heaven the cœleftial marriage, and that heaven in Scripture language is compared to and called marriage; and alfo that the Lord is called the bridegroom and hufband, and heaven with the church, his bride and wife (238).

372. Good

(238) That true conjugal love derives its origin, caufe, and effence from the conjunction [*conjugio*] of good and truth, and is therefore of heavenly extraction, n. 2728, 2729. Of the heavenly fpirits, who have a perception of it from this idea,

372. Good and truth, as conjoined in angel or man, are not two, but one, becaufe there the good is in the truth, and the truth in the good: this conjunction is as when any one thinks of what he wills, and wills what he thinks of, for fo the thinking and willing co-operate and conftitute one mind, the thought being the form to the will, and the will as the effence and life of the thought; and hence it is, that where two are joined together in this fpiritual marriage, they are not called two in heaven, but one angel. In this fenfe are to be taken thofe words of our Lord: "Have ye not read, that he who made them from the beginning, made them male and female? And faid, For this caufe fhall a man leave father and mother, and cleave unto his wife, and they twain fhall be one flefh; wherefore they are no more twain, but one flefh; wherefore what God hath joined together, let not man put afunder: all men cannot receive this faying, but they to whom it is given," Matt. xix. 4, 5, 6, 11. Mark x. 6, 7, 8, 9. Gen. ii. 24. In thefe words are defcribed the heavenly marriage of the angels, and alfo the conjunction of good and truth; and by a man's being forbid to feparate what God hath joined together, we are to underftand, that good is not to be feparated from truth.

373. Thus has been explained the origin of true conjugal love, and fhewed how it is firft formed in the minds of the parties, and thence defcending to the corporeal part, is there fenfibly experienced as love; for whatever is perceived in the bodily affections is derived from man's fpiritual part, viz. his underftanding and will, which conftitute the fpiritual man; and though in fuch defcent it affumes a different form, yet it is fimilar and confentaneous to its principle, juft as the body acts conformably to the direction of the foul, or as the effect is

---

idea, n. 10756. That conjugal love exactly refembles the conjunction of good and truth, of which, n. 1094, 2173, 2429—9206, 9495, 9637. How the conjunction of good and truth takes effect, and in whom, n. 3834, 4096, 4301—7623 to 7627, 9258. That none know what true conjugal love is, but they who are in good and truth from the Lord, n. 10171. That by marriage in the Word is fignified the marriage of good and truth, n. 3132, 4434, 4834. That in true conjugal love is the kingdom of the Lord and heaven, n. 2737.

obfequious

obsequious to the efficiency of its cause, according to what has been laid down in the two articles concerning correspondences.

374. I heard an angel describe true conjugal love, and its cœlestial delights, as divine good and divine truth from the Lord in two persons, so united, as to form in a manner but one; and he said, that every married pair in heaven was an instance of this heavenly love, forasmuch as the good and truth in every one is his proper self both in mind and body, seeing that the body is the express image of the mind, as being formed after its likeness. He inferred from hence, that a divine likeness is imaged in two persons that are in true conjugal love, and consequently that they are a similitude of heaven, as the universal heaven is divine good and divine truth proceeding from the Lord, and consequently that the whole of heaven was represented in that love, together with beatitudes and delights innumerable, which indefinite term he expressed by a word that signifies myriads of myriads. He expressed astonishment, that members of the Christian church should continue such strangers to this truth; whereas that church is the Lord's representative of heaven on earth, and heaven exhibits a complete marriage of good and truth. He likewise appeared amazed at adultery being more commonly practised within than without the church, as the inordinate gratification of that passion in every spiritual view is the love of false joined with evil, and the pleasure of it of an infernal nature, being diametrically opposite to the delights of heaven flowing from the love of truth conjoined with good.

375. Every one knows that two married persons, who are in mutual love, have an interior bond, as it is essential to the true conjugal state that there be a union of minds and affections, and according to the quality of these such is the union, and consequently the love: now the mind is entirely formed of the species of truth and good that it has imbibed, for all things in the universe have some relation to good and truth (real or apparent), and also to their conjunction; wherefore the union of minds is according to the quality and kinds of truth and good from which they are formed, and that the most perfect union where the latter are pure and genuine. It is to be remarked here,

here, that there is no stronger sympathy than between truth and good, and accordingly from this source it is that true conjugal love deduces its origin (239): there is also a sympathy between false and evil, from which proceeds a love, but of an infernal kind, and the end of which is hell.

376. From what has been here said concerning the origin of conjugal love, we may be able to pronounce who are in conjugal love, and who are not: now of the former class are all they, who, through divine truths, attain to divine good, conjugal love being only so far pure and genuine, as the truths which are joined to the good are so: and as all good in union with its truths is from the Lord, it follows, that no one can be in a state of perfect conjugal love, unless he acknowledge the Lord and his divinity, for otherwise the divine influence and presence are not in the truths, which a man has, to sanctify and make them divine.

377. From hence we may conclude, that they who come under the predicament of false (*), or opposite to the truth, [qui in falsis] more especially if from an evil principle, [in falsis

---

(239) That all things in the universal heaven and world have some relation to good and truth, n. 2451, 3166, 4390, 4409, 5232, 7256, 10122; and to their conjunction, n. 10555. That there is a marriage between good and truth, n. 1094, 2173, 2503. That good loves, and consequently desires truth, and to be joined to it, and that there is a perpetual tendency to union in both, n. 9206, 9207, 9495. That the life of truth is from good, n. 5089, 1997, 2579, 4070—5147, 9667. That truth is the form of good, n. 3049, 3180, 4574, 9154. That truth is to good as water is to bread, n. 4976.

(*) It is not easy to render our author's meaning in this place intelligible to the common reader without a paraphrase, not only on account of the difference of idioms in the two languages, but also with respect to the conception of the matter. Thus where he speaks of the false of evil, and the true of good, he not only uses those words as substantives, which are adjectives in the English, but in a sense which we have no substantives that fully express. Thus, the error, falsehood, or falsity of evil, conveys not the idea meant; but the false of evil here signifies a contrariety to whatever is right and true, proceeding from a disposition of mind or principle contrary to every thing that is good, or a wrong understanding issuing from a perverse will and depraved affections. Thus, the unconverted, natural man, who loves only himself and the world, is an enemy to all spiritual truth through the malignity of his nature; and all that such a one thinks, says, and does, is contrary to the divine order and will; as there is no divine love in his heart, there is no divine light in his mind and understanding, but such a one is in spiritual darkness, or in the false of (from) evil. Tr.

ex malo] cannot experience any thing of true conjugal love, as their inward gate is shut against the heavenly influx, and their external or natural part occupied by false and evil, which, through their close conjunction, form an infernal kind of marriage; some instances of which I have seen: they converse indeed together, and have external fellowship in lewdness; but inwardly hate one another beyond all description.

378. Neither can there be true conjugal love between two persons of different religions, as the true of one agrees not with the good of the other; but two dissimilar and discordant persuasions cannot consist with unanimity, and therefore their love cannot be of spiritual extraction; or if they cohabit and agree, such agreement is the effect only of natural causes (240); for this reason marriages in the heavens are formed only of those who belong to the same society, as being in good and truth of the same kind and quality: that all there of one and the same society are in like good and truth, and differ from those of other societies, see above, n. 41, *& seq.* This was represented among the Israelites by their marrying within their own tribes, and in particular into their own families, and not with others.

379. Neither can there be true conjugal love between a husband and different wives at the same time, as this counteracts the spiritual origin and end of marriage, which is the union of two minds, and consequently hinders the interior conjunction of good and truth, which is essential to this love: now marriage with more than one wife is like an understanding divided into many wills, or as a man that joins himself to different churches, whereby his faith is so distracted, that it comes to nothing. The angels declare, that to marry several wives is absolutely contrary to the divine order, and that they are assured of this many ways, particularly from hence, that as soon as they entertain any notion of such marriages, they lose their heavenly peace and joy, and become, as it were, intoxicated through a separation between their internal good and truth: and if their mental faculties become so disordered through thinking

(240) That it is unlawful for persons of different religions to contract marriage, as this hinders the conjunction of like good and like truth in the affections and understanding, and consequently unanimity, n. 8998.

with the least inclination on polygamy, they conclude with the strongest conviction, that the engagement itself would darken their minds, and banish their joys, and that from a heavenly conjugal love they should fall into a grofs inordinate paſſion inconſiſtent with the purity of cœleſtial delights (241) : they ſay, that it is difficult for men now o'days to form any conception of this matter, as ſo very few have any experience of true conjugal love, without which they muſt remain entire ſtrangers to that inward ſatisfaction which reſults from it, whilſt they experience nothing more than the gratification of the ſenſual part, which in a little time changes into diſguſt; whereas the ſpiritual delight of pure conjugal love not only laſts even to old age in this world, but after death makes a part of the joys of heaven, where it is exalted to higher ſpirituality and perfection in eternity : they moreover ſaid, that the beatitudes of truly ſpiritual conjugal love might be reckoned up to many thouſands, of which not one was fully known by mortal man, nor can be thoroughly experienced by any who are not in that ſtate of heavenly marriage, which conſiſts in the union of good and truth from the Lord.

380. Love of dominion in one of the married parties over the other baniſhes true conjugal love and its heavenly delight; foraſmuch as the latter, as was obſerved before, conſiſts in a conformity of wills on both ſides by mutual conſent and choice, which the thirſt of dominion in the party aiming at government totally defeats, by exalting the will of ſelf over that of the other, and obſtructing that free and equal communication of love and its friendly offices, in which the happineſs of marriage

---

(241) As huſband and wife ſhould be one in the eſſential principles of life, and as they conſtitute one angel in heaven, therefore true conjugal love cannot ſubſiſt between one huſband and different wives, n. 1907, 2740. That to have more wives than one at the ſame time is contrary to the divine order, n. 10835. That marriage can only be between two, evidently appears from thoſe who belong to the Lord's cœleſtial kingdom, n. 865, 3246, 9902, 10172 ; and that becauſe the angels of that kingdom are in the moſt intimate union of good and truth, n. 3246. That it was permitted to the Iſraelites to have more wives than one at the ſame time, and alſo to keep concubines, but not ſo to Chriſtians; and the reaſon of the difference is, becauſe the former were only in the externals of religion, but the latter are called to inward and ſpiritual religion, and conſequently to the internal marriage of good and truth, n. 3246, 4837, 8809.

conſiſts;

confifts; nay, fo oppofite is the luft of power and rule to every thing that is cœleftial and fpiritual in that ftate, as to render the very mention of it ridiculous. Where one wills and loves as the other does, there is liberty in both, for liberty is the offspring of love; but where the fpirit of governing prefides, all is fervitude, for the party, who is inftigated by the defire of dominion, is a fervant to the imperious paffion. Thefe things will not appear in their full evidence to fuch as are wholly ftrangers to the fweet liberty that is in heavenly love; but enough has been faid on this fubject to fhew, that the exercife of dominion is fo far from uniting, that nothing tends more to divide minds; it may indeed fubdue, but a mind fubdued or fubjugated, is either without a will of its own, or has an oppofite will; if it has no will, it confequently has no love; and if an oppofite will, the paffion that prevails in it is hatred and not love; and fuch married perfons as are in this condition and character, are all at ftrife and war within, however they may fmooth over their behaviour towards one another with an external decency for the fake of peace. This inward hoftility manifefts itfelf in the other world, where they attack each other with fury and open violence when they meet, as I can teftify from having been a fpectator of their quarrels and vindictive rage, as in the intermediate ftate every one appears outwardly what he is inwardly, being free there from thofe reftraints and motives to fave appearances, by which they regulate their behaviour in this world.

381. We have indeed inftances of apparent conjugal love in fome, but without the reality, if they are not in the love of good and truth; and it is not unufual to counterfeit this appearance from various motives, as for example, that the parties may live quietly and at eafe in their families, may be properly accommodated in ficknefs and old age, or that the children they are fond of may be duly taken care of; fome practife an affectionate behaviour through fear of the other party, through regard to character, to prevent bad confequences, and in fome cafes on account of natural paffion. Conjugal love has alfo its different degrees in married perfons; fome have it in a higher, and fome in a lower degree, nay, one may be in a difpofition

for it, and the other in none at all; and under such difference marriage may be to one as heaven, and to the other as hell.

382. The most perfect conjugal love is in the inmost heaven, as the angels there are most highly graduated in conjoined truth and good, and also in innocence: the angels of the inferior heavens are also (according to their degree in innocence) in pure conjugal love, which, considered in itself, is a state of innocence, and attended with heavenly delights, whilst the blessed pairs, from an infantile simplicity of disposition, receive pleasure from all that they see, and give pleasure in all that they do; for a heavenly virtue tinctures all things to them: and hence it is, that conjugal love is represented above by the most delightful emblems; accordingly I have seen it represented by a virgin of exquisite beauty, girt about, as it were, with a white cloud; and it was told me, that all the angels derive their beauty from conjugal love, that all the particular affections and sentiments, that issued from this source, were represented by adamantine atmospheres intermixed with carbuncles and rubies, exciting sensations that penetrated even to the mental affections. In a word, heaven represents itself by conjugal love, and that because the conjunction of good and truth in the angels constitutes heaven, and the same conjunction constitutes the essence of true, spiritual, conjugal love.

382. Marriage in the heavens differs from marriage on earth, and herein more particularly, that the latter is instituted for the procreation of children, whereas the end of heavenly marriages is the procreation or multiplication of good and truth, in the conjunction or union of which such marriage consists; and as the love of good and truth is the bond of it, so are these the fruit of it: hence it is, that by births and generations in the Word, we are to understand such as are spiritual, viz. of good and truth; by father and mother, truth conjoined with good as the propagating principles; and by sons and daughters, the truths and goods propagated; and by sons and daughters-in-law, the conjunctions of these, and so on (242). It is evident from

(242) That conception, delivery, nativities and generations, have also a spiritual meaning in reference to good and truth, or love and faith, n. 613, 1145, 1775.

from hence, that marriages in the heavens are very different from marriages on earth, the former being spiritual, and not so properly called nuptials, as conjunction of minds through the union of good and truth; whereas on earth they are properly nuptials, as consisting not only in a spiritual, but also a carnal conjunction; and forasmuch as such kind of nuptials is not in heaven, therefore the two mates or married persons are not there called husband and wife; but each other's partner [*conjux*] is named (from an idea in the angels of two minds united) by a term answering to his or her *mutual*, or *second self*. What has been here said may lead us to the true meaning of those words of our Lord concerning marriage, Luke xxi. 35, 36.

383. It has been given me to see how marriages are contracted in the heavens: now it must be observed, that throughout heaven, such as are of like dispositions and qualities are consociated into particular fellowships; and such as differ in these respects are dissociated or separated, so that every society in heaven consists of similar members; and these are brought together by the Lord, and not through their own seeking, see above, n. 41, 43, 44, *& seq*. In like manner the husband and wife are brought together, being such whose minds are capable of union with each other, on which they love each other with mutual cordiality at first sight, immediately perceive their appointed union, and enter into marriage: thus all marriages in heaven are from the Lord only: they also celebrate a festival on the occasion in the presence of many; these festivals differ in different societies.

384. As marriages in this world are the seminaries of mankind, and also of future angels (for, as was observed under its proper article, heaven is peopled by the human race) and being

1755, 2020—8042, 9325, 10197. That hence, by spiritual application we read of regeneration and new birth through faith and love, n. 5160, 5598, 9042, 9845. That *Mother* signifies the church in respect to true doctrine, and *Father* good, and also good of the church, n. 2691, 2717, 3703, 5580, 8897. That *Sons* signify the affections of truth, and consequently truths, n. 489, 491, 533, 8649, 9807; and *Daughters*, the affections of good, and also good in general, n. 489, 490, 491—6778, 9055. That *Son-in-law* signifies truth associated to the affection of good, n. 2389. That *Daughter-in-law* signifies good associated to its proper truth, n. 4843.

according

according to the true inſtitution of them of a ſpiritual origin through the conjunction of good and truth, and the divine bleſſing on pure conjugal love; on theſe accounts they are conſidered as holy by the angels; and, on the other hand, they look upon adultery, the oppoſite to conjugal love, as profanation; whilſt they behold in one the image of heaven, through the conjunction of good and truth therein; and in the other an image of hell, through the conjunction of falſe with evil: wherefore, on the very naming of adultery, they turn their backs in token of averſion: from this contrariety in it to every thing ſacred, it comes to paſs, that the gate of heaven is ſhut againſt the adulterer, the conſequence of which is his turning infidel, and renouncing the faith of the church (243). That all in hell are enemies to conjugal love was given me to perceive by an impreſſion on my mind by the ſphere exhaling thence, which ſeemed as a continued effort to diſſolve and violate the marriage bond; denoting thereby, that the ruling paſſion in hell is that of adultery, and conſequently an enmity to the union of good and truth, which is the foundation of heaven. From which we may conclude, that the gratification of this inordinate paſſion is nothing ſhort of an infernal pleaſure, and diametrically oppoſite to the innocent ſatisfaction of pure conjugal love, which is a heavenly pleaſure.

385. There were, on a time, certain ſpirits, who, from a practiſed behaviour in this life, followed me with an over-officious ſedulity, and with an air of ſoftneſs that reſembled the humility of good ſpirits; but by the influx from their ſpheres; I could perceive fallacy and guile within. At length I entered into converſation with one of them, who, I found, had been a commanding military officer, and, as I diſcovered ſomething of the libertine in his ideas, I turned the diſcourſe to the ſub-

---

(243) That adultery is profanation, n. 9961, 10174. That the gate of heaven is ſhut againſt adulterers, n. 275. That they, who place their delight in this ſin, diſqualify themſelves for heaven, n. 539, 2733, 2747, 2748, 2749, 2751, 10175. That adulterers are unmerciful, and without religion, n. 824, 2747, 2748. That in the other world they delight in naſtineſs, and are in hells ſuited thereto, n. 2755, 5394, 5722. That their ideas are filthy, n. 2747, 2748. That by adultery in the Word, in a ſpiritual ſenſe, is ſignified the adulterating of good; and by fornication, the perverting of truth, n. 2466, 2729, 3399, 4865, 8904, 10648.

ject of marriage, in that way of spiritual converfation which is by reprefentatives, equally expreffive with any other, and much more copious, though laconick; and he told me, that in this world he had made light of adultery: I had the freedom to tell him, that adultery was abominable, whatever pains they who were guilty of that fin might take to reafon themfelves into a perfuafion of its lawfulnefs; and that he might know this from marriage being the feminary of the human race, and alfo of the cœleftial kingdom, and confequently not to be violated, but held as facred; moreover, that, as he was in the fpiritual world, and in a ftate of perception, he ought to know that conjugal love, as a fpiritual principle, was derivative from the Lord through heaven; and that mutual love, which is the cement of heavenly blifs, proceeded from the fame fource; as likewife from hence, that adulterers, as foon as they approach the cœleftial focieties, become fenfible of their own impurity, and being unable to bear the holy efflux, fpontaneoufly precipitate themfelves down to hell: I farther obferved to him, that at the leaft, he could not but know, that to violate the laws of marriage was contrary to all laws both divine and human, as well as to the dictates of unbiaffed reafon; to which I added other arguments. To all which he only replied, that he was of a different way of thinking when in this world, and fhewed an inclination to difpute the matter with me; but I told him that plain truths did not allow of reafonings, and that arguments might be invented to plead for any thing a man liked, nay, in defence of any error or evil; and that he would do well to confider the unanfwerable reafons that had been offered; or, to view the matter in another light, that he would try the cafe by that well known unalterable rule of equity; that no man fhould do to another what he would not that another fhould do to him, and by thus making the cafe his own, afk himfelf; If any one fhould have feduced a wife he had loved, whether under the frefh fenfe of the injury he would not have expreffed the utmoft deteftation of adultery, and have employed the fkill in reafoning, to aggravate the guilt of it, which he now meant to employ in the defence of it; nay, if he would not, in the bitterness of his resentment, have adjudged the criminal to the pit of hell.

386. I have had a perception of the delights of pure conjugal love in their progression to the heavenly state, and also of the impure pleasures of adultery in theirs to the infernal state, in the other worlds; and saw how the former were sublimated by an increase of innumerable and unspeakable beatitudes, from more to more, till they were exalted to the joys of the inmost heaven, or that of perfect innocence, and that with the like increase of liberty; for all liberty proceeds from love, and the highest degree of it from conjugal, which is also cœlestial love: but the progression of adulterous love is by inverse degrees towards hell, and so on to the lowermost hell, where all is dire and horrible: such is the lot of adulterers in the other world. By adulterers is here meant, they who take delight in the gratification of this sinful passion, but have no relish for the innocent delights of pure conjugal affection.

Of the Functions of the Angels in Heaven.

387. The functions of the angels in heaven cannot be enumerated or described in particular; and therefore, being indefinite and various according to the different offices and services of the several societies, we can only speak of them in a general way. Every society has its particular offices, for they are all distinct according to their peculiar excellencies and species of good (see above, n. 41.) and consequently according to their uses; for that only is considered as good by all in heaven, which is good by operation and act: there every one performs good offices; for the Lord's kingdom is the kingdom of uses (244).

(244) That the kingdom of the Lord is the kingdom of uses, n. 453, 696, 1103, 3645, 4054, 7038. That to serve the Lord is to do uses, n. 7038. That all in the other world are appointed to usefulness, n. 1103; and that this extends even to bad and infernal spirits, and in what manner, n. 696. That all have their character and denomination from the uses they perform respectively, n. 4054, 6815. This illustrated, n. 7038. That angelical blessedness consists in doing good offices of love, n. 454.

388. There

388. There are different administrations in the heavens as well as on earth, viz. ecclesiastical, civil, and domestick; of the first has been spoken in the article concerning divine worship, n. 221 to 227; of the second, in the chapter concerning governments in heaven, n. 213 to 220; and of the last, in the chapter concerning the habitations and mansions of the angels, n. 183 to 190; and also in the last chapter concerning marriages in heaven, n. 366 to 386; all which make appear, that there are several functions and administrations established in every one of the heavenly societies.

389. All things in the heavens are instituted according to divine order, which is preserved throughout by the administrations of angels; those things which relate to more general good or use, by the angels who are most eminent for wisdom; and such as are of more private or particular consideration, by those which are less eminent, and so on; all in subordination to divine order according to their uses respectively; and hence it follows, that to every angelical office is annexed a dignity according to the dignity of its use; however, the angel assumes not the honour to himself, but assigns it to the use, and as the use is the same with the good which he administers, and all good is from the Lord, therefore to him he ascribes all the praise: nay, were any disposed to appropriate to himself any part of the honour, he would thereby disqualify himself for any high office in heaven, as seeking his own glory more than the use of his office, and the honour of God. By use here is to be understood the Lord, seeing, as was said before, use signifies the same as good, and all good proceeds from him.

390. From what has been said, a judgment may be formed concerning the nature of subordination in heaven; and how every one there not only loves, esteems, and honours the good use of administrations, but also the instruments employed in conducting them, and that in proportion to their humility and gratitude in giving glory to the Lord in that behalf; for in proportion thereto is their wisdom, and the extent of their usefulness; and as spiritual love, estimation, and honour respect the use, so the honour of the person ministering it arises thence.

thence (245). He also that considers men by the standard of spiritual truth, forms his judgment according to the same rule: he sees one man resembling another, whether in a higher or lower degree of office and dignity, and estimates the difference only by the difference of wisdom that is in him, viz. the wisdom of loving usefulness, whether for the good of his fellow-citizen, of his society, his country, or the church he is of. In this exercise of uses consists our love to the Lord, from whom proceeds all the good that is in uses; and also our love to our neighbour, whose real good and benefit is to be the object of our love and beneficence, whether considered under the character of fellow-citizen, or the complex relation of society, country, or church.

391. All the societies in the heavens are distinct [or distinguished] according to the administration of uses therein, in the same manner as they are distinguished according to their respective goods [kinds of good] and those goods are actual, or goods of charity, as observed above, n. 41, *et seq.* or, in other words, goods of uses: thus some societies are appointed to the charge of infants; others to instruct and educate them till they are grown up: there are particular societies instituted for the improvement of such young persons of both sexes as have been prepared for heaven in this world by a virtuous and pious education; and others to form for heaven such as are well disposed, but ignorant: some whose office it is to instruct those that are from the various heathen nations: some to receive the novitiate spirits, or such as are newly arrived from this world,

(245) That by the love of our neighbour is not meant the love of his person, but of his principles and qualities, which are the constituents of him, n. 5025, 10336. That they who love the person, without respecting the principle, love good and evil alike, n. 3820. That such befriend the evil as well as good, which is being injurious to the latter, and makes no part of love to our neighbour, n. 3820, 6703, 8120, 8121. The judge, who punishes criminals for their reformation, and to the end that the good may not be injured or suffer by them, thereby does an act of love for his neighbour, n. 3820, 8120, 8121. That every man and society in particular, as also our country and church, and, in an universal sense, the kingdom of the Lord, is our neighbour, and that to do good thereto from the love of good, according to their respective qualities and states, is shewing love to our neighbour, consequently their benefit, which is to be consulted by us, is our neighbour, n. 6818 to 6824, 8123.

and

and to defend them againſt all aſſaults from evil ſpirits: ſome alſo there are, whoſe deſignation is to miniſter to thoſe who are detained for a while in the inferior regions on earth (*): ſome, whoſe province it is, by turns, to preſide as overſeers in the infernal kingdom, to reſtrain the evil ſpirits from tormenting one another beyond due meaſure; and laſtly, ſome are appointed to the care of thoſe who are raiſed from death (246). In general, the angels of every ſociety are employed about men, in order to preſerve and lead them from evil affections, and the thoughts which they are apt to excite in their minds; and to inſpire them with good affections, as far as they can receive them conſiſtently with free will; and hereby they guide and influence their works and actions, and bend their inclinations from evil, as far as may ſtand with the nature of free agents. The angels, whilſt they are preſent with men, reſide, as it were, in their affections, and are nearer to or further from them, according to their degree of good life from true doctrines: but all theſe adminiſtrations are from the Lord through the angels, which act only as his inſtruments therein. Hence it is, that by angels, in the inmoſt ſenſe of the word, is meant ſome attribute or operation of the Lord, and alſo that the angels in Scripture are called gods (247).

392. The forementioned are the common functions of the angels; but beſides theſe, every angel has his charge or office in particular; for every common or general uſe is compounded of innumerable others, which are called mediate, miniſtering,

(*) By theſe probably are meant the ſouls deſcribed by St. John as under the altar, Rev. vi. 9, 10. Tr.

(246) Concerning the angels appointed to the care of infants, grown children, and ſo on in ſucceſſion, n. 2303. That man is raiſed from death by angels; this from experience, n. 168 to 189. That angels are ſent to the infernal ſpirits, to prevent their tormenting one another beyond meaſure, n. 967. Concerning the good offices of angels to men on their arrival in the other world, n. 2131. That angels and ſpirits are preſent to all men, and that man is led by the Lord through their inſtrumentality, n. 50, 697, 2796—5847 to 5866, 5976 to 5993, 6209. That angels have dominion over evil ſpirits, n. 1755.

(247) That by *angels* in the Word is ſignified ſome divine property from the Lord, n. 1925, 2821, 3039, 4085, 6280, 8192. That angels in the Word are called gods, from their reception of divine truth and good from the Lord, n. 4295, 4402, 8301, 8192.

or attendant ufes; all and every of which, whether co-ordinate or fubordinate, are according to divine order, and in their complex conſtitute and perfect the common ufe or common good.

393. They who loved the Word in this world, and ſtudiouſly inveſtigated the truths therein, not for honour or fecular advantage, but for purpofes of practice and good life, both with refpect to themſelves and others; ſuch are thofe who are appointed to the eccleſiaſtical functions in heaven, and according to the degree of ſuch their pious purſuit is their illumination and wifdom from the Word in the heavens, the fenſe of which there is not natural, as in this world, but wholly fpiritual, fee above, n. 259. Thefe exercife the office of preachers, and according to the eſtabliſhed laws of divine order excel in eminence of rank and dignity, as they are fuperior to others in divine illumination. As to matters of civil adminiſtration, they conſtitute the province of fuch as in this world loved their country, and preferred the good of it to their own private advantage, doing that which is juſt and right from affection and principle: as far as thefe took pleafure to improve their minds in the knowledge of the laws of juſtice and equity, in fuch degree are they qualified for offices in the heavenly focieties, which they adminiſter, each according to his intellectual abilities, which are in proportion to the degree of their affectionate zeal for the common good. In a word, the offices, adminiſtrations, and employments in heaven are innumerable, and far exceeding thofe that are to be found in this world, and all that are concerned therein take delight to be fo engaged from their love of ufefulnefs; where no one is actuated by felfiſh or lucrative motives, or under the temptation of anxious care for the needful accommodations of life, as thefe are all miniſtered to them gratuitouſly, as fuitable habitations, veſtments, food convenient, &c. From all which it follows, that they who have loved felf and the world above ufefulnefs, have no place nor portion in heaven; for the ruling paſſion or affection, which has taken poſſeſſion of the heart of any one in this world, follows him in the next, and is not eliminated in eternity, fee above, n. 363.

394. Every one in heaven is in his office according to correfpondency, but correfpondence refpects not merely the outward

ward office or act, but its use and tendency, see above, n. 112; and there is a correspondence in all things, n. 106. He, who in heaven is in any function or work corresponding to its use, is in a similar state of life to that which appertained to him in the body (for things spiritual and natural are the same by correspondence) with this difference, that there his delight in good is more interior and central, answerably to his spiritual life, which is more receptive of heavenly joy (*).

Of the Joys and Happiness of Heaven.

395. Few or none at this time have any conception of heaven, and the joys and happiness thereof; nay, the ideas of those, who have exercised their minds most on these subjects, are very gross, or next to none: I had the best opportunity of knowing this from the spirits, who had newly been translated from this world to the other, and which, left to themselves, think as they had done before. Now this ignorance in men concerning the joys of heaven arises from their conceiving them to be similar to the outward gratifications of the natural man in this world, and from their having no notion of the inward and spiritual man, nor of what constitutes the happiness of his condition, insomuch, that were any one to describe to them such spiritual delights from his own experience of them, the description could take no hold of their gross material ideas, nor excite any perception in their minds of what was told them, but be immediately rejected by them: and yet it is rational to conclude, that when any man is divested of the external or natural part of his composition, he must wholly enter upon that which is internal and spiritual, and consequently, that his pleasures and

(*) There is confessedly some difficulty in comprehending the sense of our author in this passage, which seems to be as follows, viz. the interior state of a good man on earth has its corresponding state in heaven, though the sweet relish and delectable sensation of it is different in these different kingdoms: thus the love of God and the peace of God are the same divine affections in the soul in both worlds, yet their beatitudes can only be fully experienced in the angelical state, as free from the imperfections and impurities of animal nature. Tr.

joys muſt be of the ſame nature with himſelf, and if inward and ſpiritual, ſo neceſſarily more pure and refined, in order to be ſuitably accommodated to the condition of a ſoul or ſpirit. This may ſerve to evince, that what his ſpirit took delight in here muſt conſtitute the delight of his ſpirit hereafter; as to the corporeal gratifications of our nature, being of the earth earthly, they can make no part of a heavenly ſtate; but the things of the ſpirit of a man follow him into the other world, where he lives ſpiritually.

396. All pleaſures flow from love as their only ſource, for what any one loves, that is pleaſant to him; conſequently, according to the kind of love, ſuch is the pleaſure it yields: all corporeal or ſenſual pleaſures iſſue from the love of ſelf, and the love of the world, from which proceed all kinds of concupiſcence and voluptuouſneſs; but all true delights of the ſoul or ſpirit originate from love to God, and love to our neighbour; and from theſe ſources are derived our affections for good and truth, and our moſt ſatisfying interior pleaſures. Theſe two loves, with their concomitant pleaſures, proceed by influx from the Lord, and from heaven by internal emanation from above, and affect the inmoſt receſſes of the ſoul; but the former ſpurious loves, with their pleaſures, iſſue from the carnal part, and from the world outwardly, or from beneath, and affect the exterior ſenſes. As far therefore as the two heavenly loves before mentioned are received and affect us, ſo far the inward gate of the ſoul or ſpirit ſtands open to the divine influences; and as far as the other two ſpurious loves are received and affect us, ſo far the outward gate of the bodily ſenſes ſtands open to this world and its evil influences: and as theſe different kinds of love gain admiſſion into our hearts, ſo alſo do their reſpective pleaſures, thoſe of heaven into the inward, and thoſe of the world into the outward man; for, as was ſaid before, every pleaſure is attendant on its parent love.

397. Heaven is ſo conſtituted, as to abound with pleaſures; inſomuch that, conſidered in itſelf, it is an aggregate of beatitudes and delectations; and that becauſe divine good, proceeding from the divine love of the Lord, conſtitutes heaven both in the general, and alſo in particular, in every one there: now it is

is the property of divine love, to will the salvation and happiness of all, and that intimately and fully; so that whether you say heaven, or the joys of heaven, it comes to one and the same thing.

398. The pleasures of heaven are unutterable, as they are innumerable; but innumerable as they are, no man that is absorbed in carnal and sensual gratifications can have the least notion of any one of them, and that because, as was said before, all his receptive faculties are turned backward from heaven to this world, and consequently, being immersed in the love of self and of the world, he is incapable of taking pleasure in any thing but the honours and riches of this world, or in sensual gratifications; whereas these things do, as it were, extinguish or suffocate all sense of the refined pleasures of heaven, even so far as to render the reality of them incredible; such a one would be ready to wonder, were you to tell him that there are pleasures, of which honours and riches make no part; and still more, should it be affirmed, that in heaven there is an endless variety of delights, to which the most splendid enjoyments of this world, added to the highest gratifications of sense, are not worthy to be compared: how can it seem strange, that persons of so gross an apprehension should be unable to form any notions of cœlestial happiness!

399. Something of an estimate may be made concerning the superlative felicity in heaven from the following single consideration, viz. that it constitutes part of the happiness of angels, to communicate their joys to one another; and as all of them are like minded in this matter, how joyous must be the effect! seeing, as was said above, n. 268, in the heavens there is a mutual communication between one and all; and this results, as was said before, from the twofold love that prevails there; love to the Lord, and love to their neighbour, both of which are of a communicative nature. Now love to the Lord is his own gift proceeding from his divine goodness, which communicates of his blessedness to all as far as they can receive it, for he wills the happiness of all: and all who love him partake of his spirit, which is the bond of communion and communication in his holy angels; and that love towards their neighbour is of

like tendency and effect will appear from what follows; though what has already been offered may suffice to indicate the natural tendency of these loves in those that possess them, to communicate of their best things: but it is far otherwise with respect to the love of self and the love of the world; for the former of these is a greedy desire of enriching self at the expence of others, and therefore draws all to it, seeking only its own things; whilst the love of the world grudges to others the share they possess of it, thinking that themselves can never have enough; so that these two loves are destructive of all pleasant and friendly communication; or where such persons do communicate to others, it is for their own sakes, and that it may some way or other redound to their own profit or pleasure: that this is the case, I have had frequent experience when in company with spirits, who had been addicted to these loves whilst they lived in the body, always finding my pleasant frames to depart from me upon the first approach of such; and I have also been told, that when they draw nigh to any angelical society, the members of it feel a diminution of their joy according to the nearness of their approach; and what is no less strange, that the evil spirits on their part receive a proportionable increase of pleasure: hence we may know, that the state of any one's spirit, after its separation from the body, is similar to what it was upon leaving it; and that those here spoken of have the same covetous desire for the goods of others in the other world that they had in this, and take the same pleasure in procuring to themselves the possession of them: and it may be farther observed from what has here been said, how destructive of heavenly joys the love of self and of this world are, and consequently how contrary to the loves of that blessed kingdom, the essential property of which is to be communicative.

400. It is here to be noted concerning those who are under the dominion of the love of self and the love of the world, that the pleasure they feel on their approach to any of the heavenly societies, is the pleasure of their own evil concupiscence, and directly opposite to every cœlestial delight, and that such pleasure proceeds from depriving others of their heavenly joy; but when no such deprivation takes place, the case is quite other-

wise

wife with them, for then they dare not advance a ſtep towards them, or if they ſhould, they would be ſure to ſuffer great perturbation and anguiſh, and therefore they ſeldom have the boldneſs to come near them; and as I have often had experience of this, I ſhall here relate ſomething by way of inſtance. There is nothing which ſpirits newly arrived in the other world more earneſtly deſire than their immediate admiſſion into heaven; this is the caſe with almoſt all, ſuppoſing that to be in heaven is no other than to be introduced and received into a certain place; and accordingly, purſuant to their longing, they are conducted to ſome ſociety in the firſt or loweſt heaven. Now as ſoon as they who are in the love of ſelf and of the world approach to the entrance of heaven, they begin to feel ſuch internal pains and anguiſh, as to find a hell inſtead of a heaven within them, and therefore precipitate themſelves thence, without being at reſt till they join company with their fellows in hell. It often happened, that ſome of this claſs had a longing deſire to experience ſomething of the joys of heaven; and upon being told that theſe were only experienced in the ſenſations of the angels, they deſired communication with them, which was granted; for what any ſpirit, which is not yet in heaven or hell, deſires, is readily granted, if it may be of any uſe: now upon ſuch communication being opened between them and the angels, they felt ſuch agonizing pains, that they could not contain themſelves, bending their heads down to their feet, rolling on the ground, and twiſting themſelves into various forms, like ſo many ſerpents, through the anguiſh they felt within. Such effects had the heavenly ſenſations of the angels, when communicated to thoſe, whoſe ſouls were immerſed in the love of ſelf and of the world, ſuch corrupt concupiſcences being quite contrary to thoſe pure affections, which are the inmates of angels: when one oppoſite acts upon another, the effect is violence and ſtrife; and thus the cœleſtial virtues of the angels, operating on the evil qualities of the other party, occaſioned the violent diſorder within them, which produced thoſe contortions and conflicts. The cauſe of this contrariety, as aſſigned before, is, that they who are influenced by the divine graces of the love of God, and charity towards their neighbour, are liberal and

commu-

communicative of what they have; whereas they who are under the dominion of those evil passions, the love of self and the love of the world, are grudging and greedy of what belongs to others: hence it is, that heaven and hell are not only separate, but opposite to each other. Now all in the latter are such as in this life abandoned themselves to temporal and carnal gratifications from the love of self and the love of the world; and all in the former, such as here took delight in spiritual things from love to the Lord, and love to their neighbour; and consequently, as their loves were opposite, so are the kingdoms to which they belong, insomuch, that were they who are in the hellish kingdom to extend but a finger beyond the sphere of it, they would suffer pain thereby. This I have often been witness to.

401. The man who is in the love of self and of the world, is, during his bodily life here, sensibly affected therewith, and the pleasures resulting from them; whereas he who is in the love of God and of his neighbour, has seldom, during his life here, the same manifest sensations thereof, nor of the sweets of the good affections resulting therefrom; but in their room feels only a kind of secret satisfaction in the center of his soul, darkened and covered, as it were, with this natural, corporeal integument, and deadened, in a manner, by the cares of this life: but these states are quite altered after death; for then the pleasures resulting from the love of self and of the world are changed into horrors, signified by the name of hell-fire, and alternately into such kinds of nastiness and filth, as correspond to those impure gratifications, in which (however strange it may be thought) he takes pleasure: but that which, as observed before, was no more than an inward, secret, and obscure satisfaction in those who were in the love of God and of their neighbour, is then changed into clear perceptions, and joyous sensations, and what was before a hidden, though spiritual root of blessedness, does, in their manifested state of spiritual life, bring forth the pleasant fruit of spiritual delights.

402. All the pleasures of heaven are connected with and inseparable from uses, these being the good fruits of love and charity in the angels; and according to the quality of the uses, and

and their alacrity to perform them, is the degree of their joy: that this is so may be illustrated by comparison with the five bodily senses in man, each of which derives its pleasure from exercise and use; the sight from beholding beautiful objects; the hearing from harmonious sounds; the smelling from odoriferous scents, and the taste from food of good savour; and the uses which they severally perform by their respective offices are well understood by those that attentively consider them, more especially if they are acquainted with their correspondent relations in respect to the intellectual and animal œconomy: thus the pleasure annexed to seeing, is from its subservient usefulness to the understanding, which is the internal sight of the mind; and the pleasure of hearing from the service it ministers to the intellect and will, by hearkening, in order to obedience (*): the sense of smelling has its pleasure from the refreshment and aid it yields to the brain and lungs; the taste from its use in supplying the stomach with food for the nourishment of the whole body; and the touch, considered in a conjugal view, from its eminent use in the propagation of the human species, and thereby providing a seminary for cœlestial inhabitants. All these pleasures with innocence are communicated to the senses by influx from the heavenly world, where every delight has its use, and is in proportion to its degree of use.

403. Certain spirits, from a notion they had entertained in this world, fancied that the happiness of heaven consisted in a life of ease and indolence, and being served in all things by others; but it was told them, that no society could subsist happily in such a state, and that where all were to be served, there could not be any to serve; moreover, that a life of idleness would render them stupid and good for nothing; that action was essential to felicity, and rest only the means of fitting them the better for it: they were likewise given to understand, that the life of angels principally consisted in doing offices of love

---

(*) Obedience is signified by *hearkening* in many places of the Sacred Writings; thus in particular, Acts iv. 19. " Whether it be right to hearken unto you more " than unto God, judge ye." To *hear* likewise has the same signification, not only in Scripture language, but also in many other writings; thus: *Neque audit currus habenas.* Virg. Georg. I. Tr.

and ufe, and that it was their higheſt delight to be ſo employed: and then, to make them aſhamed of ſo abſurd a notion, as that of happineſs in heaven confiſting in everlaſting indolence, there was given them a perception of ſuch a ſtate, by which it appeared to them moſt irkſome and melancholy, and ſuch as would not only be deſtructive of every joy, but in a little time be attended with difguſt and loathing.

404. Some ſpirits, which thought themſelves wifer than their fellows, had conceived an opinion in this world, that heavenly joy confiſted altogether in praiſing and worſhipping God, and that this conſtituted the active life of angels; but it was told them, that God needed not their praiſes and worſhip, but willed rather that they ſhould moſtly be employed in performing offices of uſe and love to one another; but this they confidered more as a taſk of ſervitude than true happineſs, although the angels aſſured them, that it was a moſt free and delightful employment, as proceeding from the moſt affectionate good will, and which they executed with unſpeakable pleafure.

405. Almoſt all, on their arrival in the other world, think that all infernal ſpirits have one and the ſame hell, and all cœleſtial ſpirits one and the ſame heaven; whereas there is an endleſs variety in both, neither is one hell or one heaven quite ſimilar to another, as there are no two men, ſpirits, or angels, that exactly reſemble each other, not even in the face; and when I went about to figure to my imagination two ſuch exactly the ſame, the angels ſeemed to ſhudder at it, telling me, that every whole was formed by the harmonizing conſent of many different parts, and that as was the harmony or agreement of the component parts, ſuch was the aggregate or whole; and that in this manner every ſociety in heaven was one body formed of ſeveral different individuals, and the univerſal complex of heaven was formed of all the different ſocieties, and that the bond of their union was love from the Lord (248). Uſes in the

---

(248) That every whole confiſts of various different parts, from which it receives its form and quality; and according to the harmony and conſent of its component parts, is the degree of its perfection, n. 457, 3241, 8003. That there is an infinite variety in the works of God, and no two things exactly alike, n. 7236, 9002. The ſame holds true in the heavens, n. 5744, 4005, 7236, 7833, 7836,

the heavens have also their like variety and diversity, no two of them being exactly similar or the same, nor yet the pleasures resulting from them, though to every use belong innumerable pleasures, and though all different, yet so orderly disposed and connected, as to harmonize together, like the uses of every member, organ, and bowel in the human body, nay, which is still more, of every vessel and fibre in each member, organ, and bowel, which are all so wonderfully adjusted, as to co-operate with their associates, and perform their distinct offices one in all, and all in every one; whilst separately, yet conjunctly, they form one regular system of complicated uses without the least confusion or disorder.

406. I have sometimes conversed with spirits newly come from this world concerning their eternal state, observing to them, that it nearly concerned them to know who was the sovereign of the kingdom, what the constitution of it, and what the particular form of its government; and that if such as travelled into a foreign country in this world considered it of consequence to be acquainted with these and the like particulars relating to it, it was of still greater importance to them to be informed of the same in reference to the kingdom in which they now were, and wherein they were to live for ever: that therefore they were to know, that the Lord of glory was the King of heaven, and also the supreme Governor of the universe, and therefore that they were his liege subjects; and moreover, that the laws of his kingdom were eternal truths founded on that universal indispensable law of loving the Lord above all things, and their neighbour as themselves; nay, what was still more, that now, if they would be as the angels, they ought to love their neighbour more than themselves: on hearing which they were struck dumb; for though in this world they might possibly have heard of such a doctrine, yet they gave no credit to it; and therefore wondered at such love, even in heaven; nay,

---

7836, 9002. Hence, that all the societies in the heavens, and every angel in each society, have their distinct characters, and their different kinds and degrees as to good and use, n. 690, 3241, 3519—7236, 7833, 3986. That the divine love of the Lord gives them their heavenly form, and makes them to be as one man, n. 457, 3986, 5598.

that it was poſſible for any one to love his neighbour better than himſelf: but they were informed, that all kinds of good became immenſely increaſed in the other world, and though in this life, few, through the imperfection of human nature, could go farther than to love their neighbour as themſelves, as being here ſubject to corporeal affections; yet on their removal from theſe impediments, true love became more pure and exalted, even to an angelical ſtandard, which is to love their neighbour more than themſelves, and to eſteem it their happineſs to do good to others without ſeeking their own good, unleſs for the ſake of their neighbour, that he may receive the benefit of it by communication; and that this was properly to love their neighbour better than themſelves: and with reſpect not only to the poſſibility, but alſo to the reality of ſuch love, they were told, that many convincing proofs might be brought from examples in this world; thus in the conjugal ſtate, where one of the parties had ſuffered death to ſave the other; in mothers, many of which would endure hunger, rather than their children ſhould want food; in inſtances of cloſe friendſhip, where the one had expoſed himſelf to the greateſt hardſhips and dangers for the ſake of the other; nay, even in decent and polite company, where ſuch kind of love is only imitated, how common is it for people of good breeding to offer preference, and the beſt things to others, from mere civility and ſhew of greater reſpect; and laſtly, they were told, that it was of the very eſſence and nature of true love to do all kind offices to the objects of it, not from ſelfiſh views, but from diſintereſted affection. But notwithſtanding the force of theſe arguments, they who were deep in the love of ſelf, and had been greedy of filthy lucre in this world, could not receive ſuch doctrine, and the covetous leaſt of all.

407. A certain ſpirit, who, in the life of the body, was in high power, and ſtill retained the love of command, was told, that his authority was now at an end, he being in a very different kingdom, where every one's eſtimation was only according to the good and truth that was in him, and from the mercy of the Lord, who had tranſlated him thither; and it was moreover told him, that the country to which he now belonged had
indeed

indeed this in common with the world he came from; that riches and the favour of the prince conferred preeminence, but then it was to be remembered, that good and truth were the only riches there accounted of; and that the favour of the prince was no other than the Lord's mercy to thofe, who had been faithful ftewards of the grace they had received from him in this world; and confequently, that to claim any farther authority than was founded hereon, would be nothing better than ufurpation and rebellion againſt the laws of his government: on hearing this he was put to ſhame and confuſion.

408. I was in converſation with fome fpirits, which had a notion that heaven, and the joys thereof, confifted in being great there, when it was told them, that he which is leaſt is greateſt in the kingdom of heaven, and that by leaſt is meant he, who, being without ſtrength and wifdom, defires not to have either from himſelf, but from the Lord only; now fuch a leaſt one is the happieſt, and confequently the greateſt, for the Lord is to him both ſtrength and wifdom; and what means greateſt but happieſt, or what do the mighty propofe by their power, or the rich by their riches, but to be happier than others? Moreover, it was told them, that it made no part of heavenly happinefs to defire to be leaſt, in order thereby to be the greateſt, for that was afpiring after grandeur; but that it confifted in heartily wifhing better to others than to themfelves, and in doing them the beſt fervices for their own fakes with a difintereſted love.

409. What heavenly joy is, in its eſſence, will not admit of defcription, as being feated in the inmoſt principles of life in the angels, from which it diffufes itfelf into all their thoughts and affections, and thence into every thing they fay and do: it is as if the fecret receſſes of their fouls were wide open to the divine influence, in order to give it free admiſſion into every fibre of their fpiritual bodies, thereby to excite perceptions and fenfations of delight furpaſſing the power of expreſſion; for what takes its rife in the center is propagated through all the derivations from it to the circumference, or external parts. The good fpirits, which have not as yet been received into heaven, nor confequently entered into this joy, are even tranfported at

the sensation of it, when communicated to them by the efflux or sphere of love issuing from any angel, as is sometimes granted to those who have an earnest desire to taste of heavenly joy.

410. Certain spirits, on a time, were anxious to feel something of this joy, and accordingly they were permitted to taste as much of it as they were able to bear; and though the quantity communicated to them was so extremely small, as scarcely to deserve the name of angelical, yet they deemed it to be highly cœlestial, as being superlative with regard to their sensations; which convinced me, not only that there are many degrees in heavenly joy, but also, that what is the highest degree to one scarcely equals the lowest degree in another; and also, that every one has his limited or utmost measure of joy, which is heaven to him, and that more, instead of increasing his happiness, would be painful and more than he could sustain.

411. There were some other spirits of no bad disposition, which sunk into a trance, and were favoured with heavenly visions; for spirits, even before the gate of communication is opened in their interiour, may be translated into heaven, and there become acquainted with the happy state of angels: I saw them in this stillness for half an hour, and then restored to their former state in full remembrance of all they had seen: they said, that they had been with the angels in heaven, and seen stupendous things glittering like gold and silver, with various forms of exquisite beauty, which changed themselves into others in a wonderful manner; but that the angels did not seem to be pleased so much with those external objects, as delighted with the things represented by them, which were unutterable, as full of divine wisdom: they likewise declared, that they had been given to know innumerable things, which could not be described in any human language to the ten thousandth part, nor quadrate with ideas conversant with material objects.

412. The ignorance of almost all that enter into the other world, in relation to cœlestial happiness, proceeds from their being such strangers to true internal joys, and having been accustomed only to relish the pleasures of sense, and of this world; and therefore what they know not passes with them for nothing; whereas sensual and worldly pleasures are as nothing when com-

pared

pared to the former: therefore it is, that for the inftruction of fome good fpirits in this matter, who are without any notion of the nature of heavenly joys, they are at firft entertained with a fight of paradifiacal reprefentations, which, for their beauty, furpafs the reach of imagination; upon which they fuppofe that they are in the true heavenly paradife; but are told, that they are as yet far fhort of it. In the next place, they are brought into a ftate of internal joy to fuch a degree as they are capable of receiving; and then into a ftate of heavenly peace; at which they exprefs a fenfe of joy that exceeds the power of words to defcribe, or even of thought to conceive: thus they are gradually formed to the experience of true fpiritual and cœleftial good.

413. That I might be inwardly convinced both of the reality and nature of cœleftial joys, the Lord has gracioufly been pleafed to grant me an experimental fenfe thereof, and this often and long together; and therefore I can teftify to them, though not defcribe them; however, a word fhall be fpoken on the fubject, in order to convey fome imperfect idea thereon. It is an affection or ftate of the foul, in which innumerable leffer pleafures and joys form one total or aggregate, in which the component particular ones harmonize, but are not diftinctly and feverally perceived, but only as forming one general or common perception or fenfation; however, I could find that there were innumerable others therein difpofed in marvellous manner according to heavenly order, for in all, even the very leaft, fuch order is obferved, though all combined form but one general fenfation according to the quality of the recipient. In a word, in every general are infinite particulars, every one of which has its vital influence and operation, and that from the inmoft ground or center from which heavenly joys proceed. I perceived alfo, that this joy and delight iffued, as it were, from the heart, diffufing itfelf gently and fweetly through all the original fibres, and from them to their feveral ramifications and complications, and that with fo exquifite a fenfe of pleafure, as if every fibre were a fountain of joyous perceptions and fenfations, in comparifon to which, grofs corporeal pleafures are but as the muddy waters of a putrid lake to the wholfome ventilations of refrefh-
ing

ing breezes. I found by experience, whenever I was prompted by a motive of benevolence to communicate the joy I felt to any other, that in the room of what was so communicated, a fresh and more copious stream of joy flowed in upon my soul, and that according to the degree of such benevolence. This I perceived to be from the goodness and free bounty of the Lord.

414. All who are in heaven continue in their progress towards the flower and perfection of life, and the more thousands of years they pass, the more pleasantly and happily they advance on in an eternal progression, according to their proficiency in love, charity, and faith (*). There such of the female sex as had departed this life broken with the infirmities of old age, but after having lived in the faith of the Lord, in charity towards their neighbour, and in all the social duties of conjugal affection, after a succession of ages appear as advancing towards perfection in the bloom of youthful beauty surpassing description, whilst goodness and charity add graces to their persons, and express themselves in every feature of their faces, insomuch that they may pass for forms of charity: certain spirits that beheld them were astonished at the sight. Such is the form of charity, which in heaven is represented to the life, for it is charity that pourtrays it, and is pourtrayed in it, and that in a manner so expressive, that the whole angel, more particularly as to the face, appears as charity itself in a personal form of exquisite beauty, affecting the soul of the spectator with something of the same grace. In a word, to grow old in heaven is to grow in youth

(*) Something has been said before in a former note concerning faith in heaven; and it may not be improper further to observe in this place, that though it be a generally received opinion in the church, that faith in heaven will cease, as being swallowed up in vision and the accomplishment of the promises, yet however a human faith, as to the reality and certainty of future things, will cease when those things now future shall come to pass; yet it follows not that a divine, dependent, confidential faith in the Lord for the continuance of his goodness and blessings will ever fail, as it is the exercise of a duty naturally springing from the relation subsisting between the most exalted of created beings, and their adorable Creator and Benefactor, to whose free bounty and goodness they stand indebted both for the continuation of their existence, and the happiness of it; of which, faith, love, and obedience, may be the absolute conditions, though no less voluntary on their part on that account. Tr.

and

and beauty, as is the case with all those who have here lived in love to the Lord, and in charity towards their neighbour. Such are the forms of the cœlestial inhabitants, though with unspeakable distinction and variety.

Of the Immensity of Heaven.

415. That heaven is of immense extent may be gathered from many things laid down in the foregoing part of this work, and particularly from what has been said concerning its being inhabited by all good people of the human race (see above, n. 311 to 317) both from within and without the church, from the creation of the earth. He that knows any thing of geography may form some judgment how vast a multitude must people this our world, and will find, upon a moderate calculation, that several thousands die every day, and some millions in the space of a year, and that mortality has been going on with us from the earliest times now for some thousands of years, passing thus continually into the world of spirits: how many of these have and do become angels cannot be known; but thus much I have been told, that very many such there were in ancient times, for then men were more spiritually minded, and more heavenly in their affections; but not so many in the following ages, as in process of time they turned more to the world, and more set their affections on things below. From this first consideration it may appear, that heaven is of great extent from the number of inhabitants therein from this world only.

416. But the immensity of heaven will still farther appear from considering, that all infants that depart this life, whether within or without the church, are adopted by the Lord, and advanced to the angelical state, and that the number of these amounts to the fourth or fifth part of the human species on earth. That every infant, wherever born, and whether sprung from good or bad parents, is after death received by the Lord, educated in heaven, and, according to an established order of that kingdom, principled with good affections, and instructed in

the knowledge of the truth; and, when perfected in underſtanding and wiſdom, adopted into the order of angels, ſee above, n. 329 to 345. How great a multitude of angels may we ſuppoſe to come from this ſingle ſeminary from the creation to this preſent time!

417. Another proof of the immenſity of heaven is deducible from hence, viz. that all the planets, ſo viſible to our ſight in this ſolar ſyſtem, are ſo many worlds or earths; and that there are alſo innumerable others in the univerſe, all inhabited, concerning which I ſhall quote the following paſſage extracted from a little work written by me, intitled, *De Telluribus in Univerſo*. " That there are many worlds inhabited by men, who afterwards become ſpirits and angels, is a truth well known in " the other life; for every one there, that deſires it from the " love of truth and uſeful knowledge, is allowed to converſe " with the ſpirits from other worlds, in order to be convinced " of the plurality of worlds, and that not this earth only, but " alſo innumerable others are peopled by the human ſpecies. " I have ſometimes converſed with ſpirits from our world on " this ſubject, and told them, that any man of rational under" ſtanding might conclude from things clearly known, that " there are more worlds beſides this, inhabited by human crea" tures, as it was highly reaſonable to conclude, that ſuch " great bodies as the planets, ſome of which exceed our earth " in magnitude, are not mere ſolitudes, and created only to " revolve round the ſun, and ſhed a little inconſiderable light " on our earth, but deſigned for far more important uſes. He " that believes, as every rational man muſt, that Divine Omni" potence created the univerſe for human creatures, and through " them for heaven, they being the ſeminary for the peopling " of heaven, cannot but believe that every world is inhabited " by mankind. That the planets, which are ſo conſpicuous to " us within the limits of our ſolar ſyſtem, are ſo many habitable " worlds, manifeſtly appears from their exhibiting all the phæ" nomena of terreſtrial bodies, ſuch as reflecting to us the light " of the ſun, and, when viewed through a teleſcope, not " ſhewing themſelves as glittering maſſes of fire, but as ſolid " globes of earth variegated with dark ſpots; as alſo from their
" reſembling

"resembling our earth in their revolutions round the sun in
"their progress through the zodiack, thereby describing their
"annual courses and seasons of spring, summer, autumn, and
"winter; and likewise in their diurnal revolutions round their
"their own axis, whereby they effect the same regular vicissi-
"tudes of morning, noon, evening, and night, as with us:
"add to this, that some of them have their moons, called Sa-
"tellites, which perform their stated revolutions round them,
"as the moon does round our earth; and that the planet Sa-
"turn, as being most distant from the sun, is surrounded with
"a large girdle or belt, that reflects much light to that ter-
"restrial globe. Who, that knows and considers these things
"in a rational light, can believe that these stupendous bodies
"are without inhabitants, and so without use. In conversation
"with the spirits before mentioned, I took occasion to observe
"further, on the great probability of there being more worlds
"than one, from the immensity of the starry heavens so be-
"spangled with shining spheres, and that it must appear highly
"credible to the attentive observer, that each of them did the
"same office with our sun to their respective planets, thus
"serving as subordinate means to the ultimate end of creation,
"which doubtless was to provide and prepare for heaven an
"infinite number of human beings, to be blessed with the
"divine presence and communications; whilst so many stars
"served as so many suns to enlighten, warm, and fructify so
"many earths for the support of men, that should in due time
"become angels in the kingdom of heaven. What rational
"man can suppose, that such an immense provision of means
"should not be in order to a proportionate end; or be weak
"enough to imagine, that so stupendous an apparatus should
"all be for the sake of the inhabitants of one earth only, when
"as myriads of worlds are but as the dust of the balance to an
"Infinite Omnipotent Creator? There are certain spirits, who
"make it their business to acquire knowledges, as placing their
"whole delight therein; and these are allowed the liberty of
"expatiating far in the universe, and to pass from one solar
"system to another, in order to procure intelligence. These
"assured me, that there were not only more terrestrial worlds
"besides

"besides this in our solar system, but also an immense number
"of others beyond it scattered throughout the starry heavens:
"these spirits were from the planet Mercury. Upon forming
"a calculation it was found, that upon the supposition of there
"being a million of worlds in the universe like ours, and inha-
"bitants to the number of three hundred millions in every world;
"and supposing two hundred generations of men to take place in
"the compass of six thousand years, and every man or spirit to
"be allowed a space of three cubical yards; that in this case
"the number of men or spirits collected together would not
"fill this our earth, nay, little more than one of the Satellites
"of the planets, which would be but as a point compared to
"the universe, as any one of the Satellites seen from our earth
"is hardly visible to the naked eye: and what is this, or an
"universe of worlds, to Infinite Power? I have had conver-
"sation with some angels on this subject, who expressed like
"sentiments on the matter, saying, that their thoughts were
"more employed about states than space; but that it was very
"evident, that all the generations of men, and countless my-
"riads of worlds, were as nothing compared to infinity." As
to the worlds in the universe, and their inhabitants, and spirits
and angels from thence, see the little work before mentioned:
all therein related was revealed and shewed to me, in order to
make manifest somewhat of the immensity of heaven, and that
all the inhabitants thereof were originally of human extraction;
and also to make known, that our Lord is every where acknowledged for the God of heaven and earth.

418. The immensity of heaven will farther appear from
hence, that heaven in its whole complex resembles one man,
and also corresponds to all and singular the parts in man, and
that such correspondency cannot be so full, as to admit of no
increase, seeing it not only has relation to all the members,
organs, and viscera of the body in general, but also to the most
minute particulars thereof, and to every vessel, nerve, and fibre;
and not only to these, but also to those most subtle organized
forms, which in the inmost recesses of material substances are
first acted upon by the heavenly influx, and whence arise those
interior active powers, which are the next immediate instruments
subservient

subservient to the operations of the human mind; for whatever internally exists in man, exists in some substantial form as its subject, without which it is nothing: now there is a correspondence between all these and the heavenly world, see ch. *Of the Correspondence of all Things in Heaven with all Things in Man*, n. 87 to 102. This correspondency can never be at its *ne plus ultra*, because the more numerous the angelical consociations, which correspond to any one member, the higher is the degree of perfection in heaven, for all perfection there increases according to plurality, and that because in the heavens one end is pursued in all things, and by the unanimous consent of all; now this end is the common good, from which arises benefit to the individuals, and from the good of the individuals arises benefit to the community; this proceeds from the Lord turning all in heaven towards himself (see above, n. 123); and thereby making them all one in himself. That the unanimity and concord of many, more especially from a divine original, and such a bond of union, must produce perfection, every one of sound judgment will readily allow.

419. I have been favoured with a sight of the heaven that is inhabited, and also of that which is not inhabited, and I saw that the former was of such vast extent, as not to be filled in eternity, on a supposition that there were many myriads of worlds like this of ours, and every one of them equally full of inhabitants, concerning which see my little work, *De Telluribus in Universo*, n. 168.

420. Some erroneously suppose, that heaven is not of such vast extent as is here mentioned, but rather comparatively small, being led into this error by some passages in Scripture ill understood, as where it seems to be implied, that the poor only are admitted into heaven; or none but the elect; or such only as are within the church; or those alone in whose behalf the Lord intercedes; as also where heaven is represented as being shut after having received its full number, and that there is a fixed time appointed for this purpose: but let them know, that heaven will never be shut; and that there is no appointed time for any such exclusion, and no certain number limited for admission thereinto; and also, that by the elect are meant all who

are in the life of good and truth (249); and that by the poor are signified such as are without the knowledge of good and truth, but earnestly desire to have it, and that from such desire they are called those that hunger (250). 'All they who have such confined notions of heaven, and of the number of its inhabitants, do greatly mistake the sense of the Scriptures, whilst they suppose that all there make up one general assembly shut up in the same place, whereas heaven consists of innumerable distinct societies (see above, n. 41 to 50); and moreover are of opinion, that every one receives his appointment to heaven by a mere arbitrary grant of immediate mercy, and consequently, that cœlestial happiness means no more than admission into a certain place by mandate or form of designation, not understanding that the Lord leads every one by his mercy that receives him; and that to receive him is to live according to the laws of divine order, or his precepts of love and faith; and that to be under his leadings from the beginning to the end of our lives in this world, and so on in eternity, is what we are to understand by his mercy: therefore let all such know, that every one is designedly born into this world for heaven, and that he is received into it, who receives into himself the qualifying heavenly principles in this world, and that no other is excluded than he who rejects them.

(249) That those are called *Elect*, who are in the life of good and truth, n. 3755, 3900. That election and reception into heaven is not according to an arbitrary distinction of mercy, as some understand it, but according to the inward life, n. 5057, 5058. That there is no such immediate arbitrary mercy respecting salvation, but mediate or through the use of means, that is, to those who live according to the Lord's precepts, and whom he mercifully guides in this world, and hereafter in eternity, n. 10659, 8700.

(250) That by *Poor* in the Word, we are to understand to be meant such as are poor in a spiritual sense, or such as are ignorant of the truth, but desirous of instruction, n. 9209, 9253, 10227. That these are signified by those that hunger and thirst, that is, desire those knowledges of good and truth, which are introductory to the church and to heaven, n. 4958, 10227.

OF THE

WORLD OF SPIRITS,

AND OF THE

State of Man after Death.

421. What is called the world of spirits is neither heaven nor hell, but a place or state betwixt both, into which man enters immediately after death, and after staying there a certain time, longer or shorter, according to what his past life had been in this world, he is either received up into heaven, or cast down into hell.

422. That there is such an intermediate place appointed for man after this life has been manifested to me from having seen hell beneath, and heaven above it, and that man whilst there is in neither of them. The heavenly state in man is from the conjunction of good and truth within him, and the hellish state in man is from the conjunction of evil and false within him; by the former he is prepared for heaven, and by the latter for hell; now this conjunction is completed in the world of spirits, or the intermediate state: whether we call it the conjunction of the understanding and will, or the conjunction of good and truth, it comes to the same thing.

423. Something must be premised here concerning this conjunction of the intellect and will, and their correlatives good and truth, as completed in the world of spirits. To man belong understanding and will; the former is the recipient of truths, and is formed by them, and the will is the recipient of goods, and is formed thereby: so that whatever a man understands, and brings into thought, that he calls truth; and what he wills and brings into thought, that he calls good. A man may think from his intellectual part, and thence perceive what is true, and what is good ideally; but he thinks it not from the will part or faculty, unless he chuses and does it; but when he wills it, and

from

from the operation of willing also does it, then it is both in the understanding and in the will, and consequently in the man, who consists of both jointly, but not of either singly and separately; and therefore in that case only it is appropriated to him, or becomes properly his own; whereas what a man has only intellectually and in theory, however it may serve him to reason upon, and to make a counterfeit show of outwardly, yet having got no hold on his will, it makes no part of himself, but is only a matter of memory and science, which he can take up or lay down, but gains no essential form in him.

424. It is provided that man should be able to think from the intellectual part separately from the will, to the end that he may be reformed and changed; for he is reformed by means of truths, and these appertain to the intellect, as was said before. Man is born into the world with natural propensities to evil, whence it is that he is so swallowed up in the love of self, as to grudge and covet the good things of others, and to take pleasure in their loss if it may turn to his gain, being only intent on the honours, riches, and pleasures of this world: now that this malignity of his nature may be reformed, he is endowed with the power of apprehending truths in his understanding, that he may thereby counteract and subdue the evil affections in his will: hence it is that he can speculate truths in his intellect, and bring forth into speech, and act according to them; yet they are not properly his own till they be dictated from his heart and will, and flow spontaneously into his life and actions; and where this is the case, the thoughts of a man's mind, or understanding, constitute his faith; and the thoughts of his heart or will, constitute his love; and so his faith and love, like his understanding and will, are united and agree in one.

425. As far therefore as truths in the understanding are conjoined with good [*bonis*] in the will, and consequently, as far forth as any one is freely actuated thereby in the practical manifestation of them, so far he has heaven in himself, or is in a heavenly state; for, as was said before, the conjunction of good and truth is heaven in the soul; but as far as the false [*falsa*] in the understanding is conjoined with evil in the will, so far a man has hell in himself, or is in a hellish state; for the conjunction of false and evil constitutes hell: but as far as truth

in

in the underſtanding is not united with good in the will, ſo far man is in a middle ſtate between both; now almoſt all at this time are in a ſtate of knowing ſomething of truth intellectually or ſcientifically, whilſt ſome live more, ſome leſs, and ſome not at all according to it, nay, ſome quite contrary to it through the love of evil, and from thence through a falſe belief; therefore, that every one may have his full preparation and fitneſs for heaven or hell, he paſſes immediately after death into the world of ſpirits, where the conjunction of good and truth is completed in thoſe whoſe lot is to heaven; and the conjunction of evil and falſe in thoſe who are to have their portion in hell: for in thoſe two kingdoms none are allowed to be divided betwixt good and evil, or to think one way, and will another; and therefore the angels in heaven, who have their wills in good, have their underſtandings in truth; and the ſpirits in hell, who have their wills in evil, know only the falſe; conſequently, in this intermediate ſtate of final preparation, whatever of falſe [*falſa*] has cleaved to the good ſpirits is done away, and ſuch truths as are accordant and conformable to their good are given them; and from the bad ſpirits are taken away ſuch adventitious or ſpeculative truths as they may have acquired, and they become poſſeſſed of ſuch falſities [*falſa*] in their room, as are accordant and conformable to their evil nature (*). Thus much may ſuffice to explain what is meant by the world of ſpirits.

426. In

(*) However obſcure at firſt ſight this and the three preceding numbers may appear to ſome of our readers (though we have uſed our beſt endeavours to render the matter intelligible to all) it muſt be obſerved, that they hold forth to us a doctrine of great importance, and worthy of their moſt attentive conſideration; and the knowledge thereof is highly conducive to the clearer underſtanding of the author in many parts of his writings: he therein treats of the two great conſtituent principles of man, the underſtanding and will, and ſhews how the depraved affections of the latter are to be ſubdued and reformed here by the light and power of truth received from the former; in which caſe the underſtanding and will are in union, and truth ſprings not ſo much from the exerciſe of reaſoning, as from the principle of good in the will; the tree being made good, the fruit is conſequently the ſame: but without this union the underſtanding and will may be contrary to each other, and the former think the things that are excellent, whilſt the latter follows thoſe that are contrary thereto, as is the caſe with the ſpeculative believer, whoſe life is not as becometh the Goſpel of Chriſt, but contrary to his faith. Now in the world of ſpirits, where all are finally prepared for heaven or hell, the underſtanding and will are united both in the good and the bad ſpirits, when the latter, having their underſtanding darkened through the evil in their will,

426. In the world of spirits is always a very great number of them, as there is the first resort of all, in order to their examination and preparation; but there is no fixed time for their stay there, for some are translated to heaven, and others consigned to hell soon after their arrival, whilst some continue there for weeks, and others for several years, though none more than thirty, this depending on the correspondence or non-correspondence between the interiour and exteriour of men. How they pass from one state to another in this world, in the course of their preparation, shall be spoken of in what follows.

427. As soon as they arrive in the world of spirits, they are all classed by the Lord according to their several qualities and dispositions, the evil with such infernal societies as they had communication with in this world in the ruling passion; and the good with such of the heavenly societies as they had communication with in love, charity, and faith: but however they are thus diversely classed, yet all meet and converse together in that world, when they have a desire so to do, who have been friends and acquaintance in this life, more especially husbands and wives, brothers and sisters: I have seen a father conversing with his six sons with a perfect remembrance of them all, and also many others with their kindred and friends; but as most of them were of different inclinations and habits of mind, according to their different ways of life here, they were soon parted; but it must be noted both concerning those that go to heaven, and those that go to hell, that after their arrival in those two different kingdoms, they no more see or know one another, unless they are of like minds and affections. The reason why they meet and know one another in the world of spirits, and not so in heaven or hell, is, because in the first of these worlds they pass through the same states they were in, in this life, and so from one to another; but afterwards, all are fixed in one

will, know only what is false, or contrary to truth, whilst the former have their understanding enlightened with the knowledge of the truth from their love of good in the will; and so both good and bad spirits think and speak and act in all things consistently with the governing principle within them respectively. Let it be noted here, that this intermediate state has nothing in it of the probationary kind, for that is all over with the life of this world, but is a state of separation, or reducing every one to his proper prevailing principle, and, as such, finally preparatory for heaven or hell. Tr.

permanent

permanent state respectively, according to the state of that love which prevails in them, in which one knows another from similarity of condition; for, as was observed above, n. 41 to 50, similitude joins, and dissimilitude separates.

428. As the world of spirits is a middle state in man between heaven and hell, so is it also a middle place, having the hells beneath, and the heavens above. All the hells are shut next to that world, except that some holes or clefts, like as in rocks, or wide mouths, are left open, and these so guarded, that none can pass through them but by permission, which is granted on particular occasions, of which hereafter: heaven likewise appears as fenced all round, so that there is no passing to any of the heavenly societies, but by a narrow way, which is likewise guarded. These outlets and inlets are what in Scripture are called the doors and gates of heaven and hell.

429. The world of spirits appears like a valley between mountains and rocks, here and there sinking and rising. The doors and gates opening to the heavenly societies are only seen by those who are in their preparation for heaven, nor are they to be found by any others: to every society in heaven there is an entrance from the world of spirits, after passing which there is a way, which, as it rises, branches into several others: nor are the doors and gates of the hells visible to any, but those that are going to enter therein, to whom they are then opened; at which time there appear, like as it were, dark and sooty caverns leading obliquely down to the deep, where there are also more gates. Through those dark and dismal caverns exhale certain fetid vapours, which are most offensive to the good spirits, but which the evil ones are greedily fond of; for as was the evil which any one took most delight in when in this world, such is the stink corresponding thereto that most pleases him in the other; in which they may be aptly compared to those birds and beasts of prey, as ravens, wolves, and swine, that are attracted by the rank effluvia emitted from carrion and putrid carcases: I once heard one of those unhappy spirits loudly bemoaning himself, as from some inward anguish, on being struck with a fragrant odour from heaven; and afterwards relieved from his misery on scenting a fetid exhalation from hell.

430. There

430. There are also in every man two gates, the one of which opens towards hell, and to all that is evil and false [*malis et falsis*] proceeding thence; the other gate opens towards heaven, and to all good and truth [*bonis et veris*] that issue thence: the infernal gate is open in those who are in evil and its false [*in malo et inde falso*] and they receive from above only some glimmering of heavenly light, just sufficient to serve them to think, reason, and talk of heavenly things; but the gate of heaven stands open in those who are in good and its truth [*in bono et inde vero*]. There are also two ways leading to the rational mind in man, the superior or internal, by which good and truth is communicated from the Lord; and the inferior or external way, by which evil and false are communicated from hell, and the rational mind is in the midst of these two ways; hence it is, that as much of the heavenly light as any man admits into his mind, so far is he truly rational; and so much as he admits not of it, in such proportion he is not rational, however he may think himself so. These things are here offered, to shew the correspondence that subsists between man and heaven and hell; for his rational mind, during the formation of it, corresponds to the world of spirits, the things above it being in heaven, and the things beneath it in hell; the former are opened, and the latter (as to all influx of evil and false) are shut with respect to those who are in their preparation for heaven; but, on the other hand, the things from beneath are opened, and the things above are shut (as to all influx of good and truth) with respect to those who are in their preparation for hell; consequently, the latter can only look down to the things beneath them, or to hell; and the former only to the things above them, or to heaven. Now to look up is, by correspondence, to look to the Lord, who is the common center to which all heavenly things point their aspect and tendency; but to look downwards is to turn from the Lord to the opposite center of attraction to all things of a hellish nature, see above, n. 123 and 124.

431. They who are in the world of spirits are spoken of in the preceding numbers under the denomination of *Spirits*, and they who are in heaven, under the denomination of *Angels*.

That

That every Man is a Spirit as to the Inner Man.

432. Whoever rightly confiders the matter, cannot but know, that it is not the body, or material part, but the foul, or fpiritual part, that thinks within him. Now the foul is his fpirit, immortal in all its properties, and receptive of what is fpiritual, as having a fpiritual life, which confifts in thinking and willing; confequently, the whole of the rational life appertains thereto, and not to the body, though manifefted therein; for the body, as obferved before, is only thoughtlefs matter, and an adjunct or inftrument to the fpirit of man, whereby it may manifeft its vital powers and functions in this natural world, where all things are material, and as fuch void of life: it is indeed cuftomary to afcribe action, motion, and power to the body in the common forms of fpeaking; but to fuppofe that thefe properties belong to the inftrument, and not folely to the principle that actuates it, is erroneous and abfurd.

433. As all vital power, both of acting and thinking, appertains folely to the fpirit, and in no wife to the body, it follows, that the fpirit is truly and properly the man, and that without its influence and operation there is neither thought nor life from the crown of the head to the fole of the foot; confequently, that the feparation of the body from the fpirit, which we call death, takes nothing from that which in reality conftitutes the man. I have been informed by the angels, that fome, even after death, before they are raifed to their fecond life, have fenfible perceptions for a while, as if ftill in the body, though without the power of bodily motion.

434. Man would not be capable of thinking and volition, unlefs there were in him a fubftance to ferve as the fubject of thefe operations, and to fuppofe otherwife would be afcribing exiftence to non-entity, as may appear from man's not being able to fee without that organ, which is the fubject of vifion, or to hear without the organ of hearing; thefe fenfes being nothing

thing without such subjects of their operations. Now thought is internal vision, or the sight of the mind, as perception is the internal hearing, and these without internal organized substances, as their proper subjects, cannot exist: so that the spirit of a man has equally a form, and that a human one, as also its sensory and senses, when divested of its material body, as it had before; for all the perceptive life of the eye and the ear, and of every other sense that appertains to man, is not from his material body, but from his spirit, and the vital powers thereof, in all and singular the organs and parts of his body: hence it is, that spirits see, hear, and feel, as well as men, in the spiritual world (*), though not in this natural world after their separation from this mortal body. That the spirit had natural sensations in this world was owing to its union with a natural or material body; but then also it had its spiritual senses exercised in the various modes of thinking and willing.

435. The foregoing doctrine is here offered, to convince the rational reader, that man, considered in himself, is a spirit, and that the corporeal part of his composition annexed to him in this natural and material world is in order to his relation thereto, and what he has to do therein, but is not the man himself, but only designed to be instrumental to the operations of his spirit: but, as few are capable of receiving abstract reasonings, and many are apt to run them into matter of doubtful disputation, by arguments drawn from fallacious appearances of sense, I

(*) To suppose a human spirit void of a human form and senses, is to annihilate the very idea of spirit; for as every essence has its proper form, and every form its own essence (they being necessary correlatives) so every spirit has its body suited to the world it belongs to, according to that distinction laid down by the apostle: " There is a natural body, and there is a spiritual body:" and indeed, it is as rational to conclude, that a human spirit should have a human, organized body endued with spiritual senses in a spiritual world, as that the same spirit should be invested with a material organized body with natural senses in this natural world. It is to be lamented, and the more for its tendency to promote infidelity, that many of the learned, so called, have in a manner defined and refined spiritual nature into nothing, by divesting it of substantiality, to which it has a more peculiar right; nor is the body of an angel less substantial in a proper sense of the word than a solid rock, though not according to the condition of material nature. Upon the whole, the common ideas of the vulgar and illiterate come much nearer to the truth and reality of heavenly things than the vain conceits of such speculating sciolists. Tr.

chuse,

chuse, for confirmation of the doctrine in hand, to appeal to truths founded on experience. Such as have confirmed themselves in the belief of the contrary side, are given to think, that as the beasts have life and sensations as well as men, so they have both the same spirit and the same end; but this is a gross error, as the spirit of a beast immensely differs from that of a man, as being destitute of that sublime principle of a heavenly life, by which the latter is made receptive of the divine influx, and capable of being exalted to a participation of the divine nature; and therefore it is that man is so highly privileged above the beasts, that he can think of God, and the things pertaining to his kingdom both in heaven and earth, and be led thereby to love the Lord, and to be united to him: now that which is in the capacity of such union is not liable to perish like that which is not. As to this inmost or supreme part in man above what the beasts possess, something has been said before, n. 39, but which it is thought proper to repeat in this place, as appofite to the subject before us, viz. " I am here led to say something
" concerning the angels of the three heavens, which has hitherto
" continued a secret, through want of knowledge as to the
" three degrees of the divine order, spoken of, n. 38, viz. that
" there is in every angel, and in every man, an inmost and
" supreme degree or part, which more immediately admits the
" divine influx from the Lord, and whereby all that is within
" man in the inferior degrees are orderly disposed and regulated.
" This inmost or supreme part of the spirit or soul, may be
" called the Lord's entrance into angels and men, nay, his very
" habitation in them; and hereby it is, that man is distin-
" guished from the brute animals (which have it not) and is
" rendered capable of near communications with the Lord in
" the inner man, of believing in him, loving him, and of seeing
" him: nay, from hence it is that man is a recipient of under-
" standing and wisdom, and also that he is endowed with a
" rational life, and an heir of immortality: but how or what
" the Lord operates in this inmost recess or supreme part of
" man, exceeds the capacity of an angel to comprehend."

436. That man is a spirit internally, has been given me to know from an experience, which would take up many sheets to relate.

relate. I have conversed with spirits, as a spirit, and also as a man in the body, and when I conversed with them in the former character, I appeared to them as a spirit in a human form like to themselves, my interior part being in all things conformable thereto, for at such times the corporeal material part did not appear.

437. That man is a spirit internally, may also be evinced from hence, that upon his separation from the body by death, he still continues a living man as before: that I might be certified of this, it has been allowed me to converse with almost all that I was acquainted with in their life-time here, with some only for hours, with some for weeks and months, and with some for years; and this was permitted, to the intent that I might be confirmed in this truth, and also be qualified by experience to bear testimony to the same.

438. To what has been said I have permission to add, that every one whilst here in the body is, as to his spirit, in some society of spirits, though he knows it not, and by means of them has communication either with some heavenly or infernal society, accordingly as he is good or bad, and also that he is joined thereto after death. This is often told and shewed to those who pass from hence into the world of spirits: not that a man appears, whilst he lives in this world, as a spirit in such society, and that because he as yet exercises his thinking faculties according to his state in nature; but where any are such as think abstractedly from the body, they being in a spiritual frame, do sometimes appear in their respective societies, and are well distinguished by the spirits that are of it; their manner is to go about musing and silent, without looking at others, and as if they did not see them; but as soon as any spirit speaks to them, they immediately disappear.

439. To illustrate that a man is interiorly a spirit, I shall here shew from experience, what it is to be withdrawn from the body, and what it is to be carried by the spirit to another place.

440. As to the first, viz. to be withdrawn from the body, it is in this manner: a man is brought into a middle state betwixt sleeping and waking, during which he knows no other than that he is perfectly awake, forasmuch as all his senses are as lively

as ever, his fight, his hearing, and what appears still more strange, even his feeling; nay, this last is at such a time more exquisite than at others. In this state I have seen spirits and angels to the life, have heard them speak, and, what will be thought still more wonderful, have touched them, though the material body then bore no part therein: it is in reference to this state that we read of being " absent from the body;" and also of " not knowing whether one is in the body, or out of " the body." Into this state I have been brought only three or four times, to the intent that I might have some experience of it, and also know that spirits and angels are possessed of every sense, and man also in spirit when withdrawn from the body.

441. As to the second of the states mentioned, viz. that of being translated by the spirit to another place; this I have had living proof of, though only twice or thrice; my experience of which is as follows. As I was walking in the streets of a certain city, and at another time out in the fields, to all seeming perfectly in the use of my bodily senses, and seeing my way as at other times, I was in a trance, conversing with spirits, and saw in the vision groves, rivers, palaces, houses, men, and many other objects; when after walking thus for some hours, I suddenly returned to my natural sight, and found myself in a far distant place; at which I was at first greatly amazed; but on recollection perceived, that I had been in the like state with those that are said to have been *carried by the spirit into another place*; for during the trance or transit, the person has no idea or thought concerning the way, though of many miles; nor of the time, though it should be of many hours, or even days; neither is he sensible of any fatigue. Thus he is conducted through ways he is an entire stranger to, by a certain direction, to the place appointed.

442. But these two states of man, as being of the more interior kind, or, which signifies the same, when he is in the spirit, are an extraordinary dispensation, and only occasionally made known to me as realities acknowledged by the church; but to converse with spirits, and to be with them as one of their own society, is a privilege which has been granted to me in the

·moſt perfect uſe of all the bodily ſenſes, and that now for many years.

443. That man, as to his interior ſtate, is a ſpirit, may further be confirmed by what has been ſaid above, n. 311 to 317, on the ſubject of heaven and hell, as conſiſting of the human race.

444. That ſuch alſo is the nature of man, may be learned from his faculties of thinking and willing, which are ſpiritual, and conſtitute the very eſſence of the human ſpecies; and alſo, according to their reſpective difference therein, the particular diſtinction of one individual of it from another.

Of Man's being raiſed from Death, and his Entrance into Immortality.

445. When the body of a man is no longer able to perform its natural functions correſponding to the thoughts and affections of his ſpirit, and which are derived to him from the ſpiritual world, then he is ſaid to die; which comes to paſs when the lungs and the heart ceaſe their reſpiratory and contractile motions, not that man then ſuffers extinction of life, but only is ſeparated from that corporeal part of his compoſition, which ſerved him for an inſtrument of uſefulneſs in this world; but he ſtill continues a living man, and that in a proper and literal ſenſe of the expreſſion, inaſmuch as man receives his denomination, not from his body, but from his ſpirit, ſince it is the latter that thinks in him, and that thought with affection eſſentially conſtitute the man; ſo that when any is ſaid to die, it means no more than that he paſſes from one world into another; and hence it is, that by *death* in the Scripture, according to the internal ſenſe of that word, is ſignified reſurrection, and continuation of life (251).

446. There is a very near communication and correſpondence betwixt the ſpirit and reſpiration, and the motion of the heart

---

(251) That *death* in the Word ſignifies reſurrection, foraſmuch as life is continued to man after death, n. 3498, 3505, 4618, 4621, 6036, 6222.

[the

[the syſtole] betwixt thinking and reſpiration, and betwixt the affection of love and the heart (252); ſo that when theſe two motions ceaſe in the body, a ſeparation preſently enſues; for theſe two motions, viz. that which is reſpiratory in the lungs, and that which is called the ſyſtole or contractile power of the heart, are the two bonds of union, which when broken, the ſpirit is left to itſelf, and the body, being deſtitute of life from the ſpirit, becomes cold and putrifies. That ſo intimate a communication ſubſiſts between the human ſpirit and reſpiration, and the heart, is becauſe all the vital motions in this world depend thereon, not only in common, but alſo in every particular part of the body (253).

447. The ſpirit of a man remains ſome little time in the body after all ſigns of life diſappear, but not longer than till a total ceſſation of all power in the heart enſues, which varies according to the nature of the diſeaſe he dies of, for the motion of the heart continues long after in ſome, but not ſo in others; but as ſoon as the total ceſſation of it happens, the reſuſcitation of man commences, and this by the ſole power of the Lord. By reſuſcitation here is meant the liberation of the ſpirit of a man from his body, and the introduction of it into the world of ſpirits, and commonly called reſurrection. That the ſpirit of a man is not ſeparated from his body before all motion and power in the heart entirely ceaſes, is becauſe the heart correſponds to the affection of love, which is the very life of man, for it is from love that every one derives his vital heat (254); therefore ſo long as this conjunction laſts, ſo long correſpon-

---

(252) That the heart correſponds to the will, conſequently to the affection of love; and that the reſpiration of the lungs correſponds to the underſtanding, conſequently to thought, n. 3888. That the heart in the Word ſignifies will and love, n. 7540, 9050, 10336; and that ſoul or ſpirit ſignifies underſtanding, faith, and truth; that therefore, *from the ſoul*, and *from the heart*, from the will, love, and good, n. 2930, 9050. Of the correſpondence of the heart and lungs with the grand man or heaven, n. 3883 to 3896.

(253) That the pulſe of the heart, and the reſpiration of the lungs, hold dominion throughout the whole body, and influence every part of it, n. 3887, 3889, 3890.

(254) That love is the eſſence of life in man, n. 5002. That love is a ſpiritual heat, and conſequently the vital principle in man, n. 1589, 2146, 3338—9954, 10740. That affection is the continuation of love, n. 3938.

dence continues, and it is from correspondency that the spirit actuates and communicates life to the body.

448. The manner in which resuscitation is performed, has not only been told to me, but also manifested to me by actual experience in myself, to the end that I might be fully certified thereof.

449. I was brought into a state of insensibility with respect to the bodily senses, and nearly into that of dying persons, the interior life, together with the power of thinking, remaining at the same time perfectly entire, so that I could perceive and retain in memory what happened, and also know how it is with those who are raised from the dead: I perceived likewise that the lungs scarcely continued their office, but there remained an interior respiration in my spirit joined with a gentle and almost imperceptible breathing of the body: I then first experienced a communication of the pulse of the heart with the heavenly kingdom, for that kingdom corresponds to the heart in man; some angels also appeared from thence, some at a distance, and two placed themselves near to my head, upon which all concern and regard for myself ceased, however thought and perception remained with me: in this state I continued for some hours. At length the spirits that were about me departed, supposing me to be dead; and at the same time an aromatick odour, like that of a body embalmed, diffused itself around; for on the presence of the cœlestial angels, that which would be otherwise a cadaverous smell, is changed into such a fragrancy (*), which is so offensive to bad spirits, as to hinder their approach; and it is by this means that they are kept from molesting such as are in their passage to eternal life. The angels which had placed themselves at my head were silent, only communicating their thoughts to mine, which being received, they know that the spirit of the man so recipient, is in a proper state to be conveyed from the body.

(*) This may serve to explain what many readers have met with, as related by authors of good credit, concerning certain persons of eminent piety, who are said to have died in the *odour of sanctity*, from the fragrancy that issued from their bodies after death. A truth easily admissible by all who believe an intercourse as subsisting between the spiritual and natural worlds; and they who do not, are ill qualified to receive benefit from our author's writings. Tr.

The

The manner of communicating their thoughts to me was by looking at me full in the face, for such is the manner of like communication in heaven. As thought and perception all along remained with me, to the end that I might know and remember the way of resuscitation, so I perceived that the angels before mentioned scrutinized into my thoughts, to know whether they were like to those of dying persons, which are generally employed on the subjects of eternal life, and also I found, that they endeavoured to direct my thoughts that way: I was told afterwards, that the spirit of every dying man was preserved in his last best thoughts, till the prevailing power of those, which proceeded from his ruling love or passion when in the world, took possession of him. I was given to perceive and experience, in a particular manner, a certain violent attraction of my inward man or spirit from my body; and it was told me, that this was from the Lord, and introductory to resurrection.

450. The cœlestial angels, after joining themselves to any raised spirit, do not leave him, for they are loving to every one; but if he be one that is not qualified to be their companion, he earnestly wishes to be separated from them, on which he is joined by some of the angels from the middle or spiritual heaven, who bring him to a sight of the external light, for hitherto all had passed with him inwardly in vision. I beheld the manner in which this appeared to be done, namely, by an evolution of the external coat of the left eye back to the fence or septum of the nose, in order to give a free ingress of light to the eye for the purpose of vision (*). This seems to be a real operation to the spirit, though it is only such in appearance: upon this

---

(*) It is easy to foresee what kind of representation men of a jesting and ludicrous turn are likely to give of this among other like passages of our author's writings: it may not therefore be amiss to caution them against indulging a vein of liberty bordering on profaneness, as far as it may extend to the parables of our Lord, and the visions in the Prophets and the Apocalypse, wherein spiritual things in the heavens are represented by natural similitudes on earth. Besides, it is very reasonable to suppose, that to spirits newly arrived from this world all things are imaged by corresponding signs or appearances accommodated to the apprehensions and ideas they carry with them; nay, that all things spiritual will eternally be visibly represented under significant emblems, both for the instruction and entertainment of the heavenly inhabitants, as this may constitute no small part of cœlestial delights.

an imperfect light at first appears, something like that which is discerned through the eye-lids upon a man's first waking in the morning: it seemed to me to be of a cœlestial colour, but I was told afterwards, that it appears differently to different persons: after this, a kind of tegument or veil is perceived to be gently removed from the face, but this also is in appearance only, such evolution representing a spiritual frame of mind and thinking, succeeding to that which before was natural only. Moreover, these angels use their best endeavours to hinder any sentiment or affection from being excited in the mind of the new raised spirit that is not tinctured with love; after this they give him to know, that he is now a spirit. After these ministrations of light and knowledge as to his condition, the spiritual angels shew all kind offices to the new spirit that accord with his state, and instruct him in things pertaining to the other life, so far as consist with his present capacity; but if he is such a one as is not capable of receiving benefit from their friendly endeavours, in that case he desires to be separated from their company, not that they leave him, but he quits them; for the angels love every one, and it is their highest delight to attend, instruct, and to conduct them to heaven. When he has thus separated himself from their society, he is next received by the good spirits [in the intermediate state] into their society, who, in like manner, do him all kind offices; but if his life in this world has been such as disqualifies him for their society, he is desirous, as before, to be separated from them also; and so on, till he can associate with such as are like himself, in whose company he finds his true enjoyment; and with them he lives (however strange it may seem) a life conformable to that which they chose in this world.

451. But this way of life in his new state lasts only for some days; after which he continues his progress from state to state, till it finally terminates in heaven or hell, as will appear in the sequel, and of which I have had convincing proof.

452. I have conversed with some the third day after their decease, when they passed through all that has been mentioned in the foregoing numbers, 449, 450; and also with three, who were of my acquaintance in this world, whom I informed, that their

friends

friends were at that time preparing their funerals, and that they were then on the point of interment; at which account they appeared aftonifhed, faying, that they knew themfelves to be alive, and therefore that they could only bury what had been of ufe to them in this world, but now belonged to them no more; and prefently after expreffed their wonder, that whilft in this world, neither they, nor fo many others in the church, truly believed in fuch a life after the death of the body. Such as in this world had little or no belief of a life after death, appear confounded and afhamed when they experience the contrary; but as to thofe who had taken pains to confirm themfelves in unbelief as to this matter, they are claffed with their fellows, and feparated from fuch as had lived in the belief of it; and as to the greater part of them, they are in chains with a certain hellifh fociety, which in this world had denied God, and held the fundamental doctrines of the Chriftian church in contempt; for as far as any one ftudies to confirm himfelf in the difbelief of a future ftate, fo far he declares himfelf an enemy to heavenly things, and to the church of God.

That Man after Death is in a perfect Human Form.

453. That the form of the fpirit of a man is in a human form, or, in other words, that the fpirit is the true formed man, may be evinced from many of the foregoing articles, particularly from thofe, wherein is fhewed, that every angel is in a perfect human form, n. 73 to 77; and alfo that every man is a fpirit as to his inner man, n. 432 to 444; and that the angels in heaven are from the human race, n. 311 to 317. This alfo more evidently appears from man's being denominated man from his fpirit, and not from his body, and becaufe the corporeal form is an adjunct to the fpirit after its form, and not contrariwife, the former being but the cloathing of the latter. Moreover, the fpirit is the fole moving power in man, acting upon and actuating every the moft minute part of the body, infomuch that

that, when any part no longer derives vital influence therefrom, it presently dies. Now the ruling powers, which govern the body as their subject, are the thought and the will; but these are from the spirit only, nay, constitute its very essence. The reason why we do not see any separate spirit, nor yet that of another man whilst in his body, in its human form, with our present organs of sight, is because these organs of vision are material, and therefore only capable of discerning objects of a material nature, whereas spiritual things must be seen by a spiritual eye (*); but when the corporeal sight is extinguished by the death of the body, and the spirit's eye is opened, then spirits appear to one another in their human form, not only in the spiritual world, but they also see the spirits of those who yet live here in the body.

454. That a human form is proper to a human spirit, follows from man's being created in the form of heaven, and also receptive of all things of a heavenly nature and order (255), consequently with the faculty of receiving understanding and wisdom; for whether we express it by the words, faculty of receiving understanding and wisdom, or, the faculty of receiving heaven, it comes to the same, as may appear from what has been said before concerning the light and heat of heaven, n. 126 to 140: concerning the form of heaven, n. 200 to 212: concerning the wisdom of angels, n. 265 to 275; and in the article wherein is shewed, that heaven, as to its form, resembles a man both in whole and in part, n. 59 to 77, and this from the Divine

---

(*) It is to be noted here, that when spirits are seen by any one in the body, they are not seen with the corporeal organs of vision, but by the spirit of the beholder abstractedly from the body, though the appearance is exactly the same in both cases, as implied in those words of the apostle, where, speaking of his visions, he says: "Whether in the body, or out of the body, I cannot tell." What is here observed is not intended by way of objection to the supposition, that spirits, for certain purposes, may be permitted to assume corporeal vehicles visible to the bodily eye. Tr.

(255) That man is the subject participating of all things relative to the divine order, and that by creation he was a form of divine order, n. 4219, 4220, 4223, 4523—9706, 10156, 10472. That as far as any one lives here according to divine order, so far he appears perfect, and of beautiful form in the other world, n. 4839, 6605, 6626.

Humanity

Humanity of the Lord, from whom heaven and its form originate, n. 78 to 86.

455. What has hitherto been faid on this fubject may be underſtood by the rational man, from his view of caufes and their effects, of premifes and their confequences; but not fo by the obſtinately irrational, and that for many aſſignable reafons; but principally, becauſe he is averfe to all doctrines which are contrary to the falfe principles that he has adopted in the room of truths; and he that has thus ſhut up his mind, hath ſhut the gate of heaven againſt himſelf, fo that no light from thence can illuminate his rational faculties; and yet that gate might be opened if his will did not refiſt, fee above, n. 424. That any man (free from natural defect) may form a rational conception of truth when offered, if his will be not averfe to it, I have had convincing proof. Thus I have known bad fpirits, who, having rendered themfelves irrational by a wilful oppofition to divine truths, and by confirming themfelves in unbelief, yet, when compelled to turn themfelves towards thofe who were in the light of truth, they became intelligent like the angels, had a clear comprehenfion of the truth, and confeſſed it; but they no fooner returned to themfelves, and the bias of their prevailing love or will, than they loſt all, and declared themfelves on the contrary fide: I have alfo heard fome infernals confefs, that their actions were indeed evil, and their thoughts contrary; but that they could not refiſt the ruling paſſion or bent of their will; and moreover, that under the influence thereof upon their minds, they faw evil as good, and falfe as truth. This makes it evident, that they who are in falfe thinking from an evil principle [*in falfis ex malo*] might be poſſeſſed of a rational underſtanding, if they were in a willing difpofition for it, and that the reafon why they are not fo, is becaufe they love the falfe above the true [*falfa præ veris*] as more agreeing with the evil they have adopted, and which they chufe to follow. It is to be obferved, that to love and to will a thing is the fame; for what a man wills he loves, and what he loves that he alfo wills. As men are thus conſtituted, to be in a capacity of receiving the truths relating to the kingdom of God both in heaven above, and in his church on earth, if their wills

wills be accordant thereto; therefore I have been called to this miniſtration of confirming the truths in both kingdoms by rational arguments, that ſo the errors which have been introduced by falſe reaſoning may be diſcuſſed and refuted by ſuch as are true, if ſo be that any by this means may be brought to the knowledge of the truth; for to confirm ſpiritual truths by rational arguments, is the proper province of thoſe who are in the principle of truth; for how ſhould any one rightly interpret or underſtand the Sacred Writings from the literal expreſſion, without the aid of reaſon enlightened from above! To the want of this qualification in expoſitors it is owing, that ſo many heretical doctrines have been introduced into the church (256).

456. That the ſpirits of men are real men after their ſeparation from the body, I can teſtify to from a daily experience of many years, and after having ſeen and heard them a thouſand times: I have alſo diſcourſed with them on the incredulity of many here on earth as to this matter, and how they who are believers in this reſpect are conſidered by the learned as weak and credulous. The ſpirits expreſſed a heart-felt grief, that ſuch ignorance ſhould prevail among men, eſpecially in the church, ſaying, that this incredulity took its riſe from the learned, who, from their groſs, ſenſual ideas of ſubſtance, as appropriated to material bodies, conceived no otherwiſe of the ſoul than as of mere thought without any viſible ſubject to inhere and ſubſiſt in, and ſo vaniſhing into a kind of volatile ſubtle æther upon its ſeparation from the body: but as the church believes in the immortality of the ſoul on the evidence of the Scriptures, they could not but aſcribe to it ſome vital property, as of thought, though they diveſt it of all human ſenſitive perception till its re-union with the body, according to their doctrine of the reſurrection at the time of the laſt judgment.

---

(256) That we ſhould ſet out with an aſſent to fundamental truths grounded on plain ſcriptural evidence, and then we may proceed to ſcientifick knowledge for the purpoſes of illuſtration, n. 6047; but that they who are in unbelief, and on the negative ſide, are in no wiſe qualified to judge of divine truths from natural knowledge, n. 2568, 2588, 4760, 6047. That it is according to divine order to proceed from ſpiritual truths to the rational inveſtigation of ſuch as are natural, and not contrarywiſe, and that becauſe influx is from the ſpiritual into the natural world, and not *vice verſâ*, n. 3219, 5119, 5259—9110, 9111.

Hence

Hence it is, that when any one thinks of the foul according to their hypothefis, he has no conception of it as a fpirit in a human form; and this falls in with the general ignorance as to the nature of fpiritual beings, whether angels or others; whence it comes to pafs, that almoſt all, upon their arrival in the other world, ſtand amazed on finding themfelves to be living men, and that they can fee, hear, fpeak, and ufe their bodily fenfes equally as in this world, fee above, n. 74. But when this wonder is over, they wonder next at the great ignorance in the church concerning fuch a ſtate after death, as alfo concerning heaven and hell, when they fee all after their departure from this life as truly living, human perfons as they were before; and as fome of them feemed to be totally at a lofs to account for fo important an article of belief not being put beyond all doubt by vifions and fupernatural appearances to men in this world; they were informed, that nothing was eafier to be done, by divine permiffion, than this; but that all fuch, as had confirmed themfelves in a contrary perfuafion, would not even believe their own fenfes on the occafion; and moreover, that it was dangerous to confirm any thing by fupernatural evidence to thofe who have grounded themfelves in falfities [*in falfis*] as after conviction at firſt by fuch evidence, they would afterwards depart from it, which would fubject them to the guilt of profaning fuch truths; for to receive a truth, and afterwards to renounce it, is the fin of profanation, and fuch profane perfons have their portion in the deepeſt lake hereafter (257). This is the great
" danger

(257) That profanation is a commixture of good and evil, and of what is true and falfe, n. 6348. That they are faid to profane good and truth, or what is facred, who at firſt acknowledge them, more efpecially if they have lived according to them, and afterwards depart from the faith, and live to themfelves and the world, n. 593, 1008, 1010—4601, 10284, 10287. That if a man relapfes, after repentance and contrition, he is guilty of profanation, and his laſt ſtate is worfe than his firſt, n. 8394. That they are not guilty of profaning facred things, who did not know or believe them to be fuch, n. 1008, 1010, 1059, 8188, 10284. That the Gentiles, who are without the church, and know not the Scriptures, cannot be guilty of this profanation, n. 1327, 1328, 2051, 2081. That therefore fpiritual truths were not revealed to the Jews, as otherwife they would not have profaned them, n. 3398, 3489, 6963. That the lot of profane perfons in the other world is the moſt miferable of all, as the good and truth which they acknowledged remains in their belief, joined with the evil and falfe they had adopted

danger signified by those words of our Lord: "He hath blinded their eyes, and hardened their hearts, lest they should see with their eyes, and understand with their heart, and be converted, and I should heal them," (*) Joh. xii. 40. And with reference to such as have so hardened themselves in unbelief, as to be proof against all conviction, are spoken the following words: "If they hear not Moses and the Prophets, neither will they be persuaded, though one rose from the dead," Luke xvi. 31.

457. When the spirit of a man first enters into the world of spirits, which is soon after his resuscitation (of which mention has been made before) he as yet retains the same face and voice that he had in this world, as being hitherto in his exterior state, that of his interiour being yet unmanifested; and this is his first state after death: but some time after, his face becomes entirely changed, so as to correspond with the particular affection or love that possessed his spirit when in the body; for the face of a man's spirit differs greatly from that of his body, the latter being derived from his parents, but the former a correspondent to his predominant affection, of which it is the signature or image, and which becomes appropriated to man in the other world, upon the manifestation of his interior state; this is his third state. I have seen some upon the first of their arrival in the other world, whom I knew by their face and voice; but, when I saw them some time after, they were so changed, that I knew them not; such of them as were endowed with good affections appeared with beautiful countenances, and they whose affections were contrary looked deformed and ugly; for the spirit of a man rightly considered is the same with his predominant affection or love, and his face is the external form of it. This change respecting faces in those who pass from hence into the other world, is founded on this law; that no dissimu-

adopted, and from this commixture their life is a state of contrariety and distraction, n. 571, 582, 6348. That therefore the Lord has provided the most effectual bars against the sin of profanation that may be, n. 2426, 10384.

(*) This passage is best understood with a supposition of apostasy foreseen in such as should otherwise have been converted, as it is less dangerous to continue ignorant of the truth, than to depart from and renounce it after having received it. Tr.

lation or counterfeiting is there allowed, but all muſt appear to be what they really are, and conſequently expreſs their thoughts in their words, and their affections and deſires in their looks and actions, ſo that the faces of all there repreſent their minds reſpectively. Hence it is, that though all who knew one another in this world are alike mutually acquainted in the world of ſpirits, yet it is otherwiſe in heaven and in hell, as ſhewed before, n. 427, (258).

458. The faces of hypocrites undergo not their proper change ſo ſoon as the faces of others, and that becauſe they have by cuſtom contracted a habit of forming their minds to a kind of imitation of good ſentiments and affections, and therefore they appear not uncomely for ſome time; but as the diſguiſe gradually wears off, and their inmoſt thoughts and affections manifeſt themſelves, they appear more ugly than others. The hypocrites here ſpoken of, are ſuch as know how to talk like angels upon divine ſubjects, and yet in their hearts exalt nature on God's throne, and diſbelieve all heavenly truths, as acknowledged in the church of Chriſt.

459. It is to be obſerved, that the human form of every man after death is beautiful in proportion to the love he had for divine truths, and a life according to the ſame, for by this ſtandard things within receive their outward manifeſtation and form, ſo that the deeper grounded the affection for what is good, the more conformable it is to the divine order in heaven, and conſequently the more beauty the face derives from its influx. Hence it is, that the angels of the third or inmoſt heaven, whoſe love is of the third or higheſt degree, are the moſt beautiful of all the angels; whereas they whoſe love for divine things had been in a lower degree, or more external than that of the cœ-

---

(258) That the face is formed for correſpondency with the inner or ſpiritual man, n. 4791 to 4805, 5693. Of the correſpondence of the face and its countenances with the affections of the mind, n. 1568, 2988, 2989—5168, 5695, 9306. That the face and inward ſtate in the angels are perfectly conſentaneous, n. 4796, 4797, 4798, 4799, 5695, 8250. That therefore by *face* in the Word is ſignified the ſtate of the mind with reſpect to its affections and thoughts, n. 1999, 2434, 3527, 4066, 4796, 5102, 9306, 9546. How the influx from the brains in proceſs of time became changed, and thereby the countenances in regard to correſpondency with the interior ſtates of the mind, n. 4326, 8250.

lestial or highest angels, possess an inferior degree of beauty; and the translucent lustre in their faces, as proceeding from a lesser degree of divine virtue within them, is comparatively dim: for as all perfection rises in degrees from the inward to the inmost, so the external beauty, to which it gives life and vigour, has its degrees in the same proportion (*). I have seen the faces of some angels belonging to the third heaven, of such exquisite lustre and beauty, as no painter on earth could describe, even to the thousandth part; though a consummate artist might be able to give us some near resemblance of the faces of the lowest angels, or such as belong to the first heaven.

460. I shall conclude this chapter with mentioning what has hitherto remained a secret to all, viz. that all that good and truth [*omne bonum et verum*] that proceeds from the Lord, and constitutes heaven, has a human form both in whole and in part, even to the least portion thereof; and that this form has respect to and influences every one that receives good and truth from the Lord, and also is the cause of every one in heaven having a human form according to his reception of it respectively: and hence it is, that heaven is similar to itself, as well in every particular, as in its complex, inasmuch as the same human form that belongs to the whole, belongs in like manner to every society, , and to every individual angel therein, as has been set forth in four articles, from n. 59 to 86; to which it must here be added, that the same holds true with respect to every thought in the minds of angels, that takes its rise from cœlestial love.

(*) That beauty springs from goodness or virtue as its source, or is the form of it, is a doctrine that seems to carry its genuine evidence with it, and is received as soon as proposed to the virtuous mind. The two last lines of the following well known epitaph express much of this idea.

"Underneath this stone doth lie
"As much virtue as could die,
"Which when alive did vigour give
"To as much beauty as could live."

Nay, the wiser heathens annexed the idea of pulchritude to the excellency of virtue; whence that saying, I think, of Tully; "That if virtue were to assume "a human form, all her beholders would be ravished with the charms of her "beauty."

But

But this doctrine will not easily gain admittance into the human mind, though it is clearly understood by the angels.

That Man, after Death, retains every Sense, as also the same Memory, Thoughts, and Affections which he had in this World, and leaves nothing behind him but his terrestrial Body.

461. That when a man passes from this natural world into the spiritual, which is at the time of his death, he takes with him all that belonged to him as man, has been manifested to me by repeated experience: for when any one enters into the spiritual world, or into the life after death, he is equally in the body as before, nor is there to all appearance the least difference: but his body then is a spiritual body, and separate from all the grossness and impurity of matter; and as when a spiritual body sees and feels that which is spiritual, it appears the same as when a natural body sees and feels that which is natural, so man, when first become a spirit, seems to himself to be as he was in this world, and knows not as yet that he has passed through death. Man, when become a spirit, possesses every sense, both external and internal, that he possessed before; he sees, hears, and speaks as before; has the same smelling, taste, and feeling as before; and he has the same appetites and desires; the same thoughts, reflexions, and affections as before; and he who took delight in studying, reads and writes as before. In a word, when a man passes from one life to another, or, which is the same thing, from one world to another, it is but as removing from one place to another; for he takes all with him that belongs to him as a man, so that he cannot be said to have left any thing behind him but his mere earthly covering: moreover, he takes with him his natural memory, retaining all that he ever heard, saw, read, learned, or thought in the world, from his infancy to his leaving it; but as to the me-

mory

mory of such natural objects, which there is nothing in the spiritual world to revive the ideas of, that is quiescent, like as in a man when he thinks not of them; however, these also are again excited in the mind occasionally, by the divine permission, to answer certain purposes: but with respect to this species of memory, and the state of it after death, more will be said hereafter. Such a state of man as this after death, will appear incredible to the mere sensualist, who is incapable of receiving any ideas even of spiritual things, but according to natural; for such a one, being led only by sense, makes no account of any thing but what he can see with his eyes, and feel with his hands, as is said of Thomas, John xx. 25, 27, 29. Concerning the sensual man, see above, n. 267, and also in the note (*b*) there.

462. But notwithstanding what has been said above, there is a very great difference between the life of any one in the spiritual world, and the life of the same in the natural world, and that with respect both to his external and internal senses, and the affections thereof respectively. Thus, for instance, all in heaven have their sight, their hearing, and all their senses, in far greater perfection than when in this world, and also their minds more abundantly replete with wisdom; for they see by the light of heaven, which greatly exceeds that of this world, see above, n. 126; and they hear through the medium of a spiritual atmosphere, to which that of our earth is not comparable, n. 235. The comparative difference between these two senses there and here, is as that of a bright sky to a thick fog, or as the lustre of the meridian sun to the dusk of the evening. Now the light of heaven, which is divine truth, makes manifest the minutest things to the perception of angels, and as their external corresponds to their internal or intellectual sight, so by mutual influx they co-operate in forming the high perfection of angelical perspicuity. In like manner their sense of hearing corresponds to their perception, both in the understanding and will; so that in the sound of the voice, and in the words of the speaker, they can trace the most minute particulars of his affections and thoughts; in the sound what relates to his affections, and in the words what concerns his mind or thoughts, see above, n. 234 to 245: but it is to be observed, that the other senses

of

of the angels are not in the same high degree of perfection with those of sight and hearing, and that because the latter are the subservient instruments to their understanding and wisdom, and not so the others, which, if equal in power, would lessen their preference to intellectual delights over and above those of their spiritual bodies, as we find to be the case with men in this world, who, according to their greater relish and indulgence as to their grosser senses, have the lesser appetite and sensibility with respect to spiritual things. That the interior or spiritual senses of the angels, (viz. such as respect their thoughts and affections) are more exquisite and perfect than they had been in this world, has been declared before, in the article *Concerning the Wisdom of Angels*, n. 265 to 275. As to the difference of state in those who are in hell, compared with those that are in this world, this also is very great; for in proportion to the exceeding excellence and perfection both of the external and internal senses in the angels above those on earth, is the comparative imperfection and degradation of those that are in hell; but of the state of the latter in what follows.

462. That man takes with him all his memory from this world into the other, has been fully shewed before: I have had much sensible and memorable experience of this, part of which shall here be orderly related. There were certain spirits in the other world, who denied the crimes and enormities which they had been guilty of in this; and therefore, to the end they might not pass for innocent in these matters, all the capital sins they had committed in the course of their past life, particularly those of adultery and fornication, were set before them in order, as they were recorded in their own memory; as likewise some others, who, by various artifices of deceit and fraud, had wronged their neighbours, to whom also their various acts of craft and injustice were enumerated, many of which were known only to themselves; and as these were discovered to them with clearness of evidence, even to all their circumstances, and also what had passed in their own minds relating thereto, they could not but confess their guilt. There were some who had sat in the seat of judgment, and suffered themselves to be corrupted by gifts and bribes, whose memories were scrutinized, and all their mal-

versations and iniquitous practices in office produced against them, to the number of some hundreds, together with the time, place, and the state of their minds during such transactions; nay, however wonderful it may appear, the very books in which they had entered these things were opened, and read to them page by page. There were others who had seduced and violated the chastity of virgins, who were brought to the same trial, and convicted by the evidence of their own memory made manifest, even as to time, place, conversation, and other particulars, nay, the very faces of the virgins and women they had seduced, were all at once fully represented, and that sometimes for hours together. A certain spirit, who in this world had been much addicted to slandering and backbiting, which he had here studiously endeavoured to conceal from the parties injured, was there exposed to open shame by a publick recital of his calumnies and defamation, and that in his own words, together with the names of the persons before whom he uttered them. Another, who had deceitfully deprived a kinsman of his inheritance, was in like manner judged and convicted, and, which will appear very strange, the letters and writings, that had passed between them, were read in my hearing; and I was told that they were exact to a word: the same spirit had a little before his death taken away the life of his neighbour by poison, which was made manifest under the following representation: he appeared as digging a hole in the ground, and having ended his work, a man was seen to rise out of it as from his grave, crying out to him, What have you done to me? Upon which he made a full discovery of the truth, and related how the poisoner bespoke him in a friendly manner, and handed to him the fatal cup; and also what passed in his mind, and what followed after: upon this evidence the delinquent was sentenced to hell. In a word, all murders, robberies, fraudulent devices, and sins and crimes of every kind, are so evidenced from the memories and consciences of all offenders to their full conviction in the other world, and all the circumstances of them set in so clear a light, that not the least room is left them for evasion or denial. I have also heard from the memory of a certain spirit, as viewed and examined by the angels, all that had passed in his mind from

day

day to day for a month together, without the least mistake, and that by a revocation of particulars as to the perception of the party himself, in as clear a manner as at the time of the first impression. These examples may serve to evince, that man retains the memory of past things after he has entered upon the other world; and that nothing is kept so secret here, as not to have its manifestation there, and that in the presence of many witnesses, according to those words of our Lord: "There is nothing covered, that shall not be revealed; neither hid, that shall not be known. Therefore, whatsoever ye have spoken in darkness, shall be heard in the light; and that which ye have spoken in the ear in closets, shall be proclaimed upon the house-tops," Luke xii. 2, 3.

463. When all that a man had done here in his natural body is made manifest to him after death, then the examining angels inspect his face, and commence their inquest, which begins at the fingers of each hand, and is from thence continued throughout the whole body: as I wondered at this way of proceeding, I was told, that as all the particulars belonging to thinking and willing have their first signatures in the brain as their subject and beginning to manifestation, so are they continued through the whole body, and terminate in its extremities; so that a man is entirely similar to himself in whole and every part, according to the quality of his will and intellect: thus an evil man is his own evil; and the derivative good in any one constitutes the good man (259). What has here been said explains what is meant by the book of life in the Word, viz. that all the deeds and thoughts of any one are so inscribed upon his whole man, that when recollected by his memory they appear legible as in a book; and are imaged in his very person, when he is viewed in the light of heaven. I shall here add the following remarkable particular concerning man's memory, as remaining with

---

(259) That the good and truth in every good man, spirit, and angel, constitutes his identity, and that he receives his particular denomination from the quality thereof, n. 10298, 10367; and that because good constitutes his will, and truth his intellect, and will and intellect are the constituent principles of life in man, spirit, and angel, n. 3332, 3623, 6065. It is of like import to say, that every man, spirit, and angel, is the same with his particular predominant love, n. 6872, 10177, 10284.

him after death; whereby I am convinced, that things not only in their general, but also in their moſt minute particulars, are never totally obliterated in him: I ſaw ſome books there written in characters like thoſe in uſe with us, and was told that they were penned from the memory of the writer, without the difference of a ſingle word from thoſe written by the ſame author in this world; which ſhews, that from the memory of any other perſon many particulars might be collected, which he himſelf had forgotten in this world; and the reaſon of this was explained to me, viz. from man's having a twofold memory (*), the one external or natural, and the other internal or ſpiritual; and that all the thoughts, deſires, and actions of a man, and the things that he had heard and ſeen, are inſcribed on his internal memory (260), nay, on the very members of his ſpiritual body, as was ſaid before, never to be obliterated, for that his ſpirit was formed according to his thoughts and acts of volition: I know that theſe things will appear as paradoxes, and gain credit with few; but they are no leſs true for that. Let no one

---

(*) That there may be a memory within a memory, unknown to that which is outward, will not appear incredible to the attentive reader, when he reflects that our minds are chiefly formed by what we learned and read many years ago, little of which we have a diſtinct remembrance of: thus we may have received much inſtruction, to the improvement both of heart and mind, from books that we do not remember to have read, nor even the names of, which muſt have been laid up ſomewhere. In a word, this diſtinction of the human faculties and powers into exterior and interior, or natural and ſpiritual, has its foundation in the nature of man, and opens many myſterious things in a being, which is an inhabitant of two worlds, even in this life, without knowing it. Tr.

(260) That man has two memories, the exterior and interior, or the natural and ſpiritual, n. 2469 to 2494. That man has no knowledge of his interior memory, n. 2470, 2471. The ſuperior excellence of his interior above his exterior memory, n. 2473. That the things of his exterior memory are in the light of the world, but thoſe of his interior in the light of heaven, n. 5212. That it is from his interior memory that man is qualified to think and ſpeak intellectually and rationally, n. 9394. That all and ſingular the things which man has thought, ſpoken, done, ſeen and heard, are recorded in his interior memory, n. 2474, 9386, 9841, 10505. That in the interior memory are the truths which conſtitute faith, and the good which conſtitutes love, n. 5212, 8067. That thoſe things which are become habitual, and have entered into the forms of life, and thereby are obliterated in the exterior memory, remain in the interior, n. 9394, 9723, 9841. That ſpirits and angels ſpeak from their interior memory, and thence have the univerſal language, n. 2472, 2476, 2490, 2493. That languages in this world belong to the exterior memory, n. 2472, 2476.

therefore

therefore flatter himself, that any thing which he has thought or done in secret will not be known after death, for all will then be made manifest as in open day.

464. Although the external or natural memory remains with man after death, yet things merely natural are not reproduced therein in the other life, but only such spiritual things as are adjuncts to the natural by correspondence, which nevertheless, when exhibited to sight, appear in the same form as in this natural world; for all things in the heavens appear in like manner as they do on earth, though in their essence they are not natural, but spiritual, as may be seen in the chapter, *Concerning Representatives and Appearances in Heaven*, n. 170 to 176. But then it must be observed, that the spirit, by means of that external or natural memory, derives no use from those appearances with respect to materiality, time, space, and other natural properties, as it did in this world; as here (when not in the use of of his intellectual powers, but of his external senses only) he thought naturally, and not spiritually; but in the other life (where he is a spirit in a spiritual world) he no longer thinks naturally, but spiritually: now to think spiritually, is to have the mind intellectually or rationally employed. Hence it is, that the external or natural memory, in respect to all things material, is quiescent in the other world, making no use of any of that nature, but such as he had applied to rational and intellectual improvement in this. The reason why the external memory is quiescent with respect to material things in the spiritual world, is through want of things of a similar nature there to excite or reproduce ideas of that kind; for spirits and angels converse from their affections, and the thoughts which spring from them in the mind; nor can they express any that are heterogeneous thereto, as may be seen in what has been mentioned before, concerning the conversation of angels in heaven with one another, and also with man, n. 234 to 257. This may serve to shew, that it is not the mere knowledge of languages and sciences as such, but the intellectual use and improvement from them that renders the spirit more rational both here and after death. I have conversed with many, who flattered themselves with a belief that they should be highly accounted of in the

other world for their learning, becaufe of their being acquainted with the ancient languages, as Hebrew, Greek, and Latin, whilft at the fame time they had neglected to cultivate their minds with the ufeful truths written therein; whereas they appeared there as arrant novices in all found literature, as they who were totally ignorant of thofe tongues; nay, fome of them ftupid, but yet elated with a fancied fufficiency of their fuperior wifdom. I have difcourfed with others, who fancied that a man's wifdom was in proportion to what he retained in his memory, and therefore had furnifhed their own with a pretty large ftock of other men's fayings; thus affecting to be rich in what did not belong to them, as not having any fund of truth in their own minds; but fome of thefe were very dullards, others of them foolifh, not being able to diftinguifh between right and wrong in common matters: and I have had converfation with fome, who had publifhed many things in the fcientifick way, and had acquired fome reputation in the world by their writings; fome of thefe could reafon about truths, whether they were fuch or not, and could alfo underftand them when they turned to thofe that were in the light of truth; but when they turned back to their own confufed dark minds, they would not receive, but rejected them; and fome of them were as void of true knowledge, as the illiterate vulgar; to fo little purpofe of real intellectual improvement had they ftudied the fciences. But as to thofe, who, by an abufe of their fcientifical learning, have ftudied to draw arguments from it againft the truths of religion, and to confirm themfelves in unbelief; all they have gained by it is a trick of difputing and reafoning without rationality (however it may pafs for fuch with the world) and of giving to error the appearance of truth by a fallacious fophiftry: it is impoffible for fuch to attain to a right underftanding, whilft they adhere to the falfe principles they have adopted; for though by the light of truth we can detect error, yet in the darknefs of error we cannot find the way to truth. Now to oppofe divine truths is to fhut the gate of communication betwixt heaven and our fouls; and as the foil of a garden or field, however fowed with feed, cannot bring forth fruit without the fructifying influence of the fun, fo neither can the rational part in man, however cultivated

by

by natural knowledge, attain to wifdom without the light of heaven, which is divine truth, and the heat of heaven, which is divine love. It is matter of great grief to the angels, that fo many of the learned, through the oppofitions of fcience, falfely fo called, fhould fo far facrifice to the pretended fovereignty of nature and natural knowledge, as to exclude all communication of divine light from their minds; on which account it is, that all fuch in the other world are deprived of the faculty of reafoning, and appointed to be in defart places, to the end that they may not ftumble or perplex the fimple, good fpirits with their infidel notions and fophiftry.

465. A certain fpirit feemed much difturbed at his not being able to remember many things that he knew in this world, and expreffed grief for the pleafure he loft thereby: but he was told, that, properly fpeaking, he had loft nothing, but was in poffeffion of all knowledge that could be of any ufe to him; that the things which he no more remembered did not fuit with his prefent ftate, and that he ought to be fatisfied that he could now think and fpeak more perfectly than before, without having his mind depraved with grofs, material ideas, which could anfwer no good end in the kingdom where he was at prefent, and where he was richly fupplied with all things conducive to an eternal happy life; and moreover, that true intellectual knowledge was fo far from being leffened by the removal of all material images from the memory, that the more the mind was difengaged from all fuch natural impediments of the outward man, the more it was at liberty to make higher advances in the contemplation of fpiritual and heavenly things.

466. Different kinds of memory are fometimes reprefented in the other world under fignificant forms known only there, many things which the mind is only fufceptible of here, being there imaged under vifible appearances. Thus the exterior memory is there reprefented under the figure of a callus, or denfe fubftance [*inflar calli*]; but the interior memory, like the medullary part of the human brain, to denote the diftinction between them: they who only ftudied to furnifh their memory here with ideas, whilft they neglected to cultivate their rational part, their callofity appears of a ftill harder texture, and ftreaked within.

within as with tendons: they who in this life ſtuffed their memory only with falſities and figments, their callus appears rough and hairy from the confuſed heap and lumber therein: they who retained nothing in their memory, but what was connected with the love of ſelf and of the world, their callus repreſented a glutinous conſiſtence bordering upon oſſification: they who ſtudied to ſearch out the divine ſecrets by their ſcientifical, and more eſpecially their philoſophical inveſtigations, with full purpoſe to believe nothing but what ſquared therewith, their memory was repreſented under the appearance of, as it were, a gloomy cavity, which abſorbed the rays of light, and converted them into darkneſs: theirs who had been given to hypocriſy and deceit, was figured by a boney ſubſtance, like as of ivory, reflecting the rays of light: but as to all thoſe who have lived in the good of love towards God and their neighbour, and in the truths of faith; with them there is no ſuch appearance of calloſity, for their interior memory tranſmits the rays of light to the exterior, in which they terminate, as their proper baſis or ground; for the exterior memory is the loweſt degree of order in man, and may be conſidered as the laſt reſidence or receptacle of ſpiritual and heavenly things, where they friendly join themſelves to the correſpondent good and truth [*bonis et veris*] they meet with therein.

467. Men who live in love towards the Lord, and in charity towards their neighbour, poſſeſs even in this life angelical underſtanding and wiſdom, but ſo hidden within the receſſes of their interior memory, that they are not manifeſted to their knowledge till they have quitted their mortal bodies; then their natural memory becomes quieſcent, or as aſleep, and they awaken to their interior memory, and ſo ſucceſſively to the angelical.

468. A few words ſhall here be ſpoken concerning the cultivation of the rational faculty in man. Genuine rationality conſiſts in truths, not in falſes [*non in falſis*]. Now truths are of three kinds, civil, moral, and ſpiritual: civil truths relate to judicial matters, and ſuch as reſpect publick government, and, in a general conſideration, juſtice and equity: moral truths have relation to the conduct of life with reſpect to ſocieties and

leſſer

lesser connexions; in general, to sincerity and rectitude; and in particular, to virtues of every class: but spiritual truths relate to the things of heaven, and of the church on earth; and in general to the good of love, and the truths of faith. There are three degrees of life in every man, see above, n. 267: the rational part in man is opened to the first degree by civil truths; to the second by moral truths; and to the third by spiritual truths. But let it here be observed, that man's rational part is not opened and formed merely by his knowing such truths, but by living according to them when known, that is, by loving them with a spiritual affection, or the affection of his spirit, or, in other words, by loving justice and equity as such, sincerity and rectitude of manners as such, and good and truth as such; whereas to love them only from external regards, is loving them for the sake of self, for one's own character, honour, or profit; and therefore such a love, as it terminates in self, gives not a man any right to the character of rational, as such a one uses truths as a lordly master uses his servants, viz. for his pleasure or interest; and where this is the case, they make no part of the man, nor open so much as the first degree of life in him, but only have a place in his memory, like other scientifical ideas under a material form, where they unite with the love of self in mere animal nature. Hence it may appear how man becomes truly and properly rational, viz. in the third or highest degree, by the spiritual love of good and truth, or the things of heaven, and its representative the church; in the second degree, by the love of sincerity and rectitude; and in the first degree, by the love of justice and equity; which two last loves become spiritual by influx of the spiritual love of good and truth from the highest degree, by joining itself to the inferior loves, and forming in them its own likeness (*).

(*) This somewhat obscure passage may be rendered more intelligible thus. There are three degrees in man corresponding to the three heavens; and as the third or highest heaven does, as it were, sanctify the two inferior heavens by the descending influx of its cœlestial superior virtue, so the spiritual love of all that is good and true in man (corresponding to the third heaven) spiritualizes or sanctifies his virtues, though of an inferior class: thus, to give a cup of cold water to another, is a little thing; but when it is the most we can do, and love is in the doing of it, the act has in it the essence of Christian charity. Tr.

469. Memory also belongs to spirits and angels in like manner as to men, and they retain whatever they hear, see, think, will, and do: hereby their rationality increases to higher degrees of improvement even to eternity, and they grow in understanding and wisdom through increasing knowledges of truth and good, as the human species here on earth. That spirits and angels are endowed with memory I have frequently been witness to, when they have given proofs of it by a recital of what they had thought and done, both openly, and also in private company with other spirits; and I have also known some simple, good spirits, with but a moderate degree of the light of truth, advanced by the gift of knowledge to higher degrees of intellectual light, and then raised up to heaven [from the intermediate state]; but then it must be observed, that the measure of such illumination is according to the kind of affection for good and truth they were in during their life in this world, and not beyond it; for every spirit and angel continues to possess the same kind of affection, or a love of the same quality that he possessed in this life, in which he advances hereafter to higher and higher degrees of perfection eternally; for there is no end to perfection there, but every good, as proceeding from an infinite cause, is capable of infinite variation and increase. That spirits and angels continue to advance to higher and higher degrees of understanding and wisdom by increasing knowledges [*cognitiones*] of good and truth, see in the chapters *Concerning the Wisdom of Angels*, n. 265 to 275: *Concerning the Gentiles and Peoples without the Church, in Heaven*, n. 318 to 328, and, *Concerning Infants in Heaven*, n. 329 to 345: and that such progression is according to the quality or kind (*) of affection in good and truth, and not beyond it, n. 349.

(*) The word *gradus* in the original, here and before in this number translated *quality* or *kind*, refers to a distinction of the author (see the foregoing number) as to the three degrees in man with respect to states, and not to degrees of the same state; which, if not kept in mind, would mislead the reader, as if implying, that the blessed in the other world did not advance in degrees of the same good begun here, in contradiction to the author's meaning, which is, that good of the same class or character in any one here, is increased in the other life by degrees *ad infinitum*, according to the quality or kind of that good, and that progression in degrees of perfection is only from good begun in this world. Tr.

That

That the Condition of Man after Death is according to his paſt Life here.

470. That every one's life follows him to the other world, is a truth known to all that believe the Bible, which tells us in many places, that every man ſhall be judged and recompenſed according to his deeds and works; and whoſoever eſtimates things according to the nature of good and of truth, cannot but conclude, that a good life leads to heaven, and an evil life to hell: but the unconverted man, eſpecially when viſited with ſickneſs, thinks otherwiſe concerning his future ſtate, not being willing to believe that his lot will be according to how he has lived here, but that admiſſion into heaven is a grant of pure favour and mercy to any one, whatever he had done in the body, provided he has but faith, which faith he conſiders ſeparately from a good life.

471. From the many declarations in Scripture, ſetting forth that man ſhall be judged and recompenſed according to his deeds and works, I ſhall here ſelect the following: "The Son of man "ſhall come in the glory of his Father, with his angels; and "then he ſhall reward every man according to his works," Matt. xvi. 27. "Bleſſed are the dead which die in the Lord: "even ſo, ſaith the Spirit, that they may reſt from their labours, "and their works do follow them," Apoc. xiv. 13. "And I "will give unto every one of you according to your works," Apoc. ii. 23. "And I ſaw the dead, ſmall and great, ſtand "before God, and the books were opened; and the dead were "judged out of thoſe things which were written in the books "according to their works: and the ſea gave up the dead which "were in it; and death and hell delivered up the dead which "were in them; and they were judged every man according to "their works," Apoc. xx. 12, 13. "And behold I come "quickly, and my reward is with me, to give every man ac-"cording as his work ſhall be," Apoc. xxii. 12. "Whoſoever "heareth theſe ſayings of mine, and doeth them, I will liken
"him

"him unto a wife man which built his house upon a rock: and every one that heareth these sayings of mine, and doeth them not, shall be likened unto a foolish man, which built his house upon the sand," Matt. vii. 24, 26. "Not every one that saith unto me, Lord, Lord, shall enter into the kingdom of heaven, but he that doth the will of my Father which is in heaven: many shall say unto me in that day, Have we not prophesied in thy name, and in thy name cast out devils; and in thy name done many wonderful works? And then will I profess unto them, I never knew you: depart from me, ye that work iniquity," Matt. vii. 22, 23. "Then shall ye begin to say, We have eaten and drunk in thy presence, and thou hast taught in our streets: but he shall say, I tell you, I know you not whence ye are: depart from me all ye workers of iniquity," Luke xiii. 26, 27. "I will recompense them according to their deeds, and according to the works of their own hands," Jer. xxv. 14. "Thine eyes are open upon all the ways of the sons of men, to give every one according to his ways, and according to the fruit of his doings," Jer. xxxii. 19. "I will punish them for their ways, and reward them their doings," Hof. iv. 9. "According to our ways, and according to our doings, so hath he dealt with us," Zach. i. 6. Our Lord, in his predictions of the last judgment, makes mention only of works, and declares that they who have done good shall enter into life eternal, and they who have done evil into everlasting fire, Matt. xxv. 32 to 46; and also in many other places, where he speaks of the salvation, and the condemnation of man. Now it is evident, that works and deeds are man's outward life, manifesting the principle of life within him.

472. But by deeds and works here, we do not mean such considered only in their external form, but according to what they are internally; for it is allowed by all, that every act and deed of man must proceed from his thought and will, otherwise it would be no better than the movement of a piece of mechanism; but what we call a man's act or deed, is an effect which has its cause and principle in the human mind, and may be said to be the thought and will of a man expressed or represented in

an external form; confequently, as is the thought and will, which give being and life to the act, fuch is the quality of the act; if the former be good, fo is the act or deed; but if evil, then fuch is the deed or work likewife, however they may both have the fame outward form. A thoufand men may do the fame act, fo like in appearance, as not to admit of diftinction, and yet the act of every one of them may be different in quality, through the difference in the will, or motive of the doer. Thus for example, in the act of dealing juftly and faithfully with one's neighbour; one may difcharge this office, as to the outward part, for the credit and reputation of paffing for an upright man; another, for the fake of lucre and worldly advantage; a third, with a view to recompenfe; a fourth, from fome particular attachments of friendfhip; a fifth, through fear of the law, lofs of character, or employment; a fixth, in order to bring fome over to his party; a feventh, that he may gain credit for an opportunity of deceiving afterwards to greater temporal benefit, and fo on: but all fuch apparent honefty and juftice, however good as to the external act, is entirely void of it, or contrary to it, relatively to the party, and to principles, as not being done for the fake of truth and juftice, but from the love of felf and of the world, to which they facrifice even the femblance of virtue, as it may ferve their turn, as an imperious mafter ufes his flaves, merely in fubferviency to his intereft, and the gratification of his paffions, and turns them off when they can no longer anfwer thefe purpofes. On the other hand, the fame external acts of juftice and fidelity towards their neighbour are done by fuch as are principled in thefe virtues; fome from the obedience of faith, as being enjoined by the authority of God's Word; others from a religious confcience; fome from charity towards their neighbour; and fome from love to the Lord, having a fincere affection for juftice, truth, and goodnefs of every kind, as proceeding from him, and partaking of his divine nature. Now as the acts of thefe perfons are from the fource of a good internal principle, fo are they properly and truly good works; for it is the quality of the thought and will, as obferved before, that determines their diftinction and kind, and without which they are no better than mere mechanical movements.

movements. Thus much may suffice to shew what is meant by deeds and works in the Scriptures.

473. As works and deeds derive their nature from will and thought, so consequently from love and faith, and are of the same quality with them; now whether we say the love or will of a man, or the faith or thought of a man, it amounts to the same, for what he loves, that he wills; and what he believes, that he thinks; and if he loves what he believes, then he wills and does it according to his power. That love and faith appertain to the willing and thinking, and are not extraneous to them, is allowed by all, as the will has its fire from love, and thought its light from faith, so that to think wisely is to have the mind or thoughts enlightened by the truths of faith. Thus every wise man thinks and wills the truth, or, in other words, believes and loves it (261).

474. But we are to observe here, that it is the will that properly constitutes the man, and thought no farther than as it issues from the will, and that deeds or works proceed from both; or, which comes to the same, that love constitutes the man, and faith only so far as it springs from love, and that works proceed from both; consequently, that will or love is the man himself, for that which proceeds belongs to the source or principle it proceeds from: now to proceed from a thing, is to be produced by it in a proper form or mode of operation, for the sake of manifestation (262). It is an obvious conclusion from the premises, that what is called faith, separated from love, has

---

(261) That as all things in the universe, which exist according to their nature, bear relation to good and truth, so in man, to will and understanding, n. 803, 10122; and that, because his will is the recipient of good, and his understanding of truth, n. 3332, 3623—9300, 9930. Whether we say truth or faith, it comes to the same, because they are correlatives like good and love, n. 4353, 4997, 7178, 10122, 10367. Hence it follows, that the understanding is the recipient of faith, and the will of love, n. 7178, 10122, 10367. And as the understanding of man is receptive of faith in God, and the will of love to God; so man, by faith and love, may be joined to God, and he that is capable of being joined to God by love and faith, cannot die eternally, n. 4525, 6323, 9231.

(262) That the will of man is the essence of his life, as being the receptacle of love or good; and that his understanding is the existence [form] of his life from thence, as being the receptacle of faith or truth, n. 3619, 5002, 9282. Therefore, that the life of the will is the principal life of man, and that the life of the under-

has no reality of faith in it, but is only a notional thing void of all spiritual life: in like manner, works, that proceed not from love, have no virtue or life in them, and consequently are dead works; and as to whatever appearance of life they may have from an evil love and a false faith, it is in Scripture deemed and stiled spiritual death.

475. It is farther to be noted, that the whole man stands represented in his deeds or works, and that his willing and thinking, or his love and faith, which are the principles of his inner man, are not complete till they are imaged in the works of his outward man, as being the ground or limit in which they terminate; and without such termination or fixedness, they are but vague, uncertain things, without residence or body. To think and will without acting, where power is not wanting, may be compared to a candle shut in a close vessel, where it is soon extinguished; or to seed sowed in the sand, where it loses its prolifick virtue, and perishes; whereas to think and will, and thence proceed to act, is like the same candle set in a proper place diffusing its light around it; or to seed sowed in good ground, where it thrives and ripens into a flower or tree. Who does not know, that to will, and not to act when one may, is the same with not willing; and to love, and not do good when opportunity serves, is not to love, but only to fancy that one loves, and but as the phantom of a thought, which vanishes into nothing: whereas love or will is the very life and soul of action, and forms to itself a body (or makes itself substantial) by operation: just so it is with the spiritual body, or the body of a man's spirit, which is formed of that which proceeds from

understanding is from thence, n. 585, 590, 3619—10109, 10110, as light issues from fire or flame, n. 632, 6314; consequently man is man from will, and its sequent understanding, n. 8911, 9069, 9071, 100-6, 10109, 10110.- That every one is amiable and estimable for the good that is in his will and understanding jointly; and that to have a good understanding, and no good will, is a contemptible character, n. 8911, 10076. That the condition of man after death is according to the state of his will and mind (or understanding) as formed thereby, n. 9069, 9071, 9386, 10153. That therefore the condition of man after death is according to his love and faith resulting therefrom; and that matters of belief called faith, which are not joined with love, then vanish into nothing, as not being in nor of the man, n. 553, 2364, 10153.

a man's

a man's love or will (*), fee above, n. 463. In a word, the works of a man are the image and likenefs of himfelf (263).

476. We have here feen what is meant by that life which remains with every one after death, viz. that of his love and faith, not only in their principle, but act, confequently in deeds and works, as thefe are the product of all that appertains to love and faith in every one.

477. There continues a ruling love in every one after he has left this world, which changes not its particular kind even in eternity; and though he may be faid to have many affections, yet they all have relation to the principal one, and co-operate with it, as many ingredients in one compound. All the operations of the will, which accord with the ruling paffion, bear the name of loves; and thefe are both interior and exterior, fome of them are immediately connected with the principal or ruling paffion, fome mediately, and many of them fubfervient to it different ways; but, confidered collectively, form, as it were, one kingdom or government in man in their different offices and places; and though a man knows nothing of their order and arrangement in this life, yet fomething of it is manifefted to him in the other, for according thereto is the direction of his thoughts and affections there; to the heavenly focieties,

---

(*) This hint of our author ftarts a fubject to the mind no lefs important, than of new and curious confideration, viz. how the fpiritual body, which we fhall have in the other world, is formed in this life from the affections, qualities, and properties of the fpirit acquired here, even (if the comparifon may be allowed) as the fhells of certain animals are formed from the juices tranfpiring from the body of the animal within: if fo, as is the nature, qualities, and properties of the fpirit of a man here, fuch will be thofe of his fpiritual body hereafter. Qu. If this is not to be underftood in Scripture as meant by the refurrection-body? N. B. Let all fuch as are in love with true beauty, be heedful what fpirit they are of. Tr.

(263) That the interior things of a man's fpirit communicate themfelves by influx to the outward man, and fubfift therein, as in their ground and limit, n. 634, 6239, 6465, 9216, 9217; and that they not only fucceffively pafs into the outward, but alfo have therein a fimultaneous fubfiftence, and in what order, n. 5897, 6451, 8603, 10099. That fo fpiritual things have a connexion and form in natural things, n. 9828. That deeds or works are their ultimate form, n. 10331. Therefore to be judged and recompenfed according to works or deeds, means the fame as according to all things appertaining to love and faith, or to the will and thoughts of man, as thefe form the effence and quality of fuch works, n. 3147, 3934, 6073, 8911, 10331, 10333.

if his prevailing love confifts of heavenly affections; and to the infernal focieties, if it confifts of infernal affections. That all the affections and thoughts of angels and fpirits have a direction or extenfion to fome particular focieties, fee above, in the chapter *Concerning the Wifdom of the Angels,* as alfo in that which treats *Of the Form of Heaven, with refpect to the Confociations and Communications therein.*

478. But what has hitherto been faid on this fubject is of deep confideration; in order therefore to render it more intelligible and plain to all, I fhall here adduce fome experiences, by way of illuftration and confirmation, to fhew, firft, that every man's ruling love or will continues after death to be his effential felf. Secondly, that his particular character or quality for ever remains according thereto. Thirdly, that every one, whofe prevailing love is fpiritual and heavenly, goes to heaven; and that every one, whofe prevailing love is fenfual and mundane, and as fuch contrary to all that is heavenly, goes to hell. Fourthly, that all faith, which has not heavenly love for its root, vanifhes into nothing after death. Fifthly, that operative love is that only which continues with him, and conftitutes his true life.

479. That every man's ruling love or will continues after death to be his effential felf, has been evidenced to me by full experience. The univerfal heaven is diftinguifhed into different focieties according to their different degrees in the good of love refpectively; and every fpirit that is exalted to heaven, and fo becomes an angel, is firft conducted to that fociety, which is in the fame love with himfelf; and when he is joined to it, he is, as it were, at home in his proper felf: this he becomes immediately fenfible of, and enters into intimacy with his friendly affociates. When he leaves them at any time to make an occafional vifit elfewhere, it is with a kind of reluctance, and he always feels an attraction to the fociety of thofe with whom he is in the clofeft fellowfhip of the fame love. In this manner confociations are formed in heaven; nor is it otherwife in hell, according to their infernal loves. That both heaven and hell confift of focieties diftinguifhed and ranked according to their refpective different loves, fee above, n. 41 to 50, and n. 200 to 212:

212 : and that it is every one's love that conftitutes his proper felf after death, may further appear from hence, that every thing is then removed or taken from a man that does not accord with his ruling love; thus all adventitious evil and falfe is removed from the good, as not agreeing with his governing principle; and every apparent good and truth from the man of evil principle; that fo every one may be wholly and confiftently in that love, which is the ruling power of his life: and this feparation is effected when a fpirit advances to his third ftate, of which in what follows. Now when this has taken place, the fpirit has always before his eyes the object of his love, which way foever he turns himfelf, fee above, n. 123, 124. All fpirits are led by thofe who have hold of their affections, even as they lift; and though the former know it, they have not power to refift, but are drawn as with a ftrong cord: I have often feen the experiment made, whether they would refift the attraction, and found they could not. The cafe indeed is much the fame with men in this world, who are under a ftrong influence of the prevailing affection, and the leading of others who have hold thereon; but the fame operates ftill with greater ftrength when they become fpirits in the other world, as then they are not fubject to the counteraction of any other paffion, which may lay a reftraint on their inclinations. The thefis at the head of this article is further confirmed by what frequently happens in the converfation of fpirits in the other world. Thus, where any one does or fays in company what is agreeable to the prevailing love of fome particular fpirit, the latter appears to be of an expanded, pleafant, and lively countenance; but when any thing is done or faid in oppofition to fuch love, his countenance prefently changes, and is obfcured, and at length becomes totally invifible, as if he were not prefent. On my fhewing fome amazement at this, as a thing unknown in this world, it was told me, that the like thing happened to the fpirit of man in this world, which, upon conceiving an averfion to another, became invifible to him (*). That every fpirit is one

and

(*) This paffage is of difficult comprehenfion, but from other parts of the author's writings feems to mean thus, viz. that the fpirits of men in this life (if

they

and the fame with his ruling love, is evident from his earneſtly coveting and appropriating to himſelf all things relative and correſponding, and his rejecting all things contrary thereto; juſt as the ſpongy root of a plant attracts and imbibes thoſe juices which favour its peculiar kind of vegetation, and repels the others; or as the brute animals are led by a native inſtinct to chuſe only that particular kind of food which is ſuitable to their nature: ſo every love is ſupported by that which is congruous to its nature, an evil love by that which is falſe, and a good love by truths. Accordingly, I have ſometimes ſeen good ſpirits apply themſelves to inſtruct ſuch as were evil, upon which the latter left them with ſpeed, and went to their fellows to feaſt on folly ſuited to their taſte; and alſo when good ſpirits have been diſcourſing together upon divine truths, to which thoſe of their own claſs liſtened with attention and delight, that ſuch as were of a contrary diſpoſition appeared quite heedleſs and unconcerned. In the world of ſpirits there is an appearance of highways or roads, ſome of them as leading to heaven, others to hell, and every one of them to ſome particular ſociety therein: the good ſpirits take thoſe that lead to heaven, and to ſuch ſocieties therein reſpectively as poſſeſs the ſame particular good love with themſelves, nor do they ſee the other ways; but the evil ſpirits take thoſe that lead to hell, and to ſuch particular ſocieties therein reſpectively as beſt ſuit with their own depravity and corrupt affections, neither do they ſee any of the other ways, or, if they do, they go not in them. Theſe appearances of ways in the ſpiritual world correſpond to verities and falſities [*veris et falſis*] and accordingly truth and error are ſignified by *ways* in the Scripture (264). Theſe proofs from experience

confirm

they are in good agreement) are viſible to each other, otherwiſe not: and though this be not known to us here, whilſt we think in or according to nature, yet it is not more to be wondered at than that our ſpirits, even whilſt connected with theſe bodies, ſhould at the ſame time communicate with ſpiritual ſocieties in the other world without our knowing it; and yet it is founded on nothing leſs than Scripture evidence, that ſpiritual Chriſtians have in this life fellowſhip with " the general " aſſembly and church of the firſt-born, and an innumerable company of angels, " and the ſpirits of juſt men made perfect," Heb. xii. 22, 23. Tr.

(264) That *way, path, ſtreet*, &c. ſignify truths leading to good, as alſo errors leading to evil, n. 627, 2333, 10422. That to prepare the way ſignifies to fit or

diſpoſe

confirm what was said before from reason, viz. that every man after death is one and the same with his ruling love or will, which are synonymous terms.

480. That man also continues for ever in the same will or predominant love that he takes with him into the other world, has been confirmed to me by many convincing proofs: it has been granted to me to converse with some that lived above two thousand years ago, whose lives and manners are transmitted down to us in history; and they in all things answered the characters therein given of them, and as to the ruling passion that influenced their actions: others I have conversed with that lived above seventeen hundred years ago, in like manner charactered in history, with others that lived above four centuries ago, others above three, and so on; and they were all found to answer the description given of them, and to possess the same predominant affection as in this life, only with this difference, that their delight was placed in the correspondences of those things which they were passionately fond of here. I was told by the angels, that the predominant affection did not change in eternity, and that because every one was the same with his governing love, and therefore to deprive a spirit of that would be to deprive him of his being: the angels farther assigned this reason for it, viz. that man was no longer capable of being reformed by instruction after death, as in his life-time here; and that because his ultimate plane or ground, which consists of natural knowledges and affections, was then quiescent, and could no more be opened, as not being spiritual, see above, n. 464: and that upon this ground or basis, as a foundation to a house, the interior things of the human mind rested, and had their fixedness; therefore a man could not change his settled affections after this life, no not in eternity. The angels greatly wonder, that man should be so ignorant of his being essentially one and the same with his predominant love, and that so many can trust for their salvation to a mere inoperative faith in immediate, unconditional mercy, however they have lived, not

---

dispose the mind for the reception of truth, n. 3142. To make known the way, when spoken of the Lord, signifies to instruct in truths leading to good, n. 10564.

knowing

knowing that the divine mercy is mediate, or through the use of means, particularly that of resigning ourselves to the divine leadings both in time and for eternity, and that they only are under the divine leadings who eschew evil, and chuse the good; and moreover, that the Gospel faith is a sincere affection for the truth proceeding from that divine love, which is the Lord's own gift.

481. *That the man who is influenced here by divine and spiritual love goes to heaven; and he who is under the dominion of carnal and worldly love, without any thing of the heavenly, spiritual life in him, goes to hell,* has been evidenced to me by all whom I have seen taken up into heaven, and cast into hell, all they of the former class being in the first, and all those of the latter class, in the second of those loves. Now it is the essential property of heavenly love to love goodness, truth, and justice for their own sake, and to be led thereby to the practice of them, which is the true heavenly life, as herein consists the love of God and of our neighbour, for these duties themselves bear to us the relation of neighbour (265): but it is the property of carnal [*corporeus*] and worldly love to love goodness, truth, and justice, not for their own sake, but the sake of self, and as the means of procuring to ourselves the glory, honour, and gain of this world. All such, as having no regard to the Lord and their neighbour in what they do, turn virtue into vice; and, whilst they appear in the garb of truth and justice, are inwardly

---

(265) That in the highest sense of the word, the Lord (considered in his Humanity) is our *proximus*, or nearest neighbour, as deserving our love above all things. Now to love the Lord, is to love all that proceeds from him, as bearing his image, and consequently all good and truth, n. 2425, 3419, 6706, 6711—8123. That to love good and truth, as proceeding from him, is to live according thereto, and that this is properly to love the Lord, n. 10143, 10153—10578, 10645. That every man and society, as also our country, the church, and in an universal sense, the whole kingdom of the Lord is our neighbour, and that to do good to them, according to their different relations, is to love our neighbour, n. 6818 to 6824, 8123. That also moral good or sincerity, and civil good, which is justice, are our neighbour; and to act sincerely and justly, from the love of sincerity and justice, is to love our neighbour, n. 2915, 4730, 8120, 8121, 8122, 8123. Therefore, that charity to our neighbour extends through the whole life of man, n. 2417, 8121, 8124. That the doctrine more particularly insisted on in the ancient church was the doctrine of charity, and that this constituted a great part of their wisdom, n. 2417, 2385, 3419, 3420, 4844, 6628.

guilty of hypocrisy and deceit. As every one's life is thus estimated according to the quality of his love, therefore all, at their first arrival in the world of spirits, undergo a scrutiny with respect to the state of their affections, and are classed with those of similar dispositions either for heaven or hell; and after having gone through their first and second states, are separated so as to see and know one another no more, for then every particular difference in their loves within becomes signatured accordingly in the form of the body, the features of the face, and the sound of the voice, so that the exterior part is a correspondent image and likeness of the interior. Thus, such as are in corporeal and earthly loves, appear gross, dark, or black, and deformed respectively; but such as are in heavenly loves, appear lively, shining, fair, and beautiful; nor is there less difference in their minds and intellectual capacities, for as the former are stupid and foolish, so the latter are intelligent and wise: also when permission is given to inspect the interior state and frame of the affections and thoughts of those who are in heavenly love, some of them appear in the form of a shining light, some of a flame colour, and such of them as are nearest to sense, beautifully variegated like rainbows; whilst the same in such as are of gross, corporeal affections, present a black appearance, and in such as are subtle and malicious, a resemblance of a dusky, fiery redness, whilst the more external state of their minds appears of a dismal hue and aspect; for it is to be noted, that both the inmost and outermost states of the mind, and its operations in the spiritual world, are at times, by divine permission, represented by visible appearances. These here last mentioned see nothing in the light of heaven, for that is to them as darkness, and that so terrifying to their inward sight or understanding, as to affect them with madness; wherefore to avoid it they hide themselves in dens and caverns, of a depth proportionate to their degree of false from evil [*falsa ex malis*]. But they, on the other hand, who are in cœlestial love, the farther they advance into the light of heaven, the more clearly they see all things, and the more beautiful do all things appear to them; and what is still more, the brighter and deeper is their understanding and wisdom. Again, they who are in

gross

grofs corporeal affections cannot live in the heat of heaven, which is cœleſtial love, but only in the heat of hell, which is the love of unmercifulneſs to all that are not obſequious to them; for contempt of others, enmity, hatred, and revenge, are the elements and comfort of their lives, whilſt they know not what it is to do good to others from any thing of benevolence; and when they do any apparent good, it is from an evil principle, and to an evil end. And, laſtly, they who are of this claſs have no uſe of reſpiration in heaven, for when any ſpirit comes thither, he gaſps as if in an agony; whereas they who are in the cœleſtial love, the farther they advance into heaven, the more free is their reſpiration, and the more complete is their enjoyment of life. From the foregoing obſervations we cannot but infer, that cœleſtial and ſpiritual love is heaven in man, as carrying with it the ſignatures of all heavenly things; and that groſs, corporeal affections are hell in man, as bearing the image and ſuperſcription of all things helliſh. Thus much may ſerve to confirm the foregoing theſis, That he who lives under the influence of cœleſtial and ſpiritual love goes to heaven, and that he who is governed by a ſenſual and earthly love, without any principle of heavenly life in him, goes to hell.

482. *That no faith abideth with man, that does not ſpring from heavenly love.* The truth of this has been manifeſted to me ſo abundantly, that were I to relate the whole of what I have ſeen and heard concerning this matter, it would fill a volume; and from which I can teſtify, that they who live to the world and to ſenſe, without any affection for ſpiritual things, neither have nor can have true faith; whilſt that which paſſes with them for ſuch, is no better than natural ſcience. or a faith of perſuaſion, which they make ſubſervient to their inclinations and wiſhes. I have known many ſuch, who fancied themſelves poſſeſſed of true faith, who, after ſome free communication with ſuch as were really in the faith, were brought to confeſs that they had no right faith, and that mere aſſent to divine truths delivered in the Scriptures was not a ſaving faith, but only the love of it from a ſpiritual principle joined to good life, and a willing obedience thereto: and it was likewiſe demonſtrated to them,

them, that the perſuaſion which they called faith, was but as the light in winter, which, being deſtitute of genial heat, had not the power of communicating the vital warmth of vegetation to the torpid earth: and not only ſo, but this glimmering light of their faith of perſuaſion, when penetrated by the rays of cœleſtial light, is extinguiſhed, nay, turned into darkneſs, which ſo far obſcures and confounds their intellectual faculties, that they become, as it were, mad with folly; and therefore the light of divine truth from the Word and ſound doctrine is withheld from them, and they are left to that falſe judgment which beſt ſuits with their evil life: for there all join themſelves to, and, as it were, incorporate with their own proper loves, and the deluſions that are ſuited thereto, and then become haters of the truth, as inimical to the principles they have adopted. This I can teſtify to from the whole of my experience, as to the things of heaven and hell; that all Solifidians, who had profeſſed the doctrine of being ſaved by faith alone, after having led wicked lives, are all in hell; I having ſeen ſeveral thouſands of them caſt in thither: concerning which ſee my little work, intitled, *Of the laſt Judgment, and Babylon deſtroyed.*

483. *That love in act, or operative love, is that which remains with man, and conſequently is the proper life of man.* This propoſition follows from what has been here advanced from experience, as its proper inference; and alſo from what has been ſaid above concerning works and deeds. Now love in act or exerciſe, is the ſame with work and deed.

484. It is to be remembered, that all outward acts and works appertain either to the moral or civil life, and comprehend all the duties of ſincerity and rectitude of manners relative to the former, and all the duties of juſtice and equity relative to the latter; and the love they proceed from as their principle, is either cœleſtial or infernal: the works and acts both reſpecting moral and civil life are cœleſtial or heavenly, if they are done from a heavenly love; for then they are of the Lord's doing in us, and by neceſſary conſequence are good; but if the ſame works are done from an infernal love, then are they alſo of an infernal nature. Now infernal love is the love of ſelf and of the world, and ſuch works, as proceeding only from man's ſelf

or

or fallen nature, are in themselves evil, because man considered singly in himself is nothing but evil (266).

That the Delights of every one's Life are changed after Death to Things corresponding thereto.

485. That the ruling affection or love continues with man for ever, has been shewed in the preceding article; and that the pleasures or gratifications of that love are changed in the other world to things corresponding thereto, will in this place be made appear. By being changed into correspondences, is meant into such spiritual things as correspond to their natural exemplars or types; and the reason of such change arises from man's different condition of existence; as, whilst in this natural world, he is in a terrestrial body, and when removed to the spiritual world, he is clothed with a spiritual body. That both angels and men appear in a perfect human form, and have spiritual bodies in the other world, see above, n. 73 to 77, and n. 453 to 460; and what is signified by correspondence between spiritual and natural things, n. 87 to 115.

486. All the delights belonging to man have relation to his ruling love; for what gives him pleasure but that which he loves, and what the greatest but that which he loves most?

---

(266) That it is the property of man in fallen nature to love himself above God, and this world above heaven, and to think lightly of his neighbour compared to himself, and consequently, that he is a lover of self and of the world, n. 634, 731, 4317. That this property is innate in man, and is essential evil, n. 210, 215, 731, 874, 875—10284, 10286, 10731. That from this innate property of man all evil and false proceed, n. 1047, 10283, 10284, 10286, 10731. That the evils which proceed from this selfish property in man, are contempt of others, enmity, hatred, revenge, cruelty, and deceits, n. 6667, 7372, 7373, 7374, 9348, 10038, 10742. That so far as self in man prevails, so far the good of love, and the truth of faith, are either rejected, extinguished, or perverted, n. 2041, 7491, 7492, 7643, 8487, 10455, 10743. That propriety, or the selfish property in man, is hell within him, n. 694, 8480. That the apparent good which man does from the principle of selfishness, or as his proper own, is not real good, but real evil, n. 8478.

Now these pleasures are as various as the different kinds of love, or as many in number as there are men, spirits, and angels; for the predominant affection is not exactly similar in all respects in any two of them; and therefore it is, that no two have exactly the same face, for the face is the image of the mind in every one, and in the spiritual world it is a true index of the predominant affection. There is also an infinite variety in their particular pleasures and gratifications, as well in those that are successive, as in those that are simultaneous; and yet these particular different pleasures in every one are all relative to the governing love, nay, are so many ingredients in it, and as such make one with it; and as all particular delights in every individual are relative to the predominant affection, so the general kinds of affection in all, both in heaven and hell, correspond in each to one universal love, viz. to the love of the Lord in heaven, and to the love of self in hell.

487. As to the kind and quality of those spiritual delights, into which those that are natural and peculiar to every one here are changed after death, this can only be known from the doctrine of correspondences; which teaches in general, that all things natural have their correlative spiritual correspondents; and in particular, the kind and quality of such correspondents; consequently, he that is an adept in this science, may judge concerning his own state after death from the knowledge of his own prevailing love, and the relation it bears to that universal love before-mentioned, to which the inferior loves are subservient and relative in their several classes: but they that are under bondage to the government of self-love cannot know it, because they take delight in it, and call their evil good, and the false [*falsa*] (*), wherewith they confirm themselves in their

---

(*) It is with reluctance that we find ourselves obliged, both here and in other parts of this translation, to render the words *falsum* and *falsa* literally as substantives; but there is no help for it, as our language affords no other word that so fully expresses the opposite to truth. The word error reaches not the full sense, as signifying mistake in judgment, or a deviation from some particular truth, rather than the contrary principle; and falsity denotes the negation of truth in this or that instance, as likewise falsehood, but not the direct contrary to truth abstractedly considered; and therefore some few authors have complied with the necessity of using the words false and falses in the sense here given them, though not so agreeable to custom and grammar.

delusion,

delusion, they call truth; and yet, were they but willing to take advice from men wiser than themselves, they might be set right in this matter, but such willingness is wanting in them: so great is the infatuation of self-love, as to shut the ear to the voice of wisdom. On the other hand, they who are influenced by heavenly love are receptive of instruction, and learn to know both their innate evils, and their propensities to them from those truths which make them manifest; for by the light of truth shining from the good principle, we may discover evil and the false belonging to it; but in the darkness of evil we see not the good and its truth, nay, all such as are blind men that grope at noon-day as in the night; nay, like owls, chuse the darkness (267) rather than the light, see n. 126 to 134. I have been confirmed in this truth by experience communicated from the angels, who immediately detect every stirring of imperfection (*) in themselves (as sometimes happens to them) and likewise all malignity in the unhappy spirits that are in the intermediate state or world of spirits, though such spirits see not their own evils, being so far gone in depravity, as not to know what is meant by the good of heavenly love, or conscience, or disinterested justice, or to be subject to the Lord; but, on the contrary, deny the reality of these things. What has been laid down in this article, is to the end that man may examine himself, and from the things he most delights in come to the knowledge of his predominant love, and thereby be able to form a judgment (according to his skill in the doctrine of correspondences) concerning his future state.

(267) That darkness in the Word signifies (by correspondency) falses [*falsa*] and thick darkness or blackness, the falses of evil, n. 1839, 1860, 7688, 7711. That the light of heaven is darkness to those that are evil, 1861, 6832, 8197. That they who are in hell are said to be in darkness, as being in the falses of evil, concerning which, see n. 3340, 4418, 4531. That by the blind in Scripture, are signified those who are in falses, and refuse instruction, n. 2383, 6990.

(*) It is highly credible, if not absolutely certain, from the distance betwixt finite and infinite, that even the highest of created beings have in them something of defect, which may be called relative evil; and this in order to preserve in them a due sense of humility, and of their dependence on their infinitely perfect Creator and Benefactor; but in order to this end, they must be conscious at times, of such imperfection, defect, or evil, and yet in a way consistent with their happiness and free will.

488. How

488. How the pleasures of this life in every one are changed after death into their figurative representations, may be learned from the doctrine of correspondences; but as that science as yet remains a secret, I shall illustrate the matter by some examples. All that are in the principle of evil, and have confirmed themselves in opposition to the truths of religion, and more especially by their disbelief of the Scriptures, all such avoid the light of heaven, and hide themselves in dark caverns and the clefts of rocks, and that because they hated the truth, and loved the false, which corresponds to darkness, as represented by such hiding places (268), wherein they take pleasure: nor is it otherwise with the insidious and subtle, who had addicted themselves to the deceitful works of darkness in this world, who, in like manner, hide themselves in caverns and obscure corners in the other, where they whisper to one another in the dark; for such sort of concealments correspond to those clandestine doings in which they had taken pleasure. They who had applied themselves to the study of the sciences merely for the sake of being accounted men of learning, priding themselves in what they could from their memory relating thereto, whilst at the same time they had neglected to cultivate their minds with knowledge useful for life; such take delight in sandy places, which they prefer to the most pleasant fields and gardens, as the former correspond to the use they had made of such studies. Such as had employed much of their time and pains to acquire a speculative knowledge in the doctrines of their own and other churches, without applying such knowledge to practical use, avoid improved and well-cultivated places, and chuse their habitations among rocks, and in stony ground. All such as had set up nature in the room of God, and had sacrificed to their own prudence, and by various political stratagems had advanced themselves to worldly riches and honours, devote themselves in the other world to the study of the magical arts, the end of which is to profane and confound the divine order in God's works. They who had indulged themselves in making false

---

(268) That the hole and cleft of a rock signifies in Scripture the obscurity and falseof faith, n. 10582; because rock signifies faith from the Lord, n. 8581, 10580; and stone the truth of faith, n. 114, 643, 1298, 3720, 6426, 8608, 10376.

applica-

applications of divine truths to the gratification of their paſſions, take delight in places of an urinous ſmell, as ſuch correſpond to that kind of profanation. They that were infected with a ſordid avarice have their abode in cells, where they take pleaſure in ſuch filth and ſtench as come from ſwine and corrupted meats. Such as lived in ſenſual pleaſures, and made their belly their God, become enemies to all cleanlineſs, and find their gratification in ordure, as ſpiritual filthineſs anſwers to filthineſs of the fleſh. They who had habituated themſelves to commit adultery dwell in as naſty brothels, having the ſtrongeſt antipathy to all purity and chaſte connexions. The cruel and revengeful delight in cadaverous ſmells, and inhabit hells adapted to their ſavage diſpoſitions: and ſo with others in like manner, according to their reſpective qualities.

489. But the delights of life in thoſe who lived here in heavenly love are changed into correſpondences of a heavenly nature from the cœleſtial ſun, in the light of which are formed repreſentations of the divine properties and qualities in the angels of ſuch exquiſite beauty, as raviſh their minds and ſenſes with unſpeakable delight; whilſt the ſame light, which illuminates their intellectual part with the knowledge of divine truths, images to their external ſight the things that correſpond thereto. That the appearances in the heavens are outward viſible ſigns of things inward in the angels appertaining to their faith and love, and conſequently to their underſtanding and wiſdom, has been ſhewed before in the chapter *Concerning Repreſentatives and Appearances in Heaven*, n. 170 to 176; and alſo in that which treats *Of the Wiſdom of the Angels*, n. 265 to 275. As I have produced ſome examples from experience in confirmation of the matter in hand, and to illuſtrate what had been advanced doctrinally, ſo I proceed to farther inſtances in reſpect to theſe correſpondent heavenly pleaſures which ſucceed to the natural ones in thoſe who live here in cœleſtial love. They who have loved divine truths and the ſacred writings with an inward affection, or from the affection of truth, have luminous dwellings in the other world upon eminences which have the appearance of mountains, where they continually enjoy the light of heaven:

they are strangers to the darkness of our nights in this world, and are blessed with a perpetual spring, whilst delightful scenes of meadows, corn fields, and vineyards are represented to their view; the splendour, like as of precious stones, beautifies their houses, and through windows, as of pure chrystal, they behold ravishing prospects; and whilst these external objects entertain the outward sense, so do they at the same time convey an inward delight to their minds from the correspondent relation they bear to the divine truths within them, which they had received from God's word. They who, upon their first receiving the doctrines of Christianity, applied them to practical use, and made them the rule of life, are in the third or inmost heaven, and enjoy the delights of wisdom above others: in every object they see something divine, and though the objects themselves are without them, yet the divine correspondence that is in them, does by a secret influx affect their minds, and fill them with blessed sensations, so that from the joy within them all things appear pleasant without them, and, as it were, to live, smile, and play, of which see above, n. 270. They who have taken pleasure in studying the sciences, so as to render them subservient to useful intellectual improvements, and to impress their minds with a deeper sense of divine things, the rational delights of such are changed in the other world into spiritual delights, as sublime attainments and discoveries in the knowledges of good and truth: such have their dwellings in beautiful gardens, curiously adorned and diversified with flowers, plants, trees, walks, porticos, &c. The flowers and trees also are varied every day, so affording fresh entertainment to the senses, and gratifying both the mind and eye with new successions of delightful scenes, whilst at the same time they exhibit instructive emblems of divine things, from which, by their skill in the doctrines of correspondences, they continually draw fresh supplies of matter for their spiritual-intellectual improvement and delight (270).

They

(270) That garden, grove, and plantation, signify intellectual knowledge, n. 100, 108, 3220. That therefore the ancients celebrated their religious worship in groves, n. 2722, 4552. That flowers and flower gardens signify scientifical truths, n. 9553.

They who faw God in all things as their creator, upholder, and governor, and confidered nature only as his inftrument in fubferviency to fpiritual ufes, and had confirmed themfelves in this belief, thefe are in cœleftial light, which gives tranfparency to every thing they behold, and by different variegations forms therein fuch beautiful reprefentations of divine things, as gives unfpeakable pleafure to their intellectual fight. Their houfes glitter with adamantine fplendour; and I was told that the walls thereof were as chryftal, and of like tranfparency (exhibiting alfo fluent reprefentations of divine things with unceafing variety) and that becaufe fuch tranfparency correfponds to a mind in illuftration from the Lord, and totally freed from all fhadow of doubting, and from every impurity from the love of natural things. Thefe, and innumerable other things, are related by thofe who have been in the [third] heaven; and moreover, that they have feen and heard there things which none elfe ever faw or heard. Such as had acted with opennefs and fimplicity, and made no fecrets of their thoughts, as far as the relations of civil life allowed of it, ftrictly adhering to the rules of truth and juftice from a divine principle, they appear in heaven with lucid faces, reprefenting, as it were, in vifible forms the thoughts and difpofitions of their minds, whilft their fpeech and actions exprefs the reality of their affections; and therefore they are beloved above others: whilft they are fpeaking there feems to be, as it were, obfcurity upon their countenances; but when they have done, what they have delivered appears legibly and in full light fignatured on their faces; and as the things about them correfpond to thofe within them, fo do they reprefent them in fo ftriking a likenefs, as to make them plainly underftood by others. Such fpirits as had been accuftomed to fubtlety and clandeftine dealings avoid coming near them, and are feen to creep away like ferpents as foon as they fpy them. Such as held adultery in horror, and lived chaftly in conjugal love, ftand in the heavenly order and form above others, and therefore appear in beauty and the bloom of youth with particular diftinction;

n. 9553. That herbs, grafs, and lawns fignify the like kinds of knowledge, n. 7571. That trees fignify perceptions and knowledges, n. 103, 2163, 2682, 2722, 2972, 7692.

the delights appertaining to their love are inexpressible, and go on increasing to eternity; for all the joys of heaven communicate by influx with it, as being that love which is derived from the conjunction of the Lord with heaven, and with his church on earth, and in a general sense from the conjunction of good and truth, which constitutes heaven in common, and in every angel in particular, see above, n. 366 to 386. In a word, the delights of those here mentioned are not to be described in words: but what has been said of the corresponding delights enjoyed in heaven by those who have lived here in cœlestial love, falls very far short of their number.

490. Thus much may suffice to shew, that the pleasures of every one in this life become changed after death into such as correspond to them in the spiritual world, the principal love continuing the same in every one to eternity; whether, for instance, it be that of conjugal love, the love of justice, sincerity, goodness, and truth, the love of scientifick knowledge, the love of intellectual knowledge and wisdom, and so on; and the pleasures which flow from them, as streams from their fountains, continue with them in like manner, but are augmented in proportion to the difference between natural and spiritual.

Of Man's First State after Death.

491. There are three states which man goes through after death, before he enters into heaven, or hell; the first respects his exterior part; the second his interior; and the third is his state of final preparation. These states man passes through in the world of spirits; however, there are exceptions, as some are immediately after death taken up into heaven, or cast into hell; of the former class are they who are regenerated, and so prepared for heaven in this world, and that in so high a degree, as to need only the putting off all their natural impurities with their bodies; these are immediately carried by the angels into heaven, and some such I have seen so conveyed thither within an hour after their departing this life. On the other hand, such as have been internally evil under the mask of externally apparent

parent goodness, and so have filled up the measure of their iniquities by hypocrisy and deceit, using the cloak of goodness as a means whereby to deceive others; these are immediately cast into hell; and this I have seen to be the case with some within an hour after their death, and in particular one such, who had been a hypocrite and deceiver above others, cast in thither with his head downward, and his feet upward; and others in a different manner. There are also some who are committed to caverns immediately after their decease, and so separated from others in the world of spirits, but afterwards released, and remanded thither by turns; such are they who, under civil pretexts, dealt fraudulently with their neighbours: but the forementioned are very few compared to the many classes of those who are detained in the world of spirits, in order to their preparation for heaven or hell, according to the established order of the divine œconomy.

492. As to the first state before mentioned, or that which respects the exterior, this, man enters upon immediately after death. Every one's spirit has belonging to it properties exterior and interior; the former are those by which he governs and accommodates the corporeal functions in this world, more especially the face, speech, and bodily gestures, according to his social connexions; the latter are proper to his will and free thoughts, which are seldom made manifest by the face, speech, and outward behaviour, man being accustomed through education and example to counterfeit friendship, sincerity, and benevolence, and to conceal his true thoughts even from his infancy. Hence it is, that so many learn the external practice of morality and good manners, however different they may in reality be within, and so, mistaking custom for principle, know not themselves, nor enter into any examination concerning the matter.

493. The first state of man after death nearly resembles his last in this life, and he is much the same in the external operations of his mind; nay, he still retains the like face, speech, and inclinations, and also the like dispositions with respect to moral and civil life, insomuch that he knows no other than that he is still an inhabitant of this world, unless he seriously reflects

on the things that prefent themfelves to him, and on what was told him by the angels, on his refufcitation, of his being a fpirit, n. 4:0. Thus one life is progreffively continued to another, and death is only the paffage between them.

494. As fuch is the ftate of man's fpirit immediately after his departing this life, he is confequently known in the other world by fuch as were his friends and acquaintance in this, not only from his face and fpeech, but alfo from the fphere of his life, and that on the firft approach. When any one there thinks intenfely of another, and is impreffed in his mind and memory with his likenefs, and certain particulars of his life [having at the fame time a ftrong defire to fee him] the perfon fo thought of becomes immediately prefent to him as if fent to him: and this comes to pafs from the nature of the fpiritual world, where thoughts are mutually communicated at any diftance, and where fpace is very different from what it is here, fee above, n. 191 to 199; by which means fuch as pafs from hence thither are readily known by their friends, relations, and acquaintance; and they converfe and affociate together after the manner of their former connexions: I have often heard their mutual congratulations on the occafion of thefe meetings. It is common for hufband and wife to meet thus, and to abide together for a longer or fhorter time, accordingly as they agreed in this world; but if they had not lived together in conjugal love, which is union of minds from a heavenly principle, after fome fhort ftay they are feparated: but if they had lived in variance and hatred, it is not unufual for them to break out into ftrife and quarreling, even to fighting; but, neverthelefs, they are not totally feparated before they enter upon their fecond ftate, concerning which hereafter.

495. As the life of men newly become fpirits is fo like to their natural life in this world, and as they are at firft ftrangers to their new ftate, without knowing any thing more of heaven and hell than what they have learned from the letter of Scripture, and their preachers; therefore after wondering for fome time at their being clothed with a body, and poffeffing every fenfe as in this world, and alfo at their feeing things under the like appearance as before, they find themfelves urged by a defire

of

of knowing what and where heaven and hell are : upon which they are inſtructed by their friends in things relating to eternal life, and are conducted to various places, and different ſocieties, and ſome into cities, gardens, and beautiful plantations, and more particularly to ſee magnificent buildings, as ſuch external objects ſuit with the preſent external ſtate of their minds. Then they are led to inſpect thoſe interior ſentiments and ideas which they had in this life concerning the ſtate of ſouls after death, and concerning heaven and hell, not without indignation to think of their own paſt ignorance, and alſo that of the church in relation to theſe important ſubjects. Almoſt all in the world of ſpirits are deſirous to know whether they ſhall go to heaven or not, and the greater part judge in favour of themſelves as to this particular, eſpecially ſuch as had lived by the external rules of morality and civil obligation here; not conſidering that both good and bad do the ſame to outward appearance, as alſo do many good offices to others, and in like manner go to church, hear ſermons, and bear a part in the publick worſhip; not reflecting that theſe external acts, and this outward form of worſhip avail nothing in themſelves, conſidered ſeparately from the diſpoſition and principle of the worſhipper, and that it is the interior or inner man that ſtamps the character and value upon the outward work and form; but ſcarcely one in a thouſand knows what is meant by the interior, and even after being taught it, place all in the words and bodily ſervice; and ſuch is the greater part of thoſe, who at this day paſs from the Chriſtian world into the other life.

496. The new comers. are tried as to their qualities by the good ſpirits, and that according to various ways; for in this their firſt ſtate the bad ſpeak and act, to appearance, like the good, and that from having kept up an outward moral deportment in the world, in conformity to the laws of government and the rules of ſociety, to preſerve character and the praiſe of men, for the ſake of worldly advantage; but the internally bad ſpirits are particularly diſtinguiſhed from the good by this among other ſigns, viz. that they eagerly attend to what is ſaid of things without them, but give little attention to inward and. ſpiritual truths. They are alſo known from turning themſelves

frequently

frequently to certain points of the compafs, and from taking the ways that lead thereto when left alone, both of which are marks in the other world of the particular kind of love that influences and directs them.

497. All fpirits, on their leaving this world, are indeed in fellowfhip with fome particular fociety either in heaven or hell; but fo only in their inner man or ground, which is not manifefted to others, whilft they are occupied in the exterior mental faculties and exercifes [fuch as border on the fenfes or outward life] for external things cover and hide what is internal, efpecially in thofe who are rooted in evil, but hypocritically good in the outward life; but afterwards, when they enter upon their fecond ftate, the outward is quiefcent, and what was inward is made manifeft.

498. This firft ftate of man after death continues to fome for days, to fome for months, and to others for a year, but rarely for longer to any one, though to all differently, according to the agreement or difagreement between their interiour and exteriour; for in the fpiritual world they muft be brought into correfpondence and confent; as it is not allowed there for any to think and will one way, and to fpeak and act another, but every one muft be an exprefs image of his thoughts and affections, or to appear outwardly as he is inwardly; and therefore the external ftate or province of the fpirit muft firft be fo manifefted and regulated, as to ferve for a correfpondent plane or ground to the internal.

Of the Second State of Man after Death.

499. The fecond ftate of man after death is called his interior ftate, as he then paffes into the more recondite things of his mind, or of his will and thoughts, whilft the more external functions of it, as exercifed in his firft ftate, are then quiefcent or dormant. Whoever carefully attends to the lives, words, and actions of men, may foon find that every one has both his exterior and interior thoughts and intentions; thus for example, the man of civil connexions and manners forms his judgment

of others by what he knows of them by character and conversation; and though he should find them to be far otherwise than men of probity and worth, yet he does not speak and behave to them according to his real sentiments of them, but with something of seeming respect and civility: and this is still more strongly exemplified in the behaviour of persons addicted to dissimulation and flattery, who speak and act quite contrary to what they think and mean; and also in hypocrites, who can talk of God, of heaven, and spiritual things, and also of their country, and neighbour, as if from faith and love, when at the same time they have neither the one nor the other, and love none but themselves. This evinces that there are thoughts in the same mind of two different complexions, the one interior, and the other exterior, and that it is common for men to speak from the latter, whilst their real sentiments in the interior are contrary thereto; and that these two arrangements of thoughts are of distinct and separate apartments in the mind, appears from the pains such persons take to prevent those that are interior from flowing into the exterior to manifestation. Now man was so formed by his original creation, that both these were as one by correspondence and consent, as is the case now with the good, who both think and speak what is good and true; whereas in the evil the interior and the exterior are divided, for they think evil, and speak good, thus inverting the order of things, whilst the evil is innermost, and the good outermost, the former exercising rule over the latter, and using its services for temporal and selfish ends, so that the seeming good which they say and do is corrupted and changed into evil, however the undiscerning may be deceived by its outward appearance. On the other hand, they who are in the good principle stand in the divine order of God's creation, whilst the good in their interiour flows into the exteriour of their minds, and thence into their words and actions. This is the state in which man was created, and thus they have communication with heaven, and have the Lord for their leader. Thus much may serve to shew, that man thinks from two distinct grounds, the one called the interior, the other the exterior; and when we speak here of

R r r r   his

his thinking, we include likewise his faculty of willing, as his thoughts are from his will, neither can they exist separately.

500. When willing and thinking are considered under their particular distinctions, then by the will is also to be understood the affection or love, with the particular pleasures annexed to it, as these also have relation thereto, as the subject in which they inhere; for what a man wills, that he loves and takes pleasure in, and so reciprocally, what he loves and takes pleasure in, that he also wills: and by thought is meant that operation of the mind by which a man confirms and fixes his affection or love, it being the form of the will made manifest in the light of the understanding. This form of the will may be considered under various relations to the spiritual world, and is properly the spirit of a man.

501. It must be noted, that man is to be estimated according to what he is inwardly, and not according to what he is outwardly only, and that because his interior things appertain to his spirit, which is the proper life of man, and is that which animates his body; and therefore accordingly as man is in his interiour, such he remains for ever; whereas exterior things, as appertaining to the body and its senses, are separated after death, so much of them only remaining (and that in a quiescent, dormant state) as may serve as a plane or ground to his interiors, as was shewed before in the article treating of the memory retained by man after death. Hence it may appear what properly belongs to man as himself, and what not; thus for example, the good that bad men speak and do from their exterior thought and will, is not their proper own, but only that which proceeds from their inner man, or the ground of the heart.

502. After that man, now become a spirit, has gone through his first state, which is that of his exterior thoughts and will, he passes into his second or interior state, and this he enters upon insensibly, which resembles that of a man in this world, who, finding himself at liberty from every restraint and dissipation, recollects himself, and enters into the most secret recesses of his soul. Now in this state of introversion, when he thinks freely from his inmost disposition and affections, he is properly himself, or in his true life.

503. When

503. When a spirit is in this state of thinking from his will, consequently from his ruling affection or love, thought and will in him appear so much one and the same, that he seems only to be in the exercise of the latter: and the case is nearly the same when he speaks, only with this difference, that then he is not without some little fear of betraying the whole of his affections, and that through a habit contracted in this world from the reserves practised in ordinary conversation.

504. All without exception enter into this state in the other world, as proper to spirit, for the former is assumed and practised in accommodation to society and transactions in this world; and therefore, though it remains with man for some time after death, yet it is not long continued in, as not being suitable to the nature of a spirit, for the following reasons: First, Because a spirit thinks and speaks from the governing principle of life without disguise, see article *Concerning the Conversation of Angels*, n. 234 to 245; nay, the same is the case of man in this world, when he enters into his inmost self, and takes an intuitive view of his outward man, in which kind of survey he sees more in a minute than he could utter in an hour. Secondly, Because in his conversation and dealings in this world, he speaks and acts under the restraint of those rules which society has established for the maintenance of civility and decorum. Thirdly, Because man, when he enters into the interior recesses of his spirit, exercises rule over his outward economy, prescribing laws thereto, how to speak and act in order to conciliate the good will and favour of others, and that by a constrained external behaviour. These considerations may serve to shew, that this interior state of liberty is not only the proper state of the spirit of a man after death, but even in this life.

505. When a spirit has passed into his second or interior state, it then appears outwardly what manner of man he had been in this world, as he now acts from his proper self; thus if he had been a wise and good man before, he now manifests still higher degrees of rationality and wisdom in his words and actions, as being freed from those corporeal and earthly embarrassments which had fettered and obscured the inward operations of his mind, whereas the bad man evidences greater folly

than

than before, for whilst in this world he fashioned his external behaviour by the rules of prudence, in order to save appearances; but not being under the like restraints now, he gives full scope to his infamy. A bad man, that apes the manners and behaviour of a good one, is nothing better than a neat vessel well covered, but replete with filthiness; and answers to that comparison of our Lord: "Like unto a whited sepulchre, which "indeed appears beautiful outward, but is within full of dead "mens bones, and of all uncleanness," Matt. xxiii. 27.

506. All who in this world lived uprightly, and preserved a good conscience, walking in the fear of God, and in the love of divine truths, applying the same to practical use, seem to themselves as men awaked out of sleep, and as having passed from darkness to light, when they first enter upon their second or interior state; they think from the light of pure wisdom, and they do all things from the love of goodness; heaven influences their thoughts and affections, they are in communication with angels; and they love and worship the Lord from the very principle of life: for they have entered into the holy of holies, in which the true worship consists, and is to them and in them a service of perfect freedom, such is the state of those hereafter, whose life here has been according to the Gospel of Christ. But very different is the condition of those, whose lives have been contrary thereto, and therefore have denied the Lord in their works, however they may have confessed him with their lips; all such, when they enter upon their interior or second state, and so are set free from outward restraints, appear as infatuated and mad in all they say and do; for being now under the full uncontrolled dominion of their evil lusts and passions, they commit all iniquity with greediness, as contempt of others, mockery, hatred, revenge, and blasphemy, and some of them are crafty and malicious to a degree exceeding belief; in a word, they appear wholly destitute of rationality, though wise in their own conceits: they are sometimes, during short intervals, restored to their external state, together with the remembrance of these flagrant enormities; at which some of them seem ashamed, and to confess their madness; but others are void of all shame. Some of them also appear indignant, that they are not suffered

to

to continue in their former exterior state; when it is told them, that this would prove to their detriment; for that they would go on to commit the same things in a clandestine manner, would do evil under the appearance of good, and defraud the simple-hearted by their dissimulation, till by degrees they waxed as wicked openly, as they were inwardly, and so increased their condemnation and wretchedness.

507. The spirits of this state appear outwardly such as they were inwardly whilst in this world, and also publickly declare the things they had spoken and done here in private, and endeavour to repeat the same without regard to decency and character; and this is permitted, that they may be known to the angels for what they are. Thus their hidden things are made manifest, and their secret things declared openly, according to those words of the Lord: " There is nothing covered, that " shall not be revealed; nor hid, that shall not be made known. " Therefore, whatsoever ye have spoken in darkness, shall be " heard in the light, and that which ye have spoken in the ear " in closets, shall be proclaimed upon the house-tops," Luke xii. 2, 3. " I say unto you, That every idle word that men " shall speak, they shall give account thereof in the day of " judgment," Matt. xii. 36.

508. The condition of the evil in this state respectively cannot be described in a few words, as every one's infatuation there, is according to his particular concupiscence: from the following examples we may form some judgment of the rest. They who had been absorbed in self-love, so as not to attend to the good uses of their respective offices and functions, but discharged them only with a view to their own estimation and honour, appear more stupid than others; for in proportion to the degree of self-love in any one is his distance from heaven, and consequently from wisdom: but they who to the evil of self-love had added crafty devices, and by means thereof advanced themselves to worldly honours, they associate themselves to the worst of spirits, and addict themselves to the magical arts, which are profane abuses of the divine order, by means of which they molest and vex all that pay them not honour; the practising of insidious wiles, and to kindle strife and hatred yield

them the highest pleasure; they burn with revenge, and long for nothing more than to tyrannize over all that submit not to their will; and all these wicked passions they gratify as far as their evil associates give them assistance; nay, so far does madness hurry them on, as to make them wish to scale heaven, either to subvert the government of the holy kingdom, or to cause themselves to be worshipped for gods therein. Such of this class as were of the papal church are more mad than the rest, as vainly thinking that they have power over heaven and hell, and can forgive sins at pleasure: some of these arrogate to themselves divine honour, and exalt themselves into the place of Christ. Such diabolical persuasions spread darkness and distraction upon their minds; they are indeed similar in both the fore-mentioned states, but in the latter of them they totally lose their reason. As concerning their madness, and their ensuing lot, something shall be particularly said in a little piece, intitled, *Of the Last Judgment, and Babylon destroyed*. As to those who in this world ascribed all creation to nature, and so in effect denied a God, and consequently all divine truths, such herd together in this state, calling every one a god who excelled in subtlety of reasoning, and giving him divine honour. I have seen some such in their conventicle worshipping a magician, holding conferences concerning nature, and behaving more like brute beasts than human creatures, and among them some who were dignitaries in this world, and had the reputation of being learned and wise, and others of a different character. From thus much we may gather what they are, the interior of whose minds is shut against divine things, as theirs is, who receive no influx from heaven through looking up to God, and a life of faith. Now let every one judge from himself, what sort of creature he should be, were he to live without regard to laws both human and divine, and without all external restraints arising from fear in respect to life, character, honour, advantage, and the pleasures resulting therefrom. However, the madness of those before mentioned is so far restrained by the Lord, as not to break all bounds of uses, for even a use arises from every one of them, evil as they are; for in them the good spirits see the odiousness of evil, and what man is, separate from the divine direction

tion and leadings. Another ufe is, that all evil is fo collected into a vifible body, and that all apparent good and truth, which ferved them only for a cover to their malignity, is taken from them, and they fo left to their own evil, and the falfe iffuing from their evil, that they may be totally difqualified for all fociety with the good, and fitted for their own place: for no one is allotted to his portion in hell before evil and the falfe from evil have taken full poffeffion of him, and that becaufe it is contrary to the laws of the other world to have the mind fo divided, as to think and fpeak one way, and to have the will fet the contrary way; but every evil fpirit muft think and fpeak there from the falfe of his own evil or proper affection, as he did in this world, when under no conftraint or reftraint; and that becaufe the affection or love is the fame with the will, and the will is man's proper felf or nature, which is formed according to his life in this world, and never forfakes him, as it is not to be reformed by any power of thinking, or knowledge of the truth in the next.

509. As bad fpirits in this their fecond ftate are given to evils of all kinds, fo do they frequently fuffer fevere punifhment. Now punifhments in the world of fpirits are manifold, and they are inflicted on all alike without refpect of perfons, had he been a king, or the meaneft fervant; for fin carries its fuffering with it by neceffary conjunction, and confequently, he that is in evil is alfo in the pain of evil; neverthelefs, no one fuffers there for the evils he had committed in this world, but for thofe which he is in, loves, or does in the other; for it comes to the fame, whether we fay, they are punifhed for paft or prefent fins, as every one after death returns to the ftate of his own life, and confequently into all the evils belonging to it: for the fpirit of a man is the fame that it was in the body, fee n. 470 to 484. The reafon of inflicting punifhment here, is becaufe the fear of it is the only means of fuppreffing evil in thofe on whom exhortation, inftruction, confcience, or regard to character have no influence, but they act folely from the bent of their nature, which can only be awed and reftrained by punifhment. On the other hand, the good fpirits fuffer no punifhment, and though they had done evils in this world, yet they make no part of them in

the

the other; and it is also given them to know, that the evils which they had done, were of another kind or nature, and not of set purpose and determined oppofition to the truth, nor from any other bad difpofition than what was derived to them from their parents, or which they were inftigated to commit by the urgency of fome blind paffion, when they forfook their inward guide.

510. Every one betakes himfelf to that fociety to which his fpirit belonged in this world, for every man in this life was joined to fome fociety in fpirit, either to an infernal or cœleftial one, the bad to the former, and the good to the latter, fee n. 438; and after fome fucceffive experiments with refpect to other focieties after his departure hence, he is at laft conducted to his own, which he joins himfelf to. An evil fpirit, when in his interior ftate, gradually turns towards the particular fociety he belongs to, till at length he fully faces it, and that before his ftate of preparation for it is quite finifhed; and when this is effected, he cafts himfelf into hell, to join his proper companions: his manner of cafting himfelf thither has the appearance of one falling down headlong from a precipice with his feet upwards; and the reafon of fuch appearance is, becaufe he had inverted the order of things in himfelf, by having loved the infernal, and rejected the cœleftial. Some evil fpirits in this their fecond ftate go in and out of hell by turns, but appear not to be caft down in the manner juft now mentioned, as when in full preparation for their final abode there: they have alfo fometimes, when in their external ftate, a fight of the fociety they had fellowfhip with in fpirit, when in this world, to give them to underftand, that they belonged to the infernal kingdom even in this life, though they were not at the fame time in a like condition with thofe that are actually in hell, but only with thofe that were in the world of fpirits on their way to it; of whofe condition, in refpect to the infernal fpirits, fomething fhall be faid hereafter.

511. The feparation of the evil from the good fpirits takes effect in this fecond ftate, for they are both together in the former ftate; for fpirits, whilft they are in externals, are in the fame condition of ftate as in this world, the bad with the good,

and

and the good with the bad; but it is otherwife when they are in their internals, and fo entirely under the dominion of their own nature and will (*). It is an ufual way for them to be led round the other focieties in a wide circle, and to be exhibited to the good fpirits in their proper form and afpect, on which the good fpirits all turn their backs to them, and the evil fpirits, on their part, do the fame to them, with their faces towards fuch infernal focieties as they refpectively belong to, and are appointed for; not to mention many other ways by which this feparation is conducted.

Of the Third State of Man after Death, which is the State of Inftruction for thofe that go to Heaven.

512. The third ftate of man, or of his fpirit, after death, is the ftate of inftruction, which is appointed for thofe that go to heaven, and become angels; but not for thofe that go to hell, as fuch are not in a capacity of inftruction, and therefore their fecond ftate is their laft, and anfwers to the third in others, as it terminates in their total change into that prevailing love which conftitutes their proper principle, and confequently into a conformity to that infernal fociety with which they have fellowfhip. When this is accomplifhed, their will and thoughts flow fpontaneoufly from their predominant love, which, being infernal, they can only chufe the evil and falfe, and reject all that apparent good and truth which before they had adopted, folely as means fubfervient to the gratification of their ruling paffion. On the other hand, the good fpirits are introduced from their fecond into their third ftate, which is that of preparation for heaven by the means of inftruction; for none can be qualified

---

(*) Some capital error plainly appears to have crept into the text in this place, to the caufing of a manifeft contradiction in the fenfe, and to an important doctrine of the author, as difcovered and explained to us in other parts of his writings: it was therefore thought proper to leave thefe four lines untranflated.

Tttt   for

for heaven, but through the knowledges of spiritual good and truth, and their opposites, evil and false, which can only come from previous instruction. As to good and truth in a civil and moral sense commonly called justice and sincerity, these may be learned from the laws of nations, and from conversation in virtuous company; but spiritual good and truth, as ingrafted principles in the heart, are only received by the teachings of a divine light: for though they are literally set forth in the Scripture, and the doctrines of the Christian churches founded thereon, yet they only gain the efficacy of a vital principle from a cœlestial influence manifesting itself in a conscientious obedience to the divine laws, as promulgated in the written word, and that in respect to the divine authority of them, and not from selfish and worldly motives; then a man is in the heavenly life, or in heaven, even whilst in this world. But in order to this, he must first be taught, that there is a God, a future state, a heaven and hell; and that God is to be loved above all things, and his neighbour as himself; and that the Holy Scriptures are the rule of faith, together with other rudiments of the Christian religion, without which a man attains not to that spiritual understanding and will, which are the proper recipients of the heavenly influx and divine wisdom. Thus the spirituality of religion is by vital influence from the Lord, which, when received into the heart of man, enters even into all his moral and civil virtues, and sanctifies them also, as being done from and to the Lord; so that all the common offices of life, proceeding from this divine source or principle, are so many effects of the spiritual life; and as every effect partakes of the nature of its efficient cause, so it makes one with it.

513. The angels appointed for instructors are from several societies, but chiefly from such as are in the north and the south, as their understanding and wisdom more particularly consist in the distinct knowledges of good and truth. The places set apart for instructing are towards the north, and are various, well-ordered, and divided, according to the particular classes of the disciples to be instructed in heavenly things, that so all may have their proper portion according to their particular capacity and genius respectively. These places extend far and wide in a circular

a circular form, and thither are led by their divine guide, the good spirits that are to receive their instruction, after having passed their second state in the world of spirits, but not all of them, as some of their number received their full instruction in this world, and so were here prepared for heaven by the Lord, and are conducted thither another way; some immediately after death, some after a short stay with the good spirits in the world of spirits, in order to be defecated and purified from some impurities contracted in their thoughts and affections from the honours and riches of this world; and some not till they have undergone vastation (*), which is performed in subterraneous places called the lower earth [*terra inferior*] where some pass

(*) The words *vastatio* and *vastati*, as here used by our author, with respect to good spirits, and more particularly in his large work, intitled *Arcana Cœlestia*, are difficult to translate by any single words in the English language: those of purgation and purification, or the physical terms, depuration and defecation, come the nearest to what he means by *vastation*, viz. a kind of refining or separating discipline, by which a spirit, whose radix or principle is good, is cleansed from those stains and pollutions, which it had contracted in its passage through this naughty world, and as yet hinder its fitness for heaven. Some who have a bigoted aversion to every doctrine indiscriminately that is held by the Romish church, and not adopted by the Protestants, will doubtless be offended at one so nearly bordering upon purgatory as this before us; but that we cannot help: it is for men of more enlarged minds, to seek out and embrace truth wherever they find it; nor is a pearl the less valuable, because it has lain among rubbish. In a word, it is the doctrine of a Romish purgatory, as stuffed with absurd figments, and the gainful superstitions introduced into it by the priests, that is to be repudiated, and not that of a state of purification after death, which, as it is consonant both to the goodness of God, and to our most rational ideas of a future happy state, so is it no less comforting to the mind of the serious Christian: for few, I think, are so well satisfied with their condition and state of acceptance at the time of their departure hence, as to think themselves entirely meet for the kingdom of heaven, so it cannot fail to minister great consolation to their spirit, to believe that the Lord hath appointed a state hereafter, wherein every thing that hinders shall be removed out of their way to the heavenly inheritance. But the word vastation [*vastatio*] relates also to evil spirits, and, in such application of it, signifies the divesting them of that seeming good which they might derive from mere outward nature or practice, and used as a cover to the predominant evil principle within, and therefore to be done away by this vastation or separating discipline, that they may be wholly in their own proper principle, and so fitted for the kingdom to which they belong. Thus both the good and the evil spirits become entirely their real selves without any heterogenous mixtures. N. B. The word [*vastatio*] will be translated by that of vastation in the following note, and where else it may occur; but as the participle *vastati* literally translated *vastated* would sound more harsh to an English ear, the word divested will be used in its place.

through

through a very painful difcipline; fuch in particular as had confirmed themfelves in grofs errors, whilft at the fame time they led good lives: for falfe doctrines, confirmed by reafonings into a belief of them, flick very clofe to the mind, and muft firft be difcuffed and difcharged from it, before truths can be clearly perceived and gain admiffion. But concerning vaftations, and the different ways whereby they are effected, much has been related in the ARCANA COELESTIA, from which fome particulars are extracted in the note here referred to (271).

514. All that are in the places fet apart for inftruction have diftinct habitations; for every one, in refpect to his interior ftate, is in communion with that heavenly fociety to which he is to be joined; and therefore, as the heavenly focieties are all according to a heavenly form and order (fee above, n. 200 to 212) fo are the places where thefe inftructions are held; and therefore, when

(271) That vaftations are appointed in the other world, or that they who pafs from hence thither are divefted of all that does not properly belong to them, n. 698, 7122, 7474, 9763. That good fpirits are divefted as to falfes, and evil fpirits as to truths, n. 7474, 7541, 7542. That the good fpirits are divefted of the earthly and mundane infections which they had contracted in this life, n. 7186, 9763; and likewife of all evil and falfe adhering to them, that fo they may become receptive of all good influxes from the Lord, n. 7122, 9331. That without fuch a feparation none can be qualified for the kingdom of heaven, n. 6928, 7122, 7136, 7541, 7542, 9763. That all are thus prepared before their exaltation thither, n. 4728, 7090. That without fuch preparation, admiffion into heaven would be attended with danger, n. 537, 538. Of the ftate of illuftration, and of the joy of thofe who have paffed through their vaftation for heaven, and their reception there, n. 2699, 2701, 2704. That the region appointed for vaftations is called the lower earth, n. 4728, 7090. That it is fituated directly under the feet, and furrounded with infernals; a defcription of it; n. 4940 to 4951, 7090. From experience, n. 699. Vaftations of the infernal kinds, what, n. 7317, 7502, 7545. That fuch of the evil fpirits as are employed in the vaftations of the good, do afterwards fear and fhun them, and have an averfion to them, n. 7768. That fuch infeftations and vaftations are different according to the different adherence of evil and falfe, and continue according to their difference in quality and degree, n. 1106 to 1113. That fome are willing to undergo vaftation, n. 1107. That fome are divefted through fears, n. 4942. Some through infeftations from the evils they were chargeable with in this world, and through anxiety and remorfe of confcience for the fame, n. 1106. Some through fpiritual captivity confifting in ignorance, and a withholding from them the light of truth joined to a ftrong defire of knowing it, n. 1109, 2694. Some in their fleep; and fome in a middle ftate betwixt fleeping and waking, n. 1108. That they who place merit in works, feem to themfelves as hewers of wood, n. 1110. Others differently, in many various ways, n. 699.

they

they are seen from heaven, they appear from thence as a heaven, of a lesser form : they extend in length from east to west, and in breadth from south to north, but appear of less breadth than length. The order of classes is as follows : foremost are they who died infants, and were educated to their early part of youth in heaven, and after such their first tuition in infancy, are appointed hither by the Lord for instruction in knowledge. Behind these are the places for the instruction of those who died adults, and who in this world were in the affection of truth from the good of life. Next to them are such as had professed the Mahometan religion, led a moral good life, believed in one God, and acknowledged the Lord for his prophet, who, after death, finding no help to be had from Mahomet, go to the Lord, and worship him, and acknowledge his divinity, after which they are instructed in the Christian religion. Behind these more to the north are the places appointed for the instruction of the various Gentiles, who had led a good life according to the religion they professed, and that from a conscience agreeing thereto, and so practising what is just and right from an inward law, and not merely in obedience to civil institutes. All such are soon brought to the knowledge of and belief in the Lord through the means of instruction; and the more so, as it is a fundamental of their creed, that God is visible in a human form. These are the greater number [of the appointed for heaven] and the best of them are from Africa.

515. But all are not instructed in the same manner, nor by angels of the like societies: such as were educated in heaven from their infancy, are instructed by angels of the two interior heavens, as not having imbibed dangerous errors [*falsa*] from false principles of religion [*ex falsis religionis*] nor defiled the spiritual part with the pollutions of worldly honours and riches. They who died in their adult state, are, as to the greater part of them, instructed by the angels of the lowest or first heaven, as being of an order better suited to their capacity than the former, who are of too interior a wisdom for their recipiency in their present state. The Mahometans are instructed by angels, who had been of the same religion in this world, and afterwards converted

converted to the Chriſtian; and the Heathens in like manner by their angels.

516. All inſtruction there, is by way of doctrines drawn from the written Word, and not from the Word itſelf ſeparately from the doctrinal form. Thus for example: The Chriſtians are inſtructed from ſuch heavenly doctrines as are moſt adapted to the internal or ſpiritual ſenſe of the Word; others, as the Mahometans and Gentiles, from ſuch as are moſt adequate to their capacity and genius, and may lead them to the ſpiritual life by the way of a Chriſtian morality in a ſort conformable to the beſt and moſt ſublime of their own moral precepts.

517. The way of conveying inſtruction in the other world differs from that on earth, inaſmuch as truths there are committed, not to the memory, but to the life; for the memory of ſpirits is in their life's principle, and they receive and imbibe only what is conformable thereto, for ſpirits are ſo many human forms of their own affections. As the nature of ſpirits is ſuch, therefore they are continually inſpired with an affection for truth for the uſes of life; for the Lord has ſo ordered it, that every one ſhould love the uſes that accord with their particular gifts and qualities; which love is likewiſe heightened by the hope of their becoming angels; for in heaven all particular and ſingular uſes have relation to the general uſe or good of the Lord's kingdom, and may be conſidered as ſo many parts of one whole, ſo that the truths which they learn are both truths and the uſes of truths conjunctly: thus the angelical ſpirits are prepared for heaven. The affection or love of truth for the purpoſes of uſe is inſinuated into them many ways not known in this world, more particularly by various repreſentations of uſes under ſuch delightful forms as affect both their minds and ſenſes with unſpeakable pleaſure, ſo that when any ſpirit is joined to the ſociety for which he was prepared, he then enjoys life moſt when he is in the exerciſe of its proper uſes (272). Hence it may appear,

(272) That every good receives its joy and delight [*ſuum jucundum*] from and according to uſes, and that their particular qualities are reciprocal, n. 3049, 4984, 7038. That the angelical life conſiſts in the goods [*in bonis*] of love and charity, and accordingly in the exerciſe of uſes, n. 453. That the Lord, and his angels from him, have reſpect only to the ends or uſes of things in man, n. 1317, 1645, 5844.

pear, that not the ideal knowledge of truths, as things without us, but an implantation of them in the affections and life for the purpose of uses, is that which qualifies for the kingdom of heaven.

518. There were certain spirits who had flattered themselves in this world, not only with the expectation of going to heaven, but also of being received there with particular marks of distinction on account of their learning, and for their great scientifical knowledge in the Scriptures and the doctrines of the several churches, supposing this to be wisdom, and that such as themselves were meant by those in Dan. xii. 3. "They that be wise "shall shine as the brightness of the firmament." These were consigned over for examination, whether their knowledge resided in their memory only, or was carried also into practical use. There were others who possessed a genuine affection for truth, for the sake of spiritual use and improvement, who, after they had passed through their course of instruction, were received into heaven, and given to know the cause of splendor there, viz. that it was divine truth (which is the essence of light in heaven) in use, which use is the plane or ground that receives the rays of that light, which it converts into various splendors; whereas they whose knowledge resided only in their memory for the purposes of reasoning about truths, and oftentimes to confirm their belief in error; such not being in the light of heaven, but self-exalted through their pride of knowledge into a fancied superiority above angels; these, in order to cure them of their vain conceit, were introduced into the first or lowest heaven, as though to be joined to some society there; but upon their first entrance, the brightness of the light struck them with dimness; their minds were perturbated and confused, and they gasped for breath like dying persons; and upon feeling the heat of heaven (which answers to heavenly love) they were tormented with inward excruciating pains, and immediately cast down from thence; so learning by experience, that it is not knowledge, but

---

5844. That the kingdom of the Lord is the kingdom of uses, n. 453, 696, 1103, 3645, 4054, 7038. That the service of the Lord consists in the exercise of uses, n. 7038. That according to uses in man, such is his quality and distinction, n. 1568, 3570, 4054, 6571, 6934, 6938, 10284.

life

life influenced by knowledge that qualifies for the angelical state: whilst the former, considered in itself alone, is but as a foreign plant; but the latter as a tree of life in the midst of paradise.

519. After that the angels are duly prepared for heaven in the places before described, which comes to pass in a short time, as spiritual minds are of quick comprehension, they are then clothed in angelical garments, which, for the most part, are white as of fine linen, and conducted to the way which leads up to heaven, and delivered to the guardian angels there; after which they are received by other angels, and introduced to different societies, where they partake of various delights: after this every one is led by the Lord's guidance to his particular proper society, and this by various ways, sometimes direct, sometimes otherwise, not known to any of the angels, but to the Lord only. Lastly, When they are come to their own society, their inmost thoughts and affections [*interiora illorum*] open and expand themselves, which meeting with the like returns of cordial sympathy from their fellow-angels, they are immediately known and received by them with a joyful welcome.

520. I am led here to mention a memorable particular concerning the ways which lead from the places before mentioned to heaven, through which the novitiate angels pass thereto: there are eight such, two from every place of instruction, the one of which ascends to the east, the other to the west: they who are appointed to the Lord's cœlestial kingdom [the third heaven] take the eastern way; but they who are appointed to his spiritual kingdom [the second heaven] take the western way. The four ways which lead to the former kingdom are beautifully planted with olive and other fruit bearing trees of various kinds; the other four leading to his spiritual kingdom, with vines and laurels; and this from correspondency, as vines and laurels correspond to the affection of truth and its uses; and olives and fruits, to the affection of good and its uses.

That

That no one is appointed for Heaven by an immediate [arbitrarious] Act of Mercy.

521. They who are not rightly inftructed concerning heaven, and the heavenly life in man, are apt to fuppofe, that admiffion into heaven is by a particular grant of favour and mercy in behalf of certain perfons who are in a particular belief, and have the privilege of a peculiar election through our Lord's interceffion in their behalf; and fome, that all men may be faved by an arbitrary will, without refpect to meetnefs or qualification, nay, even the very devils: but all fuch are utter ftrangers to the nature of man, viz. that he is identically one and the fame with his life's principle, and that this is one and the fame with his predominant love, not only with refpect to his interior, but alfo to his exterior life, for the latter is only the external form, in which his will and intellect manifeft themfelves in vifibility and effect; and therefore, that man is wholly according to his love or ruling paffion, fee above, n. 363: nor do they underftand, that the body lives not from itfelf, but from its fpirit, and that the fpirit of a man is his affection; and that his fpiritual body is no other than his affection in that human form, in which he appears after death, fee above, n. 453 to 460. Ignorance, as touching thefe things, leads many to think, that falvation is nothing more than a mere gratuitous act of favour and good pleafure, called mercy, without any refpect to means or qualification.

522. Something fhall here be faid concerning the divine mercy: and this is no other than the divine compaffion towards all men, to the end that they may be faved, abiding with every one, and never departing from him; and therefore all may be faved, whom it is poffible to fave, but that only in the way of divine means. Thefe are revealed to us in the Scriptures, and are called divine truths, teaching us by what kind of life falvation is attainable; and by thefe truths the Lord, who is loving to every man, directs all in the way to heaven, and imparts to

them a principle of life, provided they refrain from evil, but otherwife they are not receptive of his gift, for evil hinders. This is that pure mercy of the Lord to every one that walketh not in the ways of evil, and which abides with him from infancy to the end of his days here, and forfakes him not in eternity; but not fuch an immediate arbitrarious kind of mercy, as fome falfely fuppofe, by which all may be faved, however unrightcoufly they had lived.

523. The Lord never does any thing contrary to order, for he is himfelf the fountain of it, and the divine truths proceeding from him are the laws of it, by which he conducts the falvation of men, and to which an immediate or arbitrary mercy, with means and fitnefs in the fubject of it, would be a manifeft contrariety. Divine order is heaven in man, which he had perverted by difobedience to its laws, or to divine truths; and therefore muft be reduced by the pure mercy of the Lord by divine truths to the fame order from which he had fallen, and as far as he recovers this ftate, fo much of heaven he receives here, and becomes meet to be a partaker of its joys hereafter; thus he receives all from mere mercy, but not by an immediate unconditional act of it (273).

524. If men might be faved by immediate, arbitrarious mercy, then all would be faved, even the devils, nay, in that

(273) That divine truth proceeding from the Lord conftitutes order, and that divine good is the effence of it, n. 1728, 2258, 8700, 8988. That therefore the Lord is the fountain of order, n. 1919, 2011, 5110, 5703, 10336, 10619. That divine truths are the laws of order, n. 2247, 7995. That the univerfal heaven is difpofed by the Lord according to his divine order, n. 3038, 7211, 9128, 9338, 10125, 10151, 10157; and receives its form from thence, n. 4040 to 4043. That as far as any one lives according to the divine order, or in good according to divine truths, fo much of heaven he receives into himfelf, n. 4839. That man by creation was a form of the divine order as a recipient of it, n. 4219, 4220, 4223—10156, 10472. That man by birth inherits not good and truth, but only evil and falfe, and confequently is in contrariety to the divine order; therefore he is born in mere ignorance, and muft be born again, or regenerated by divine truths, that fo he may be reftored to order, n. 1047, 2307, 2308—10286, 10731. That when the Lord regenerates man, he difpofes all things in him according to the form of heaven, n. 5700, 6690, 9931, 10303. That all evil and falfe is contrary to order, and that fuch as are therein are governed by the Lord not as regulars, but irregulars, n. 4839, 7877, 10778. That it is impoffible for any one that is in the evil principle to be faved by an immediate, inftantaneous act of mercy, as this would be contrary to the divine order, n. 8700.

cafe,

case, there would be no such place as hell; for seeing that the Lord is all mercy, love, and goodness, it would be nothing less than denying his nature, to say, that he could save all men immediately if he would, but is not willing; whereas it is declared in his Word, that the Lord willeth not the death of a sinner, but that all should be saved.

525. The greater part of those, who pass into the other world from Christendom, retain the belief, that they are to be saved by an immediate act of mercy, and accordingly they implore it; but upon examination it is found, that they have no other idea of the happiness of heaven than by admission into it as a place of all delights (without considering the necessity of preparation and fitness for it) thus shewing their ignorance as to the nature of heaven and heavenly joys; upon which it is told them, that the Lord denies entrance into heaven to no one, and that if they desire it, they may not only be admitted, but stay there: accordingly some that were so desirous were admitted; but no sooner did they enter, and feel the heat of heaven, which is that love in which the angels are; and were struck by the influx of the heavenly light, which is divine truth, than they were seized with such an heart-felt agony, that instead of heavenly joy they were racked with infernal pains, and, as it were, mad through anguish, cast themselves down headlong; thus learning, by dear-bought experience, that the fruition of heaven, though all from pure mercy, yet is not from an immediate act of mercy separate from the means of meetness, through preparation, for the heavenly inheritance.

526. I have sometimes conversed with the angels on this subject, and told them, that the greater part of those in this world, who live in sin, in the freedom of conversation concerning heaven and eternal life, speak of going to heaven, as a mere admission into such a place through a mere act of gratuitous favour, and unconditional mercy; and they in particular who lay down faith as the only means of salvation: for having fixed upon this as the fundamental principle of religion, they pay little regard to life, nor to those operations of love which constitute the essence of life, nor to any other means which the Lord has appointed, whereby to render man a recipient of the

spiritual

spiritual life, and of heavenly joys; and thus having rejected the use of all preparatory means, they by necessary consequence from the principle they have adopted, maintain, that God the Father is prevailed upon, by the intercession of his Son, to advance some particular favourites to the kingdom of heaven by special grants of mercy. To which the angels replied, that such a belief was a necessary consequence of the Solifidian doctrine; and as this was the foundation of their creed, no wonder that from an error, so far distant from all truth, should proceed such ignorance among Christians concerning the Lord, concerning the state of life after death, and the joys of heaven; or that they were so little acquainted with the true nature of love and charity, and the necessity of good being joined with truth, to constitute the divine life in man, which consisted no less in the will and its operations, than in thoughts of the mind; and consequently not a persuasion called faith, separate from love, and the effects of love. The angels shew concern for their folly, in supposing that true faith can subsist in any one singly and alone; as faith separated from its origin, which is love, is no other than science, or a certain kind of persuasion, which is no better than a counterfeit of faith (see above, n. 482) and makes no part of the life of man, as not being conjoined with love. Moreover, the angels said, that all of the Solifidian persuasion must necessarily believe, that salvation must be by favour or grant, or from immediate, unconditional mercy (separate from the use of means) as they know both from the light of nature, and from experience, that such kind of separate faith makes no essential part of life, and therefore that evil doers may work themselves into the same doctrinal persuasion of their own salvation with others: and hence it is, that the bad are believed by such to be equally in a salvable state with the good, provided they have but confidence sufficient to apply the merits and intercession of Christ to themselves in their last hours, and to rely on an immediate act of mercy. The angels declared, that they had never known any one that had passed his life in sin, to be made partaker of heavenly joy, whatever confidence he might have had in this world, under the name of faith, as touching his salvation; and being asked as concerning Abraham, Isaac, Jacob,

Jacob, David, and the Apoſtles, whether their portion in heaven was not by a ſpecial grant of immediate mercy and favour; they anſwered, that not one of them, but each had his reception and portion according to what his life had been in this world; that they knew their place and lot, and that they were in the ſame degree of eſtimation and honour with others of their own claſs; that the reaſon of the honourable mention made of them in the written Word, is becauſe, that in the internal ſenſe of it they were ſo many typical repreſentatives of the Lord in their ſeveral characters and callings; thus he was repreſented by Abraham, Iſaac, and Jacob, as to his Divinity and Divine Humanity; by David, as to his Divine Sovereignty; and by the Apoſtles, as the fountain of Divine Truths. Moreover they ſaid, that when the Word was read by any man, they [the angels] received not the ideas of the perſons repreſenting (for names enter not heaven) but inſtead thereof ſo much of the Lord as was repreſented by them; and therefore no mention was made of them in the written Word in heaven (of which ſee above, n. 259) as that Word contains only the inward and ſpiritual ſenſe of that which we have in this world (274).

527. That it is impoſſible for thoſe to receive the principle of heavenly life in the other world, who have rejected and lived contrary to it in this, I can witneſs to from abundant experience in many. There were certain ſpirits which poſſeſſed the notion, that they could readily receive divine truths after death, as ſoon as they ſhould be declared to them by the angels, and that in

(274) That by Abraham, Iſaac, and Jacob, in the inward ſenſe of the word, is meant the Lord, in reſpect to his Divinity, and Divine Humanity, n. 1893, 4615, 6098, 6185, 6276, 6804, 6847. That the name *Abraham* is not known in heaven, n. 1834, 1876, 3229. That by David is to be underſtood the divine ſovereignty or royalty, n. 1888, 9954. That the twelve apoſtles repreſented all divine truths in the Chriſtian church, conſequently, all things appertaining to faith and love, n. 2129, 3354, 3488, 3858, 6397. That Peter repreſented the Lord as to faith; James, as to charity; and John, as to the works of charity, n. 3750, 10087. That the twelve apoſtles, ſitting on twelve thrones to judge the twelve tribes of Iſrael, ſignify that the Lord will proceed in judgment according to the truths and goods of faith and love, n. 2129, 6397. That the names of perſons and places mentioned in the Word have no place in heaven, but are changed into things and ſtates; and that ſuch names cannot be uttered in heaven, n. 1876, 5225, 6516, 10216, 10282, 10432. That the angels alſo think abſtractedly from perſons, n. 8343, 8945, 9007.

confequence thereof, they fhould believe, and change their courfe of life, and become qualified for heaven. An experiment of this kind was made on many who were of the like perfuafion, to the end they might be convinced, that there is no repentance after death: fome of thofe on whom the trial was made, appeared to underftand the truths that were announced to them, and alfo to admit them at firft; but no fooner did they return to their ruling love or life's principle than they immediately rejected them, and argued againft them; and others rejected them as foon as offered, and would hear no more of them. There were fome in particular, who were defirous to be wholly deprived of that governing love, or life's principle [*vita amoris*] which they had contracted in this world, and that the angelical life, or life of heaven, might be infufed inftead thereof: their requeft was granted; but no fooner did the change take effect, than they lay as dead without any power over themfelves. From thefe and other means of experience the fingle-hearted, good fpirits were convinced, that every one's ftate abideth the fame after death; and that beyond this period an evil life cannot be changed for a good one, nor that which is infernal, for one that is angelical; becaufe that every fpirit is in every part throughout the fame with the love that predominates in him, and that a change of it to its contrary would be to deftroy the fpirit. The angels affirm, that a night-owl may fooner be changed into a pigeon, or a buzzard into a bird of paradife, than an infernal fpirit into an angel of heaven. That man continues after death in a ftate conformable to his life in this world, fee above in its proper article, n. 470 to 484. Thus far may fuffice to fhew, that no one is made a partaker of the kingdom of heaven by an act of immediate, unconditional mercy, or without the means and fitnefs of a qualifying preparation.

That it is not so difficult a Thing to live for Heaven, as some suppose.

528. Some suppose that the spiritual life, or that which qualifies for heaven, is extremely difficult; and that because we are told, that we must renounce the world, and die to the lusts of the flesh, and live to the spirit; which they so construe, as if we were to reject all worldly things, particularly the riches and honours of this life; to be constantly exercised in pious meditations of God, salvation, and eternal life, and to employ a great part of our time in prayer, and reading the Word, and other pious books. This they call renouncing the world, and to live, not after the flesh, but after the spirit: but that the truth of the matter is otherwise, I can testify both from experience, and from conversation with the angels; nay, that they who so renounce the world, in order to become spiritual, are such, for the most part, as contract a melancholy and sourness of spirit, as indisposes them for the reception of heavenly joys; whereas in order to qualify and form himself for a heavenly life, is to bear his part in the relative duties and offices of this; and by a life of morality, and a discharge of the duties respecting civil society, ascend to the spiritual life, as preparatory for heaven: for to live an internal life separate from the external, is like dwelling in a house without a proper foundation, which therefore necessarily sinks into the earth, divides, or falls into a ruin.

529. The life of man, when considered in a rational view, will appear to be threefold; the spiritual, the moral, and the civil life; and these three are distinct; for some lead a civil, but not moral and spiritual life; some, both civil and moral, but not spiritual; and some, a civil, moral, and spiritual life also; and the last are they who live a heavenly life, whilst the other two live only the life of this world. From this view it may appear, that the spiritual life, though distinct, is not separate from the natural, or life of this world, but closely con-

nected with it, as the foul with the body, and if feparated from it, would be like the houfe before mentioned; for the moral and civil life conftitute the activity of the fpiritual life; and as the will to good is the property of the latter, fo the doing good is the property of the former, and if this were feparated from the other, then the fpiritual life would confift only in thinking and fpeaking, and the will would remain folitary and inactive, as having no outward termination to reflect and difplay its operations; and yet it is the very principle of the fpiritual life in man.

530. That it is not fo difficult a thing to live for heaven, as many think, may appear from the following confiderations. Who can fay, that he has no power to lead a civil and moral life, when every one from his infancy is educated to it, and may eftablifh his ideas of it from what he fees around him in the world; nay, even the bad (if not abandoned to profligacy) as well as the good, act it externally, and to fave appearances with the world, for the fake of intereft and character? The fpiritual man does but the fame, with this difference, that he has faith in God, and does it, not only in obedience to the laws of fociety, and of moral obligation, but in obedience to the authority of the divine laws; for as he fets God always before him, he has fellowfhip with the angels in heaven, having his inmoft or fpiritual man open to fuch communion; and in this ftate he is an adopted child, under the Lord's leadings, even when he knows it not, difcharges all the duties both of civil and moral obligation from a principle of vital love, and fo ferves the Lord with his whole heart. His juftice and truth, as to external manifeftation and form, appear indeed like the fame in natural men, even of the moft infernal difpofitions, but inwardly they are totally different; for the evil fay and do the fame things from felfifh and worldly refpects only; but having neither confcience, nor fear of God, were it not for human laws, and the fear of fuffering in character, intereft, or other ways, they would give full fcope to their wicked wills, to commit all iniquity with greedinefs, as evidently appears in the other world in fuch as are of the like difpofitions; who, being no longer under fuch outward reftraints, manifeft openly the malignity that is within them,

them, turning into mockery all virtue and godlinefs, and holding on in the fame courfe to eternity, n. 499; whilft they who have the divine laws written in their hearts do all things well, and that more abundantly, as their liberty and freedom from reftraints is the greater (*); adding to their goodnefs wifdom, which is miniftered unto them from the Lord by the angels of wifdom, with whom they are in bleffed fellowfhip. Thus we fee, that the fpiritual man may act in all the relations both of moral and civil life as the natural man does, provided that he adheres clofely to that divine principle within, which is to be the regulator of his will and thoughts, fee above, n. 358, 359, 360.

531. The laws of the fpiritual life, as alfo of the civil and moral life, are laid down in the ten precepts of the decalogue; in the firft three are the laws of the fpiritual life; in the four following, the laws of the civil life; and in the three laft, the laws of the moral life. Now the mere natural man [of decency] pays an external obedience to thefe precepts, as well as the fpiritual man: thus he is prefent at the celebration of divine worfhip in the church, hears preachings, and compofes his exteriour to a form of devotion; he refrains from committing murder, adultery, and theft, bears not falfe witnefs, and defrauds not his neighbour of his goods; but in all thefe things he has regard only to himfelf, and to fave appearances with the world, being inwardly the reverfe of what he appears outwardly, as having no fenfe of God in his heart, playing the hypocrite with the form of religion, and fecretly deriding things facred, as only fo many inventions of ftate policy to keep the fimple multitude in awe and order; and therefore fuch a one ftands in no relation to heaven; and being deftitute of all fpirituality, fo neither can he be faid to poffefs either moral or civil virtue: for though he does not kill, yet he hates and wifhes vengeance on all that oppofe or provoke him, and but for human laws

---

(*) The different motives in thefe two forts of perfons for refraining from the fame things, are well expreffed in the following lines:

" Oderunt peccare boni virtutis amore:
" Tu nihil admittes in te formidine pœnæ."   Hor.

would

would execute his wrath upon them, and therefore is in heart no better than a murderer; nor is it from any better principle that he refrains from adultery, theft, or other crimes and immoralities prohibited in the decalogue. Such a one is every man that difbelieves a God, and has no principle of confcience formed in him by a fenfe of religion: and that this is the cafe with all fuch, appears from like fpirits in the other world, who, being left to their freedom, openly declare againft every thing that is heavenly; and as they think and act like devils, fo with them is their everlafting portion: but they that fear the Lord, and walk in the ways of his commandments with a pure heart, and faith unfeigned, are after death brought into their full interior liberty, and into a degree of wifdom that far furpaffes what they poffeffed before, their forrow is turned into joy, and all being divine within them, makes all things heaven without them. So different are thefe two claffes in the other world, who, to appearance, were fo much alike as to the outward life in this.

532. It is well known that the thoughts, or intellect, which is the eye of the mind, receives that direction, like the eye of the body, which the intention or will gives it, and alfo takes its delight therein. Thus if the intention be directed to heaven, the thoughts become heavenly; if to felf, fenfual; if to this world, earthly; and as the ruling love makes one with the intention, fo from the direction and employment of the thoughts may be known what any one loves moft, and what the interior ftate of his mind is with refpect to things above, and things beneath. Such, for example, as love themfelves, and the world above all things, have the inward gate of their minds fo fhut to all heavenly influx and heavenly things, that they fee not the truths of religion at all, or fo very obfcurely, that they either deny, or underftand them not; the things of fenfe and of this world are all in all with them, and thefe are continually fuggefting many grofs, impure, or profane ideas incompatible with heavenly influx, and the due confideration of divine things. It is the intention or will of man, as obferved before, that directs his thoughts, or internal fight, and if heaven is the object, his whole mind is there, from whence he looks down on this

world,

world, as on things beneath him; and from the same elevation sees and judges all that is evil and false in his inferior nature; which he who is destitute of the same spiritual sight cannot discover, because he is in it, and not above it. Hence we learn from what sources man derives his wisdom, or his folly, which respectively determines his state after death, when he will be left at liberty, not only to will and think, but also to act and speak without disguise, according to the ruling principle within him. Thus much for the distinction between the inward and the outward man.

533. It is not so difficult a thing, as many imagine, for a man so to live, as might qualify him for the heavenly inheritance, were he, when tempted to evil, to stop, and reflect that he ought not to consent to it, as being forbidden by God's command; some such reflection [like that of Joseph] often repeated, would beget an habitual fear of offending, by degrees draw the attention to heavenly things, and open the inward gate of the mind to the divine influx, whereby it would obtain a full sight of the deformity of sin. Every one has received power and freedom so to think and reflect, in order to this process, till the operations of divine grace should overcome all the reluctances of the will, excite an abhorrence to sin in the mind, and subdue the power of it in the soul, till the man experience the truth of those words of our Lord: " My yoke is easy, and my bur- " den is light," Matt. xi. 30. The difficulty with regard to serious consideration and reflection, in the first instance, arises from a hasty surrender of the will to the temptations of evil, till custom in sinning reconciles to it, and then begets love for it; and so the unhappy proficient goes on to excuse, and then to defend it by every kind of fallacious arguments, till at last he confounds all distinction of right and wrong, putting evil for good, and good for evil. Such is the case of those, who, in the early part of life, rush into evil courses, like the horse into the battle, and so, losing all sight of divine truths, become infidels.

534. I had formerly represented to me the way which leads to heaven, and also the way which leads to hell, in the following manner. There was first a broad way bearing to the left or

north, in which many spirits appeared as walking; and at a distance where the broad way terminated was seen a large stone, from which went two ways, the one to the left, and the other to the right; the former was narrow and straight, leading westward to the south; the other broad and spacious, leading obliquely downwards towards hell. They all appeared to hold on their way together, as far as to the great stone; but when they came thither they separated, the good taking the left-hand narrow road leading to heaven; but the bad, not seeing the stone, fell upon it, and received hurt, but recovering themselves went fast on in the broader way to the right, leading to hell. The interpretation of it was given to me afterwards as follows, viz. that by the first broad way, in which both good and bad spirits went together conversing as friends, without any apparent difference between them, are signified those who lived so alike in the way of an external righteousness, as not to be distinguished. By the corner stone at the end of the common broad road, on which the bad stumbled, and afterwards took the way leading to hell, was signified divine truth, denied by those that walk therein, and in the highest sense was signified by that stone the Divine Humanity of our Lord: but they who acknowledged and believed divine truth, and also his Divine Humanity, were conducted in the way leading to heaven; shewing hereby, that the principle from which men act, is that which determines the difference of their states after death; the thoughts of the mind proceeding from the heart and will, being represented in the other life by *ways*; and accordingly in Scripture, the internally righteous are said to walk in the ways of the Lord; and there the quality of spirits is known by the ways that they are seen to walk in. What has been said above may serve to illustrate those words of our Lord: " Enter ye in at the strait gate; for " wide is the gate, and broad is the way that leadeth to de- " struction, and many there be which go in thereat; because " strait is the gate, and narrow is the way which leadeth unto " life, and few there be that find it," Matt. vii. 13, 14; not implying that the way is difficult to find, but only that it is sought, and therefore found by few. By the corner stone before mentioned, seen where the common broad way terminated, and

the

the two opposite ways took their direction, is plainly given to understand the meaning of those other words of our Lord: " The stone which the builders rejected, the same is become " the head of the corner: whosoever shall fall upon that stone " shall be broken; but on whomsoever it shall fall, it will " grind him to powder," Luke xx. 17, 18. The stone signifies divine truth, and the stone or rock of Israel, the Lord as to his Divine Humanity; the builders are the rulers in the church; the head of the corner signifies where the two ways meet; and to fall upon, and be broken to powder, signifies a denial of the truth, and destruction ensuing thereon.

535. It has been given me to converse with some in the other life, who had sequestered themselves from all connexions and commerce with society, and others that placed religion in macerations of the body, and such like austerities of discipline, under the notions of renouncing the world, and of attaining to higher degrees of purity in the spiritual life; but most of these, from having contracted a severity and sourness of mind contrary to a life of charity, had rendered themselves unfit for the society of angels, who are pleasant and amiable, and take delight in exercising offices of kindness and love towards one another. Besides, they who so devote themselves to a life of solitude and abstraction from all social relations, are for the most part deeply infected with conceits of their own fancied merit, whence they are led to look upon heaven as their reward by debt; so that when they are permitted to come into the company of angels, and are witnesses to their joys (which they ascribe solely to the divine goodness) and when they behold their innocent liberty, and free communications, and the pleasure they take in their affectionate exchange of good offices, they are offended, as at things contrary to the strictness of religion; and being not capable of partaking in their joys and delights, they quit their company to consociate with those that are like-minded with themselves, and had lived in the same manner in this world. As to those who affected a sanctimonious shew of godliness in their outward religious forms and mortifications, to pass for saints both here and hereafter, thinking highly of themselves, and despising others; they have no lot with the saints in the

other world, as having profaned sacred things with the impurities of self-love; nay, some of them there become so infatuated and mad with pride, as to fancy themselves gods, and so are consigned over to such infernal societies as resemble themselves. Some are full of subtlety and deceit, who have also their lot among those, who, by various crafty devices, had bewitched the vulgar with a belief of their extraordinary sanctity. Many of these were of the Romish religion, and appeared in like form and outward demeanour, as when in this world; I have conversed with some of them in the other. Hence it may appear, that it is not the solitary life, or life of recluse piety separate from charity, but such a one as may consist with the relative and social duties that best qualifies for the kingdom of heaven, as that wherein truth and justice, benevolence, and acts of charity, in conformity to the divine laws, may have their scope and exercise. These virtues proceeding from, and sanctified by a divine principle within (and not a life of recluse, religious exercises, void of charity towards our neighbour) render the way to heaven both easy and delightful, exalt the soul in all its faculties, and give it a meetness for the participation of cœlestial joys (275).

(275) That a life of piety, separate from a life of charity, avails nothing; but joined therewith is profitable to all things, n. 8252, 8253. That charity to our neighbour consists in truth, justice, and integrity in all our dealings and relations towards him, n. 8120, 8121, 8122. That charity towards our neighbour extends to every thing that a man thinks, wills, and does, n. 8124. That the life of charity is to live according to the divine commands, n. 3249. That to live according to the divine commands is to love the Lord, n. 10143, 10153, 10310, 10578, 10648. That genuine charity is free from all taint of fancied merit, as proceeding from interior affection, and taking delight in the exercise of it, n. 2340, 2373, 2400, 3887, 6388 to 6393. That man continues after death in the same state of charity he was in during this life, n. 8256. That cœlestial happiness is by influx from the Lord into the life of charity, n. 2363. That no one is admitted into heaven merely for thinking, but for also willing and doing the same, n. 2401, 3459. Unless the doing good [according to the power] be joined with willing and thinking it, it avails not to the conjunction of the inner and outward man, nor consequently to salvation, n. 3987.

CONCERNING

CONCERNING

HELL.

That Hell is under the Lord's Government.

536. THroughout the foregoing treatife on heaven it has been fhewed, that the Lord is the God of heaven (fee in particular, n. 2 to 6.) confequently, that the whole government of the heavens is in his hands; and as heaven and hell are to each other as two contraries in mutual oppofition, from the action and reaction of which refults that equilibrium by which all things fubfift; therefore, in order to the prefervation of fuch equilibrium, it necefsarily follows, that he who governs the one muft alfo govern the other; for unlefs the fame Lord were to reftrain the fury and madnefs of hell, the equilibrium would be loft, and all would be deftroyed.

537. But to fay fomething firft concerning equilibrium. It is well known, that when two things are fo in mutual oppofition, that reaction on one fide is equal to action on the other, there remains no excefs or fuperiority of power on either fide; fo that through fuch extinction of power by their equality of oppofition, they become fubject to the difpofal and will of any third agent. Such is the equilibrium betwixt hell and heaven, but not as betwixt two bodies of equal powers; for it is of a fpiritual nature, viz. of falfe againft true, and of evil againft good; from hell proceeds falfe from the root of evil, and from heaven truth from the root or principle of good; and from this equilibrium in fpirituals it is that man's freedom of thinking and willing arifes; for whatfoever a man thinks and wills has relation to evil and its falfe, or to good and its true; therefore when

when the mind is in this balance, it is at full liberty to admit the former from hell, or the latter from heaven; and in this equipoise man ſtands by appointment of the great Governor of heaven and hell: but why this is the caſe with him, and that he is not wholly ſeparated from the ſphere of evil and falſe, and fixed in that of good and true, ſhall be ſpoken of under its proper article.

538. It has ſometimes been given me to perceive the ſphere of falſe from evil iſſuing from hell, as a perpetual endeavour or malignant will [*conatus*] to deſtroy all good and truth, joined to rage and madneſs at not being able to effect it; but this efflux of malice was principally directed againſt the Divinity of the Lord, as the fountain of all good and truth: on the other hand was perceived a ſphere of truth from good from heaven oppoſing and reſtraining the fury and madneſs of the former, from whence proceeds an equilibrium. The heavenly ſphere was perceived to be an emanation from the Lord, though it appeared as proceeding from the angels; but the latter could not really be the caſe, as every angel knows and acknowledges, that no good and truth originates in them, but all from the Lord.

539. All power in the ſpiritual world appertains to truth iſſuing from good, and none to falſe iſſuing from evil, and this, becauſe the Deity, who is the ſource of all power, is alſo the ſource of all good and truth, which being only in heaven, and their contraries in hell, therefore to the former kingdom belongs all power, and none to the latter: ſee in the articles concerning the firſt, ſecond, and third ſtate of man, n. 491 to 520: and that all power belongs to truth from good, ſee the chap. *Concerning the Power of the Angels*, n. 228 to 233.

540. Such is the equilibrium betwixt heaven and hell; and all in the world of ſpirits are in this equilibrium, as being betwixt both; and hence it is, that all men in this world are in the like equilibrium, as being under the Lord's government through the miniſtry of the ſpirits in the world of ſpirits; of which hereafter. Thus all things are balanced by the wiſdom, power, and goodneſs of the Great Sovereign of the univerſe, who keeps hell within its bounds, and preſerves the world from

being

being deftroyed by evil. In this equilibrium ftands the liberty or free will of men.

541. Hell has its diftinct focieties as well as heaven, and as many in number, every fociety in the one having its oppofite in the other, and that in reference to equilibrium; and as the focieties in heaven are claffed according to their diftinctions as good and truth, fo are the infernal focieties, according to their diftinctions as to evil and falfe: for every good has its oppofite evil, and every truth its oppofite falfe, there not being any thing without its relation to a contrary, by which it is diftinguifhed both in quality and degree; nay, this gives the difference to all perception and fenfation. And thus the Lord difpofes and regulates the evil in hell into focieties of contradiftinction and oppofition to the focieties in heaven, for the fake of order and equilibrium.

542. As there is the fame number of focieties in hell as in heaven, fo there are as many different hells; for as every fociety in heaven, is heaven in a leffer form (fee above, n. 51 to 58) fo every fociety in hell, is hell in a leffer form; and as in the general divifion there are three heavens, fo alfo three hells, the loweft of which is refpectively oppofite to the inmoft or third heaven; the middle hell, to the middle or fecond heaven; and the uppermoft, to the firft or loweft heaven.

543. A word here, as to the adminiftration of the Lord's dominion over the hells, which, in general, is (by a common efflux of divine good and truth from the heavens, by which the evil efflux from the hells is obftructed and reftrained) and alfo by a fpecial efflux from each of the heavens, and from each fociety therein: and in particular, they are governed by fuch angels as are commiffioned to infpect and ftill the tumults and madnefs that may arife therein; and fometimes angels are fent to the infernal focieties to reduce them to order by their perfonal prefence. In general, the infernals are governed by their fears, and fome by thofe of the fame kind which awed them here; but as thefe for. the moft part wear off by degrees, or are infufficient to influence them, they are chiefly deterred from perpetrating their wickednefs by the dread of fuffering for it. Now the punifhments in their ftate are multifarious, more gentle, or more

B b b b b

more severe, according to their malefactions: for the most part, they are placed under discipline to such as are more malignant than themselves, who keep them under subjection by subtle arts and devices, or by severity and dread of punishment, but are not allowed to extend their severity beyond the bounds appointed. But it must be observed, that the only means of keeping these rebellious spirits in order, is the dread of punishment.

544. It has hitherto obtained in the world, as an article of belief, that there is one certain Devil, who rules as a king over hell; and that he was created an angel of light, but, upon his rebelling against the Almighty, was cast down from heaven with his apostate followers: and this belief is grounded on a literal intepretation of those passages of Scripture, where the words Devil, Satan, and Lucifer occur; whereas by Devil and Satan in those places is meant hell; by the former, that hell which is hindermost [*quod à tergo*] and occupied by the worst of the devils, called evil genii; and by Satan, that hell which is foremost, and occupied by such as are of lesser malignity, and called evil spirits: and by Lucifer, such are meant as are from Babel or Babylon, who are for usurping a dominion and power even to heaven. That there is no one particular Devil that rules as chief in the hells may be gathered from hence, that all both in the heavens and in the hells are from the human race (see n. 311 to 317) in which are myriads of millions from the creation to this time; and that every one in the latter, is a Devil of the same quality, which distinguished his particular enmity against all that is divine and good when in this world, see above, n. 311, 312.

That the Lord casts none into Hell, but that the Spirits cast themselves into it.

545. It is a prevailing opinion with many, that God turns away his face from man, rejects and casts him into hell; in a word, that he is angry with him for sin, and inflicts vindictive punishment upon him on that account; and they confirm themselves

selves in this belief from like expressions in the Scriptures, not considering, that the spiritual sense of the word, which is the true interpreter of the letter, is very different. Now the genuine doctrines of the Christian church, as founded on the spiritual sense of the word, teach us, that God is not inexorable, nor implacable, neither hath any vindictive wrath, nor casts any one into hell: and this all may plainly know, that read the Scriptures with any degree of divine light in their understandings, as He is there represented as the fountain of all good, love, and mercy, and consequently, that it is contrary to his nature and essence to reject and cast away any: but contrariwise, that he willeth the good and happiness of all men, and dealeth with them according to his infinite love and mercy. They that so read the Word of God will not fail to discern therein that hidden, spiritual sense which gives light and life to the letter, which is written in a sense accommodated to our natural capacities, and first rudiments of knowledge.

546. Men of an enlightened understanding, moreover, see good and evil in the same fulness of contrariety and opposition that heaven and hell stand in to each other, and how all good comes from the former, and all evil from the latter (n. 7 to 12) and consequently, that man is continually drawn to good by the Lord of heaven, as well as to evil by the attraction of hell; and that unless man stood between these two contrary attractions, he would neither have thought, will, nor liberty, these being the effects of his equilibrium betwixt good and evil; consequently, were the Lord so to turn away from man, as to leave him wholly to the power of evil, he would immediately cease to be human. This divine influence extends to every man both bad and good, only with this difference, that in respect to the former, its operation consists in withdrawing from evil; in respect to the latter, in attracting to all good; and the cause of the difference is the quality or will of the recipient.

547. It has here been shewed, that the evil which a man does, is by influx from hell; and that the good which he does, is by influx from the Lord; but by believing [and consenting to it as such] that the evil which he does, is from himself, he makes it his proper own, and therefore is the cause of his own evil.

evil. Evil in man [as his choice] is hell within him; for whether we call it evil or hell, it amounts to the same. Now as far as man is the cause of his own evil, so far he is his own leader to hell; and so far is the Lord from being chargeable with his deſtruction, that He does all that divine goodneſs can do to deliver him from it, as far as can conſiſt with his choice and free will. All that becomes eſſential in a man's will and love remains with him after death (n. 470 to 484); he that wills and loves evil in this world, wills and loves the ſame after death, and then it is no longer ſeparable from him; and therefore it is, that he who by choice continues in evil here, binds himſelf to hell, and is actually in it in ſpirit, even in this life, and after death deſires nothing more than to be where his own beloved evil may be in its proper province and exerciſe; conſequently, ſuch a one is caſt into hell by himſelf, and not by the Lord.

548. How the above is effected ſhall here be mentioned: When any one firſt enters the other world, he is received by angels, who do him all kind offices, enter into converſation with him concerning the Lord, heaven, and the angelical life, and inſtruct him in various kinds and relations of good and truth; but if the perſon (now become a ſpirit) be one that was acquainted with the like things in this world, but in his heart had rejected and deſpiſed them; in this caſe, after ſome ſhort conference with the angels, he deſires his diſmiſſion: upon which they leave him. He then, after ſome conferences with others, aſſociates with ſpirits like unto himſelf (ſee above, n. 445) which done, he turns away from the Lord, and ſets his face towards that particular hell which he had fellowſhip with in this world, and where the infernals are of the ſame evil affections with himſelf. By this we may learn, that the Lord ſtrives with every ſpirit to draw him to himſelf by the miniſtry of angels, and by an influx from heaven; but that ſuch as are under the dominion of ſin are reluctant to all his gracious means for good to them, being drawn away from them as by a rope by their evil propenſities, and ſo voluntarily caſt themſelves into hell. This will ſeem incredible to moſt in this world, from the general idea conceived of hell; nor do thoſe miſerable wretches think that they ſo

precipitate

precipitate themſelves, but only that they enter in of their own accord, though ſuch of them as enter their diſmal priſons under ardent propenſities to evil, appear to the good ſpirits as if they were caſt headlong thither; and from this appearance of precipitation comes the notion of the Lord's caſting them into hell by his Almighty power; ſee more on this ſubject hereafter, n. 574. Let thus much ſuffice to ſhew, that the ſinner's deſtruction and caſting into hell, is not from the Lord, but from himſelf both in this world and the other.

549. That the Lord, who is the eſſential good, love, and mercy, cannot exerciſe them towards all alike, is becauſe of the hinderances which evil and falſe lay in the way, and ſo weaken or repel the divine emanations. Evils and falſes are as ſo many black clouds, which, by their interpoſition between the ſun and the human eye, intercept its lovely light and cheering influences, whilſt the ſun continues the ſame, all glorious, and ſtrives to diſſipate the obſtructing medium, nay, tranſmits, though a fainter, light through the intermediate vail. The caſe is ſimilar in the ſpiritual world: the Lord and his divine love are there repreſented by the ſpiritual ſun (n. 116 to 140) and the light thereof is divine truth, n. 126 to 140; the black clouds are the falſes from evil; and the eye ſignifies the underſtanding; and as far as any one there, is in the falſes of evil [*in falſis ex malo*] in the ſame degree of darkneſs and thickneſs is the cloud that ſurrounds him. This compariſon may repreſent to us how the Lord is preſent to every man, but differently according to his recipiency.

550. Severe puniſhments are appointed for the evil ſpirits in the ſpiritual world, to deter them from the commiſſion of evil; and the infliction of them appears as if from the Lord; but in reality it all proceeds from the evil that is in them; for evil and its puniſhment are inſeparable companions. Infernal ſpirits wiſh and delight in nothing more than to do miſchief, and torment others that are not under the divine protection; and as all that offend through malicious wickedneſs withdraw themſelves from that protection, on ſuch they ruſh and exerciſe their cruelty. This may be illuſtrated from the adminiſtrations in this world, where the puniſhment alſo follows its evil. Thus human laws have

have provided a penalty for every crime, and which the delinquent brings upon himself, only with this difference, that offences may be concealed here, but not in the other life. Thus the Lord can no more be said to be the author of the sinner's misery, than the king, the judge, or the law to be the cause of the criminal's punishment, as having nothing to do with the guilt that entails it upon him.

All that are in the Hells, are in the very Principle of Evil, and in Oppofition to Truth from the Love of Self, and the Love of the World.

551. All that are in the hells are in evil and its refpective falfes, and none in evil and truth conjunctively. The greateft part of evil fpirits had been taught the rudiments of religion in this world in their very childhood, and afterwards further inftructed in the knowledge of the truth by their paftors, and in converfation; nay, fome of them, by hypocritical appearances in their words and actions, had paffed for fincere Chriftians, whilft at the fame time they had abftained from evil, only through fear of the laws, human refpects, or other felfifh confiderations; but in the other world (where all external motives and reftraints are removed) they fhew outwardly what they are inwardly, and that all their knowledge and practice of truth and good were nothing but fpeculation and imitation, without reality and principle. In this their internal ftate they can no longer fpeak the truth, or counterfeit the good; but the evil that rules within them, and exercifes dominion over them, manifefts itfelf in all their words and actions. Every evil fpirit is brought into this ftate before he is caft into hell (fee above, n. 499 to 512); and this is called vaftation as to good and truth (276), which means

(276) That the evil, before they are caft into hell, are divefted of all that is good and true, on which they betake themfelves to hell of their own accord, n. 6977,

means the reducing any one to his proper principle, or condition of fpirit, and to the free liberty of acting according thereto; fee above, n. 425.

552. In this ftate of man after death, when he is no longer between man and fpirit, as in his firft ftate (of which above, n. 491 to 498) but is truly and properly a fpirit, having both face and form correfponding to the inward difpofition of his mind, or, in other words, being an external type of his fpiritual life; in this their third ftate the fpirits appear to be what they really are at firft fight, and are known, not only by their countenances, and the forms of their fpiritual bodies, but alfo by their fpeech and geftures, for now they are uniformly their proper felves; and as there is a mutual communication of the thoughts and affections in the world of fpirits, fo they naturally turn to and confort with fuch as are like themfelves, for with them only they have liberty and true enjoyment. We are to know, that mutual communications in the fpiritual world are according to the converfion of the face, and that they who are in the fame kind of love, conftantly front one another, which way foever they turn their bodies; fee above, n. 151. Hence it is, that all the infernal fpirits have their faces averted from the Lord towards an oppofite black fpot, that is to them inftead of the fun and moon of this world; but that all the angels of heaven turn their faces to the Lord, as to the fun and moon of heaven; fee above, n. 123, 143, 144, 151. From what has here been faid it will appear, that all the infernals are in the elements of evil, and all its derivations of falfe, and that their fole bent and direction is towards it.

553. All fpirits in the hells, when feen in the light of heaven, appear in the feveral forms of their particular evils refpectively, as fo many types or portraits thereof; for in every one the interiour manifefts itfelf in the exteriour, and exhibits the fignatures of his particular diftinction, fo as to be vifibly known

6977, 7039, 7795, 8210, 8232, 9330. That it is not the Lord, but they who diveft themfelves, n. 7642, 7926. That all evil has its refpective falfe, and therefore all who are in evil, are likewife in falfe, though fome know it not, n. 7577, 8094. That they who are in evil cannot but think falfe from themfelves, n. 7437. That all that are in hell fpeak only falfe from evil, n. 1695, 7351, 7352, 7357, 7392, 7698.

to be what he is, by his face, by his spiritual body, his speech, and his geſtures. Theſe forms in general, are ſuch as expreſs contempt of others, and threatening of thoſe that refuſe them homage; forms of hatred and revenge of various kinds; forms of rage and cruelty, &c. But when ſuch ſpirits receive adulation, homage, or worſhip from others, their features ſoften into a ſhew of ſelf-complacency and ſecret ſatisfaction. It is no eaſy matter to deſcribe theſe forms under their various appearances, as no two are exactly alike; only it muſt be obſerved, that among all that are in the ſame ſpecies of evil in any ſociety, there is one common ground of ſimilitude, or, as it may be called, of family likeneſs, however it may be diverſified in the individuals. In general, their faces are hideous and ghaſtly, like thoſe of carcaſſes, ſome black, ſome reſembling firebrands, and ſome deformed and ugly with warts, carbuncles, and running ſores; many appear as having no face, but in the room of it ſomething of a viſage of hair or bone; and ſome only a kind of ſnout with prominent teeth; their bodies alſo are monſtrous; and their ſpeech ſounds as from anger, hatred, or revenge; for, as every one ſpeaks from his own falſe, ſo he ſounds his voice from his own evil; in a word, they are all ſo many images of their particular and proper hell. It has not been given me to ſee the form of hell in the whole of it, but only it has been told me, that as the univerſal heaven reſembles in form one man, ſo the univerſal hell reſembles in form one devil, and may be conceived under that image, ſee above, n. 544; but as to the form of particular hells, or infernal ſocieties, it has often been given me to ſee it, for at the apertures or mouths of thoſe hells, which are called the gates of hell, there for the moſt part appears a monſter, repreſenting the general form of thoſe that are within it: their rage and cruelty likewiſe are repreſented by ſuch horrid images, as I am reſtrained from mentioning. But it is to be remarked, that though the infernal ſpirits appear thus like hideous monſters in the light of heaven, yet to one another they appear as men, and that from divine mercy, that they may not be ſo abominable to one another, as they are to the angels. But ſuch appearance is all deception, for no ſooner does the light of heaven appear, than their human forms exhibit

them-

themselves in their real monstrosity, for in that light every thing appears as it is; for this reason they shun the heavenly light as much as possible, and seek to appear in their own light, which resembles that which comes from fire coals, or burning brimstone; but even this light is turned into mere darkness by any influx of that from heaven. Hence it is, that darkness and thick darkness are predicated of hell, to denote the falses from evil that are there.

554. Upon a narrow inspection into those monstrous forms of the infernal spirits, expressing, as was observed before, contempt of others, and also hatred and vindictive anger towards such as did not favour and honour them, it appeared, that they were in general so many forms of the love of self and of the world, and that their particular differences were but so many derivations from thence; and it was also told me by the angels, and also confirmed by much experience, that these two loves were their ruling passions in hell, and were fundamental in the constitution of it; and that love to the Lord and our neighbour were the prevailing and constituent principles of the kingdom of heaven; and that those two infernal, and these two heavenly loves, were diametrically opposite.

555. At first I was in wonder how it came to pass, that the love of the world, and the love of self, should be of so diabolical a nature, as to give such monstrous forms to such as were under the dominion of these passions; whereas in this world we are not apt to pass condemnation on the love of self further than it manifests itself in that elation of mind with respect to external things, which we call pride; and that short of this, the love of man's self is a becoming vivacity of spirit, inciting to a laudable ambition in quest of honourable employments and offices of publick usefulness; and that without sense of honour, and love for distinction and glory, the mind of man would be torpid and inactive. Thus the men of this world reason, little considering that the love of self, considered in its own nature, is of infernal extraction, and that which is the beginning of hell in man; which leads to the saying something concerning this love, and to shew how all evils and their respective falses [*omnia mala et inde falsa*] originate in it.

556. Self-

to be what he is, by his face, by his spiritual body, his speech, and his gestures. These forms in general, are such as express contempt of others, and threatening of those that refuse them homage; forms of hatred and revenge of various kinds; forms of rage and cruelty, &c. But when such spirits receive adulation, homage, or worship from others, their features soften into a shew of self-complacency and secret satisfaction. It is no easy matter to describe these forms under their various appearances, as no two are exactly alike; only it must be observed, that among all that are in the same species of evil in any society, there is one common ground of similitude, or, as it may be called, of family likeness, however it may be diversified in the individuals. In general, their faces are hideous and ghastly, like those of carcasses, some black, some resembling firebrands, and some deformed and ugly with warts, carbuncles, and running sores; many appear as having no face, but in the room of it something of a visage of hair or bone; and some only a kind of snout with prominent teeth; their bodies also are monstrous; and their speech sounds as from anger, hatred, or revenge; for, as every one speaks from his own false, so he sounds his voice from his own evil; in a word, they are all so many images of their particular and proper hell. It has not been given me to see the form of hell in the whole of it, but only it has been told me, that as the universal heaven resembles in form one man, so the universal hell resembles in form one devil, and may be conceived under that image, see above, n. 544; but as to the form of particular hells, or infernal societies, it has often been given me to see it, for at the apertures or mouths of those hells, which are called the gates of hell, there for the most part appears a monster, representing the general form of those that are within it: their rage and cruelty likewise are represented by such horrid images, as I am restrained from mentioning. But it is to be remarked, that though the infernal spirits appear thus like hideous monsters in the light of heaven, yet to one another they appear as men, and that from divine mercy, that they may not be so abominable to one another, as they are to the angels. But such appearance is all deception, for no sooner does the light of heaven appear, than their human forms exhibit

them-

themselves in their real monstrosity, for in that light every thing appears as it is; for this reason they shun the heavenly light as much as possible, and seek to appear in their own light, which resembles that which comes from fire coals, or burning brimstone; but even this light is turned into mere darkness by any influx of that from heaven. Hence it is, that darkness and thick darkness are predicated of hell, to denote the falses from evil that are there.

554. Upon a narrow inspection into those monstrous forms of the infernal spirits, expressing, as was observed before, contempt of others, and also hatred and vindictive anger towards such as did not favour and honour them, it appeared, that they were in general so many forms of the love of self and of the world, and that their particular differences were but so many derivations from thence; and it was also told me by the angels, and also confirmed by much experience, that these two loves were their ruling passions in hell, and were fundamental in the constitution of it; and that love to the Lord and our neighbour were the prevailing and constituent principles of the kingdom of heaven; and that those two infernal, and these two heavenly loves, were diametrically opposite.

555. At first I was in wonder how it came to pass, that the love of the world, and the love of self, should be of so diabolical a nature, as to give such monstrous forms to such as were under the dominion of these passions; whereas in this world we are not apt to pass condemnation on the love of self further than it manifests itself in that elation of mind with respect to external things, which we call pride; and that short of this, the love of man's self is a becoming vivacity of spirit, inciting to a laudable ambition in quest of honourable employments and offices of publick usefulness; and that without sense of honour, and love for distinction and glory, the mind of man would be torpid and inactive. Thus the men of this world reason, little considering that the love of self, considered in its own nature, is of infernal extraction, and that which is the beginning of hell in man; which leads to the saying something concerning this love, and to shew how all evils and their respective falses [*omnia mala et inde falsa*] originate in it.

556. Self-

556. Self-love is that principle in any one that leads him to seek his own good only, and that of others no further than it may be subservient thereto; nay, such a one is a mercenary in the whole of his zeal and regards for his religion, his country, or any human society, and all his wishes and endeavours for their respective interests center in views to his own private advantage, honour, or welfare, and therefore he cannot so properly be said to love them, as himself in them, for self is the root of his love; and as the root is evil, so is the fruit also. Such a one may indeed love his children and descendants, and those who are nearly connected with him by the ties of consanguinity or interest, and such he calls his own, but still the matter reverts to the same, for he loves them only as so many parts of his own dear self; and the same holds good in regard to the affection he bears to those who shew him respect and honour.

557. The odiousness of self-love will manifestly appear by comparison with its opposite; or that love which is cœlestial, consisting in the love of uses for the sake of usefulness, and the love of good for the sake of goodness, whether a man exercise himself therein in behalf of religion, his country, or fellow-citizens, studying and labouring to promote their interest and welfare with all the sincerity of a cordial affection, and takes pleasure in the work, without any view to consequences respecting self. This is to love God with all our heart, and our neighbour as ourselves; and as we do this from the love which is from God, so in doing it we glorify him, who is the giver of every good and perfect gift. But how different is the man of self, who, being the idol of his own vanity, considers others as his slaves, and only estimates them by the service and worship they pay him; little knowing, that so far as he departs from the disinterested principle of cœlestial love, so far is he distant from the kingdom of heaven.

558. As far as any one is actuated by this divine principle of heavenly love in the conscientious and affectionate discharge of all the relative duties of religion and morality, so far he is under the divine guidance and safeguard, whilst the man of self-love takes the government out of the Lord's hands into his own, and becomes a slave to the hereditary corruptions of his nature; and

and as in man, through his original depravity, dwelleth no good thing, so in his unconverted state evil appears to him as good, and good as evil, " becaufe of the blindnefs of his heart," loving himfelf more than God, and earth above heaven (277), nay, corrupting the very good that he does, by placing felf in the center of it, as the object of his affections. There are certain evil fpirits that dwell in thofe regions under the heavens that lie between the north and the weft, which with great fubtlety know how to practife on the minds of virtuous fpirits, fo as to give them a turn to the felfifh and other bad properties of nature, and this either by means of open flattery, or by artful infinuations into their affections; and fo far as they fucceed in their wicked devices, they draw, for the time, the minds and thoughts of fuch virtuous fpirits from heavenly things, darken their underftanding, and call forth and ftir up the corrupt properties of their nature.

558. That the love of felf is oppofite to the love of our neighbour will appear from the origin and effence of both: they who are led by the former principle go by this maxim, that charity begins at home, and as every one is his own neareft, fo he fhould be his own deareft neighbour. Thus his love to others originates in felf, and iffuing thence, as from its center, leffens as it proceeds, according to the diminution of his interefting connexions, making no account of the wifdom or probity of others, but only of their fubferviency to his own private ends, and holding all for his enemies that crofs them. Such is the corrupt tree of felf-love, and fuch the corrupt fruit that it brings forth; whereas true and genuine love to our

(277) That all that conftitutes man's felf, as derivative from his parents, is entirely evil, n. 210, 215, 731, 876—10284, 10286, 10731. That it is the original fin of man's nature to love himfelf more than God, and this world more than heaven, and his neighbour only for his own fake, and confequently, that he may be called a compound love of felf and of the world, n. 694, 731, 4317, 5660. That from the predominant loves of felf and of the world proceeds evil of every kind, n. 1307, 1308, 1321—9348, 10038, 10742; fuch as contempt of others, enmity, hatred, revenge, deceit, cruelty, n. 6667, 7372, 7374, 9348, 10038, 10742: and that from thefe evils come falfes of every kind, n. 1047, 10283, 10284, 10286.

neigh-

neighbour (278) is of heavenly extraction, a stream from the fountain of all perfection, the gift of the Lord, communicating itself, like its Divine Author, to all that are receptive of it : " It suffereth long, and is kind ; it seeketh not its own things ; " it beareth all things, believeth all things, hopeth all things, " endureth all things, and never faileth ; and it comprehendeth " all the properties of that wisdom which is from above, being " pure, peaceable, gentle, easy to be entreated, full of mercy " and good fruits, without partiality, and without hypocrisy."

559. So unbounded is the ambition, so insatiable the thirst of rule in self-love, that were it free from all restraints, and had power equal to its will, it would aim at the sovereignty, not only of the whole earth, but of heaven also. What examples have we of this unlimited ambition in those greedy conquerors, who, not satisfied with kingdoms and empires, have aspired after universal dominions ; and also in Ecclesiastical Babylon the Great, by her arrogant, usurping claims to divine authority and power. All of this character after death are on the side of hell against the Lord and his kingdom : see a little piece, *Concerning the Last Judgment, and the Destruction of Babylon.*

560. If we figure to our minds a society of such as love themselves only, and others but for their own sakes, such a love must appear to us no other than that of a company of robbers,

(278) They who have not a right understanding concerning the duty of love to our neighbour, are apt to suppose, that every man falls under this denomination, and that therefore we must be beneficent to all indiscriminately, n. 6704 : and some, that every man is nearest neighbour to himself, and therefore that charity is founded in self, n. 6933. That they who are under the dominion of self-love go by that maxim, n. 8120. How every one is neighbour to himself explained, n. 6933 to 6938. That the Christian, who loves God above all things, loves his neighbour from a divine principle, n. 6706, 6711, 6819, 6824. That the differences, as to our neighbour, are as many as the differences of good in him ; and that to regulate and proportion our beneficence towards him is the office of Christian prudence, n. 6707, 6710, 6818. That these differences are innumerable, and therefore the ancients, who understood them, reduced the exercises of charity into classes, and distinguished them by their proper names, by which their several specifick differences were noted, and rules of religious prudence laid down for the direction of their charity, n. 2417, 6629. 6705, 7259 to 7262. That the principal doctrine in the ancient church was the doctrine of charity towards our neighbour, and that therein consisted their chief wisdom, n. 2417, 2385, 3419, 3420, 4844, 6628.

who

who continue in all good agreement and friendlinefs whilſt they are confederates in their iniquity, but are no ſooner ſeparated than they are ready to exerciſe the ſame villany on one another, as on ſtrangers. Self-love, where intereſt is concerned, is the ſame principle in others, however covered with the vail of an external decorum, as being equally void of juſtice, conſcience, and religion. This will appear ſtill more evidently from the infernal ſocieties of this character mentioned hereafter.

561. The inmoſt thoughts and affections of thoſe abovementioned being thus turned wholly to ſelf and the world, and ſo from the Lord and the things of his kingdom, they fall under the power of infection from their other natural corruptions, and this, becauſe they ſo render themſelves unreceptive of the divine influence, which can alone ſubdue their evil, and renovate their nature; ſo impoſſible it is for thoſe to be helped, who turn their backs upon the Lord, and wilfully oppoſe the corruptions of their nature to the influences of his grace. Hence it is, that in the other world all ſuch turn their faces from the Lord towards a certain dark orb, which is to them a ſubſtitute for the ſun of this world, and diametrically oppoſite to the ſun of heaven, the repreſentative of the Lord; ſee above, n. 123. Darkneſs alſo ſignifies evil, and the ſun of this world emblematically ſignifies the love of ſelf (279).

562. Such as are abſorbed in the love of ſelf are addicted to the following evils in general, contempt of others, envy, enmity towards thoſe that ſide not with them, and hatred, if againſt them, revenge, craft, deceit, uncharitableneſs and cruelty; and with reſpect to ſpirituals, an averſion to divine things and religious worſhip, which in the other life becomes changed into hatred towards them, and thoſe that are addicted to them. I once converſed with a certain ſpirit that had been in great power in this world, and in the ſuperlative love of ſelf, who was poſſeſſed with ſuch an abominable hatred to all that was divine, that he could not bear to hear the name of God mentioned,

---

(279) That the ſun of this world is an emblem of the love of ſelf, n. 2441. In what ſenſe to worſhip the ſun, is to worſhip thoſe things that are contrary to divine love, and to the Lord, n. 2441, 10584. That an ardent ſun emblematically ſignifies evil concupiſcence, n. 8487.

E e e e e   more

565. As to the love of the world; though it be highly dangerous and pernicious to the foul of man, yet it has not altogether the fame degree of malignity with the forementioned love, as not ſtanding in the fame direct oppoſition to all love of heavenly things. It ſhall ſuffice here to obſerve, that it conſiſts in the general, in an eager deſire after the riches of this world, and to acquire them by any means, however indirect; and alſo in ſuch a paſſionate fondneſs for them, as alienates the affections from all love of ſpiritual things, and from true love towards our neighbour, which is of ſpiritual extraction. This love of the world is multifarious in kind; thus it is the love of riches, as theſe may be the means to worldly honour and eminence of ſtation; or it is the love of dignity and eminence, as theſe may be the means ſubſervient to the acquiſition of riches; it is the love of riches, in order to a fuller gratification of the ſenſes, for oſtentation, and the pride of life; or it is the love of riches for their own ſake, and ſo the fame with avarice. Theſe, with many others, are the ſnares and hinderances that the love of the world lays in our way to heaven: to guard us againſt the dangers and deluſions of which is that important caution given; " Love not the world, neither the things that " are in the world. If any man love the world, the love of " the Father is not in him," 1 John ii. 15.

What is meant by Hell Fire, and Gnaſhing of Teeth.

566. Hitherto very few have rightly underſtood what is meant in Scripture by hell fire, and the gnaſhing of teeth, as ſpoken of thoſe that are in hell, and that becauſe they have taken theſe expreſſions, not in their ſpiritual, but literal ſenſe only; and accordingly ſome have thereby underſtood material fire, ſome torment in general, ſome remorſe of conſcience, and others that it was only made uſe of to deter men from ſin by the conſideration of its penal conſequence; whilſt by gnaſhing of teeth, they have underſtood as meant ſuch an actual ſound, or
a horror

a horror like that occasioned by it; but these words, like the rest of the Scriptures, have a more inward signification; for though the spiritual things contained therein must be expressed by such as are natural, in accommodation to the natural understanding of man, yet to the mind that is capable of receiving it, they are to be interpreted according to their recondite and spiritual sense; it shall therefore here be explained what is meant by fire and gnashing of teeth, as applied to the sufferings of evil spirits in the other world.

567. There is a twofold origin of heat, the one from the sun of heaven, which is the Lord, and the other from the sun of this world; the heat from the former is spiritual, and in its essence is love (see above, n. 126 to 140); the heat from the latter is natural, and has not love for its essence, but serves as a receptacle to spiritual heat or love. That love in its essence is heat or fire, is indicated by the fervor it communicates, first to the mind, and then to the body of man, according to its degree and quality, in winter as well as summer; and also from the increasing heat of the blood from its influence. That natural heat serves as a receptacle of the spiritual heat, or love, appears from the desire in all animals towards the other sex in the spring and summer seasons; not that this orgasm proceeds from natural heat, any farther than as this disposes their bodies to receive the spiritual heat (the essence of which is love) from the spiritual world; for the spiritual world operates by influx on the natural, as cause on effect, but not so the natural on the spiritual; and therefore it is a great error to think that animal love is caused by the natural heat, for love is a property of life, and all life is spiritual; nay, the whole natural world exists and subsists by influx from the spiritual world. To this all the subjects of the vegetable kingdom owe their vegetation, virtues, and increase, whilst the natural heat only does the office of opening and expanding their seeds and vessels, and of disposing them for the reception of the genial and fructifying influences of the spiritual world; thus joining in concurrent evidence to this truth, that there are two kinds of heat, the one spiritual, and the other natural, the former of which is from the sun of heaven, and the latter from the sun of this world; and that by influx

influx from the first, and the co-operation of both, are produced those visible effects which present themselves to us in this natural world (280).

568. The spiritual heat in man is his vital heat; for, as was said before, its essence is love. This is the heat which is signified by fire in the Word; love to the Lord and our neighbour by the heavenly fire; and the love of self and the world by the fire of hell.

569. Both infernal and cœlestial love originate from the same divine principle, but the former becomes infernal only from the will and disposition of the recipient; for all influx from the spiritual world is according to the condition or state of the subject receiving it, in like manner with the heat and light from the sun of this world, which, operating in odoriferous plants and flowers, produces the most grateful and delicious scents; whilst the same falling upon putrid carcases, and fœtid bodies, gives them to exhale the most offensive stinks. Thus likewise the same light from the same sun which strikes the eye with pleasing and refreshing colours from some objects, causes others to reflect a sad and mournful hue. The case is the same with respect to the heat and light proceeding from the heavenly sun; for when these enter by influx into good subjects, as good spirits, good men, or angels, they advance their good properties to higher degrees of perfection, by augmenting the vigour and lustre of them. On the other hand, when they fall upon the ungodly, they produce the contrary effect, for the evils within them reverberate, suffocate, or pervert the good influx, and so turn it to their own greater detriment. Thus the light of heaven, incident on the truths of good, increases understanding and wisdom; but the same, when incident on the falses of evil, is transmuted by the recipients into the most extravagant phantasies and madness. Thus all things become in quality according to that of the receiver.

(280) That the spiritual world acts by influx on the natural world, n. 6053 to 6058, 6189—6598 to 6626. That this holds true with regard to the life of animals, n. 5850; as also with regard to the subjects of the vegetable kingdom, n. 3648. That this influx is a continual tendency of things subservient to the wonderful system of divine order in the world, n. 6211.

570. As

570. As the infernal fire confifts in the love of felf and the love of the world, fo likewife in all the inordinate paffions and evil concupifcences which fpring from thofe loves, and confequently in the gratification of them; for what a man loves he paffionately defires, and what he defires he takes delight in. Now thefe are all the evils before mentioned, viz. contempt of others, enmity to thofe that are not on his fide, envy, hatred, and revenge, and in confequence thereof, unmercifulnefs and cruelty; and with regard to things divine and facred, unbelief, contempt, derifion, and blafphemy, which after death become changed into indignation and hatred againft them; fee above, n. 562. And as thefe infernal paffions naturally aim at the ruin and deftruction of thofe who are the objects of them, fo where fuch evil-minded perfons have it not in their power to effect this, they however give the fulleft fcope they can to their diabolical malevolence and hatred. Thefe are the things meant by fire in the Scriptures, as applied to evil men and evil fpirits, as will appear from the following quotations: " Every one is
" an hypocrite, and an evil-doer, and every mouth fpeaketh
" folly; for wickednefs burneth as the fire: it fhall devour the
" briars and thorns, and it fhall kindle in the thickets of the
" foreft, and they fhall mount up like the lifting up of fmoke:
" and the people fhall be as the fuel of fire," Ifa. ix. 17, 18,
" 19. The land fhall become burning pitch; it fhall not be
" quenched night nor day; the fmoke thereof fhall go up for
" ever," Ifa. xxxiv. 9, 10. " Behold, the day cometh that
" fhall burn as an oven; and all the proud, and all that do
" wickedly, fhall be as ftubble, and the day that cometh fhall
" burn them up," Mal. iv. 1. " Babylon is fallen, and is
" become the habitation of devils: and they cried when they
" faw the fmoke of her burning: and her fmoke afcended up
" for ever and ever," Apoc. xviii. 2, 18. xix. 3. " And he
" opened the bottomlefs pit, and there arofe a fmoke out of
" the pit, as the fmoke of a great furnace; and the fun and
" the air were darkened by reafon of the fmoke of the pit,"
" Apoc. ix. 2. And out of their mouths iffued fire and fmoke,
" and brimftone: by thefe three was the third part of men
" killed," Apoc. ix. 17, 18. " If any man worfhip the beaft
" and

" and his image, the fame fhall drink of the wine of the wrath
" of God, and be tormented with fire and brimftone," Apoc.
xiv. 9, 10. " And the fourth angel poured out his vial upon
" the fun, and power was given unto him to fcorch men with
" fire ; and men were fcorched with great heat, and blafphemed
" the name of God," Apoc. xvi. 8, 9. " Every tree that
" bringeth not forth good fruit, fhall be hewn down and caft
" into the fire," Matt. iii. 10. " Where their worm dieth not,
" and the fire is not quenched," Mark ix. 44. In thefe and
many other places, by fire, is meant the inordinate and evil
affections proceeding from the love of felf and of the world;
and by fmoke we are to underftand the falfe proceeding from
evil.

571. It has been fhewed in the foregoing article, that by
the fire of hell is meant all thofe evil affections and propenfities
which proceed from the love of felf and of the world, and with
which all the inhabitants of the infernal regions are infected,
fo that when the gates of the hells are fet open, there appears
a column of fire mixed with fmoke afcending from the pit, as
from a houfe on fire, more thick and dark from the hell where
felf-love is predominant, and of a flame colour from that where
the love of the world prevails; but when the hells are fhut, no
fuch phænomenon of fire is feen, but in the room of it a denfe
exhalation as of fmoke, which affects the fenfes as from a heat
within, in fome places refembling that of a ftove, in others the
vapour of a hot bath; when this heat extends its influence to
a man on earth, it excites in him inordinate appetites and defires; it inftigates the wicked to hatred and revenge, and fometimes caufes infanity in fick perfons; and this heat or fire is the
prevailing element in fuch as are under the dominion of the
above mentioned loves, as having communication in fpirit with
thofe hells whilft here in the body. It muft be obferved in this
place, that they who are actually in hell, have no fenfation of
fire or burning, as is commonly imagined, but only experience
fuch a kind of heat or fire as inflamed their irafcible and other
evil paffions in this world: that all about them appears in the
form of fire, is from correfpondency, and that becaufe every
love, according to its kind, correfponds to fire, and in the fpiritual

ritual world all things have their reprefentations and vifible forms according to the laws of correfpondency.

572. It is to be noted here, that this infernal heat or fire is changed into intenfe cold on any influx of heat from heaven, and at fuch times the infernals are feized with a convulfive fhivering and rigour like perfons in an ague fit, and that becaufe of the contrariety between the elements of heaven and hell, infomuch that the heat of the former, which is divine love, extinguifhes the heat of the latter, which is the love of felf, thefe being oppofite to each other. The dufky light that is from the fire of hell is likewife at fuch times turned into darknefs, and the infernal fpirits are fo overcome by the divine influx, as to fall into aftonifhment and extreme infatuation: but fuch a vifitation feldom happens, except when the tumult and uproar in hell requires fuch a difcipline to reduce them to order and fubjection.

573. As this fire of hell fignifies every propenfity to evil flowing from the love of felf, fo likewife it fignifies its punifhment in thofe felf-tormenting paffions of hatred, revenge, and cruelty towards thofe who are the objects of them; for this kind of love is the root of all tyranny and arbitrary power, and the enemy of God and man; it quits not the foul even in death, but follows it to hell, and there becomes its confirmed infernal paffion, for ever excluding divine light and love, and binding itfelf in chains of darknefs, and the penal fire of its own evil.

574. It was faid before, that the evil fpirits caft themfelves into hell of their own accord; now how it comes to pafs that they fhould voluntarily commit themfelves to a place of fuch miferies muft be explained. From every particular hell exhales a fphere of effluvia from the paffions and qualities of the inhabitants therein, which ftriking the fenfes of thofe who are of fimilar affections, it excites in them the moft grateful perceptions, as every one's pleafure is according to the kind of his love. The fpirit that is thus agreeably affected, prefently turns himfelf to the quarter from whence the fphere arofe, and wifhes to be there, for as yet he is unacquainted with the miferies it is replete with, nay, otherwife he would wifh the fame: for in the fpiritual world no one can refift the propenfities of his ruling paffion

passion or love, for therein is his will, and thefe conftitute his nature, and there every one goes by the bent of his nature. On the fpirit's firft arrival in hell, he is received with a fhew of kindnefs, infomuch that he now thinks that he is with his friends; but this lafts only a few hours; for after fifting into his genius and particular turn of mind, they begin to moleft and vex him different ways, and fo go on to greater provocations, till they lead him to a deeper hell; for the more interior and deep the hell, the more malignant the fpirits that dwell there; and here, after other exercifes of difcipline, they torment him, till they have entirely brought him under fubjection to their will. But as there arife continual tumults and infurrections where all hate one another, and every one ftrives to be the greateft; fo they who were lately fubdued to the will of others, become in turn confederates with fome more potent infernal, to ftrengthen his faction, and fupport his pretenfions to fuperiority. Thus the fcene of diforder and confufion continually varies, whilft all according to their power evilly intreat and tyrannize over others. Such are the miferies and fufferings which go by the name of hell fire.

575. By gnafhing of teeth is fignified the difcordance and contradiction betwixt falfe and falfe [*pugna falforum*] and the various difputes and wranglings of fuch as are in error from the ground of falfe (*) joined with contempt of others, enmity, mockery, railings, and bitter ftrife, whilft every one fights for falfity [*pro fuo falfo*] and calls it truth. Thefe wrathful contentions, as heard by thofe that are not within thofe hells, found like the gnafhings of teeth, and are changed into fuch when truths from heaven are manifefted there. In thefe hells are all

(*) Error is to be diftinguifhed from *falfe*, where it proceeds from miftake, defect of underftanding, influence of education, or deference to the judgment of thofe whom we deem to be wifer than ourfelves. In thefe and fuch like cafes it is innocent error, or matter of infirmity, and demands all candid allowances, as fuch perfons, through fimplicity, fincerity, and an earneft defire of finding the truth, may be in the principle, though without the knowledge of it; but it is far otherwife where error in the judgment proceeds from evil in the will, as from attachment to vice, any falfe intereft, or the love of felf, &c. Here the judgment is infected and determined by the will, and makes part of it, and fuch error has in it the nature of *falfe*, and is properly what our author calls *falfum ex malo*. Tr.

thofe

thofe who fet up nature for God; and in ftill deeper hells fuch as had confirmed themfelves by ftudied arguments in this atheiftical perfuafion. All of this clafs, as being unreceptive of light from heaven, and confequently having no perception of truth within them, are merely fenfual and corporeal, believing nothing but what they can fee with their eyes, or touch with their hands; whence it is, that all the fallacies of the fenfes pafs with them for real truths, and all that is fpiritual for fallacy; which is the caufe of all their difputes and vain janglings having a refemblance to the gnafhings of teeth in the fpiritual world, where all falfes have that found. Now teeth correfpond to the extremities in nature, and to the loweft things in man, fuch as thofe which are fenfual and corporeal. As to gnafhing of teeth in hell, fee Matt. viii. 12. xiii. 42, 50. xxii. 13. xxiv. 51. xxv. 30. Luke xiii. 28.

Of the Malignity and wicked Devices of the infernal Spirits.

576. Every one that is given to introverfion, when he reflects upon the operations of his own mind, may form an idea of the fuperiority of fpirits over man as to the intellectual powers, as knowing, that he himfelf can conceive, reafon upon, and form a judgment of more things in a minute, than he can exprefs or commit to writing in half an hour; learning hereby, how far a man under the exercife of his intellectual or fpiritual faculties excels himfelf at another time, and confequently how much more he fhall excel when he comes to be a pure fpirit divefted of his earthly body; for it is the fpirit alone that thinks in him, whilft the body is no more than the inftrument whereby he expreffes his thoughts: and hence it is, that the angels poffefs unfpeakably greater underftanding and wifdom than when they were joined to this material world by their corporeal vehicles, in connexion with which the mind is for the moft part fufceptible only of general and obfcure notices of things, and unable to difcern innumerable others pertaining to fpiritual

know-

knowledge; not to mention the many hinderances in the way to it from worldly cares and connexions: but when man is freed from thefe defects and impediments by a tranflation to the angelical ftate (for every angel once lived here as man, and in the fame low degrees of knowledge) he no longer fees as through a glafs darkly, but a new intellectual world opens to his view, and he has clear perceptions of things unconceivable by the mind of the natural man.

577. In the fame degree that the angels excel in underftanding and wifdom, the infernal fpirits increafe in ferpentine craft and deceit; for after this life every fpirit enters into the whole of its good or evil, and thinks, wills, and acts therefrom without difguife; whereas in this life the evil of a man's fpirit was curbed by legal reftraints, regards to character, intereft, and other human confiderations, nay, fometimes fo artfully concealed under an outfide fhew of juftice, fincerity, and the form of godlinefs, that he did not know himfelf, nor difcover the latent evils in his heart and nature, which manifeft themfelves to his aftonifhment when he arrives in the world of fpirits. The number and different kinds of evil that there appear in their feveral hideous forms, are not to be defcribed in any human language, and this I can teftify, as having been witnefs thereto feveral times; for the Lord has granted me the privilege to be in [as one of] the fpiritual world as to my fpirit, whilft in this natural world as to my body: and this I can affirm, that fo great is the malice of evil fpirits againft man, that except the Lord did take him under his protection by the miniftry of angels (for both attend him here, fee n. 292, 293), it would be impoffible for him to deliver himfelf from the power of hell. But man withdraws himfelf from this protection by denying his divinity, and renouncing a life of faith and charity, for fo he turns away from the Lord to the evil fpirits, and enters into fellowfhip with the powers of darknefs; yet even fo (when loft to all fenfe of confcience) the Lord makes ufe of external reftraints and fears, in order to deter him from the commiffion of outward evils; but then thefe means are unavailable to introduce him into the fpiritual life, feeing this can only be effected by a real converfion of his mind, will, and affections.

578. The

578. The worst of spirits are those, who in this life were immersed in the principle of self-love, and at the same time actuated by a serpentine subtlety; for all deceit and craft enter deep into the thoughts and intentions, and so poison the very root of life in man, as to destroy every seed of spiritual good therein. Most of these are in the hells behind, and are called genii; their pleasure is to make themselves inconspicuous, fluttering about like bats by night, that they may do their works of darkness in secret: these suffer more than any other of the evil spirits. Such as were in the like principle of self-love, but not actuated by the like subtlety and deceit, are also in the hells behind, but not of like depth. And as to those who were possessed by the evils proceeding from the love of the world, but not so deep in the love of self, nor alike addicted to hatred and revenge, deceit and subtlety, they are called evil spirits, and their hells are milder, as they suffer less from their lesser degrees of malignity.

579. It has been given me to know experimentally the particular kind of malicious wickedness in those spirits which are called genii. Now these do not practise their diabolical subtlety on the thoughts, but on the affections, which they scent by a peculiar sagacity, like as dogs do their game; and when they have made the discovery, they make it their business to turn and wind the good affections of any one, all they can, to their contraries, and this by drawing them off to other objects by allurements suited to their particular inclinations and complexions; and this they manage with such art and cunning, that the party is not aware of the deceit, as they hinder him by various crafty devices from attending to and making reflexions upon the matter. Their situation, when with man, is under the occiput, or hinder part of the head. These, when living in this world, were such as cunningly applied to the ruling passions of men, and by artfully insinuating themselves into their affections captivated their minds, in order to lead them more easily into the traps and snares they laid for them: but all, of whose reformation and regeneration there are the least hopes, are carefully preserved by the goodness of the Lord from these insidious spirits, whose power and subtlety are otherwise sufficient to remove the barriers

of confcience, and to awaken and put in motion all the hereditary evils in man's nature; and therefore they are not permitted to infeſt fuch perfons. Such are the companions, and fuch the manfions to which all crafty and malicious deceivers are configned after death: when viewed in the other world in their proper form and character, they appear in the fhape of vipers.

580. The malignity of the infernal fpirits manifeſts itſelf in fo many wicked arts and devices (unknown in this world) that to enumerate them would fill a volume, and to defcribe them many volumes. One kind of them refpects the abufe and perverting of correfpondences: another, in difturbing the divine order in its loweſt claſſes: a third, is by the influxive communication of evil thoughts and affections, and this by falfe converfions, infpections, and emiſſary fpirits: a fourth, by operations on the mind by phantafies: a fifth, by falfe appearances of themfelves, where in reality they are not: and fixthly, by counterfeiting other characters, by evil perfuafions and lies. By thefe and various other deceitful arts they vex and torment one another in their miferable focieties: but as all thefe wicked arts, except the laſt mentioned, are unknown in our world, I forbear to defcribe them, not only becaufe they would not be underſtood, but alfo becaufe they are not fit to be mentioned.

581. This feverity of fufferings and tormenting difcipline is permitted by the Lord, to keep within certain bounds the flagrant evils of the infernal fpirits, by their mutual oppofition, as they are fubject to no other reftraint than the fear of fuffering for them, without which, hell would be tenfold itfelf in uproar, rage, and madnefs; a picture of which we may form to ourfelves by the idea of an earthly kingdom without coercive laws with penal fanctions (*).

Of

(*) This obfervation of our author may fuggeſt to us a good additional argument in vindication of the Divine Providence in permitting the calamities of tumults, infurrections, and wars, in the prefent degenerate ſtate of mankind; for though thefe are confeffedly great evils, yet they ferve as means preventive of greater, by operating on the fears and paſſions of men various ways: thus, by reftraining the oppreffions, tyranny, and cruelty of wicked rulers on the one hand, and by experience of the evils and miferies thereof curbing the licentioufnefs of

the

Of the Appearance, Situation, and Plurality of the Hells.

582. In the spiritual world, where spirits and angels have their abodes, there are the same appearances of things as in this our natural world, as of plains, mountains, hills, rocks, vallies, waters, &c. but all from a spiritual origin, and therefore only visible to those spiritual beings, and not to man whilst in this natural state, unless it be given him to be conversant in the spiritual world as a spirit: nor can an angel or spirit behold the material things of this world, except he be joined to man in like manner; for as the sight of the former is adapted only to natural light, so is the sight of the latter to spiritual light, though the eyes of both are to appearance the very same. This will hardly be received by the natural man, much less by the sensualist, who, being governed in all things by his bodily senses, can form no conception of reality and substance, as pertaining to any thing beyond material nature; but notwithstanding this, the resemblance between the spiritual and natural world is such, that man for some time after his departure hence, knows not but that he is still in the latter, insomuch that his death may very properly be termed a translation from one world to another like it; and that there is such similitude betwixt them has been shewed before in the chapter *Concerning Representatives and Appearances in Heaven*, n. 170 to 176.

583. The heavens there appear above; the world of spirits beneath; and the hells are under both. The heavens are not seen by the spirits that are in the world of spirits, except when their interior sight is opened; at other times they appear only as through a mist, or as light clouds, and that because the angels of heaven are in a more interior state of understanding and wisdom, and accordingly above the sight of those that are in the

---

the multitude on the other, which is only awed by fear of sufferings from venting their malignity every man on his neighbour, and from turning all things into chaos and confusion. Tr.

world of spirits: but the spirits, who are in the plains and valleys, see each other, except when they are internally separated by intromission into their interior states; for at such times the evil spirits do not see the good, but the good spirits see the evil ones, but turn away their faces from them, and so become invisible to the others. As to the hells, they are not seen in this world, as being shut, but only the entrances into them, called their gates, when they are opened for the admission of those that are consigned to them. These gates are visible in the world of spirits, but not in heaven.

584. There are hells every where under the mountains, hills and rocks; and the holes or gates leading into them, appear as so many clefts or fissures in rocks, some of larger, and some of narrower extent, and they all appear dark and dismal, though the spirits within have a kind of light like that from burning coals, to which their sight is accommodated; and that because in this world, being in darkness as to divine truths through unbelief, they had no other light than what proceeded from vain reasonings and error, and therefore they can see nothing in the light of heaven, when they quit their gloomy mansions; such opposites are the light of faith, and the darkness of unbelief.

585. The openings or gates leading to the hells, which are underneath the plains and valleys, have different aspects; some resemble those which are underneath the mountains, hills and rocks; some of them look like dens and caves; some like wide mouths and gulfs, and others like lakes and pools of water. They are only open when evil spirits come thither from the world of spirits, to be passed into their respective hells, at which times are seen to issue from them fire, and flame with or without smoke, as also thick clouds of fuliginous vapour; though it is said, that they do not appear as such to the infernal spirits, as being then in their own proper atmosphere, and the elements that are congruous to their nature; for they correspond to the evils and falses thereof: for example, such fire to hatred and revenge; smoke and soot to the falses belonging thereto; flame to the evils of self-love; and black clouds and vapour to the falses thereof.

586. I was

586. I was allowed to look into the hells, and take a view of their infide; for the power of fuch infpection is, by divine permiffion, granted at times to the angels and fpirits above them, even when they are not open: fuch an infide view of them I had. Some of the hells appeared like caverns in rocks, firft proceeding far horizontally, and then defcending either perpendicularly, or by windings, to a great depth. Some refembled the dens of wild beafts in the woods; others the fubterraneous works in mines, with different chambers and defcents to ftill lower floors. Moft of them are of three degrees of defcent, the uppermoft dark, as correfponding to the falfes of evil; the loweft of a fiery appearance, as correfponding to the evils themfelves. In the loweft hells are thofe who acted immediately from the root or principle of evil; but in fuch as are lefs deep, thofe who acted from evil errors, or the falfes of evil. In fome hells appear, as it were, ruins of houfes and towns after fome dreadful conflagration, in which the infernal fpirits fkulk; and in the milder hells are feen a kind of rude cottages, and in fome places contiguous in the form of a city or large town, with ftreets and lanes, inhabited by infernal fpirits that live together in ftrife, hatred, quarrellings, and fightings even to blood, whilft in the ftreets and publick ways are committed thefts and robberies; and in fome of the hells are places like publick ftews fhocking to behold, as full of uncleannefs and filth of all kinds. There are alfo gloomy woods, in which the infernal fpirits wander about like wild beafts, and alfo fubterraneous caves, into which fuch as are purfued by others fly for refuge. Moreover, there are barren and fandy defarts, ragged rocks with caverns, and fcattered cottages; and to thefe defert places are configned fuch in particular as had paffed through fevere fufferings in the other hells, and had been foremoft among thofe who deceive others by crafty devices and wicked ftratagems. This is the laft ftate of their appointment.

587. The exact particular fituation of the hells is not known even to the angels, but to the Lord only, though their general diftinctions are known from the quarters refpectively where they lie; thefe diftinctions being the fame as in the heavens,

where they are regulated according to the kinds and degrees of heavenly love, beginning with the Lord as the sun of heaven, which is called the east; and as the hells are in all things opposite to the heavens, so the principal or regulating quarter there is the west (see the chapter *Concerning the Four Quarters of Heaven*, n. 141 to 153). Hence it is, that the western hells are the worst and most horrible of all, and that in proportion to their greater degrees of distance from the east. To these are appointed such as in this world were so swallowed up in the love of self, as to hold in contempt and bitter hatred all that were not of their party and in their interest, or refused to honour them: and in the remotest of those regions are those in particular of the Romish religion, who had arrogated to themselves divine worship, burning with rage and revenge against all that denied their power and heavenly jurisdiction over the souls of men; and as they still retain the same proud vindictive spirit, so to shew their rage and cruelty is their greatest pleasure; but this turns to their greater misery in the other world, for all of their class being actuated by the same infernal passion of domineering, they exercise their fury and malice upon one another: but more of this in a small work *Concerning the Last Judgment, and the Destruction of Babylon*. As to the particular circumstances relative to the hells, it can only be said, that the worst of them are to the northward; that they abate in degree of malignity towards the south, and still more towards the east. Towards the last also are many who were high-minded and atheistical, but not of like savage cruelty and infernal subtlety as those nearer to the west. At this time there are no infernal societies in full east, they having been translated nearer to the western regions; but the hells in the north and south are very many, and inhabited by such as were immersed in the love of the world, and the various evils derived from that source, as enmity, hostilities, extortion, wrong and robbery, artifice, avarice and uncharitableness, increasing or decreasing in degrees of malignity, as was said before, according to their greater or lesser degrees of distance from the east. Behind the hells in the western and northern divisions are the gloomy woods and deserts

before

before mentioned. Thus much concerning the situation of the hells.

588. With regard to plurality of hells, it is here to be noted, that they equal in number the angelical societies in the heavens; for there is a society of infernals answering to every society of angels, according to the nature of opposites. That the heavenly societies are innumerable, and all distinct, according to the different kinds and degrees of their goods of divine love, charity and faith, see under the article, *Concerning the Societies of which the Heavens consist*, n. 41 to 50: as also in that, *Concerning the Immensity of Heaven*, n. 415 to 420. In like manner the infernal societies are distinct, according to their respective evils opposite to the goods before mentioned. Every evil, as well as every good, is a genus or general, which contains in it innumerable species or particulars; however, this may not appear to those who form to themselves only one simple idea of every evil; as for example, of contempt, hatred, enmity, revenge, deceit, and the like; whereas every one of these contains so many specifick differences, and under them as many particular subdivisions as would more than fill a volume to enumerate them all. According to these manifold distinctions in evil, and their nearer or more remote distances from one another, are the several hells divided and regulated with the utmost exactness and congruity. There are also hells under hells, communicating with one another, some by passages, and some by exhalations, according to the agreement or affinity betwixt evil and evil. That the hells are so many and various appears from its being given me to know, that under every mountain, hill, rock, plain and valley, there were particular hells of different extent in length, breadth, and depth. In a word, both heaven and the world of spirits may be considered as convexities, under which are arrangements of those infernal mansions. So much concerning the plurality of hells.

Of the Equilibrium betwixt Heaven and Hell.

589. An equilibrium is neceffary to the exiftence and fubfiftence of all things, and confifts in the equality of action and reaction between two oppofite powers, producing reft or equilibrium; and this according to an eftablifhed law throughout the natural world, obferved in the very atmofpheres, in which the lower and denfer air reacts on the fuperincumbent columns; nay, even betwixt heat and cold, light and darknefs, dry and moift; and the middle point is the temperature or equilibrium. The fame law obtains throughout the three great kingdoms of this world, the mineral, vegetable, and animal; wherein all things proceed and are regulated according to action and reaction, or actives and paffives, producing or reftoring an equilibrium in nature. In the phyfical world, the agent and reagent are called Power and Conatus; and in the fpiritual world, life and will, as being living power and conatus; and here the equilibrium is called liberty. Thus there exifts a fpiritual equilibrium or liberty betwixt good and evil, by the action of one, and the reaction of the other; for example, in good men this equilibrium is effected by the action of the good principle, and the reaction of the evil principle; but in bad men, evil is the agent, and good is but the reagent. That there is a fpiritual equilibrium betwixt good and evil, is becaufe every thing appertaining to the vital principle in man has relation to good or evil, and the will is the receptacle of both. There is likewife an equilibrium betwixt true and falfe; but this depends on the equilibrium betwixt good and evil, according to their kinds refpectively. The equilibrium betwixt truth and falfe, is fimilar to that which is betwixt light and darknefs [*umbram*] which operate, according to the heat and cold therein, on the fubjects of the vegetable kingdom; for that light and darknefs have no fuch operation in themfelves alone, but only through the heat in them, may appear from the fimilarity that is betwixt the

light

light and darknefs in winter and in fpring. The comparifon of truth and falfe with light and darknefs is from correfpondency, for truth correfponds to light, and falfe to darknefs, and heat to the good of love. Spiritual light alfo is the fame with truth, and fpiritual darknefs is the fame with falfe, concerning which, fee the chapter, *On the Light and Heat in Heaven*, n. 126 to 140.

590. There is a perpetual equilibrium betwixt heaven and hell; from the latter continually exhales and afcends a conatus of doing evil; and from the former continually emanes and defcends a conatus [tendency to or will] (*) of doing good. In this equilibrium is the world of fpirits, which is fituated in the midft betwixt heaven and hell (fee above, n. 421 to 431); and this may appear from hence, that every man immediately after death enters into the world of fpirits, and there continues in the fame ftate in which he died; is examined and proved thereby, as a touchftone of his principles; and remains under the fame free will, which all indicate an equilibrium; for fuch a fpiritual equilibrium there is in every man and fpirit, as obferved before. The particular kind and tendency of this liberty or free will, is well known by the angels in heaven by the communication of thoughts and affections; and it appears vifibly to the angelical fpirits (*), by the paths and ways which they chufe to walk in, as the good fpirits take thofe which lead to heaven, and the evil fpirits thofe which lead to hell; for fuch ways and walks have actually a vifible appearance in that world; and this is the reafon, that the word *way* or *ways* in Scripture fignifies thofe truths which lead to good, and in an oppofite fenfe, thofe falfes which lead to evil; and hence alfo it is, that to go, walk, or journey, fignify the progreffions of life in the fame Sacred Writings (281). It has oftentimes been given me to fee fuch ways

or

(*) It will not appear ftrange, that in the fpiritual worlds the fpiritual mental powers, fuch as willing, defiring, &c. fhould have their extrinfick operations and effects at great diftances, when we reflect on the like diftant operations and effects of bodies upon one another in this material world, in their different propertics of attraction, repulfion, gravitation, &c. Tr.

(*) By angelical fpirits is here meant fuch fpirits as are yet in the intermediate world of fpirits, in their ftate of final preparation for heaven. Tr.

(281) That to journey, in Scripture fignifies progrefs in life, as does likewife to go,

or roads, and the spirits walking and passing therein, as they were led to chuse one or the other by the particular bent of their minds and affections.

591. That evil continually exhales and ascends from hell, and that good continually flows and descends from heaven, is because every one is surrounded by a spiritual sphere flowing or transpiring from his vital affections and thoughts (282), and consequently the same from every society cœlestial or infernal, and collectively from the whole heaven and the whole hell. This universal efflux of good from heaven originates in the Lord, and passes through the angels without any mixture of their propriety [*proprium*] or self-hood; for this is suppressed in them by the Lord, who grants them to live in his own divine property; whereas the infernal spirits are in their own property of selfish nature, or what only belongs to themselves [*proprium*] which, as unblessed with divine communications from the sole fountain of all good, is only evil in every one continually (283). This may suffice to shew, that the equilibrium both of the angels and devils differs from that in the middle world of spirits; the equilibrium of the former being according to their free will in the principle of good from a life and love of good, and hatred to evil in this world; but the equilibrium of the latter, according to their free will in evil from a life and love of evil, and a hatred to good in this world.

go, n. 3335, 4375, 4554—8417, 8420, 8557. That to walk with the Lord signifies to lead a spiritual life, or to live to him, n. 10567. That to walk signifies to live, n. 519, 1794, 8417, 8420.

(282) That a spiritual sphere, which is the sphere of life, proceeds from every man, spirit, and angel, and forms a kind of atmosphere around them, n. 4464, 5179, 7454, 8630. That this flows from their inmost affections and thoughts, n. 2489, 4464, 6206. That the quality of spirits is known at a distance by their spheres, n. 1048, 1053, 1316, 1504. That the spheres of evil spirits are opposite to those from good spirits, n. 1695, 10187, 10312. That these spheres extend far to the heavenly societies, according to their quality and degree of good, n. 6598 to 6613, 8063, 8794, 8797. And likewise to the infernal societies, according to their quality and degree of evil, n. 8794, 8797.

(283) That the property or nature of man is altogether evil, n. 210, 215, 731, 874—10283, 10284, 10286, 10731. That the selfish property in man is hell within him, n. 694, 8480.

592. Except

592. Except the Lord kept the government of the heavens and hells in his own hands, there would be an end of equilibrium, and confequently both of heaven and hell; for all things in the natural and fpiritual worlds fubfift thereby, and the balance once deftroyed, all things would neceffarily run into diforder and confufion. Suoh would be the cafe in the fpiritual world, unlefs the power of evil were reftrained by the reaction of the good principle, and fo hindered from acquiring the fuperiority. Unlefs this were effected by the fole government of the Lord, there would be an end of heaven and hell, and of the whole human race: the words, *fole government of the Lord*, muft here be repeated, as He alone is fufficient for this work; for every thing belonging to the creature as his proper own or felf, whether it be angel, fpirit, or man, is nothing but evil, and therefore abfolutely incapable of making any refiftance to the efflux and powers of hell, as being more on their fide; fo that the whole of falvation in every creature is folely owing to the government and grace of the Lord: nor can it be fuppofed, that lefs than his omnipotent arm can be fufficient to keep within bounds the hoftile fury and malice of all the hells, which join in one common confederacy againft heaven, and all that are therein.

593. The equilibrium between the heavens and the hells is determined by the number of thofe that enter therein, which amounts to feveral thoufands every day; and to adjuft a matter of fuch univerfal importance can only belong to that omniprefent Lord, who weighs all things in the balance of infinite wifdom; for wife as the angels are, they fee comparatively but a little way, nor know all things that pafs within the circle of their own focieties.

504. Something has been offered before on the government of the heavens and the hells with relation to the fubferviency of all therein to the prefervation of equilibrium; as that all the focieties in both are difpofed and regulated according to their general and fpecifick diftinctions in good and evil; and that under every cœleftial there is an infernal fociety anfwering thereto as its oppofite, from which oppofite correfpondence refults the equilibrium, whereby the evil is reftrained from over-
powering

powering the good, and a provifion made by the divine wifdom to check every tendency to fuperiority in the former over the latter: and this is effected by various means; as by a ftronger operation of the divine prefence; or by a ftricter confederacy in good among particular angelical focieties. There are alfo other means made ufe of, in order to this end, by various regulations as to the hells; thus, by dividing particular focieties therein, and by ejecting a certain number into the deferts before mentioned; by the tranflation of fome infernals from one hell to another, and divers other adminiftrations of government both in the heavens above, and in the hells beneath. By fo many ways does the Lord provide for the prefervation of that equilibrium between good and evil, on which the falvation and happinefs of men and angels fo much depend.

595. The hells are continually plotting againft heaven, and exerting their hoftile malice for its deftruction; though impotent and vain are all their endeavours againft thofe who are under the defence of the Lord omnipotent. I have often feen their enmity and hatred to all things divine and facred reprefented by the form of a fphere afcending from the infernal regions, as if to infult and affault heaven; whereas the heavens, on the contrary, make no affault on the hells, the divine fphere proceeding from the Lord being an efflux of love for the falvation of all; but as thofe miferable fpirits, through the evil they are in and chufe, render themfelves incapable of fuch falvation, therefore this emanation of the divine goodnefs can effect nothing more in their behalf, than to reftrain, as far as poffible, their vindictive malice from wreaking itfelf with unbridled fury and madnefs on one another; and to this end He is gracioufly pleafed to employ various means; fo merciful is the Lord even towards the impenitent and incorrigible.

596. The heavens, in the general, are diftinguifhed into two kingdoms; the one of which is called the cœleftial, the other the fpiritual kingdom; of which fee above, n. 20 to 28. The hells likewife are diftinguifhed into two kingdoms; the one of which is oppofite to the cœleftial, the other to the fpiritual. That which is oppofite to the cœleftial is in the weft, and they who belong to it are called genii; and that which is

oppofite

oppofite to the fpiritual kingdom is in the north and fouth, and they who belong to it are called evil fpirits. All in the cœleftial kingdom excel in love to the Lord, and all that are in the hells oppofite to that kingdom, are under the prevailing power of felf-love; all that belong to the fpiritual kingdom are diftinguifhed in excellence by love to their neighbour, and all that are in the hells oppofite to this kingdom are flaves to the love of the world; fo that love to the Lord and the love of felf are in the fame diametrical oppofition to each other, as the love of our neighbour and the love of the world. Effectual provifion is made by the Lord, that no power of evil from the hells, that are in oppofition to the cœleftial kingdom, may reach the fubjects of the fpiritual kingdom, as the confequence in that cafe would be the fubverfion of the latter, for the reafon given in n. 578, 579. Thus does the Lord keep the balance betwixt good and evil in his own hand for the prefervation of his kingdoms.

That the Liberty or Free Will of Man, is from the Equilibrium that fubfifts between Heaven and Hell.

597. In the foregoing chapter we have treated of that equilibrium which fubfifts betwixt heaven and hell, and fhewed, that it is no other than an equilibrium betwixt the good that proceeds from the former, and the evil that proceeds from the latter, and fo conftituting the effence of human liberty: and as good and evil, truth and falfe, are of a fpiritual nature, fo alfo is that equilibrium in which confifts the power of thinking and willing the one or the other, and the liberty of chufing or refufing accordingly. This liberty or freedom of the will originates in the divine nature, but is given to every man by the Lord for a property of his life, nor does He ever take it back again. This good gift to man is to the end that he may be regenerated and faved, for without free will there is no falvation for him; but that he actually poffefles it, he may know from the operations of his own mind, and what paffes inwardly in his

his spirit, he being able to think and chuse either good or evil, whatever restraints he may be under from uttering or acting the latter in respect to laws divine or human. Now this inward experience evinces beyond a thousand arguments, that liberty belongs to man, as his spirit is his proper self, and it is that which freely thinks, wills, and chuses; consequently, liberty is to be estimated according to the inner man, and not from what he may be outwardly through fear, human respects, or other external restraints.

598. That man would not be capable of being reformed or regenerated without free will, is because he is by the original constitution of his nature born to evils of every kind, which must be removed in order to his salvation; and that can only be by his knowing, owning, renouncing, and abhorring them. To this end, he must be instructed in the nature of good; for it is by good only that he can see the evil, but by evil he cannot see the good: accordingly, he must be early educated in the knowledge of spiritual truths by teaching, by reading the Scriptures, and by the preaching of the Word, that so he may attain to a right understanding of what is good; as he is likewise to cultivate his mind with the knowledge of moral and civil truths from his intercourse with society in the different relations of life; all which imply the use and exercise of freedom. Another thing to be considered is, that nothing becomes appropriated to man, or can be called his own, that is not received into the affectionate part; other things he may apprehend or form an ideal knowledge of, but what enters not his will or love, which is the same thing (for what a man wills he loves) that makes no part of him, nor abides with him. Now man being naturally prone to evil, he could not receive its contrary, the good, into his will or love, so as to become appropriated to him, unless he were endowed with liberty or freedom of will, seeing that the good is opposite to the evil of his nature.

599. That man may be possessed of liberty or free will, in order to be capable of regeneration, therefore he can have communication in spirit with heaven, or with hell; for evil spirits from the one, and angels from the other, are present with him; by the former he possesses his own evil; by the latter he is in the principle of good from the Lord; and herein stands his

equili-

equilibrium or liberty. That every man has both angels and evil spirits attending him in this world, see the chapter *Concerning the Conjunction of Heaven with the Human Race*, n. 291 to 302.

600. Not that this conjunction of man with heaven or hell is an immediate conjunction, but mediate only, and that through the spirits that belong to the world of spirits; for these are the spirits that attend on man, and not any immediately from heaven or hell (*). By the evil spirits belonging to the world of spirits man joins himself to hell; and by the good spirits of the same world he has communication with heaven; for the world of spirits is intermediate between heaven and hell, and constitutes the true equilibrium; for these two particulars, see above, n. 421 to 431, and n. 589 to 596. Thus much for the origin of human liberty.

601. Let it be observed, as touching those spirits that are appointed to be man's associates here, that a whole society may hold communication with another society, and also with any individual wheresoever, by means of an emissary spirit, which spirit is called, *The Subject of many* [*Subjectum plurium*]. The cause is similar with respect to man's communication [*conjunctio*] with the societies in heaven and in hell by the intervention of his associate spirits from the world of spirits.

602. As to that common impression of belief concerning a future life on the human mind, which some call innate, or natural, though in reality it be from cœlestial influx, the following memorable particular shall here be related. Certain spirits, which in their life-time here had been of that simple plebeian class which live in all good faith, were reinstated in the same low degree of understanding and thinking that they

---

(*) This is entirely consistent with what was affirmed by the author in the foregoing number, as the good spirits belonging to the world of spirits, being in their final preparation for the angelical state, are called angelical spirits; and as they have immediate communication with the heavenly angels, so has man, through them, a mediate communication with the same. On the other hand, the bad spirits belonging to the world of spirits, being in their final preparation for hell, are called infernal spirits, and have immediate communication with devils; and wicked men, through them, a mediate communication with the same. Thus all communications between man, and the highest and lowest in heaven and hell, are conducted through mediums adapted to his nature and states respectively. Tr.

possessed in this world (as may be the case of every one, by the divine permission, to answer certain ends). On this change they discovered what ideas they had here concerning the state of man after death, and related as follows; viz. that they were asked on a time by some learned men when in this world, what they thought of their souls after death? To which they answered, that they did not know what the soul was. They then asked them, what their belief was concerning their state after death? To which they replied, that they believed they should be living spirits. They asked them, what their faith was, as to spirits? They said, that a spirit was a man. They asked them, how they knew that? They answered, after their simplicity, that they knew it, because it was so. On which these learned querists stood astonished, to find such simple illiterate people possessed of a stronger faith than what they had themselves; manifesting hereby, that in all who are in communion with heaven there is a principle of faith, as touching the immortality of the soul by a divine influx from the Lord, through the medium of those spirits which belong to the world of spirits, but not received by such as, through a vain philosophy and science falsely so called, poison their minds with corrupt doctrines concerning the soul, as that it is nothing else than mere thought, or a certain animated something proceeding from matter; and then go to find out the particular place of its residence in the body; whereas the immortal spirit is the man himself that animates his body, and uses it only as its instrument or servant to perform the functions of life in this natural world, according to his different states and relations therein, on his pilgrimage to and preparation for a better country, even a heavenly one.

603. What has been delivered in this work concerning heaven, the world of spirits, and hell, will appear obscure to those who have no relish for spiritual truths, but clear to such as take delight therein, more especially to all who are in the love of Truth for its own sake. What we love, we readily receive and understand; and where Truth is the object of our affections, it recommends itself to the mind by the evidence it brings with it; for Truth is Light.

F I N I S.

www.ingramcontent.com/pod-product-compliance
Lightning Source LLC
Chambersburg PA
CBHW051859300426
44117CB00006B/461